Paper Sack Puppets

Paper Sack Puppets

60+ Easy Patterns and Activities for Librarians, Teachers and Parents

Eunice Wright

Illustrated by Juli Wright

McFarland & Company, Inc., Publishers
Jefferson, North Carolina

Library of Congress Cataloguing-in-Publication Data

Wright, Eunice, 1950–
Paper sack puppets : 60+ easy patterns and activities for librarians, teachers and parents /
Eunice Wright ; illustrated by Juli Wright.
p. cm.
Includes bibliographical references and index.

ISBN 978-0-7864-4567-7 (softcover : acid free paper) ∞

1. Puppet making. I. Wright, Juli, 1981– illustrator. II. Title.

TT174.7.W65 2015 745.592'24–dc23 2015029397

British Library cataloguing data are available

Front cover: children and mother holding the 3 little pigs puppets (photograph courtesy author)

Printed in the United States of America

McFarland & Company, Inc., Publishers
Box 611, Jefferson, North Carolina 28640
www.mcfarlandpub.com

TABLE OF CONTENTS

Section Two. ABC Puppets

Section Three. Family Members

Preface

I love puppets! And I love making and playing with puppets. It's fun to use your imagination to create characters that you can "bring to life." They can be whatever you want them to be and do things that you might feel silly doing yourself. Puppets can do and say things that regular people cannot, and their silliness makes people laugh. They can also be wonderful teaching tools. Puppets come in many shapes and sizes, but this book focuses on using paper sacks to create puppets—an easy and economical option for teachers, librarians, and storytellers.

Puppets can be wonderful little creatures, especially when you make them yourself, and that is half the fun. Add embellishments to the puppets, such as fake fur, pom-poms, fabric, lace, glitter, jewels, yarn, etc. People make puppets to entertain, teach, amaze, or just for the fun creative process. So use your imagination and put on your very own puppet show with puppets you make yourself!

In this book are many possible activities and ideas to get your creative juices flowing, along with many resources using puppets with groups of children. Many adults enjoy the creative ways to use puppets while working with children, and children enjoy a rhyme or song to chant or sing while performing. Sometimes teachers search for a play, an art and craft activity, a book or visual aid to tie in with a theme or lesson. They may want to teach a specific idea or develop or supplement a unit, and a puppet can help children learn those lessons.

Some activities might be useful for a class presentation or a program for parents. Librarians might enjoy using puppets or some of the activities to promote a particular book. Perhaps the list of ideas and activities will inspire you and/or your children to create poems and songs of your own. Have fun experimenting and creating your own special puppets and change or adapt the puppet or activity to meet your needs.

Many of the puppets can be repurposed. For example, there is one basic pattern for a mouse. This basic pattern, with the addition of a few embellishments, can become the Country Mouse, the City Mouse, the Three Blind Mice, the mouse from Aesop's fable about the lion's paw, the mouse that ran up the clock, and many more. Most of these options are covered in this book, but the real possibilities are endless with a little imagination.

There are three kinds of paper sack puppets covered in this book. Section One includes story book characters, Section Two is alphabet puppets (useful when teaching very young children) and Section Three, called "Family Members," includes people puppets. Within these sections each chapter is numbered. Many of the chapters in Section One include more than one puppet, so each subsequent puppet is numbered with the chapter number plus a letter. The first appendix includes lists of animal puppets, alphabetically and by groups and themes, while a second appendix includes many resources, print, electronic and musical.

Remember, there are no hard and fast rules (except that puppets *never* fight with each other, unless it is part of the "act"). This is what I always tell my students, because I don't want them to start out by "puppet-fighting," when there are so many other wonderful things puppets can do!

I hope you will enjoy making up your own poems, songs and activities and creating your own puppets to suit your children's needs. Be creative, but most of all—HAVE FUN!

Using This Book

Classroom teachers and librarians may reproduce materials in this book for non-profit classroom use or for children's group use only. Pages may also be photocopied for personal use. (Please apply to the publisher for permission to reproduce the patterns in bulk.)

Enlarging Patterns and Making Puppets

Patterns that are too large to fit at full size on the pages in this book have been reduced. The approximate percentage you will need to use to enlarge the pattern in order to fit a standard sack is noted.

1. Choose the puppet pattern, pieces and accessories you will need.
2. Copy all the pieces of the pattern and test them for a correct fit, particularly if you need to enlarge any portions of the pattern.
3. When you are happy with the fit of the pattern on the sack, make as many copies as you need for the number of participants you will have, or the particular story you are telling. I recommend using card stock as it is sturdier than copy paper. You may also wish to make copies of the song, finger play, or poem for each participant (on regular copy paper).
4. Color and cut out the pieces. If at all possible, laminate the pieces. If you wish to add any embellishments with dimension, such as jewels, pom-poms, yarn, cloth, streamers, cotton balls, etc., do it after the pieces are laminated
5. Cut out the laminated pieces, leaving about a ¼-inch border of plastic.
6. Mount the laminated pieces (with tape) to the paper sack, and tape or glue the song or poem on the back of the sack. By doing this, you will be able to see the words of the song or poem on the back of the puppet when performing with your hand in the sack.

For example, if you are making "Five Little Speckled Frogs," copy the frog pattern five times to glue on five sacks, and also copy the song five times. Glue or tape the song on the back of the paper sack so it can be easily read while performing. For the benefit of younger children, you can also write the numbers from 1 to 5 on the front of the sacks.

How to Make a Paper Sack Puppet

The paper sacks that I use for making puppets are regular-sized lunch bags, 10½ × 5¼ inches with a "bottom" of 3⅝ × 5¼ inches. They generally come in packages of 50, either brown or white, and can be found in most grocery stores. (You can use any size paper sack—just enlarge the pattern to fit the sack.) The puppet will have the opening at the bottom for your hand to go inside. The plain side of the bag will be facing you with the bottom flap facing the audience. This will be the face.

The process is very simple:

1. Place the mouth piece under the flap. Temporary positioning is recommended at this point.

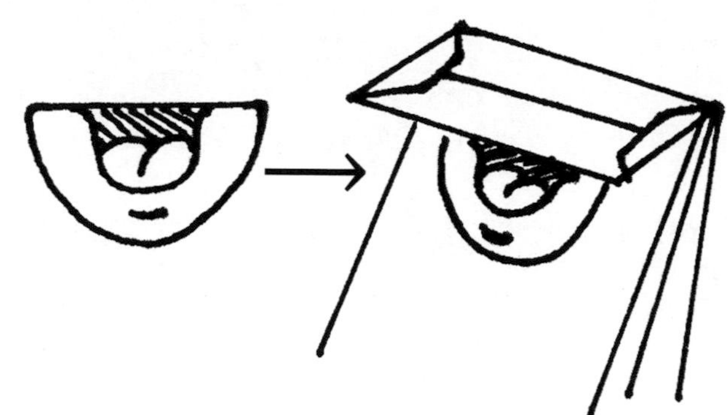

2. Place the face of the puppet on the bottom flap of the sack. Do not adhere yet.

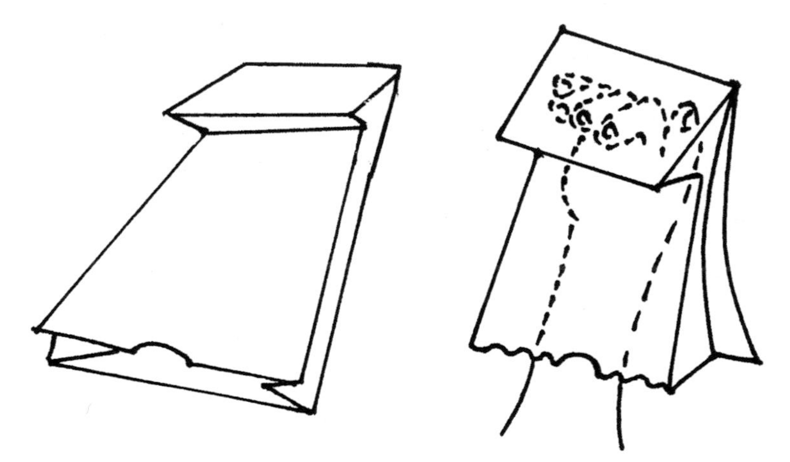

3. Adjust the head piece and the mouth piece so that the head overlaps the mouth and joins together the way you like it *before you adhere them*. Do the same with body pieces and accessories. When everything is in place the way you like it, glue or tape the parts in place.

Left and middle: Breanna colors and cuts a giraffe paper sack puppet pattern at the Learning Landing Preschool. *Right:* Eunice places the mouth piece of the Fawn puppet under the sack flap.

I copy the patterns onto colored card stock, then embellish them with colored pencils or markers, and cut out and laminate the puppet for durability. I usually use doubled-over clear plastic tape to secure the laminated puppet to the sack, so adjustments of the head, mouth and body pieces can be made easily.

Add any embellishments you wish. For example, the wolf in sheep's clothing or the lamb could have cotton balls glued on to look like wool. Brown and yellow yarn could be the lion's mane, add a stick or some straw for the Three Little Pigs. A red plastic cherry could be taped to the top of the ice cream cone. Glitter glue or confetti might be the "sprinkles." Fake jewels (with one flat side) look impressive on the crown. Let your imagination soar!

Note: If young children are making puppets, close supervision is advised. Avoid using materials that babies or toddlers could choke on or swallow.

Make a Puppet Play from a Picture Book

Picture books are an excellent source for puppet plays. There are many great colorful and well-known picture books available. Perhaps your class has a favorite story they love to hear over and over, and have memorized some of the lines. Choose one and read it to the children several times, then make puppets and act it out.

Often, teachers already have favorite books for use in a themed unit. Add puppets for an exciting reinforcement of the theme or unit idea. For the preschool classroom, use related material to reinforce the theme. Use books that have repeated phrases, humorous stories, stories involving movement or travel or problem-solving, have inspiring pictures, an element of surprise, animal or people characters, an interesting storyline or atmosphere or setting, and

Tyler, Breanna and Tammy display the Three Little Pigs puppets, easily turned into a puppet play.

one with possible parts for all children (they could all be the main character and the teacher take the other parts, or vice versa).

Librarians can use children's favorite books to promote reading in the same way.

Choose books that use a series of items or people for sequencing or simple math activities, and a plot that promotes problem-solving opportunities. Choose a book that emphasizes the curricular goal being presented, or the unit being studied. Shorten books that are too long, and simplify language that is too difficult. You can even make up new endings and change characters to fit your needs. See the book lists at the end of each puppet group for ideas.

Remember, puppets are *tools* to bring variety, fun and adventure to the learning process.

Turn a Finger Play, Poem, Song, Story or Chant into a Puppet Show

Children love listening to and participating in poems, songs, finger plays chants and stories, so turn this opportunity into a puppet show. For a finger play, five (or more) children can participate in a puppet show with five of the same puppet (Five Little Speckled Frogs, Five Little Monkeys, etc.) Other children can be given props to hold and move, or music or sound effects to make or start. Color and decorate each puppet differently, or have a collection of puppets that the children can move when it is their turn. (Example: Old MacDonald Had a Farm is a great way to use a variety of animals.)

Tyler and Breanna are ready to put on a "finger play" puppet show, using a finger play from the book.

The children can stand on a stage or in a row at the front of the room, and can enter or exit depending on the rhyme, song, poem or story (count up, count down, enter or move the puppet as each puppet is named). You can use several related rhymes so all the children in the class can participate.

Another idea is to watch a children's movie together, then convert that into a puppet play. For example, you would watch the movie *Heidi* then perform the story with puppets. Other examples are doing an all nursery rhyme theme, fairy tales, counting songs or chants, like "Five Little

Ducks" or "Ten Little Indians." Don't limit yourself too much—why not use 20 or 30 little Indians? Or create a math lesson by counting by twos, fives or tens.

Ideas for Follow-up Activities After a Puppet Show

Take Home Activity

Give the audience something to take home after the puppet show. (This reinforces the story and continues to make good memories and experiences of the play.) Examples: a coloring sheet, a bookmark featuring characters from the play, patterns for other puppets to make at home, or a list of library books to be checked out. If the puppet show is in a library, have related books on the theme available for check out at that time.

Tyler is holding a giraffe puppet and is ready to put on his own puppet show at the Learning Landing Preschool, using an idea from a puppet show.

Group Activity

Following the puppet play, children can make their own puppets to take home and put on a puppet show for their family, or color a related page or bookmark to take home. Or you could repeat the puppet play, allowing the audience to participate in making the sound effects, singing the song or reciting the finger play or poem, repeating a phrase that reoccurs throughout the play, or reading a sign at an appropriate time. (The signs might say, "yeah!" "boo!" "hiss," "sigh," "groan," "whine," "grunt," "Oh!" etc.—or it could be a repeated phrase: "You can't catch me, I'm the Gingerbread Man!")

Teach Something Related to the Puppet Show

Teach the group a song, finger play or poem relating to the puppet show. Give parents a copy with directions for performing it at home. Give them ideas to carry out a home puppet show.

Let's Put on a Puppet Show!

Here are the basic steps that will get you started putting on a show. They are adapted from my own ideas as well as those from other puppeteers and teachers.

1. **Decide on a "story," plot, theme, unit, finger play, poem, song, etc.** If this is your first puppet play, choose something easy, and that the children like.

2. **Make puppets.** Use your imagination, be creative. You don't *have* to use patterns!
3. **Write and assign character lines and narrative parts.** For a large audience (like a classroom), I recommend recording the play on a tape with music and sound effects at appropriate places. Try to use animated voices. When performing, use a microphone (if appropriate) when playing the tape for amplification so that everyone can hear the lines. Then the puppeteers' hands will be free of papers, and the performers will not have to read or memorize their lines.
4. **Prepare stage**. Use a designated area for performances using tape on the floor, a rug, or rope off an area. For the stage, use a table lying on its side, a doorway with a spring curtain rod and curtains, a rod or broom with draped material placed across the backs of two tall chairs which are turned sideways or a large folded cardboard screen. Paint, decorate, drape material, and attach items as needed.
5. **Prepare lighting, music (I recommend pre-recorded music), scenery, props, etc.**
6. **Practice the play.**
7. **Make invitations.**
8. **Make refreshments (optional).** Popcorn, popsicles, cookies, carrot sticks—make it simple and easy and something that ties in with the theme.
9. **Prepare audience seating, stage, lights, music, microphones, scenery, props, etc.** Don't forget to have a dress rehearsal!
10. When the play is ready to perform, the audience is ready, and it's time to start, **welcome everyone, thank them for coming, and announce the actors, narrators, parts, story title, etc.** Announce the refreshments available during or after the play if you are having any.
11. **Have fun** putting on your puppet show! (Don't forget to record it!)
12. After the show, **discuss** areas for improvement. **Modify** and **adapt** as needed. Watch the video and treat/reward and praise the children for participating.
13. **Plan to have another puppet show** for a new audience, or a new puppet show for the same audience. HAVE FUN planning and creating. Be enthusiastic!

1. CHICKEN LITTLE

An acorn falls on Chicken Little's head. She thinks the sky is falling, panics and runs to tell the king this important news. On the way, she encounters Goosey Loosey, Ducky Lucky, Henny Penny, Turkey Lurkey and Cocky Locky. All the friends then run into Foxy Loxy, who threatens to eat them.

1a. Chicken Little

Acorn pattern is on page 343.

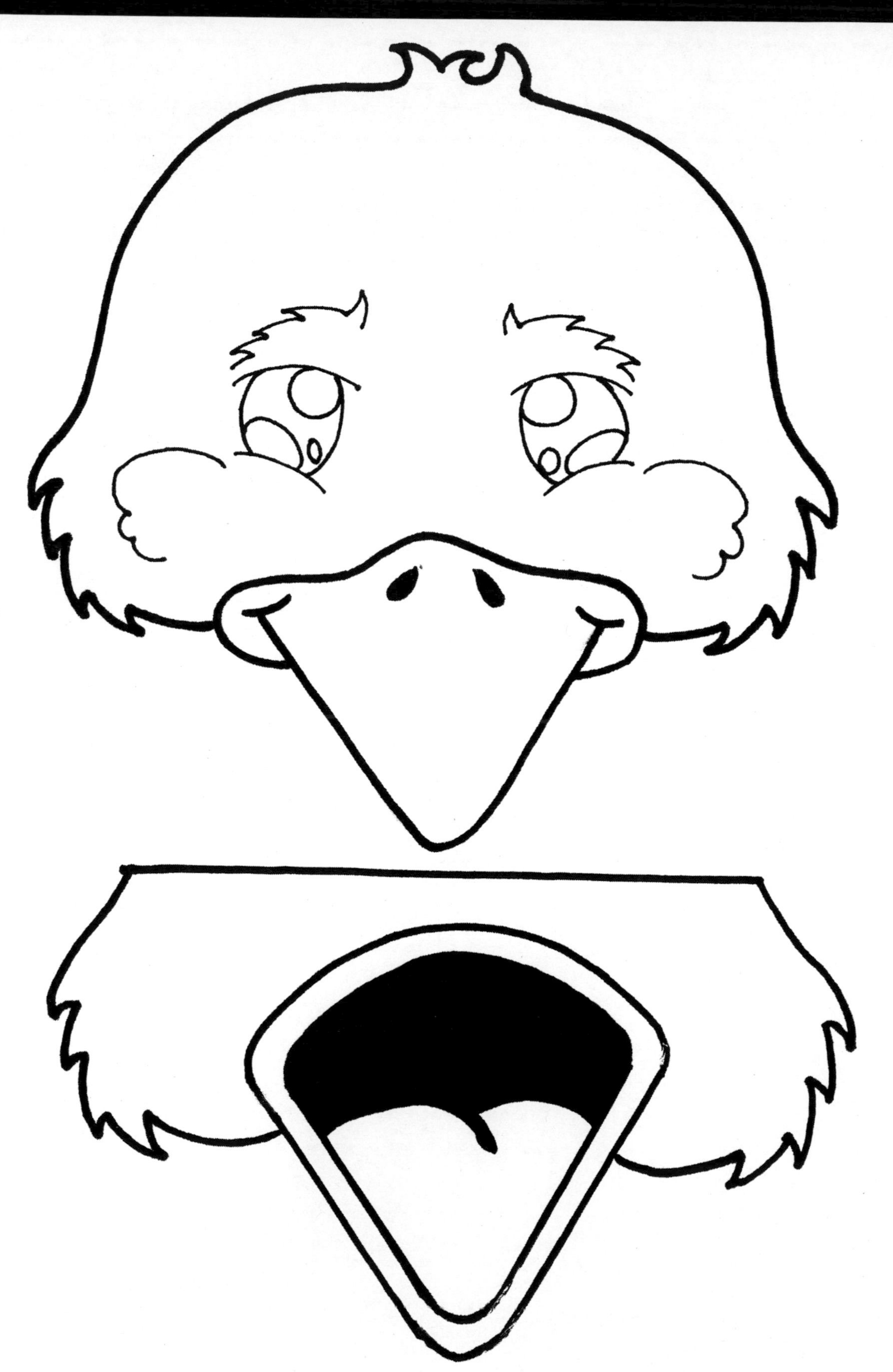

Chicken/Chicks Activities

For additional ideas see Goosey Loosey (#1b) puppet activities.

Songs to Sing and Play

Chicken Little Song
(tune: The Wheels on the Bus)

Uses all characters in the Chicken Little story; words by Eunice Wright

Chicken Little said, "The sky is falling!
The sky is falling! The sky is falling!"
Chicken Little said, "The sky is falling!"
When the acorn fell on her head.

Chicken Little told Goosey Loosey,
Goosey Loosey, Goosey Loosey.
Chicken Little told Goosey Loosey,
"Let's go tell the King."

Chicken Little told Ducky Lucky,
Ducky Lucky, Ducky Lucky.
Chicken Little told Ducky Lucky,
"Let's go tell the King."

Chicken Little told Henny Penny,
Henny Penny, Henny Penny.
Chicken Little told Henny Penny,
"Let's go tell the King."

Chicken Little told Turkey Lurkey,
Turkey Lurkey, Turkey Lurkey.
Chicken Little told Turkey Lurkey,
"Let's go tell the King."

Chicken Little told Cocky Locky,
Cocky Locky, Cocky Locky.
Chicken Little told Cocky Locky,
"Let's go tell the King."

Chicken Little told Foxy Loxy,
Foxy Loxy, Foxy Loxy.
Chicken Little told Foxy Loxy,
Who wanted to eat them all up!

Chicken Little and Goosey Loosey,
Ducky Lucky and Henny Penny.
Turkey Lurkey and Cocky Locky
All ran for their lives! *(Scream and run away!)*

Tune: Oh Where, Oh Where Has My Little Dog Gone?

Words by Eunice Wright

Oh where, oh where are the chickens on the farm?
Oh where, oh where can they be?
Are they laying some eggs
or eating some seed?
Oh where, oh where can they be?

Tune: The Wheels on the Bus

Words by Eunice Wright

The chickens on the farm
Go cluck, cluck, cluck
Cluck, cluck, cluck
Cluck, cluck, cluck
The chickens on the farm
Go cluck, cluck, cluck
All around the farm.

The chicks on the farm
Go peep, peep, peep.
Peep, Peep, Peep
Peep, Peep, Peep
The chicks on the farm
Go Peep, Peep, Peep
All around the farm.

Tune: Baa Baa Black Sheep

Words by Eunice Wright

Red hen, red hen, did you lay today?
Yes, sir. Yes, sir, right here in the hay.
One egg for my master,
One egg for the dame,
And one egg for a little boy
Who lives down the lane.
Red hen, red hen, did you lay today?
Yes, sir. Yes, sir, right here in the hay.

Tune: I'm a Little Teapot

Words by Eunice Wright

I'm a little chick, yellow and sweet.
Here is my beak, I use it to eat.
When I get real hungry, I say, "Peep!"
Then I find a worm that I can keep.

Tune: Old MacDonald Had a Farm

Old MacDonald had a farm, E-I-E-I-O
And on this farm he had [a chicken, some chicks, *or* a hen], E-I-E-I-O, etc.

Tune: The Farmer in the Dell

The farmer takes a [chicken, chick *or* hen]

Down on Grandpa's Farm

Written by Robert D. Singleton/Traditional
See songs for teaching.com or One Light, One Sun *by Raffi to listen to the tune.*

Down on grandpa's farm there is a ... [big white hen, brown chicken, black hen, a little chick, a red hen].

Chicken

Author Unknown

Chicken, chicken, you can't cluck too much for me ...
"C" is for the little chick, "H" for the momma hen ...

For more, visit nancycassidymusic.com, kididdles.com, songlyrics.com, theteachersguide.com.

Mother Gilligan (tune: Father Abraham)

Mother Gilligan [*or* Mother Chicken *or* Mother Hen] had some chicks,
Some chicks had Mother Gilligan. And they didn't dance...

For more information, visit Pete's Activity Advice for Camps and All (http://campsongs.blogspot.com/)

Bought Me a Hen

See Cat (#6e) Song section for entire song.

Bought me a hen and the hen pleased me,
I fed my hen under yonder tree.
Hen goes chimmy-chuck, chimmy-chuck,
Cat goes fiddle-i-fee.

Song to play

"Chickens in the Barnyard," *I Have a Song for You,* by Janeen Brady, page 12.

Poems and Nursery Rhymes

Forehead, Eyes, Cheeks, Nose, Mouth, and Chin

Love and Law in Child Training: A Book for Mothers, *by Emilie Poulsson, 1899.*

Here sits the Lord Mayor;
Here sit his two men;
Here sits the cock
And here sits the hen;
Here sit the little chickens
And here they run in;
Chin chopper, chin chopper, chin chopper, chin!

Higgledy, Piggledy My Black Hen

The Real Mother Goose, *by Blanche Fisher Wright, 1916.*

Higgledy, Piggledy, my black hen,
She lays eggs for gentlemen;
Sometimes nine, Sometimes ten,
Higgledy, Piggledy, my black hen.

Little Hen
(a term of endearment for a daughter)
Or Clever Hen

The Real Mother Goose, *by Blanche Fisher Wright, 1916.*

I had a little hen, the prettiest ever seen,
She washed up the dishes and kept the house clean.
She went to the mill to fetch us some flour,
And always got home in less than an hour.
She baked me my bread, she brewed me my ale,
She sat by the fire and told a fine tale!

Five Little Chicks
(Make 5 chick puppets and a mother hen)

Children's Corner, June 11, 1904.

Said the first little chick with a queer little squirm,
"I wish I could find a fat little worm."
Said the next little chick with an odd little shrug,
"I wish I could find a fat little slug."

Said the third little chick with a sharp little squeal,
"I wish I could find some nice yellow meal."
Said the fourth little chick with a sigh of grief,
"I wish I could find a little green leaf."
Said the fifth little chick with a faint little moan,
"I wish I could find a wee gravel stone."
"Now, see here," said mother hen from the green garden patch,
"If you want any breakfast, just come here and scratch!"

The Ambitious Chicken

In My Nursery: A Book of Verse,
by Laura E. Richards, 1890.

It was an Easter chicken
So blithesome and so gay;
He peeped from out his plaster shell
All on an Easter Day.

His wings were made of yellow down,
His eyes were made of beads;
He seemed, in very sooth, to have
All that a chicken needs.

He winked and blinked and peeped about,
And to himself he said,
"When first a chicken leaves the shell,
Of course he must be fed.

"And though I may be young in years,
And this my natal morn,
I'm quite, quite old enough to know
Where people keep the corn."

He winked and blinked and peeped about,
Till in a corner sly
He saw a heap of golden corn
Piled on a platter high.

"Now, this is well!" the chicken cried;
"Now, this is well, in sooth.
This corn shall nourish and sustain
My faint and tender youth.

"And I shall grow and grow apace,
And come to high estate,
With mighty feathers in my tail,
And combs upon my pate.

"To see my beauty and my grace
The feathered race will flock,
And all will bow them low before
The mighty Easter Cock."

Books

Charlie Chick, by Nick Denchfield (Harcourt, 2007).
The Chick and the Duckling, by Mirra Ginsburg (Macmillan, 1972).
Chicken Little, by Paul Galdone (Seabury Press, 1973).
Chicken Little, by Rebecca Emberley (Roaring Book Press, 2009).
Chicken Little, by Sally Hobson (Simon & Schuster, 1994).
Chickens Aren't the Only Ones, by Ruth Heller (Grosset and Dunlap, 1981).
The Cinnamon Hen's Autumn Day, by Sandra Dutton (Macmillan, Atheneum, 1988).
Cluck, by Alan Snow (Bantam, Doubleday, 1995).
Daisy and the Egg, by Jane Simmons (Little, Brown and Co., 1998).
The Egg, by Gallimard Jeunesse, a Scholastic First Discovery Book (Scholastic, 1992).
Five Little Chicks, by Nancy Tafuri (Simon & Schuster, 2006). *The chicks hunt for food at the farm. Short text, beautiful illustrations.*
For Sure! For Sure! A tale by Hans Christian Andersen (August House Little Folk, 2004). Illustrated by Stefan Czernecki. Translation by Mus White. *A gossip-spreading humorous story.*
The Golden Egg Book, a Golden Book by Margaret Wise Brown (Golden Press, 1975).
Hattie and the Fox, by Mem Fox (Bradbury Press, 1986).
Interrupting Chicken, by David Ezra Stein (Candlewick Press, 2010).
The Little Hen and the Giant, by Maria Polushkin (Scholastic, Robbins-Harper and Row, 1977).

Merry Christmas, Cheeps! by Julie Stiegemeyer (Bloomsbury, 2007).

The Most Wonderful Egg in the World, by Helme Heine (Aladdin, 1987).

Mrs. Chicken and the Hungry Crocodile, by Won-Idy Paye (Henry Holt, 2003). *African tale. Mrs. Chicken tricks the crocodile, and saves herself. Easy to read, basic illustrations for young children.*

The Plot Chickens, by Mary Jane Auch (Holiday House, 2009).

The Runaway Chick, by Erica Briers (Templar, 2012).

Something Is Coming, by Bernice Chardiet (Puffin, 1994).

Stuck in the Mud, by Jane Clarke (Bloomsbury, Walker Pub. Co., 2008). *Baby chick gets stuck in the mud and this begins a chain reaction of helpers. Kids will enjoy the muddy tug of war as the farm animals all lend a hand.*

Super Cluck, by Robert and Jane O'Connor (HarperCollins, 1991).

This Little Chick, by John Lawrence (Candlewick Press, 2002).

When the Chickens Went on Strike: A Rosh Hashana Tale, by Erica Silverman (Dutton, 2003). *Beautiful illustrations; a Jewish story of customs and trying to be a better person.*

Movies and Television

Chicken Little (2005), Walt Disney Buena Vista

Chicken Run (2000), Dream Works

FogHorn LegHorn (1946–1964) Warner Brothers Entertainment, Inc. *Banty Raids* (1963); *Of Rice and Hen* (1953); *The Dixie Fryer* (1960); *Little Boy Boo* (1954); *Feather Dusted* (1955); *Henhouse Henery* (1949); *Lovelorn Leghorn* (1951)

The Hoboken Chicken Emergency (1984), Martin Tahse Productions, WonderWorks

Hop (2011), Universal Pictures and Illumination Entertainment

The Muppets (1976–1992), ITC Entertainment Henson Associates, distributed by Disney: *"Forget You,"* performed by Camilla and the Chickens (2011); *Classical Chicken*, "The Blue Danube Waltz," conducted by The Great Gonzo and featuring the lovely Camilla (2009); *Chicken in the Basket* (1977–1978), The Muppet Show Swedish Chef, season 3, episode 11; *Ping Pong Ball Eggs* (1976–1977), The Muppet Show Swedish Chef, episode 214; *Spring Chicken* (1979–1980), The Muppet Show Swedish Chef, Episode 512; *Baby Face*, performed by a chorus of chickens (1977), season 2, episode 28; *Muppet News Flash*: chicken dances ballet (1976), season 1; Gonzo interviews hopefuls for a new dancing chicken act (1977), season 2, episode 26; "Tea for Two" by Gonzo and his dancing chicken, Lolita (1977), season 2, episode 26; Song pecked out by chickens on a piano (1977), season 2, episode 28; Chickens peck out "Chopsticks" on the piano (1977), season 2, episode 32; Rowlf and a chicken play a song on the piano (1977), season 2, episode 36; The Swedish Chef chases a chicken, and performs "Egg du Chef," (1978), season 2, episode 39; "Cluckitis" disease (1979), season 3, episode 21; Wonder Pig battles a giant chicken (1980), season 4, episode 19; Gonzo and the chickens (1980), season 5, episode 11.

The Natural History of the Chicken (2003), PBS

Our Feathered Friends: Adventures on a Chicken Farm. (2007), Choices Inc.

Return to Oz (2004), Walt Disney Home Entertainment

Robin Hood (Animated, 1973), Disney

Rock-A-Doodle (1991), Don Bluth Entertainment

Toy Story 2 (1999), Disney (man in chicken costume)

1b. Goosey Loosey

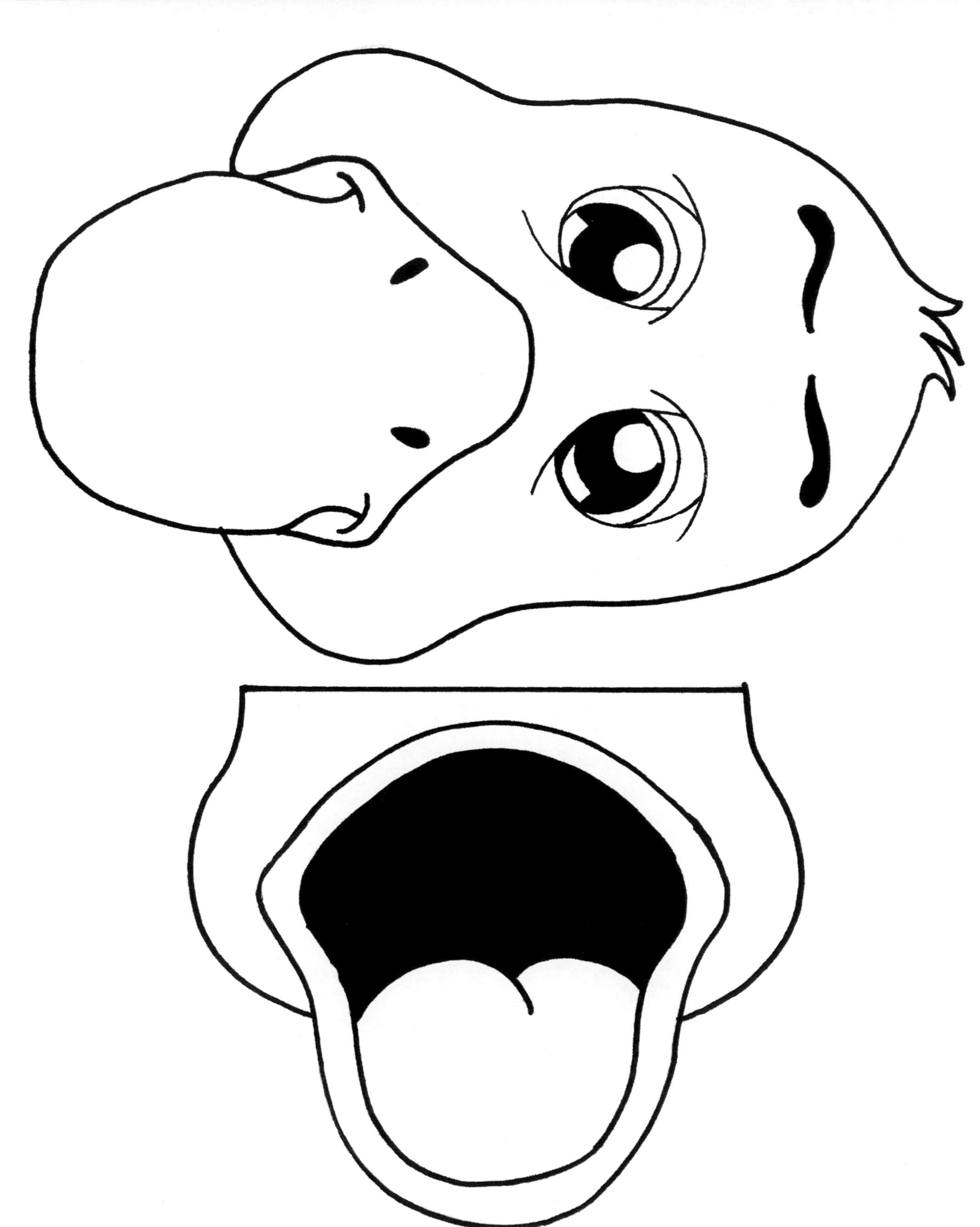

Goose Activities

Songs to Sing and Play

Go Tell Aunt Rhody

Traditional, 1844; roots traced to a 1752 opera by Rousseau. For sheet music, see warrenemilyswan.us. Listen to the song on Ballad of America, *Vol. 2 by Matthew Sabatella.*

Go tell Aunt Rhody,
Go tell Aunt Rhody,
Go tell Aunt Rhody
The old gray goose is dead.

The one she's been saving,
The one she's been saving,
The one she's been saving
To make a feather bed.

She died in the mill pond,
She died in the mill pond,
She died in the mill pond
From standing on her head.

She died on a Friday,
She died on a Friday,
She died on a Friday,
With an aching in her head.

The goslings are mourning,
The goslings are mourning,
The goslings are mourning.
Because their mother's dead.

The old gander's weeping,
The old gander's weeping,
The old gander's weeping
Because his wife is dead.

Go tell Aunt Rhody,
Go tell Aunt Rhody,
Go tell Aunt Rhody
The old gray goose is dead.

Down on Grandpa's Farm

Written by Robert D. Singleton/Traditional. See songs for teaching.com or One Light, One Sun *by Raffi to listen to the tune.This song is suitable for use with many other animals by substituting the animal names and the sounds they make and sometimes changing the settings.*

Down on grandpa's farm there is... [an old gray goose ... she makes a sound like this: "Honk, honk."]

Down on Grandpa's farm there is a tiny baby lamb.
Down at the zoo there is a hungry striped tiger.
Over in the jungle there is a hungry wild lion.
Living with the giant is a golden goose.
Once upon a time there lived Goosey Loosey.
Flying overhead is a Canadian Goose.

Bought Me a Goose

See Cat (#6e) for entire song.

Bought me a goose and the goose pleased me
I fed my goose under yonder tree.
Goose goes hissy, hissy,
Duck goes quack, quack,
Hen goes chimmy-chuck, chimmy-chuck,
Cat goes fiddle-i-fee.

Song to play

"Grandma's Feather Bed" by Jim Connor, sung by John Denver. (There is a great version sung by the Muppets and John Denver.) Also sung by Brenda Lee, from the Music for Little People album, *Big Country (For One and All)*. "It was made from the feathers of forty eleven *geese...*"

Poems and Nursery Rhymes

Goosey, Goosey, Gander

The Real Mother Goose, *by Blanche Fisher Wright, 1916.*

Goose-a goose-a gander,
Where shall I wander?
Up stairs or down stairs,
In my lady's chamber;

There you'll find a cup of sack
And a race of ginger.

Old father long legs
Can't say his prayers.
Take him by the left leg,
And throw him down the stairs.

The stairs went crack,
He nearly broke his back.
And all the little ducks went,
"Quack, quack, quack."

The Goose in the House

Aunt Kitty's Stories, *1870.*

This goose got in the house,
He'd the courage of a mouse,
So he quacked, and he hissed at the kitten;

But as she stood at bay,
He quickly ran away;
Afraid of being scratched as well as bitten.

The Canada Goose

The Peter Patter Book of Nursery Rhymes, *by Leroy F. Jackson, 1918.*

A Canada goose
On the South Palouse
Is singing her summer song.
Her words are wise,
And she greets the skies
With a voice like a steamer gong:
"If you harbor your wealth
And keep your health,
You'll always be rich and strong."

Old Mother Goose

The Real Mother Goose, *by Blanche Fisher Wright, 1916.*

Old Mother Goose, when
She wanted to wander,
Would ride through the air
On a very fine gander.

Intery, Mintery

The Real Mother Goose, *by Blanche Fisher Wright, 1916.*

Intery, mintery, cutery corn,
Apple seed and apple thorn;
Wire, brier, linber-lock,
Five geese in a flock,
Sit and sing by a spring,
O-u-t, and in again.

Games and Group Activities

Feathers

Let children glue goose feathers on the goose puppet or stuff a pillow case with goose feathers to make a small feather bed.

Blowing the Feathers

From Games for Everybody, *by May C. Hofmann (Dodge Publishing Co., 1905).*

Seat the children around a small sheet or tablecloth. This is held tight by the players about 1½ feet from the floor, and a feather is placed in the middle.

One is chosen to be out, and at a given signal from the leader, the feather is blown from one player to another by small movements of the sheet, back and forth, high and low, never allowed to rest once.

The player outside tries to catch the feather. When he does succeed, the person on whom it rested or was nearest to must take his place.

Duck, Duck, Goose

Everyone sits in a circle. One player is "It" and goes around the circle patting heads (gently!) and saying "Duck." "It" then chooses one player to be "Goose" by patting her head and saying "Goose." The Goose jumps up and chases "It" around the circle. If It is tagged before sitting in the Goose's empty spot, he remains "It." If "It" makes it to the empty spot before being tagged, Goose becomes "It." An alternate is to say "Goose, Goose, Golden Egg.")

Drama

Dramatize the story of Jack and the Beanstalk using boy (#47), mother (#46), cow (#21), troll (#14d), and goose (#1b) puppets.

Goosey-Gander

This is a play with sheet music: *The Cat and the Fiddle Book*, 1922.

Books

Barnyard Banter, by Denise Fleming (Henry Holt, 1997). *Ages 3–6, board book. Goose and farm animals.*

Blue Goose, by Nancy Tafuri (Simon & Schuster, 2008). *The farm animals are different colors (blue goose, red hen, yellow chick, white duck) and decide to mix paint to paint the farm. Great simple story line and pictures to teach children color mixing.*

Boo to a Goose, by Mem Fox (Hodder Children's Books, 1996). *Great for rhyming and repetition.*

The Daddy Goose Treasury, by Vivian French (Chicken House, 2006). *Nursery rhymes.*

The Day the Goose Got Loose, by Reeve Lindbergh (Penguin Group, 1995). *Nice Illustrations.*

Duck and Goose, by Tad Hills (Schwartz and Wade, 2006). *They work together to take care of an egg.*

Gertrude the Goose Who Forgot, by Joanna and Paul Galdone (Methuen Young Books, 1976).

The Golden Goose, by Dick King-Smith (Knopf, 2005). *Beautiful Illustrations. A farmer experiencing hard times could really use a golden goose to change his luck.*

Goose Goofs Off, by Jacquelyn Reinach (Sweet Pickle Series, Holt, 1997).

A Goose Named Gilligan, by Jerry M. Hay (HJ Kramer, 2004).

The Goose That Laid the Golden Egg, an Aesop Fable by Mark White (Picture Window, 2004).

Goose's Story, by Cari Best (Farrar, 2002). *A story about an injured Canada goose.*

Honk, Honk, Goose! By April Sayre (Henry Holt, 2009). *Two Canada geese start a family.*

Lucy Goosey, by Margaret Wild and Ann James (Little Hare Books, 2007). *When all the ducks leave the pond to fly away, Lucy doesn't want to go. A very cute story of a mother's love. Nice illustrations.*

Monster Goose, by Judy Sierra (Harcourt, 2001). *Twenty-five Scary Nursery Rhymes.*

Never Say Boo to a Goose! By Jakki Wood (Barefoot Books, 2002).

The Perfect Nest, by Catherine Friend (Candlewick Press, 2007). *A chicken, duck, and goose try to lay eggs on the farm. Humorous, fantastic illustrations, good text, a great preschool book. Recommended!*

The Real Mother Goose, by Blanche Fisher Wright (Rand McNally and Co., 1916).

Silly Goose, by Marni McGee (Good Books, 2008). *Goose and friends outwit fox. Cute illustrations, okay for preschool age.*

Silly Little Goose, by Nancy Tafuri (Scholastic Press, 2001). *Preschool age; a goose looks for a nest. Good book!*

Movies and Television

Abbott and Costello in *Jack and the Beanstalk* (1952), Exclusive Productions Inc.

The Aristocats (animated, 1970), Disney

Beanstalk (1994), Paramount Family Favorites

Fly Away Home (1996), directed by Carroll Ballard

The Giant Killer (1924), J.R. Bray Studios (silent, black and white)
Giantland (1933), Disney. *Mickey tells a story, with himself as Jack.*
Jack and the Beanstalk (1955), Directed by Lotte Reiniger
Jack and the Beanstalk (1967), Hanna-Barbera Productions
Jack and the Beanstalk (2010), Avalon Family Entertainment
Jack and the Beanstalk: The Real Story (2001), Jim Henson company (Hallmark)
Mickey and the Beanstalk (1947), Disney
The New 3 Stooges: Three Jacks and a Beanstalk (1965), TV Classics Collection, Golden Age of Television
Puss in Boots (2011), DreamWorks Animation
Tales from Europe: The Golden Goose (1964), released 2001 by First Run Features studio

1c. Ducky Lucky

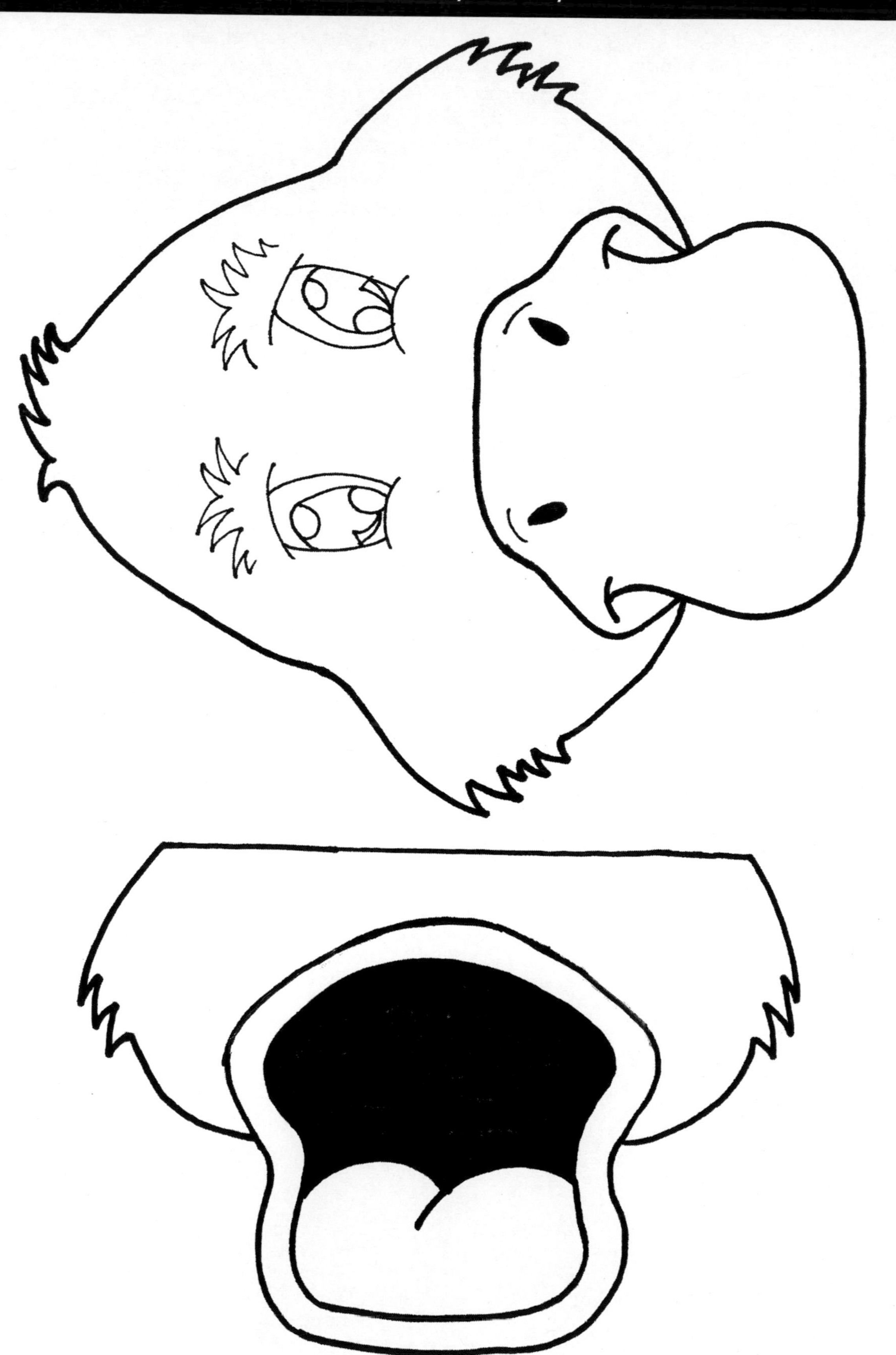

Duck Activities

Songs to Sing and Play

Six Little Ducks

Unknown Author

Six little ducks
That I once knew,
Fat ones, skinny ones,
Fair ones, too…

Five Little Ducks

Unknown author. Raffi sings a good version of this song.

Five little ducks went out one day
Over the hills and far away.
Mommy [or Daddy] duck called, "Quack, quack, quack,"
But only four little ducks came waddling back.

Four little ducks went out one day
Over the hills and far away.
Mommy [or Daddy] duck called, "Quack, quack, quack,"
But only three little ducks came waddling back.

Continue the song to zero.

Web-footed Friends (Tune: Stars and Stripes Forever)

By Fred Allen (1950)

Change lyrics to "Be kind to your web-footed friends, / For a duck may be somebody's mother…"

She Waded in the Water (Tune: Battle Hymn)

Original author unknown. Adapted by Eunice Wright. See entire song with sheet music in Wee Sing Silly Songs, *pp. 20–21.*

She [*the duck*] waded in the water and she got her feet all wet,
She waded in the water and she got her feet all wet, (*repeat*)
But she didn't get her (clap, clap) wet, (clap) yet. (clap)…
…She finally got her *feathers* wet!…

Tune: I'm a Little Teapot

Words by Eunice and Juli Wright

I'm a little duck, fluffy and white.
When I walk, I'm quite a sight!
I like to "quack, quack" with my bill,
While waddling up and down the hill.

Alternate:

I'm a little duck, fluffy and white.
I have feathers, soft and light.
Here are my wings that I use for flight.
"Quack" is the sound I make day and night.

Tune: Are You Sleeping?

Words by Juli Wright

Fuzzy duckling,
Fuzzy duckling,
In the creek;
In the lake.
Swimming upstream,
There he goes.
Quack! Quack! Quack!
Quack! Quack! Quack!

Bought Me a Duck

See cat (#6e) for entire song.

Bought me a duck and the duck pleased me,
I fed my duck under yonder tree.
Duck goes quack, quack,
Hen goes chimmy-chuck, chimmy-chuck,
Cat goes fiddle-i-fee.

Quack, Quack, Quack

In I Have a Song for You About Animals, *by Janeen Brady, p. 7.*

There's a Little White Duck

Written by Bernard Zaritzky and Walt Barrows © 1950.

"There's a little white duck sitting in the water..."

Down on Grandpa's Farm

Written by Robert D. Singleton/Traditional. See songsforteaching.com or One Light, One Sun *by Raffi to listen to the tune.*

Down on grandpa's farm there is a little white duck [a lonely little duck, an ugly duckling, etc.]

I Had a Rooster

Performed by Pete Seeger

Change words to "I had a duck, my duck pleased me / I fed my duck 'neath the greenberry tree..."

Songs and Albums

The Duck Song, by Bryant Oden (2009), Songdrops.com

Five Little Ducks (*Raffi Songs to Read)* by Raffi (1992), Random House (1989), Crown.

Six Little Ducks, by Al Dana (1997), music CD by Kimbo Educational.

Six Little Ducks, by Chris Conover (1976), Crowell.

Six Little Ducks, by Kim Mitzo Thompson. Sing a Story Book and CD (2006), School Specialty Publishing. Also: Twin Sisters, 2010.

Six Little Ducks, Classic Children's Songs, by Dennis Buck (1997), Kimbo Educational

Six Little Ducks Primary Concepts, Illustrated by Brendan Flannelly-King (Read Along Songs).

Poems and Nursery Rhymes

Ducks and Drakes

The Little Mother Goose, by Jessie Willcox Smith, 1918.

A duck and a drake,
And a halfpenny cake,
With a penny to pay the old baker.
A hop and a scotch
Is another notch,
Slitherum, Slatherum, take her.

6 Little Ducks (Count Up)

By Juli Wright

One little duck, feeling blue,
He found a friend, now there are two.
Two little ducks, happy as can be,
They saw father duck, now there are three.
Three little ducks, swimming to shore,
Along came mother, now there are four.
Four little ducks, they love to dive,
Up swam brother duck, now there are five.
Five little ducks, doing some tricks,
Happy little sister came, that made six.
Six little ducks, swimming away,
I really wish that they would stay.

The Duck and the Kangaroo

Nonsense Songs, Stories, Botany, and Alphabets, *Edward Lear, 1894.*

I.
Said the Duck to the Kangaroo,
"Good gracious! how you hop
Over the fields, and the water too,
As if you never would stop!
My life is a bore in this nasty pond;
And I long to go out in the world beyond:
I wish I could hop like you,"
Said the Duck to the Kangaroo.

II.
"Please give me a ride on your back,"
Said the Duck to the Kangaroo:
"I would sit quite still, and say nothing but 'Quack'
The whole of the long day through;
And we'd go the Dee, and the Jelly Bo Lee,
Over the land, and over the sea:
Please take me a ride! oh, do!"
Said the Duck to the Kangaroo.

III.
Said the Kangaroo to the Duck,
"This requires some little reflection.
Perhaps, on the whole, it might bring me luck;
And there seems but one objection;
Which is, if you'll let me speak so bold,
Your feet are unpleasantly wet and cold,
And would probably give me the roo-
Matiz," said the Kangaroo.

IV.
Said the Duck, "As I sat on the rocks,
I have thought over that completely;
And I bought four pairs of worsted socks,
Which fit my web-feet neatly;
And, to keep out the cold, I've bought a cloak;
And every day a cigar I'll smoke;
All to follow my own dear true
Love of a Kangaroo."

V.
Said the Kangaroo, "I'm ready,
All in the moonlight pale;
But to balance me well, dear Duck, sit steady,
And quite at the end of my tail."
So away they went with a hop and a bound;
And they hopped the whole world three times round.
And who so happy, oh! who,
As the Duck and the Kangaroo?

Dame Duck's Lessons to Her Ducklings

Mother Goose's Nursery Rhymes, 1877.

Old Mother Duck has hatched a brood
Of ducklings, small and callow:
Their little wings are short, their down
Is mottled grey and yellow.

There is a quiet little stream,
That runs into the moat,
Where tall green sedges spread their leaves,
And water-lilies float.

Close by the margin of the brook
The old Duck made her nest,
Of straw, and leaves, and withered grass,
And down from her own breast.

And there she sat for four long weeks,
In rainy days and fine,
Until the Ducklings all came out—
Four, five, six, seven, eight, nine.

One peeped out from beneath her wing,
One scrambled on her back:
"That's very rude," said old Dame Duck,
"Get off! quack, quack, quack, quack!"

"'Tis close," said Dame Duck, shoving out
The egg-shells with her bill,
"Besides, it never suits young ducks
To keep them sitting still."

So, rising from her nest, she said,
"Now, children, look at me:
A well-bred duck should waddle so,
From side to side—d'ye see?"

"Yes," said the little ones, and then
She went on to explain:
"A well-bred duck turns in its toes
As I do—try again."

"Yes," said the Ducklings, waddling on.
"That's better," said their mother;
"But well-bred ducks walk in a row,
Straight—one behind another."

"Yes," said the little Ducks again,
All waddling in a row:
"Now to the pond," said old Dame Duck—
Splash, splash! and in they go.

"Let me swim first," said old Dame Duck,
"To this side, now to that;
There, snap at those great brown-winged flies,
They make young ducklings fat.

"Now when you reach the poultry-yard,
The hen-wife, Molly Head,
Will feed you, with the other fowls,
On bran and mashed-up bread;

"The hens will peck and fight, but mind,
I hope that all of you
Will gobble up the food as fast
As well-bred ducks should do.

"You'd better get into the dish,
Unless it is too small;
In that case, I should use my foot,
And overturn it all."

The Ducklings did as they were bid,
And found the plan so good,
That, from that day, the other fowls
Got hardly any food.

The Forty Little Ducklings

In My Nursery: A Book of Verse, *by Laura E. Richards, 1890.*

The forty little ducklings who lived up at the farm,
They said unto each other, "Oh! the day is very warm!"

They said unto each other, "Oh! the river's very cool!
The duck who did not seek it now would surely be a fool."

The forty little ducklings, they started down the road;
And waddle, waddle, waddle, was the gait at which they goed.

The same it is not grammar,—you may change it if you choose,—
But one cannot stop for trifles when inspired by the Muse.

They waddled and they waddled and they waddled on and on.
Till one remarked, "Oh! deary me, where is the river gone?

We asked the Ancient Gander, and he said 'twas very near.
He must have been deceiving us, or else himself, I fear."

They waddled and they waddled, till no further they could go:
Then down upon a mossy bank they sat them in a row.

They took their little handkerchiefs and wept a little weep,
And then they put away their heads, and then they went to sleep.

There came along a farmer, with a basket on his arm,
And all those little duckylings he took back to the farm.

He put them in their little beds, and wished them sweet repose,
And fastened mustard plasters on their little webby toes.

Next day these little ducklings, they were very very ill.
Their mother sent for Doctor Quack, who gave them each a pill;

But soon as they recovered, the first thing that they did,
Was to peck the Ancient Gander, till he ran away and hid.

Group Activity

Fuzzy Duckling

Make 10 little duck puppets of different colors, insert color words into the rhyme to reinforce learning colors. Use the words in *The Fuzzy Duckling* by Jane Werner (a Little Golden Book).

"One little baby duck, looking out at you, He has a fuzzy sister, now there are two..."

Books

Angus and the Ducks, by Marjorie Flack (Square Fish, 1997).
Animal Hospital, by Judith Walker-Hodge (DK Pub., 1999). *Two children find an injured duck and take it to the veterinarian.*
The Chick and the Duckling, by Mirra Ginsburg (Aladdin, Simon & Schuster, 1988). *Duck can swim well. But what about Chick?*
The Chick and the Duckling, by V. Suteev (Macmillan, 1972).
Cold Little Duck, Duck, Duck, by Lisa W. Peters (Greenwillow Books, 2000).
Days of the Ducklings, by Bruce McMillan (Houghton Mifflin, 2001), Co.

Delilah's Delightful Dream, by Ruth Lerner Perle (Grolier, 1990). *A cute story for K+ children about cooperation and being bossy.*

Dick the Duckling, by Mrs. Herbert Strang (Oxford Univ. Press, 1932).

Duck, by David Lloyd (Lippincott, 1988).

Duck, by Janet Anne Holmes (Little Hare Books, 2009).

Duck for President, by Doreen Cronin (Simon & Schuster, 2004).

Duck! Rabbit! by Amy Krouse Rosenthal (Chronicle Books, 2009).

Duck Soup, by Jackie Urbanovic (Harper-Collins, 2008). *Max the duck is cooking an amazing soup.*

Duckling, by Lisa Magloff (DK Publishing, 2003).

Duckling Days, by Karen Wallace (Dorling Kindersley, 1999), Level 1 reader.

Ducks Disappearing, by Phyllis Reynolds Naylor (Athenium Books for Young Readers, 1997).

Ducks Don't Wear Socks, by John Nedwidek (Viking, 2008). *Humorous story, cute illustrations, great for young children.*

Duncan the Dancing Duck, by Syd Hoff (Clarion Books, 1994).

Farmer Duck, by Martin Waddell (Candlewick, 1996).

Five Little Ducks, by Ian Beck (Henry Holt & Co., 1993).

Five Little Ducks, by Penny Ives (Swindon Child's Play, 2002).

The Fuzzy Duckling, a Little Golden Book, by Jane Werner (Golden Press, 1977).

The Fuzzy Duckling: Quack, Quack! by Melissa Lagonegro (Golden Books, 2004).

Giggle, Giggle, Quack, by Doreen Cronin (Simon & Schuster, 2002).

Goodnight, My Duckling, by Nancy Tafuri (Scholastic Press, 2005). *Very simple text, beautiful illustrations.*

Have You Seen My Duckling? By Nancy Tafuri (Greenwillow Books, 1984).

I Wish That I Had Duck Feet, by Theo LeSieg (Random House, 1965).

In the Rain with Baby Duck, by Amy Hest (Candlewick Press, 1995). *A series.*

Little Chick's Friend, Duckling, by Mary DeBall Kwitz (HarperCollins, 1992).

The Little Duck, by Judy Dunn (Random House, 1976). *Full color photographs with humorous facts of a year in a duck's life.*

Little Quack, by Lauren Thompson (Simon & Schuster, 2003).

Little White Duck, by Walt Whippo (Little, Brown, 2000).

Lucky Duck, by Ellen Weiss (Aladdin, 2004). *A duck, oblivious to dangers, has a day filled with near misses.*

The Magic String, by Francene Sabin (Troll Associates, 1981). *A beautifully illustrated book and wonderful story. Highly recommended.*

Make Way for Ducklings, by Robert McCloskey (Viking, 1976). *A mother duck and ducklings cause a traffic jam when they cross the road. Winner of the Caldecott Medal for illustrations.*

Mr. Duck Means Business, by Tammi Sauer (Paula Wiseman Books, Simon & Schuster, 2011).

One Duck Stuck, by Phyllis Root (Candlewick, 1998). *A duck gets one foot stuck in the mud ... which of her ten animal friends will help?*

Quack and Count, by Keith Baker (Harcourt Brace, 1999). *How many different ways can you make the number 7 using addition? Count the ducks as they play in the pond.*

Quack! Quiet! Quick! by Kathleen Kuchera (Scholastic, 2000).

Quick and Quack, by John Van Hunnik (W. Walker and Sons Ltd., 1935).

Quick, Duck, by Mary Murphy (Walker Books, 2012).

Quick, Quack, Quick! by Marsha Arnold (Random House, 1996).

Rainy-Day Duckling, by Ruth Martin (Templar Publishing, 2011).

Six Little Ducks (lap book), by Kim Mitzo (Twin Sister, 2010).

The Story About Ping, by Marjorie Flack (Viking, 1933). *Things are kind of cramped on the boat in the Yangtze River where Ping the duck lives with his parents, siblings and 42 cousins. It gets very exciting when one day Ping wanders off all by himself.*

Super Duck, by Jez Albourough (Kane Miller, 2008). *Duck and his friends, frog, sheep, goat, and frog try to fly a kite.*

10 Little Rubber Ducks, by Eric Carle (HarperCollins, 2005).

Three Ducks Went Wandering, by Ron Roy (Seabury Press, 1979).

What's Up, Duck?: A Book of Opposites, by Tad Hills (Schwartz and Wade, 2008).

Wiggle! March! by Karen Pixton (Workman Press, 2009).

Wow! It's Great Being a Duck, by Joan Rankin (Simon & Schuster, 1997). *Fair illustrations, text okay.*

Movies and Television

The Adventures of Dynamo Duck (1960), a French children's TV show.

Aflac Duck (1999), the duck mascot for *Aflac* insurance company (TV commercials)

Babe (1995), Universal Pictures (one character is Ferdinand, the adventurous duck). Also: *Babe: Pig in the City*.

Chicken Little (2005), Disney Buena Vista

Daffy Duck (1939), Warner Brothers Looney Tunes (many episodes)

Duck Amuck, *Porky's Duck Hunt* (1937), Warner Brothers Looney Tunes

Duck Tales Episodes (1987–1990), Disney (characters Scrooge McDuck, Daisy, Hewey, Dewey, Lewey, and Donald).

Edd the Duck, a puppet mallard from CBBC's *The Broom Cupboard* (1988)

Journey to the Center of the Earth (1959), Twentieth Century–Fox.

Leafie, A Hen into the Wild (2011), South Korean animated film

Mickey's Christmas Carol (1983), Disney's Scrooge

The Million Dollar Duck (1971), Disney (Charlie)

The Muppets (1976–1992), ITC Entertainment Henson Associates, distributed by Disney: "The Muppets, Veterinarian's Hospital: Duck!" (12/4/1976), season 1, episode 12; "Talk Spot: Bruce rents a duck" (12/4/1976), season 2, episode 12; The Swedish Chef: "Pressed Duck" (1978), season 2, episode 40

Orville the Duck, a green duckling puppet (1982–1990), *The Keith Harris Show*

Peep and the Big Wide World, episodes (2004), National Film Board of Canada (PBS series)

Plucka Duck, from the Australian television program, *Hey Hey It's Saturday.* Also on *Plucka's Place* (1997).

64 Zoo Lane, a children's cartoon, by An Vrombaut (1999), CBBC, Millimages, HiT Entertainment

The Ugly Duckling (1939), Disney

1d. Henny Penny

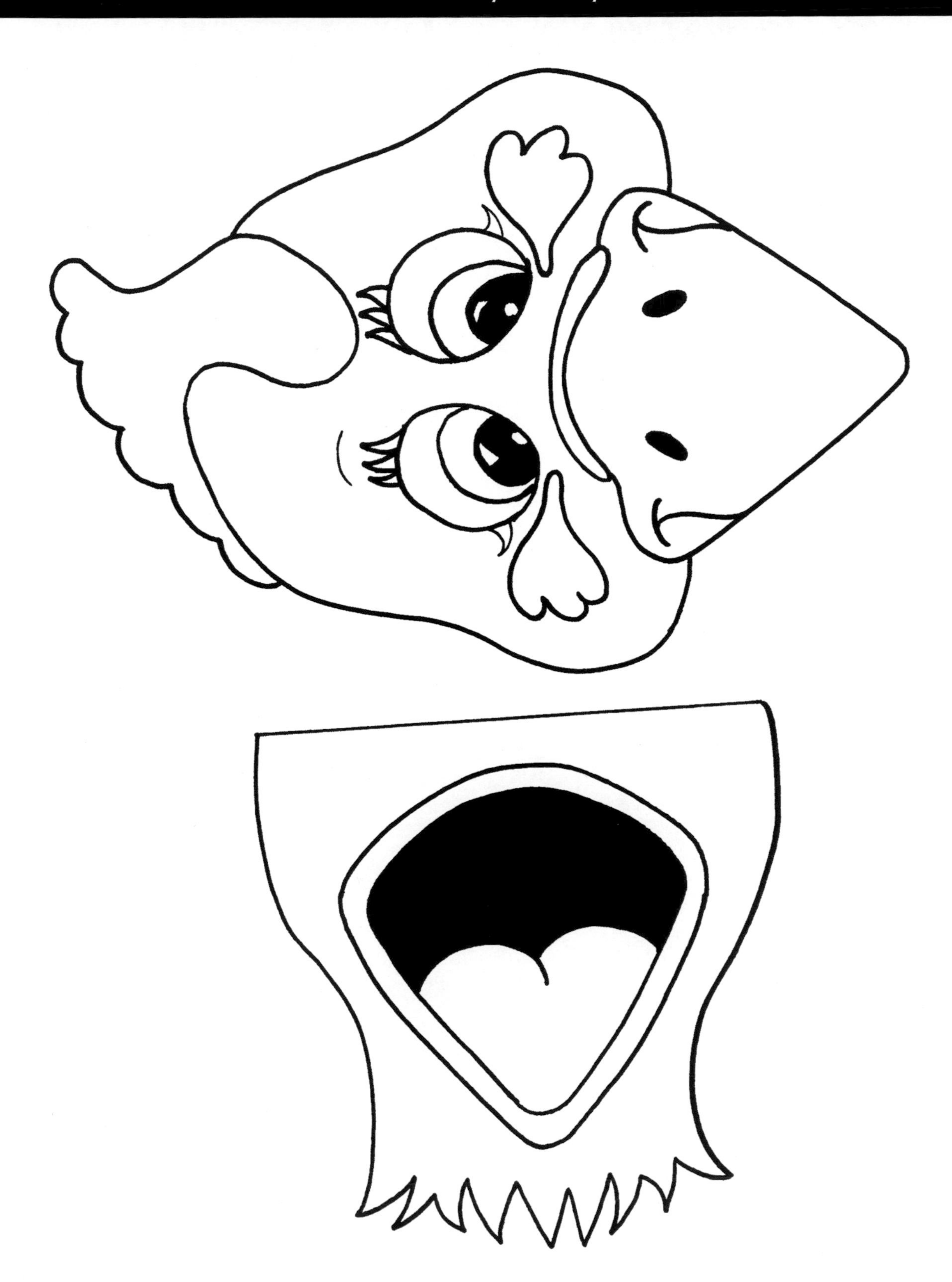

Hen Activities

Songs to Sing and Play

Tune: Oh Where, Oh Where Has My Little Dog Gone?

Words by Eunice Wright

Oh where, oh where is the hen (Henny Penny) on the farm?
Oh where, oh where can she be?
Is she laying some eggs
Or eating some seed?
Oh where, oh where can she be?

Tune: Three Blind Mice

Words by Eunice Wright

Little Henny Penny,
And Chicken Little,
And Goosey Loosey,
And Ducky Lucky,
They all ran to tell the King their strife,
Cocky Locky, and Turkey Lurkey both ran for their life,
Did you ever see such a sight in your life,
As they all—ran to tell—the King?

Little Henny Penny

© 2011 by Ronald J. Brown. All rights reserved. Used with permission. This song is available on Intelli-Tunes' Storybook Friends.

Little Henny Penny
thought the sky was falling,
falling to the ground.

Little Henny Penny
said the sky was falling,
It almost knocked her down!

Run, Little Henny Penny!
Tell your friends!
Run, Little Henny Penny,
before it ends!
Run, Little Henny Penny!
Tell the king!

Tell the king the sky is falling,
falling right down.

Little Henny Penny
told Lucy Goosey
the sky was falling down.
Little Henny Penny
told Turkey Lurkey,
and all his friends around.

Run, Little Henny Penny!
Tell your friends!
Run, Little Henny Penny,
before it ends!
Run, Little Henny Penny!
Tell the king!

Tell the king the sky is falling,
falling right down.

Little Henny Penny
told Foxy Loxy
the sky was falling down.
Little Henny Penny
and all her friends,
followed him to town.

Run, Little Henny Penny!
It's a trick!
Run, Little Henny Penny!
You're in a fix.
Run, Little Henny Penny!
Run right home.

The sky was never falling,
falling right down!

Bought Me a Hen

See Cat (#6e) for entire song.

Bought me a hen and the hen pleased me,
I fed my hen under yonder tree.
Hen goes chimmy-chuck, chimmy-chuck,
Cat goes fiddle-i-fee.

Down on Grandpa's Farm

Written by Robert D. Singleton/Traditional. See songsforteaching.com or One Light, One Sun *by Raffi to listen to the tune.*

Down on grandpa's farm there is a big white hen [brown chicken, black hen, etc.]

Tune: Old MacDonald Had a Farm

And on this farm he had a hen...

Tune: The Farmer in the Dell

The farmer takes a hen...

Poems and Nursery Rhymes

Ten Red Hens

Use 10 Red Hen puppets. Insert child's name in the blanks.

By Eunice Wright

Ten red hens,
all of them mine.
_____ came over to play,
And now there are nine.

Nine red hens,
On their nests to wait.
_____ came and scared one off,
And now there are eight.

Eight red hens,
And one named Kevin.
_____ wanted one,
And now there are seven.

Seven red hens,
All in the sticks.
_____ chased one,
And now there are six.

Six red hens,
Right next to a hive.
_____ ran around them,
And now there are five.

Five red hens,
Sitting by the door.
In came _____,
And now there are four.

Four red hens,
That's all I see.
_____ picked up one,
And now there are three.

Three red hens,
None of them are new.
_____ took one,
And now there are two.

Two red hens,
The chicken coop is done.
_____ made a nest,
And now there is one.

One little hen,
She is the hero.
_____ shut the door,
And now there is zero.

One, Two, Buckle My Shoe

The Little Mother Goose, *by Jessie Wilcox Smith, 1918.*

1, 2—buckle my shoe;
3, 4—shut the door;
5, 6—pick up sticks;
7, 8—lay them straight;
9, 10—a good fat hen;
11, 12—Who will delve;
13, 14—maids a-courting;
15, 16—maids a-kissing;
17, 18—maids a-waiting;
19, 20—my stomach's empty.

The Hen and Chickens

Finger Plays for Nursery and Kindergarten, *by Emilie Poulsson, 1893.*

Good Mother Hen sits here on her nest,
Keeps the eggs warm beneath her soft
breast,
Waiting, waiting, day after day.

Hark! there's a sound she knows very well:
Some little chickens breaking the shell,
Pecking, pecking, pecking away.

Now they're all out, oh, see what a crowd!
Good Mother Hen is happy and proud,
Cluck-cluck, cluck-cluck, clucking away.

Into the coop the mother must go;
While all the chickens run to and fro,
Peep-peep, peep-peep, peeping away.

Here is some corn in my little dish;
Eat, Mother Hen, eat all that you wish.
Picking, picking, picking away.

Happy we'll be to see you again,
Dear little chicks and good Mother Hen!
Now good-bye, good-bye for to-day.

The Pig and the Hen

Poems by Alice and Phoebe Cary, *Book 2, 1850.*

The pig and the hen,
They both got in one pen,
And the hen said she wouldn't go out.
"Mistress Hen," says the pig,
"Don't you be quite so big!"
And he gave her a push with his snout.

"You are rough, and you're fat,
But who cares for all that;
I will stay if I choose," says the hen.
"No, mistress, no longer!"
Says pig, "I'm the stronger,
And mean to be boss of my pen!"

Then the hen cackled out
Just as close to his snout
As she dare: "You're an ill-natured brute,
And if I had the corn,
Just as sure as I'm born,
I would send you to starve or to root!"

"But you don't own the cribs;
So I think that my ribs
Will be never the leaner for you:
This trough is my trough,
And the sooner you're off,"
Says the pig, "why the better you'll do!"

"You're not a bit fair,
And you're cross as a bear;
What harm do I do in your pen?
But a pig is a pig,
And I don't care a fig
For the worst you can say," says the hen.

Says the pig, "You will care
If I act like a bear
And tear your two wings from your neck,"
"What a nice little pen
You have got!" says the hen,
Beginning to scratch and to peck.

Now the pig stood amazed
And the bristles, upraised
A moment past, fell down so sleek.
"Neighbor Biddy," says he,
"If you'll just allow me,
I will show you a nice place to pick!"

So she followed him off,
And they ate from one trough
They had quarreled for nothing, they saw;
And when they had fed,
"Neighbor Hen," the pig said,
"Won't you stay here and roost in my
straw?"

"No, I thank you; you see
That I sleep in a tree,"
Says the hen; "but I must go away;
So a grateful good-by."
"Make your home in my sty,"
Says the pig, "and come in every day."

Now my child will not miss
The true moral of this
Little story of anger and strife;
For a word spoken soft
Will turn enemies oft
Into friends that will stay friends for life.

Come and See

Chinese Mother Goose Rhymes, *1900; adapted by Juli Wright.*

All come and see!
All come and see!
A black hen laid a white egg for me!
Oh, look there!
Oh, look there!
A great, big egg we can all share!

The Egg

In My Nursery: A Book of Verse, *by Laura E. Richards, 1890.*

Oh! how shall I get it, how shall I get it,—
A nice little new-laid egg?

My grandmamma told me to run to the barnyard,
And see if just one I could beg.

"Moolly-cow, Moolly-cow, down in the
meadow,
Have you any eggs, I pray?"
The Moolly-cow stares as if I were crazy,
And solemnly stalks away.

"Oh! Doggie, Doggie, perhaps you may have
it,
That nice little egg for me."
But Doggie just wags his tail and capers,
And never an egg has he.

"Now, Dobbin, Dobbin, I'm sure you must
have one,
Hid down in your manger there."
But Dobbin lays back his ears and whinnies,
With "Come and look, if you dare!"

"Piggywig, Piggywig, grunting and squealing,
Are you crying 'Fresh eggs for sale'?"
No! Piggy, you're very cold and unfeeling,
With that impudent quirk in your tail.

"You wise old Gobbler, you look so knowing,
I'm sure you can find me an egg.
You stupid old thing! just to say 'Gobble-
gobble!'
And balance yourself on one leg."

Oh! how shall I get it, how shall I get it,—
That little white egg so small?
I've asked every animal here in the barn-yard,
And they won't give me any at all.

But after I'd hunted until I was tired,
I found—not one egg, but ten!
And you never could guess where they all
were hidden,—
Right under our old speckled hen!

The Intelligent Hen

The Jingle Book, *by Carolyn Wells, 1901.*

'Twas long ago,—a year or so,—
In a barnyard by the sea,
That an old hen lived whom you may know
By the name of Fiddle-de-dee.

She scratched around in the sand all day,
For a lively old hen was she.

And then do you know, it happened this way
In that barnyard by the sea;
A great wise owl came down one day,
And hooted at Fiddle-de-dee,
Just hooted at Fiddle-de-dee.
And he cried, "Hi! Hi! old hen, I say!
You're provincial, it seems to me!"

"Why, what do you mean?" cried the old red
hen,
As mad as hops was she.
"Oh, I've been 'round among great men,
In the world where the great men be.
And none of them scratch with their claws
like you,
They write with a quill like me."

Now very few people could get ahead
Of that old hen, Fiddle-de-dee.
She went and hunted the posy-bed,
And returned in triumphant glee.
And ever since then, that little red hen,
She writes with a jonquil pen, quil pen,
She writes with a jonquil pen.

Two Riddles

The Home Book of Verse, *Vol. 1 (of 4) edited by Burton Egbert Stevenson, 1912.*

Riddle 1:
In marble walls as white as milk,
Lined with a skin as soft as silk,
Within a fountain crystal clear,
A golden apple doth appear.
No doors there are to this stronghold,
Yet thieves break in and steal the gold.

Answer: An egg.

Riddle 2:
Elizabeth, Lizzy, Betsy and Bess,
All went together to seek a bird's nest;
They found a nest with five eggs in it;
They each took one and left four in it.

Answer: There was only one girl (three of the four names are nicknames for Elizabeth); she took only one egg.

White Hen

Sing Song: A Nursery Rhyme Book, *by Christina G. Rossetti, 1893.*

A white hen sitting
On white eggs three;
Next, three speckled chickens
As plump as plump can be.

An Owl, and a Vulture,
And a Quail come to see;
But chicks beneath their mother's wing
Squat safe as safe can be.

Games and Group Activities

Hen Colors—Guess the Rhyme

By Eunice Wright
A little hen sat down by a sack,
She was completely dressed all in _____ (black).

A big fat hen slept all day in bed,
Her feathers were a brilliant _____ (red).

A sorry hen with a great big frown,
Wore a funny hat with colors of _____ (brown)

This smart little hen was nice and mellow,
Her sunny colors were bright and _____ (yellow)

This little hen sat under a light,
Her feathers were a dazzling _____ (white).

A little hen ran in a dizzy circle,
She wore a vest made all in _____ (purple).

This little hen is never mean,
She always wears the color _____ (green).

This nice little hen lays eggs for you,
She wears a dress the color _____ (blue).

This little hen gave me a wink,
The clothes she wore were all in _____ (pink).

These colorful hens live on a farm,
They live and eat near the rainbow barn.

Books

Big Fat Hen and the Hairy Goat, by Vivian French (David and Charles Children's, 1999).

Big Fat Hen, by Keith Baker (Harcourt Brace, 1994). *1, 2, buckle my shoe, etc. This simple nursery rhyme has bright illustrations, full page.*

Can Hens Give Milk? By Joan Betty Stuchner (Orca Book Pub., 2011).

The Fox and the Hen, by Eric Battat (Battut-Sterling Pub. Co., 2010).

The Hen House, by Allan Ahlberg (Viking, 1999).

The Hen That Crowed, by Shelia Cole (Lee and Shepard Books, 1993).

The Hen Who Wouldn't Give Up, by Jill Tomlinson (Harcourt Brace, 1980).

Henny Penny, by Paul Galdone (Houghton Mifflin, 1979).

Hen's Pens, by Phil Roxbee Cox (Usborne, 2001), Pub.

Hens Say Cluck, by Hannah Giffard (Tambourine Books, 1993).

Hungry Hen, by Richard Waring (HarperCollins, 2001).

Jen and the Ten Hens, by Cindy Clements (Modern Curriculum Press, 1979).

Jen the Hen, by Colin Hawkins (Dorling Kindersley, 1995). *Great rhyming and learning to read book series.*

Jen the Hen and the Golden Pen, by Colin Hawkins (Family Learning, 2001).

The Little Hen and the Giant, by Maria Polushkin (Harper and Row, 1977).

The Loopy Coop Hens, by Janet Morgan Stoeke (Dutton Children's Books, 2011).

Nine Men Chase a Hen, by Barbara Gregorich (School Zone Pub. Co., 1992).

Red Hen, by Janis Asad Raabe (Modern Curriculum, 1986).

Ren Hen and Sly Fox, by Vivian French (Simon & Schuster, 1995).

Three French Hens, A Holiday Tale, by Margie Palatini (Hyperion, 2005).

Three Hens and a Peacock, by Lester L. Laminack (Peach Tree, 2011).

Movies and Television

The Muppets (1976–1992), ITC Entertainment Henson Associates, distributed by Disney. Gonzo and his chickens; some of the Swedish Chef's skits include chickens.

The Wise Little Hen (1934), Mickey Mouse presents Walt Disney's Silly Symphony.

Also see Chicken (#1a) and The Little Red Hen (#12) for more.

1e. Turkey Lurkey

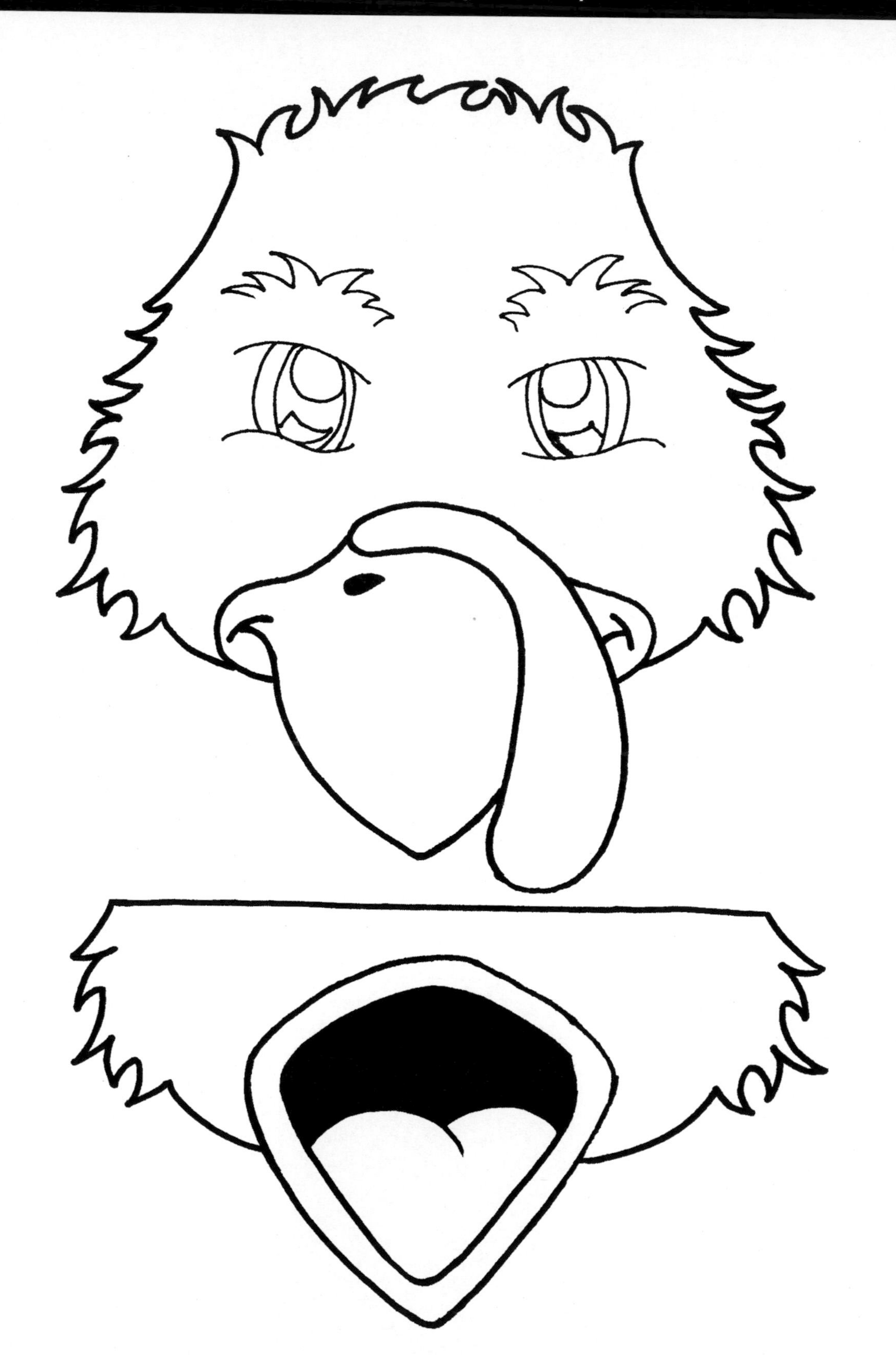

Turkey Activities

Songs to Sing and Play

Turkey in the Straw

Unknown author; American folk song, early 19th century.

Well, I hitched up the wagon and I drove down the road,
With a two horse wagon and a four horse load,
Well I cracked my whip and the lead horse sprung,
And I said "Goodbye" to the wagon tongue.

Chorus:
Turkey in the straw, in the straw, straw, straw.
Turkey in the hay, in the hay, hay, hay!
Funniest thing I ever saw
It's a tune called Turkey in the Straw.

Went out to milk and I didn't know how,
I milked the goat instead of the cow,
A monkey sittin' there on a pile of straw
A-winkin' his eye at his mother-in-law.

Chorus

Well, I came to the river and I couldn't get across,
So I paid five dollars for an old blind horse,
Well, he wouldn't go ahead and he wouldn't stand still,
So he went up and down like an old saw mill.

Chorus

Did you ever go fishin' on a warm summer day
When all the fish were swimmin' in the bay
With their hands in their pockets and their pockets in their pants
Did you ever see a fishie do the Hootchy-Kootchy Dance?

Chorus

Well, if frogs had wings and snakes had hair:
And automobiles went flyin' thru' the air,
Well, if watermelons grew on a huckleberry vine,
We'd still have winter in the summer time.

Chorus

Alternate:

Well I had a little chicken and she wouldn't lay an egg
So I poured hot water up and down her leg.
Well the little chicken cried and the little chicken begged
and the darned old chicken laid a hardboiled egg.

Well I had a little monkey and his name was Tiny Tim
And I put him in the bathtub just to see if he could swim.
And he drank up all the water and he ate up all the soap
And he tried to eat the bathtub but it wouldn't fit down his throat.

Mama called the doctor and the doctor called the nurse
and the nurse called the lady with the alligator purse.
Well the monkey ate the doctor and the monkey ate the nurse
and the monkey ate the lady with the alligator purse.

Did you ever go fishing on a hot summer day
and you're sittin' on a rail and the rail gives away?
With your hands in your pockets and your pockets in your pants
Watchin' the fishes do the Hoochie Kootchie dance.

Did you ever go huntin' for a fat bullfrog
and you find one sittin' on a bumpety log.
And you yell, "Here's a frog!" and the frog says, "Nay!
I'm a little green birdie with my feathers washed away!"

Well I walked around the corner and I walked around the block.

And I walked right in to a donut shop.
And I pulled up a donut out of the grease.
And I handed the lady a five cent piece.

She looked at the nickel, and she looked at me.
She said, "This nickel is no good, you see!
It's got a hole in the middle, all the way through
and I said, "There's a hole in your donut too!"

Down on Grandpa's Farm

Written by Robert D. Singleton/Traditional. See songsforteaching.com or One Light, One Sun *by Raffi to listen to the tune.*

Down on grandpa's farm there are some big, fat turkeys.

Tune: Michael Finnegan

Author unknown. Found on everythingpreschool.com and KIDiddles.

"This old road is hard and bumpy, Our new turkey's wild and jumpy..."

Albuquerque Turkey (Tune: Oh My Darling, Clementine)

Change words to: "Albuquerque is a turkey and he's feathered and he's fine..."

Other Songs

"Gobble, Strut, Strut," *I Have a Song for You* by Janeen Brady, p. 13.
"Five Fat Turkeys Are We," finger-play and traditional song.
"Except for the Turkey (The Turkey Song; A Funny Thanksgiving Song)," by Bryant Oden, 2009. Songdrops.com
"Five Little Turkeys," by The Learning Station, *Thanksgiving Songs for Children.*

Poems and Nursery Rhymes

Five Big Turkeys (Count Up)

By Eunice and Juli Wright

1 big turkey, eating a shoe,
He found a friend, then there were 2.
2 big turkeys, having a jubilee,
Along came a cousin, then there were 3.
3 big turkeys, eating more and more,
Along came sister, then there were 4.
4 big turkeys, all still alive,
Along came brother, then there were 5.
Five big turkeys, all wanting to play,
They'll change their mind on Thanksgiving Day.

There Once Was a Young Turkey

Nonsense Books *by Edward Lear, 1894; adapted by Juli Wright.*

There once was a Young Turkey,
Who wept when the weather was murky;
When the day turned out fine, she ceased to repine,
That capricious annoying Young Turkey.

Five Colorful Turkeys (Count Down)

By Eunice and Juli Wright

Five colorful turkeys, with feathers to adore,
One lost a red feather, then there were four.
Four colorful turkeys, so beautiful to see,
One lost a yellow feather, then there were three.
Three colorful turkeys, with colors so true,
One lost a blue feather, then there were two.
Two colorful turkeys, sparkling in the sun,
One lost a green feather, then there was one.
One colorful turkey, with a rainbow tail,
Granted wishes in the children's fairy tale.

The Girl in the Lane

The Real Mother Goose, *by Blanche Fisher Wright, 1916; adapted by Juli Wright.*

The turkey in the lane,
That couldn't speak plain,
Cried, "Gobble, gobble, gobble."
On the hill, he couldn't stand still,
And went hobble, hobble, hobble.

Christmas Turkey

Folk Rhymes Wise and Otherwise *by Thomas W. Talley, 1922; adapted by Juli Wright.*

I asked for a turkey,
I waited for that turkey to come.
I waited and waited,
I really want some.

Christmas Day is almost here;
And I am really mad,
I want that turkey more and more
I want him really bad.

The Turkey's Reply

By Juli Wright

I dreamed my turkey spoke
and when I awoke,
I gobbled in my throat
and couldn't sing a note.

I promised that on Thanksgiving Day,
I wouldn't eat him, if he'd let me say.
Now he is happy and so am I
Because "Gobble, gobble" is his reply.

When Daddy Carves the Turkey

By Jack Prelutsky (1940)

"When Daddy carves the turkey, / It is really quite a sight..."

Games and Group Activities

The Turkey with the Terrible Temper

This is a good group story (a flannel board or puppet story), and can be found on Sugardoodle.net and allmylittlegems.com.

Books

Beauty and the Beaks: A Turkey's Cautionary Tale, by Mary Jane Auch (Holiday House, 2007). *Grades 2–4. The most conceited bird in the hen yard is the new turkey.*

Five Silly Turkeys, by Salina Yoon (Price Stern Sloan, 2005).

Gobble Gobble Crash! A Barnyard Counting Bash, by Julie Stiegemeyer (Dutton Children's Books, 2008).

Gracias the Thanksgiving Turkey, by Joy Cowley (Scholastic, 2005). *A turkey to fatten up for the holiday becomes a pet. Ages 4–8.*

Over the River; A Turkeys' Tale, by Derek Anderson (Simon & Schuster, 2005).

The Perfect Thanksgiving, by Eileen Spinelli (Square Fish, 2007).

A Plump and Perky Turkey, by Teresa Bateman (Winslow Press, 2001).

T Is for Turkey: A True Thanksgiving Story, by Tanya Lee Stone (Price Stern Sloan, 2009). *A group of children put on a play using rhymes for each letter of the alphabet.*

Ten Fat Turkeys, by Tony Johnston (Scholastic, 2004). *Count down 10 fat turkeys, as each turkey leaves the fence in a creative way (teaches subtraction).*

Thanks for Thanksgiving, by Julie Markes (HarperCollins, 2004). *Detailed and funny illustrations with a rhyming text. Ages 3–6.*

Thelonius Turkey Lives! (on Felicia Ferguson's Farm), by Lynn Rowe Reed (Knopf, 2005). *Mixed media illustrations, ages 4–9. Great for reading aloud.*

Tobias Turkey: A Thanksgiving Tale, by Sandra Robbins (See-More's Workshop, 1990).

The Turkey Ball, by David Steinberg (Price Stern Sloan, 2005).

A Turkey for Thanksgiving, by Eve Bunting (Clarion Books, 1991).

Turkey Trouble, by Wendi Silvano (Marshall Cavendish Children, 2009).

'Twas the Night Before Thanksgiving, by Dav Pilkey (Scholastic, 2004).

Why We Have Thanksgiving, by Margaret Hillert (Follett Pub. Co., 1982), *Easy reader story of the first Thanksgiving with reading activities.*

Movies and Television

The First Thanksgiving, BC, by Johnny Hart (1973).

"Holiday for Drumsticks" (1949), Daffy Duck, Looney Tunes.

Montana's Wild Turkeys (2010), CBS news online.

The Muppets (1976–1992), ITC Entertainment Henson Associates, distributed by Disney: Swedish Chef cooks a turkey (1979), season 4, episode 8; Swedish Chef finds the greatest Christmas bird of all, Big Bird; Swedish Chef and his uncle prepare a turkey (1979), Season 3, episode 16.

Nature: My Life as a Turkey (A new mother) (2011), PBS.

Nature: Wild Turkeys (2012), CBS news online.

Pluto Cold Turkey (1951), Buena Vista Disney.

Tom Turk and Daffy, featuring Porky Pig, Warner Brothers, Looney Tunes.

Turkey Catchers (1999), Disney.

Turkeys Gone Wild, National Geographic, 2004.

1f. Cocky Locky

Rooster Activities

Songs to Sing and Play

Tune: Three Blind Mice

Words by Eunice Wright

Roosters crow,
Greeting the sun.
"Wake up now!"
They tell everyone.
It's time to eat breakfast with fork and knife.
The farmer has chores, and so does his wife.
Did you ever see such a sight in your life,
As roosters that crow.

Tune: The Wheels on the Bus

Words by Eunice Wright

The rooster on the fence says, "cock-a-doodle do,"... all morning long.

Tune: Old MacDonald Had a Farm

And on this farm he had a rooster...

Tune: The Farmer in the Dell

The farmer takes a rooster...

Tune: Row, Row, Row Your Boat

Words by Eunice Wright

Crow, Crow, Crow all day,
A rooster loves to crow.
In the morning or at night,
The rooster loves to crow.

Tune: 10 Little Indians

Words by Eunice Wright

1 little, 2 little, 3 little roosters ... down on grandpa's farm.

A Hunting We Will Go

Adapted by Eunice Wright

A hunting we will go, a hunting we will go,
We'll catch a rooster and give him a booster,
And then we'll let him go!

Tune: Mary Had a Little Lamb

Words by Eunice Wright; fill in blanks with child's name.

_____ had a little rooster, little rooster, little rooster.
_____ had a little rooster, its crow was loud and strong.
And everywhere that _____ went ... the rooster was sure to crow.

It followed her to bed one night ... and woke her early next day.

And so the family put him out ... to crow another day.

Tune: Oh, Have You Seen the Muffin Man?

Adapted by Eunice Wright

Oh, have you seen the rooster yet?
The rooster yet? The rooster yet?
Oh, have you seen the rooster yet?
I haven't heard him crow.

He's in the barn fast asleep...
He crowed too late last night.

Down on Grandpa's Farm

Written by Robert D. Singleton/Traditional. See songsforteaching.com or One Light, One Sun *by Raffi to listen to the tune.*

"Down on grandpa's farm there is a rooster that crows..."

I Had a Rooster

Traditional, performed by Pete Seeger. Also in I Had a Rooster: A Traditional Folk Song *by Laura Vaccaro Seeger, 2001.*

"I had a rooster, my rooster pleased me.
I fed my rooster 'neath the greenberry tree..."

Poems and Nursery Rhymes

Five Loud Roosters (Count Down)

By Eunice Wright

5 loud roosters, crowing by the door,
1 ran away, then there were four.
4 loud roosters, up in a tree,
1 ran away, then there were three.
3 loud roosters, under the sky so blue,
1 ran away, then there were two.
2 loud roosters, sitting in the sun.
1 ran away, then there was one.
One loud rooster, having lots of fun,
He ran away, then there were none.

Cock-A-Doodle-Do!

The Real Mother Goose, *by Blanche Fisher Wright, 1916.*

Cock-a-doodle-do!
My dame has lost her shoe,
My master's lost his fiddle-stick
And knows not what to do.
Cock-a-doodle-do!
What is my dame to do?
Till master finds his fiddle-stick,
She'll dance without her shoe.

Cock-Crow

The Real Mother Goose, *by Blanche Fisher Wright, 1916.*

Cocks crow in the morn
To tell us to rise,
And he who lies late
Will never be wise;
For early to bed
And early to rise,
Is the way to be healthy
And wealthy and wise.

A Cock and Bull Story

The Real Mother Goose, *by Blanche Fisher Wright, 1916.*

The cock's on the housetop blowing his horn;
The bull's in the barn a-threshing of corn;
The maids in the meadows are making of hay;
The ducks in the river are swimming away.

The Cock and the Hen

The Real Mother Goose, *by Blanche Fisher Wright, 1916.*

"Cock, cock, cock, cock,
I've laid an egg,
Am I going to be bare-foot?"
"Hen, hen, hen, hen,
I've been up and down
To every shop, in town,
And cannot find a shoe
To fit your foot,
If I'd crow my heart out."

Cock-a-doodle-do

The Real Mother Goose, *by Blanche Fisher Wright, 1916.*

Oh, my pretty cock, oh, my handsome cock,
I pray you, do not crow before day,
And your comb shall be made of the very beaten gold,
And your wings of the silver so gray.

The Cock Doth Crow

The Little Mother Goose, *by Jessie Willcox Smith, 1918.*

The cock doth crow,
To let you know,
If you be wise,
'Tis time to rise.

The Cock

Chinese Mother Goose Rhymes, *by Isaac Taylor, 1900.*

Cock's comb flower he wears on his head.
For his clothes he needs neither thimble nor thread;
Though you be a great Cock, I'd have you know,
Ten thousand doors would open if *I* should crow.

The Little Rooster

Folk Rhymes Wise and Otherwise, by Thomas W. Talley, 1922; adapted by Juli Wright.

I had a little rooster,
He crowed all day.
Along came an owl,
And "who'd" him away.

The owl beat the rooster
Then he made him go.
Now all the pretty hens
Want him for their beau.

Books

Brewster the Rooster, by Devin Scillian (Sleeping Bear Press, 2013).
Cock-a-Doodle-Doo! by Janet Stevens (HMH, 2005).
Cock-A-Doodle Doo! by Tracey Moroney (Five Mile Press, 1995).
Cock-A-Doodle-Doo: A Farmyard Counting Book, by Steve Lavis (Dutton, 1997). *One noisy rooster wakes everyone on the farm, including 2 hungry horses, etc.*
Cock A Doodle Doo! Farmyard Poems, by Anna Currey (Macmillan Children's Books, 2000).
Cock-A-Doodle Doo: The Story of a Little Red Rooster, by Berta Hader (Macmillan, 1939).
The Day the Dog Said, "Cock-A-Doodle Doo," by David McPhail (Scholastic, 1997).
Four Hens and a Rooster, by Lena Landstrom (Sweden) (R&S Books, 2005). *Four hens are bullied out of their fair share of food by the rooster.*
Rooster Can't Cock-A-Doodle-Do, by Karen Rostoker-Gru (Penguin, 2004).
The Rooster Crows: A Book of American Rhymes and Jingles, by Maud and Miska Petersham (Simon & Schuster, 1969).
The Rooster Who Went to His Uncle's Wedding, By Alma Flor Ada (Puffin, 1998). *A Latin American folktale, colorful illustrations.*
Rooster's Off to See the World, by Eric Carle (Simon & Schuster, 1992). *Beautiful illustrations.*
Wake Up, Henry Rooster, by Margaret Ruurs (Fitzhenry & Whiteside, 2006). *Henry is just not a morning rooster. Ages 4–8.*

Movies and Television

Babe (1995), Universal Pictures.
Chicken Run (2000), Dream Works.
FogHorn LegHorn character (1946–1964). Warner Brothers Entertainment, Inc.
Quack A Doodle Doo, by Famous Studios; (1950), Paramount Pictures.
Robin Hood (1973), Disney.
Rock-A-Doodle (1991), Don Bluth Entertainment.

1g. Foxy Loxy

Fox Activities

Songs to Sing and Play

The Fox

The Nursery Rhymes of England, *by Halliewell Phillipps, 1842.*

The fox went out on a chilly night,
He prayed for the moon to give him light,
For he'd many a mile to go that night,
Before he reached the town-o, town-o, town-o,
He'd many a mile to go that night,
Before he reached the town-o.

He ran 'til he came to a great big pen,
Where the ducks and the geese were put therein,
"A couple of you will grease my chin,
Before I leave this town-o, town-o, town-o,
A couple of you will grease my chin,
Before I leave this town-o."

He grabbed the gray goose by the neck,
Throwed a duck across his back,
He didn't mind their quack, quack, quack,
And their legs a-dangling down-o, down-o, down-o,
He didn't mind their quack, quack, quack,
And their legs a-dangling down-o.

Then old Mother Flipper-Flopper jumped out of bed,
Out of the window she cocked her head,
Crying, "John, John! The gray goose is gone,
And the fox is on the town-o, town-o, town-o!"
Crying, "John, John! The gray goose is gone,
And the fox is on the town-o!"

Then John, he went to the top of the hill,
Blowed his horn both loud and shrill,
The fox he said, "I better flee with my kill,
Or they'll soon be on my trail-o, trail-o, trail-o!"
The fox he said, "I better flee with my kill,
Or they'll soon be on my trail-o!"

He ran till he came to his cozy den,
There were the little ones, eight, nine, ten,
They said, "Daddy, better go back again,
'Cause it must be a mighty fine town-o, town-o, town-o!"
They said, "Daddy, better go back again,
'Cause it must be a mighty fine town-o!

Then the fox and his wife without any strife,
Cut up the goose with a fork and knife,
They never had such a supper in their life,
And the little ones chewed on the bones-o, bones-o, bones-o,
They never had such a supper in their life,
And the little ones chewed on the bones-o.

A Hunting We Will Go

By Thomas Arne, 1777; adapted by Eunice Wright.

A hunting we will go, a hunting we will go,
Heigh ho, the dairy-o, a hunting we will go!
A hunting we will go, a hunting we will go,
We'll catch a fox and put him in a box,
And then we'll let him go!

A hunting we will go, a hunting we will go,
Heigh ho, the dairy-o, a hunting we will go!
A hunting we will go, a hunting we will go,
We'll catch a fish and put him on a dish,
And then we'll let him go!

A hunting we will go, a hunting we will go,
Heigh ho, the dairy-o, a hunting we will go!
A hunting we will go, a hunting we will go,
We'll catch a bear and cut his hair,
And then we'll let him go!

A hunting we will go, a hunting we will go,
Heigh ho, the dairy-o, a hunting we will go!
A hunting we will go, a hunting we will go,
We'll catch a pig and dance a jig,
And then we'll let him go!

A hunting we will go, a hunting we will go,
Heigh ho, the dairy-o, a hunting we will go!
A hunting we will go, a hunting we will go,
We'll catch a giraffe and make him laugh,
And then we'll let him go!

A hunting we will go, a hunting we will go,
Heigh ho, the dairy-o, a hunting we will go!
A hunting we will go, a hunting we will go,

We'll catch a goose and meet a moose,
And then we'll let him go!

A hunting we will go, a hunting we will go,
Heigh ho, the dairy-o, a hunting we will go!
A hunting we will go, a hunting we will go,
We'll catch a duck and wish him luck,
And then we'll let him go!

Make up more animal rhyming verses for your puppets—cat/hat, dog/hog, fawn/yawn, chicken/licken, hen/pen, hippo/zippo, rhino/line-o, gater/later, squirrel/pearl, etc.

Tune: 10 Little Indians

Words by Eunice Wright

1 little, 2 little, 3 little foxes...
All with fluffy tails.

Tune: The Farmer in the Dell

Words by Eunice Wright

The farmer takes the fox...
Heigh ho, the dairy-o, the farmer takes the fox.

Tune: The Wheels on the Bus

Words by Eunice Wright

The fox on the farm runs round and round...
Until he gets a meal. (Until he gets caught, until the farmer shoots his gun, etc.)

Tune: Old MacDonald Had a Farm

And on this farm he had a fox...

Tune: A Rig-A-Jig Jig

The Best College Songs for Union College, *p. 185, 1897; words adapted by Eunice Wright.*

As I went walking down the street, down the street, down the street,
A sly, cunning fox I happened to meet,
Hi ho, hi ho, hi ho.

A rig-a-jig jig and away we go,
Away we go, away we go.
A rig-a-jig jig and away we go,
Hi ho, hi ho, hi ho.

Tune: I'm a Little Teapot

By Eunice and Juli Wright

I'm a little fox, cunning and sly,
Here is my tail, fluffy and spry.
When I get real hungry, and a chicken I spy,
I run and chase, to catch her I'll try.

Poems and Nursery Rhymes

5 Little Foxes (Count Down)

By Eunice Wright

5 little foxes, playing on the floor,
1 found a friendly dog, then there were 4.
4 little foxes, running 'round the tree,
1 found a friendly pig, then there were 3.
3 little foxes, chewing on a shoe,
1 found a friendly cat, then there were 2.
2 little foxes, playing in the sun,
1 found a friendly duck, then there was 1.
1 little fox, ate a bakery bun,
He found a friendly chicken, then there was none.

Fatima Fox Found Four Friends

By Eunice Wright

Fatima Fox found four friends,
Fatima frolicked, and four friends followed.
Far, far away frolicked the fast friends.
Frustratingly, Fatima fell forward flat.
Fortunately, four friends finally found Fatima,
And frankly flew frantically fast for Father.
Father flew to Fatima's flop,
And ferried Fatima and friends to father's farm.

The Fox and the Crow: A Fable

Childhood's Favorites and Fairy Stories: The Young Folks Treasury, *Volume 1, edited by Jennie Ellis Burdick, 1919.*

In a dairy a crow,
Having ventured to go,

Some food for her young ones to seek,
Flew up in the trees,
With a fine piece of cheese,
Which she joyfully held in her beak.

A fox, who lived by,
To the tree saw her fly,
And to share in the prize made a vow;
For having just dined,
He for cheese felt inclined,
So he went and sat under the bough.

She was cunning, he knew,
But so was he too,
And with flattery adapted his plan;
For he knew if she'd speak,
It must fall from her beak,
So, bowing politely, began.

"'Tis a very fine day"
(Not a word did she say):
"The wind, I believe, ma'am, is south:
A fine harvest for peas":
He then looked at the cheese,
But the crow did not open her mouth.

Sly Reynard, not tired,
Her plumage admired,
"How charming! how brilliant its hue!
The voice must be fine,
Of a bird so divine,
Ah, let me just hear it, pray do.

"Believe me, I long
To hear a sweet song!"
The silly crow foolishly tries:
She scarce gave one squall,
When the cheese she let fall,
And the fox ran away with the prize.

Stories with a Fox

Adapt stories like "The Gingerbread Boy" (#10) to create a puppet play. Also, many of Aesop's Fables have a fox in the story, such as "The Fox and the Grapes" and "The Cock, the Dog and the Fox."

Games and Group Activities

The Chickens and the Fox

Divide the room into thirds; chicks in first section, fox in middle, Mother Hen in third. Mother Hen calls, "Little chicks, little chicks, won't you come home?" Chicks try to run to Mother without getting caught by fox. The ones that are caught then become foxes and help catch more chicks. Last chick caught becomes the new fox.

Fox and Geese

From Games for the Playground, Home, School and Gymnasium, *by Jessie H. Bancroft, 1922, p. 92.*

10 to 30 or more players. Venue: playground or gymnasium.

One player is chosen to be fox and another to be the gander. The remaining players all stand in a line behind the gander, each with his hands on the shoulders of the one in front. The gander tries to protect his flock of geese from being caught by the fox, and to do this spreads out his arms and dodges around in any way he sees fit to circumvent the efforts of the fox. Only the last goose in the line may be tagged by the fox, or should the line be very long, the last five or ten players may be tagged as decided beforehand. The geese may all cooperate with the gander by doubling and redoubling their line to prevent the fox from tagging the last goose. Should the fox tag the last goose (or one of the last five or ten, if that be permissible), that goose becomes fox and the fox becomes gander.

This game is found in almost all countries, under various names and representing different animals.

Fox and Squirrel

From Games for the Playground, Home, School and Gymnasium, *by Jessie H. Bancroft, 1922, p. 93.*

20 to 60 players. Venue: A room with enough chairs for each player.

The players sit in their seats facing each

other in two lines, so that each two adjacent lines have their feet in the same aisle. The game consists in passing or tossing some object (the squirrel), such as a bean bag, basketball, or hand ball, from one player across the aisle to another and back again, zigzagging down each aisle, to be followed at once by a second object (the fox); the effort being to have the fox overtake the squirrel before the end of the line is reached.

With very little children, passing is better than tossing; but with older children, or even with little ones, when more experienced, it is well to use the game as a practice for tossing and catching. The action should be very rapid. The game makes much sport for young children, and they are very fond of it.

Hunt the Fox

From Games for the Playground, Home, School and Gymnasium, *by Jessie H. Bancroft, 1922, p. 111.*

20 to 60 or more players. Venue: Playground or gymnasium.

The players stand in two parallel lines, with about five feet distance between the lines, and considerable distance between each two players in a line, so that the runners may have space to run between them. The head player of one line is a fox and the head player of the opposite line the hunter.

At a signal the fox starts to run, winding in and out from one side to the other of his line until he reaches the bottom, when he turns and comes up the opposite line. The fox is not obliged to run between each two players, but may skip any number that he wishes, and choose his own track. The hunter must follow in exactly the same trail. If he makes a mistake, he must back to the point at which he diverged from the path of the fox. If the fox succeeds in getting back to the head of the second line without being caught, he is considered to have escaped, and takes his place at the foot of his own line. Should he be caught by the hunter, he changes places with the latter, the hunter going to the foot of the fox's line, and the fox taking the hunter's original place at the head of his line. The second player in the fox's line, who should have moved up to the front to keep the lines even, is then fox for the next chase.

Books

Basho and the Fox, by Tim Myers (Marshall Cavendish, 2000).

Basho and the River Stones, by Tim Meyers (Marshall Cavendish, 2004).

Fox, by Edward Marshall (Listening Library, 1993).

Fox All Week, by Edward Marshall (Puffin, 1995).

Fox and His Friends, by Edward and James Marshall (Puffin, 1982).

Fox at School, by Edward and James Marshall (Puffin, 1993).

Fox in Love, by Edward Marshall (Dial Press, 1982).

Fox in Socks, by Dr. Seuss (Random House, 1965).

Fox on the Job, by Edward Marshall (Puffin, 1996).

Fox Outfoxed, by James Marshall (Puffin, 1996).

Fritzi Fox Flew in From Florida, by Leah Komaiko (HarperCollins, 1995).

Hattie and the Fox, by Mem Fox (Bradbury Press, 1986).

The Midnight Fox, by Betsy Cromer Byars (Puffin, 1968).

Oh, a-Hunting We Will Go, by John Langstaff (Atheneum, 1974).

The Rabbit, the Fox, and the Wolf, by Sara August (Orchard Books, 1990).

Raven and Fox, by Gerald Rose (Macmillan, 1988).

The Rooster and the Fox, Retold and illus. by Helen Ward (Millbrook Press, 2003). *A beautifully illustrated book and a good story; teaching as well as entertaining.*

Saving Samantha: A True Story, by Robbyn Smith van Frankenhuyzen (Sleeping Bear Press, 2004). *A fascinating true account of the rescue, rehabilitation and eventual release of a red fox. Beautiful illustrations.*

Movies and Television

Fantastic Mr. Fox (2009), Fox Home Entertainment

The Fox and the Hound (1981), Disney

Mary Poppins (1964), Disney

Pinocchio (1940), Disney

Robin Hood (1973), Disney

2. Goldilocks and the Three Bears

When their breakfast is too hot to eat, the Three Bears go for a walk. Goldilocks enters their house, eats their porridge, sits in their chairs, breaking the smallest one, and sleeps in their beds. When the bears return, Goldilocks is scared away.

2a. Goldilocks

Goldilocks Activities

Songs to Sing and Play

Tune: She'll Be Coming Round the Mountain

Words adapted by Juli Wright

She'll be coming to the bears' house when she comes, Oh, boy!
She'll be coming to the bears' house when she comes, Oh, boy!
She'll be coming to the bears' house, coming to the bear's house,
She'll be coming to the bears' house when she comes, Oh, boy!

She'll be eating all their porridge when she comes, Yum, Yum!
She'll be eating all their porridge when she comes, Yum, Yum!
She'll be eating all their porridge, she'll be eating all their porridge,
She'll be eating all their porridge when she comes.

She'll be breaking all their chairs when she comes, Crack! Crack!
She'll be breaking all their chairs when she comes, Crack! Crack!
She'll be breaking all their chairs, breaking all their chairs,
She'll be breaking all their chairs when she comes, Crack! Crack!

She'll be sleeping in their beds when they come, Snore! Snore!
She'll be sleeping in their beds when they come, Snore! Snore!
She'll be sleeping in their beds, sleeping in their beds,
She'll be sleeping in their beds when they come, Snore! Snore!

She'll be wearing pink pajamas when she sleeps, scratch, scratch!
She'll be wearing pink pajamas when she sleeps, scratch, scratch!
She'll be wearing pink pajamas, wearing pink pajamas,
She'll be wearing pink pajamas when she sleeps, scratch, scratch!

Oh, 3 bears go up to meet her when she sleeps, Growl! Growl!
Oh, 3 bears go up to meet her when she sleeps, Growl! Growl!
Oh, 3 bears go up to meet her, 3 bears go up meet her,
Oh, 3 bears go up to meet her when she sleeps, Growl! Growl!

She'll be running for her life when they come, Scream! Scream!
She'll be running for her life when they come, Scream! Scream!
She'll be running for her life, running for her life,
She'll be running for her life when they come, Scream! Scream!

Hey There, Goldilocks

"Hey there, Goldilocks!
I see you there in the three bears' house.
Don't you know what you're doing is such a crime?"
You tried the porridge
Some was much too hot.
You tried another then you ate a lot.
Don't you know what you're doing is such a crime?
Sitting right there in the baby bear's chair
Broke it all to pieces, it went everywhere.
Tired and sleepy you went up the stairs
And, were caught by three mad bears.
Hey there, Goldilocks!
I see you there in the three bears' house.
Don't you know what you're doing is such a crime?
You learned a lesson and you won't be back.
You're never ever gonna come right back.
Forever you'll be on the right track.
Be good now, Goldilocks!

The Three Bears Rap

Three bears, three bears,
Walking through the forest
You'd better go home now
ready or not...
Three bears, he bear,
Baby and a she bear,
Going for a walk because the
porridge was hot....
Three bears, three bears...
Three bears, three bears...
G-r-o-w-l

Tune: The Lion Sleeps Tonight

Words by Eunice and Juli Wright

In the forest, the mountain forest, the bears go out tonight. (repeat)
In the bears' house, the three bears' house, Goldilocks walks in. (repeat)
Uninvited, lost and hungry, Goldilocks eats porridge. (repeat)
Careless, bold and clumsy too, Goldilocks breaks chairs. (repeat)
Exhausted, scared and sleepy, too, Goldilocks finds beds. (repeat)
In the forest, the mountain forest, the bears are coming home. (repeat)
In the house, the three bears' house, the bears find Goldilocks. (repeat)
In the forest, the mountain forest, Goldilocks screams and runs. (repeat)
In the forest, the mountain forest, the bears go out tonight. (start over)

Tune: Oh, My Darling, Clementine

By Percy Montrose, 1884; words adapted by Juli, Glen and Eunice Wright.

Oh my darling, oh my darling,
Oh my darling Goldilocks,
You are lost and gone for a long walk,
Oh my darling, Goldilocks.

Found a house, and entered inside,
Her search for shelter now was done.
She was hungry, ate the food,
And broke the chair, the little one.

Went upstairs, found the beds there,
Too tired to even talk.
Soon the owners of the house came,
The three bears, back from their walk.

Oh my darling, oh my darling,
Oh my darling Goldilocks,
Three bears growled, she woke and ran,
Oh my darling, Goldilocks.

Tune: Three Blind Mice

Words by Eunice Wright

Goldilocks, Goldilocks.
See how she runs, see how she runs.
She ate their porridge with fork and knife,
She broke baby's chair and slept without strife,
Did you ever see such a sight in your life?
As Goldilocks, Goldilocks.

Tune: Mary Had a Little Lamb

Words by Eunice Wright

Goldilocks had a dish of porridge, dish of porridge, dish of porridge.
Goldilocks had a dish of porridge, and promptly ate it up!
Goldilocks had a seat in a chair...
And promptly broke it up.
Goldilocks had a nap in a bed...
And promptly woke right up.
Goldilocks had a dreadful scare...
And quickly screamed and ran.

Poems and Nursery Rhymes

Chant: Teddy Bear, Teddy Bear, Turn Around

Words by Eunice and Juli Wright

Goldilocks, Goldilocks, went for a walk.
Goldilocks, Goldilocks, didn't knock.

Goldilocks, Goldilocks, porridge she ate.
Goldilocks, Goldilocks, this tastes great!
Goldilocks, Goldilocks, not your chair!
Goldilocks, Goldilocks, for baby bear.
Goldilocks, Goldilocks, go upstairs.
Goldilocks, Goldilocks, beds for bears.
Goldilocks, Goldilocks, hit the sack.
Goldilocks, Goldilocks, bears are back.
Goldilocks, Goldilocks, wake with a fright.
Goldilocks, Goldilocks, run out of sight!

Naughty Little Gold-i-locks

Mother Goose: The Complete Book of Nursery Rhymes, *1941 (see donaldsauter.com).*

"Naughty little Gold-i-locks left her home one day;
Wand'ring up and down a wood, soon she lost her way..."

Curly-Locks

Mother Goose's Nursery Rhymes, *by Walter Crane, 1877.*

Curly-locks, Curly-locks, wilt thou be mine?
Thou shalt not wash the dishes, nor yet feed the swine;
But sit on a cushion, and sew a fine seam,
And feed upon strawberries, sugar, and cream.

The Little Girl with a Curl

Henry Wadsworth Longfellow (1850–1880)

There was a little girl, who had a little curl,
Right in the middle of her forehead.
When she was good she was very good indeed,
And when she was bad she was horrid.

One day she went upstairs, when her parents, unawares,
In the kitchen were occupied with meals,
And she stood upon her head in her little trundle-bed,
And then began hooraying with her heels.

Her mother heard the noise, and she thought it was the boys
A-playing at a combat in the attic; but when she climbed the stair,
And found Jemima there, she took and she did spank most emphatic.

Games and Group Activities

Peas, Porridge Hot (Group clapping game)

The Real Mother Goose, *by Blanche Fisher Wright, 1916; words adapted by Eunice Wright.*

Peas, Porridge hot.
Peas, Porridge cold.
Peas, Porridge in the pot,
Nine days old.

Some like it hot.
Some like it cold.
Some like it in the pot,
Like *Goldilocks* bold.

Books

The Apple Dumpling, and Other Stories for Young Boys and Girls, by Aunt Fanny (1852/1894). *Contents include "The Three Bears."*

Denslow's Three Bears, adapted and illustrated by W. W. Denslow (1903). *The story of Golden Hair and the jolly bears—beautiful old illustrations.*

Dusty Locks and the Three Bears, by Susan Lowell (Henry Holt, 2001).

Goldilocks and the Three Bears: Bears Should Share, Another Point of View, by Alvin Granowsky (Steck-Vaughn, 1996).

Goldilocks and the Three Bears, by Barrie Wade (Picture Window Books, 2003).

Goldilocks and the Three Bears, by Candice Ransom (School Specialty Children's Pub., 2005).

Goldilocks and the Three Bears, by Caralyn and Mark Buehner (Dial Books, 2007). *A rude little girl helps herself to the belongings of a nice family of bears.*

Goldilocks and the Three Bears, by Emma C. Clark (Candlewick Press, 2010).

Goldilocks and the Three Bears, by Gennady Spirin (Marshall Cavendish Children, 2009).

Goldilocks and the Three Bears, by James Marshall (Puffin, 1998).

Goldilocks and the Three Bears, by Jan Brett (G. P. Putnam's Sons, 1987). *Great illustrations, simple story, great puppet play material.*

Goldilocks and the Three Bears, by Jim Aylesworth (Scholastic, 2003). *Great but old-fashioned illustrations, simple story, great puppet play material.*

Goldilocks and the Three Bears, by Lauren Child (Hyperion, 2008). *Real photos as illustrations, Goldilocks is an actual doll. A different kind of story with a twist, and a comical spin on text; best for older children.*

Goldilocks and the Three Bears, by Robbin Cuddy (Preschool Press, 1993).

Goldilocks and the Three Martians, by Stu Smith (Dutton Children's Books, 2004). *A cute rhyming story, nice illustrations, good for preschool age children.*

Goldilocks Returns, by Lisa C. Ernst (Simon & Schuster, 2000).

Little Curly-Locks (Series), by Peter G. Thompson (1885).

Mother Hubbard's Picture Book, by Walter Crane (1897). *Contents include "The Three Bears."*

The Three Bears, by Paul Galdone (Seabury Press, 1972).

The Three Snow Bears, by Jan Brett (G. P. Putnam's Sons, 2007). *Beautiful illustrations, with a funny story variation set in Alaska. Great twist on the Three Bears story. Polar bears live in an igloo. Recommended.*

Movies and Television

Goldilocks and the Three Bears (1939), MGM

Goldilocks and the Three Bears (1995), Twin Dolphin Santa Monica Pictures, a Brent Loefke film. Mama Papa Baby Productions, Inc. *Story involves a human girl and talking animals.*

2b. Father Bear, 2c. Mother Bear, 2d. Baby Bear

Use this pattern for Father Bear and Mother Bear.

Patterns for hats and bowtie can be found on page 137.

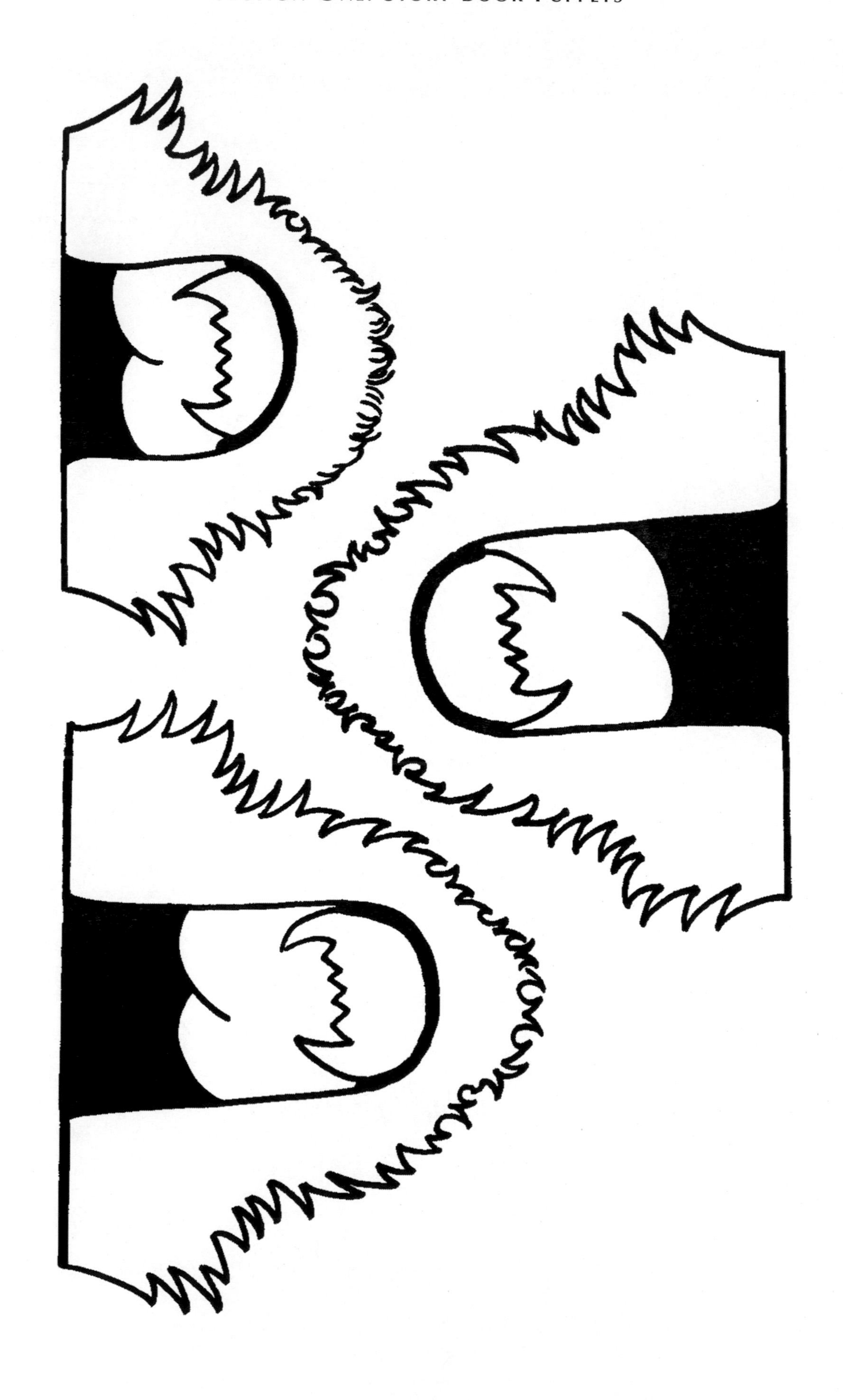

Bear Activities

Songs to Sing and Play

Tune: A Rig-A-Jig Jig

Words adapted by Eunice Wright

As we went walking down the mountain,
Down the mountain, down the mountain,
A Big Brown Bear we happened to meet,
Hi ho, hi ho, hi ho.

A rig-a-jig jig and away we run,
Away we run, away we run.
A rig-a-jig jig and away we run,
Hi ho, hi ho, hi ho.

Alternate verses: A little bear cub I happened to meet, a big polar bear, a hungry black bear, a dancing bear, a bear named Pooh, a hibernating bear, Smokey the bear.

Tune: Mary Had a Little Lamb

Words by Eunice Wright

Substitute child's name and kinds of bears: brown bear, black bear, polar bear, grizzly bear, Pooh bear, Smokey the bear, hibernating bear, hungry bear, dancing bear, bear cub, fishing bear.

Susie saw a brown bear, a brown bear, a brown bear,
Susie saw a brown bear, its fur as brown as dirt.

David saw a hibernating bear ... asleep until spring.

Tune (and Book): Brown Bear, Brown Bear, What Do You See?

Book by Bill Martin, Jr. (Holt, 1983)

"I see a _____ _____ looking at me." *(Repeat song, changing color and animal as desired.)*

Tune: Today Is Monday

Traditional; words adapted by Eunice Wright. Also read Today Is Monday *by Eric Carle.*

Today is Bear day.
Tall bears, fat bears, baby bears, grizzly bears.
All you hungry bears, come and eat it up.

Repeat, adding names of bears in place of week-day names.

Tune: Did You Ever See a Lassie?

Words adapted by Eunice Wright

Did you ever see a brown bear,
A brown bear, a brown bear?
Did you ever see a brown bear,
Go this way and that?

Alternate verses: That lives in the zoo, that lives on the mountain, in a cave, eats fresh fish, loves to eat honey, hunts for grubs, etc.

Tune: 10 Little Indians

Words by Eunice Wright

1 little, 2 little, 3 little bear cubs... (Black bears, brown bears, etc.)
Playing on the mountain.

Tune: London Bridge

Traditional; adapted by Eunice Wright

Now it's time to _____ _____ _____ *(find the bear, follow the bear, catch the bear, run from the bear, etc.)*
For it is _____ o'clock (or *And take a long bear nap*)

Tune: Are You Sleeping?

Words adapted by Eunice Wright

I hear bears growl, I hear bears growl,
Grrrrowl! Grrrrowl! Grrrrowl!
Grrrrowl! Grrrrowl! Grrrrowl!
In a cave or by a tree,

Eating berries or honey.
Grrrrowl! Grrrrowl! Grrrrowl!
Grrrrowl! Grrrrowl! Grrrrowl!

Tune: The Farmer in the Dell

Words by Eunice Wright

The bear in the zoo,
The bear in the zoo,
Hi ho, the beary-O,
The bear in the zoo.

(The bear takes a...)

Tune: She'll Be Coming 'Round the Mountain

Words by Eunice and Juli Wright

He'll be coming down the mountain when he comes. (growl, growl)
He'll be coming down the mountain when he comes. (growl, growl)
He'll be coming down the mountain,
He'll be coming down the mountain,
He'll be coming down the mountain when he comes. (growl, growl)

Alternate verses:

He'll be eating all the honey when he comes... (yum, yum)
He'll be hibernating in a cave all winter long... (snore, snore)
He'll be looking for a fish when he comes... (splash, splash)
He'll be eating grubs and berries when he comes... (yum, yum)
He'll be scratching all the trees when he comes... (scratch, scratch)

Tune: The Wheels on the Bus

Words by Eunice Wright

The bears in the zoo go growl, growl, growl... (*prowl, sleep, scratch, eat, snore, etc.*)
All around the zoo.

Tune: There Were Three Jolly Fishermen

Words by Eunice Wright

Use 3 paper sack bear puppets while singing this song (or use Cinnamon, Gummy, or Graham Cracker Bears)

There were three jolly (Gummy or other) bears.
There were three jolly _____ bears.
(Gummy, Gummy), bears, bears, bears.
(Gummy, Gummy), bears, bears, bears.
There were three jolly (Gummy) bears.

There were two jolly (Graham or other) Bears
There were two jolly _____ bears.
(Graham, Graham), bears, bears, bears.
(Graham, Graham), bears, bears, bears.
There were two jolly (Graham) bears.

There was one jolly Cinnamon bear.
There was one jolly Cinnamon bear.
Cinna, Cinna, mon, mon, mon.
Cinna, Cinna, mon, mon, mon.
There was one jolly Cinnamon bear.

If children are eating the bears as they sing, or subtracting puppet bears, then sing:

There were no little bears left,
There were no little bears left,
Little, little, bears, bears, bears
Little, little, bears, bears, bears
There were no little bears left.

Song: The Bear Went Over the Mountain

The American Folk Lore Society, 1920. The Journal of American Folk Lore, *Vol. 55, Boston: Houghton, p. 91.*

The bear went over the mountain
The bear went over the mountain
The bear went over the mountain
To see what he could see.

And all that he could see
And all that he could see
Was the other side of the mountain,
The other side of the mountain,
The other side of the mountain,
Was all that he could see.

Tune: Are You Sleeping?

Words adapted by Eunice Wright

Are you sleeping,
Are you sleeping,
Little bear,
Little bear?
You hibernate all winter
Through the cold, cold winter,
Little bear, Little bear.

Are you sleeping,
Are you sleeping,
Little bear,
Little bear?
You wake up in springtime,
In the warm, warm springtime,
Little bear, little bear.

Tune: "B-I-N-G-O"

Words by Eunice Wright

There was a boy (girl, child) who had a bear,
and Teddy was his name-O.
T-E-D-D-Y, T-E-D-D-Y, T-E-D-D-Y,
and Teddy was his name-O.

Tune: You Are My Sunshine

Words by Eunice and Juli Wright

Use "Care Bears"; add verses for each bear.

I Love my Sunshine bear,
My little Sunshine bear.
He fills my heart
With love and joy.
He always has a cheerful smile,
I'm so glad you're my
Sunshine Bear toy.

The Bear (tune: Sipping Cider Through a Straw)

Traditional American camp echo song; original author unknown

The other day (the other day),
I met a bear (I met a bear),
Away up there (away up there) *or,* Out in the woods
A great big bear (a great big bear)
The other day I met a bear,
A great big bear a way up there.
He looked at me (he looked at me)
I looked at him (I looked at him)
He sized up me (he sized up me)
I sized up him (I sized up him)
He looked at me, I looked at him,
He sized up me, I sized up him.
He said to me (he said to me)
"Why don't you run? (why don't you run?)
I see you don't (I see you don't)
Have any gun (have any gun)
He said to me, "Why don't you run?
I see you don't have any gun."

And so I ran (and so I ran)
Away from there (away from there)
And right behind (and right behind)
Me was that bear (me was that bear)
And so I ran away from there,
And right behind me was a that bear.

Ahead of me (ahead of me)
I saw a tree (I saw a tree)
A great big tree (a great big tree)
Oh, golly gee (oh, golly gee)
Ahead of me there was a tree,
A great big tree, oh, golly gee.

The lowest branch (the lowest branch)
Was ten feet up (was ten feet up)
I had to jump (I had to jump)
And trust my luck (and trust my luck)
The lowest branch was ten feet up,
I had to jump and trust my luck.

And so I jumped (and so I jumped)
Into the air (into the air)
And missed that branch (and missed that branch)
Away up there (away up there)
And so I jumped into the air,
And missed that branch away up there.

Now don't you fret (now don't you fret)
And don't you frown (and don't you frown)
I caught that branch (I caught that branch)

On the way back down (on the way back down)
Now don't you fret and don't you frown,
I caught that branch on the way back down.

That's all there is (that's all there is)
There is no more (there is no more)
Until I meet (until I meet)
That bear once more (that bear once more)
That's all there is, there is no more,
Until I meet that bear once more.
The end, the end (the end, the end)
The end, the end (the end, the end)
The end, the end (the end, the end)
The end, the end (the end, the end)
The end, the end, the end, the end,
This time it really is *the end*!

Tune: A Hunting We Will Go

Adapted words by Eunice Wright

Make up more rhyming verses for other bears and actions. See Fox (#1g) puppet music activities for another bear verse and examples.

A hunting we will go, a hunting we will go,
We'll catch a bear and sit him in a chair,
And then we'll let him go!

Grizzly Bear (tune: "Beverly Hillbillies" by Paul Henning)

Performed by Harry Belafonte (grizzlybear.wmv)

"I'm gonna tell ya all a story 'bout a grizzly bear...
A great big grizzly, grizzly bear."

Tune: I'm Bringing Home a Baby Bumble Bee

Words by Eunice Wright

I'm bringing home a baby grizzly bear (Polar bear, Koala bear, Brown bear, etc.),
Won't my mommy pull out all her hair!
I'm bringing home a baby grizzly bear,
OHH! A Big Bear Hug!

Tune: Little Peter Rabbit Had a Fly Upon His Nose

Words adapted by Eunice Wright

Little brown bear had a honey tree to find,
Little brown bear had a honey tree to find,
Little brown bear had a honey tree to find,
He followed his nose all the way.

Little brown bear had a bee upon his nose,
Little brown bear had a bee upon his nose,
Little brown bear had a bee upon his nose,
He licked it and it flew away.

Big brown bear found a honey pot to lick,
Big brown bear found a honey pot to lick,
Big brown bear found a honey pot to lick,
So he licked it all clean away.

Brown bear chased a salmon up the stream,
Brown bear chased a salmon up the stream,
Brown bear chased a salmon up the stream,
He caught it and he ate his lunch.

Black bear found a nice little cave,
Black bear found a nice little cave,
Black bear found a nice little cave,
And then he took a nice long nap.

(Let the children make up other things bears do.)

Other Songs

"A Bear, Bear, Bear," in *I Have a Song for You About Animals*, by Janeen Brady, page 32.
"The Bear Hunt," *Movin' & Groovin'* by The Learning Station. DVD, Vids for Kids. This song is from the award-winning DVD, *Movin' & Groovin' Vids for Kids* and award-winning CD, *Here We Go Loopty Loo*.
"Grizzly Bear," by Harry Belafonte, 1960 (grizzlybear.wmv).
"Grizzly Bear," by Jack Scott, 1962.
Song, movie and story of "*Smokey, the Bear*," 1960 (smokeybear.com).
"The Teddy Bear's Picnic," by Henry Hall and His Orchestra, 1932.

"The Teddy Bear's Picnic," by Jimmy Kennedy, 1932.
"Winnie the Pooh," Disney song.

Poems and Nursery Rhymes

Fuzzy Little Caterpillar (Bear)

Fingerplays for Nursery and Kindergarten, 1893, by Emilie Poulsson; adapted by Juli Wright

Fuzzy little brown bear,
Sleeping, sleeping under ground!
Fuzzy little brown bear,
Nowhere, nowhere to be found,
Tho' we've looked and looked and hunted
Everywhere around!

Fuzzy little bear,
Slept in his cave, day and night.
Fuzzy little bear,
Found his furry coat too tight,
So he stretched, yawned, and then
Awoke, walking into the light.

Fuzzy little bear,
See how he welcomes spring!
Fuzzy little bear,
Doesn't really know how to sing.
The free and happy creature,
Wonders what the new year will bring.

Nonsense Books

By Edward Lear, 1894; words adapted by Eunice Wright.

There was a Young Lady of Clare,
Who was madly pursued by a Bear;
When she found she was tired, she abruptly perspired,
That unfortunate Lady of Clare.

Five Sleeping (Hibernating) Bears

Words by Eunice and Juli Wright

5 little bears went to sleep in a cave,
One woke up, to his mother he did wave.
Four little bears, asleep in a sack,
One was hungry, and went for a snack.
Three little bears, left there to dream,
One woke up to drink from a stream.
Two little bears, so tired in bed,
One rolled over, and bumped his head.
One little bear, hibernated until spring,
He woke up to hear the birds sing.

Five Little Bears (Count up)

By Eunice and Juli Wright

One little bear, feeling really blue,
Along came another, then there were two!
Two little bears, stung by a bee.
Along came another, then there were three!

Three little bears, wishing there were more,
Along came another, then there were four!
Four little bears, happy and alive,
Along came another, then there were five!

Five Little Bears (Count Down)

By Eunice and Juli Wright

Five little bears, asleep by the door,
One ran away, then there were four!
Four little bears, chased by a bee.
One ran away, then there were three!

Three little bears, watching you,
One ran away, then there were two!
Two little bears, heard a loud gun,
One ran away, then there was one!
One little bear, too hot in the sun,
Ran home to mother, then there was none!

Teddy Bear, Teddy Bear (Jump Rope Chant)

Words by Eunice Wright

Teddy Bear, Teddy Bear, turn around.
Teddy Bear, Teddy Bear, touch the ground.
Teddy Bear, Teddy Bear, say, "I love you."
Teddy Bear, Teddy Bear, that will do.

Teddy Bear, Teddy Bear, go upstairs.
Teddy Bear, Teddy Bear, say your prayers.
Teddy Bear, Teddy Bear, turn off the light.
Teddy Bear, Teddy Bear, say Good Night.

Teddy bear, teddy bear, Dance on your toes,
Teddy bear, teddy bear, touch your nose.

Teddy bear, teddy bear, stand on your head,
Teddy bear, teddy bear, go to bed.

Teddy bear, teddy bear, say good-night,
Teddy bear, teddy bear, turn out the light.
Teddy bear, teddy bear, wake up now,
Teddy bear, teddy bear, take a bow.

Games and Group Activities

Tune: Row, Row, Row Your Boat

Bring a stuffed toy bear or use a bear puppet for this musical activity. Sing the song slowly, while the children do the actions with their bears. Add additional actions.

Hug, hug, hug your bear,
Squeeze him very tight.
Hold him high
Help him fly,
Then hug with all your might.

Tune: Turkey in the Straw

19th century American Folk Song; words adapted by Eunice Wright.

The children bring a Teddy Bear from home to use in this song activity. Make up more verses with help from the children. This activity is great for teaching prepositions, opposites, following directions, social interaction and cooperation.

Pick your teddy bear up from the ground,
Then go dancing all around.
Hold him high and hold him low,
As round and round and round you go!
Hold him left and hold him right,
Hold him tight with all your might!
Hold him close and hold him far,
Pretend that he can drive a car!

Hold him in front and hold him in back,
Sit down with him on your lap!
Rock him gently, to and fro,
Hold him tight, don't let him go.

Now, place him on the top of your head,
And walk a straight line to your "bed."
Give him a kiss, and say, "Good night,"
This sweet Teddy Bear is just right!

Teddy Bear's Picnic (book)

This book is a pop-up picnic basket with working fork, knife, and spoon, with an interactive story, by Margaret Wang and Paulina Malinen (Barrons Juveniles, 2008). *It's Teddy Bear's birthday, and all the other bears are organizing a surprise picnic!*

Group Activity: *Let children bring stuffed toy bears to class, lay out a blanket on the floor and have a class picnic.*

Teddy Bears Picnic Game

This game can be purchased online or at retailers. It consists of a game board with a built-in spinner with two different games: Rhyming and Colors and Shapes and Counting. In each game, a child draws a card, uses a complete sentence, spins, moves the number of spaces and finally arrives at Teddy Bear's Picnic. The games are educational for classroom use and fun for home use. They promote social, language arts and math skills. The game board comes with 23 rhyming cards, 23 shapes, colors and counting cards, and 6 player pieces. For 2–6 players, ages 4 and up.

Going on a Bear Hunt

Kids love this chant! If you need ideas of how to do it, find "Cool Bear Hunt" by Dr. Jean on the internet; also Darren 988 on YouTube has a good version. Michael J. Rosen's book *We're Going on a Bear Hunt* may also be helpful.

Baste the Bear

Games for the Playground, Home, School and Gymnasium by Jessie H. Bancroft, 1922, p. 50.

10 to 30 or more players.
Playground; gymnasium; large room.

One player is chosen to be the bear and sits in the center on a stool. The bear chooses a second player to be his keeper. The keeper stands by the bear, each of them holding an end of a short rope about two feet in length and knotted at either end to give a firm hold. The rest of the players stand in a circle around these two. The object of the players is to tag (baste or buffet) the bear, without themselves being tagged by the bear or his keeper. The players may only attack the bear when the keeper calls "My bear is free!" Should a player strike at the bear before the keeper says this, they change places, the striker becomes bear, the former bear becomes the keeper, and the keeper returns to the ring. The keeper does his best to protect his bear by dodging around him on all sides to prevent the attacks of the players who dodge in from the circle to hit him. Should the keeper or bear tag any player, the same exchange is made; that is, the player tagged becomes bear, the former bear the keeper, and the keeper returns to the ring.

Should a rope not be conveniently at hand, the game may be played in any of the three following ways: (1) by the bear and his keeper clasping hands; (2) a circle may be drawn around the bear beyond which the keeper may not go; (3) the keeper may be subjected to the general rule of not going more than two steps away from the bear in any direction.

Where there are more than thirty players, two or more rings should be formed, each having its own bear and keeper.

This is an old game, popular in many countries. It contains excellent sport, with opportunity for daring, narrow escapes, and much laughter.

Bear in the Pit

Games for the Playground, Home, School and Gymnasium by Jessie H. Bancroft, 1922, p. 50.

10 to 30 players.
Playground; gymnasium.

A bear pit is formed by the players joining hands in a circle with one in the center as the bear. The bear tries to get out by breaking apart the bars (clasped hands), or by going over or under these barriers. Should he escape, all of the other players give chase, the one catching him becoming the bear.

This is a favorite game with boys, and is not so rough a game as Bull in the Ring, the means of escape for the bear being more varied. He can exercise considerable stratagem by appearing to break through the bars in one place, and suddenly turning and crawling under another, etc.

Look Out for the Bear!

Games for Everybody, by May C. Hofmann, Dodge Publishing Co., 1905.

Any number of children can play this game. One is chosen to be the "bear," and he hides in some part of the room or garden, while the rest, with their backs turned, are standing at their goal.

As soon as the children have counted to 50 or 100, they all scatter and hunt for the "bear." The child who finds him first calls out "Look out for the bear," and all the children run to their goal.

If the bear catches anyone while running for the goal, they become "bears." These "bears" hide together and the game continues until all the children are "bears."

Books

The Adventures of Baby Bear, by Aubrey Lang (Fitzhenry, 2001). *Cute photos of baby bears. Series: Nature Babies.*

Baby Bear's Bedtime Book, by Jane Yolen and Jane Dyer (Harcourt, 1990).

Bear About Town, by Stella Blackstone (Series: Barefoot Board Book, 2001). *Each week, a friendly bear makes his way around town visiting the neighborhood businesses.*

Bear Snores On by Karma Wilson (Margaret K. McElderry, 2002).

The Bear Went Over the Mountain, by Rosemary Wells (Environments, Inc., 2002).
Bears, by Bobbie Kalman (Crabtree, 1994).
Bears, by Helen Gilks (Ticknor and Fields, 1993).
Bears, by Ian Stirling (Sierra Club Books for Children, 1992).
Bears, by John B. Wexo (Creative Education, 1989).
Bears, by Laura Bour (Scholastic, 1992).
Bears, by Mark Rosenthal (Children's Press, 1983).
Bears! by Nicole Iorio (HarperCollins, 2005).
Bears, by Ruth Krauss (HarperCollins, 1948).
Bear's First Christmas, by Robert Kinerk (S.S., 2007). *After a young bear finds just the right cave for his long winter's nap, he notices a little tree at the cave's entrance.*
The Bears in the Bed and the Great Big Storm, by Paul Bright (Scholastic, 2008). *One by one, bears crawl into bed with mom and dad.*
Bear's New Friend, by Karma Wilson (McElderry, 2006). *Bear and friends play with a bashful owl.*
Bears on Wheels, by Stan and Jan Berenstain (Series Scholastic, 2014). *Bears on bicycles? Count them as they go speeding past. Beginning reader.*
Berlioz the Bear, by Jan Brett (Penguin, 1996).
Black Bears, Our Wild World series (North-Word Press, Cooper Square, 2000).
Blueberries for Sal, by Robert McCloskey (Viking, 1948). *A girl and a baby bear each go picking blueberries with their respective mothers.*
Brown Bear, Brown Bear What Do You See? by Bill Martin, Jr. (Holt, 1996). *Children see a variety of animals, each one a different color.*
Can't You Sleep, Little Bear? by Martin Waddell (Candlewick, 1994).
Corduroy and *A Pocket for Corduroy*, by Don Freeman (Viking, 1968).
Don't Worry Bear, by Greg Foley (Viking, 2008). *A friendship develops between a bear and a caterpillar as it is transformed into a beautiful silk moth.*
Every Autumn Comes the Bear, by Jim Arnosky (Puffin, 1996).
Good Night, Little Bear, by Richard Scarry (Little Golden Book, 1961). *Father bear plays hide and seek with little bear. Very cute pictures and story for preschool children.*
Gotcha! by Gail Jorgensen (Scholastic, 2001). *Will a pesky fly ruin the bears' picnic? Math concepts.*
Jamberry, by Bruce Degen (Harper Festival, 1995).
Jesse Bear, What Will You Wear? by Nancy White Carlstrom (Aladdin, 1996). *Series.*
A Kiss for Little Bear, by Else Holmelund Minarik (HarperCollins, 1984).
The Legend of Sleeping Bear, Kathy-Jo Wargin (Sleeping Bear Press, 1998).
The Legend of the Teddy Bear, by Frank Murphy (Sleeping Bear Press, 2000).
Let's Count It Out, Jesse Bear, by Nancy White Carlstrom (Series; Aladdin, 2001). *A series of 10 poems celebrate all the fun counting activities Jesse Bear enjoys doing.*
The Little Mouse, the Red Ripe Strawberry and the Big Hungry Bear, by Don and Audrey Wood (Scholastic, 1984). *A little rodent learns to protect the things he treasures, sharing the fun.*
Mama's Little Bears, by Nancy Tafuri (Scholastic, 2002). *A simple and beautifully illustrated story for preschool children.*
Maybe a Bear Ate It! by Robie H. Harris (Orchard Books, 2008). *Imagine you've lost your favorite book and discover that a bear ate it.*
Mooncake, by Frank Asch (Simon & Schuster, 1986). *Bear builds a rocket to try and taste the moon.*
Paddington, by Michael Bond (series; HarperCollins, 2007).

Roawr! by Barbara Joosse (Philomel, 2009). *A hungry bear says, "Roawr!"*

Teddy Bear, Teddy Bear: A Classic Action Rhyme, by Michael Hague (Harper Festival, 1997).

The Teddy Bears' Picnic, by Jimmy Kennedy (Aladdin, 2000).

This Is the Bear, by Sarah Hayes (Candlewick Press, 2004).

The Valentine Bears, by Eve Bunting (HMH, 1985).

We're Going on a Bear Hunt, by Michael J. Rosen (Candlewick, 2014).

What About Bear? by Suzanne Bloom (Boyds Mill Press, 2010). *Good illustrations, short text, good story. Preschool level.*

Where's My Teddy, by Jez Alborough (Candlewick, 1994).

Movies and Television

The Adventures of the Wilderness Family (Trilogy: Part 2 and 3) (Lions Gate, 1975).

The Amazing Panda Adventure (Warner Bros., 1995).

Balto (Universal, 1995).

The Bears and I (Disney, 1974).

The Berenstain Bears (PBS, animated TV series, 1985–1986).

Brave (Pixar/Disney, 2012).

Brother Bear (1 and 2, Disney, 2004).

The Care Bears (TV series, 1985–1988).

Coke bears (commercials with polar bears) (Coca-Cola, 1993).

The Country Bears (Disney, 2002).

Disney—Adventures of the Gummi Bears (1985–1991 TV series).

Escape to Grizzly Mountain (Part 1 and 2, Miracle Entertainment, 2000).

Gold Diggers: The Secret of Bear Mountain (Universal, 1995).

The Great Outdoors, 1988.

Grizzly Bear, *Ultimate Predators* (National Geographic, 2012).

The Jungle Book.

Kung Fu Panda 1 and 2.

The Life and Times of Grizzly Adams, 1974.

Little Bear (TV series).

Little Bear Movie.

Little House on the Prairie.

Madagascar 3.

The Muppets (Fozzie Bear, Kermit's best friend).

Open Season 1 and 2.

Snuggles (commercial with teddy bear).

Spirit Bear: The Simon Jackson Story, 2006.

The Teddy Bear's Picnic (TV movie, Lacewood Productions, 1989).

The Three Bears (animated).

Toy Story 3.

We Bought a Zoo, 2011.

Winnie the Pooh.

Yogi Bear, cartoon character.

3. Hansel and Gretel

Hansel and Gretel are led away from their house because there is not enough food to feed them. They leave a trail of bread crumbs, but the crumbs are eaten by birds and the siblings are lost in the woods. They come across a house made of gingerbread and start eating it. Caught and imprisoned by the witch who lives there, they are fattened up for cooking. The pair tricks the witch and manages to escape.

3a. Hansel

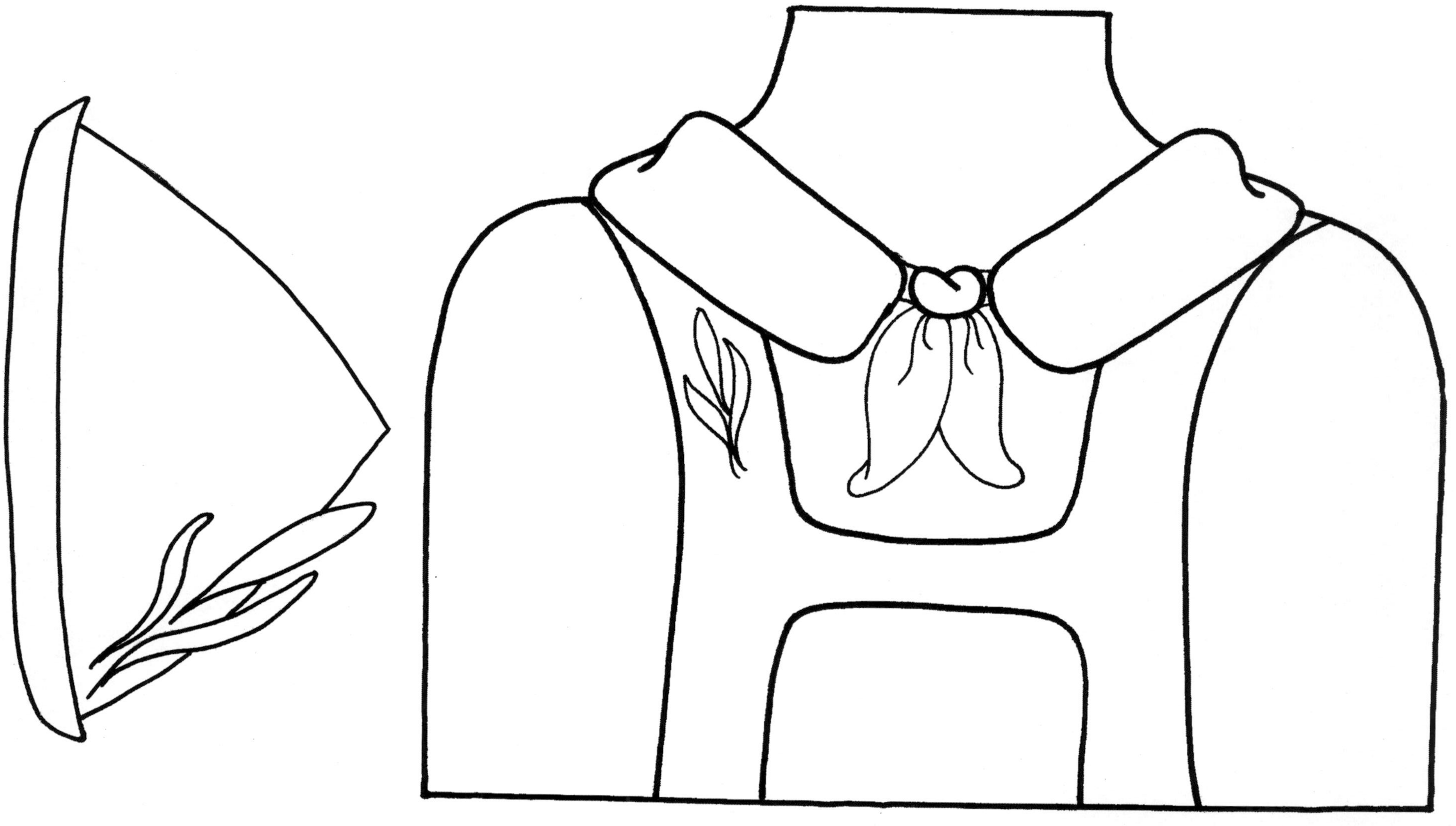

3b. Gretel

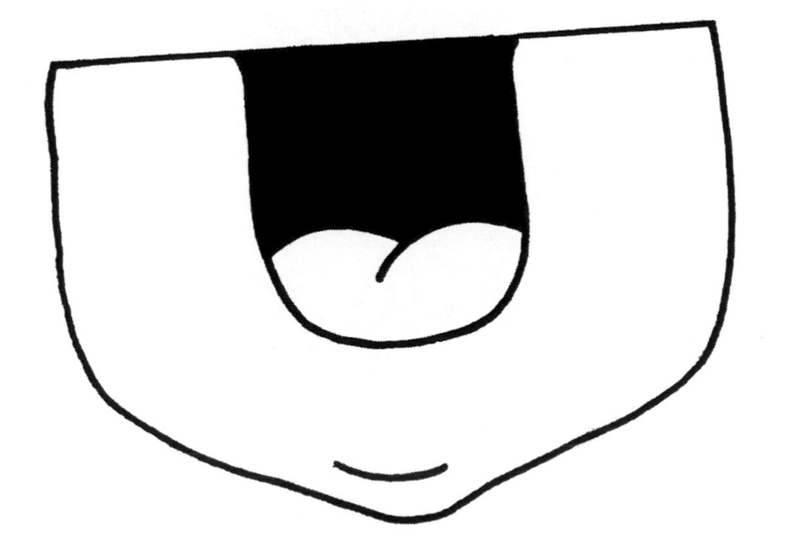

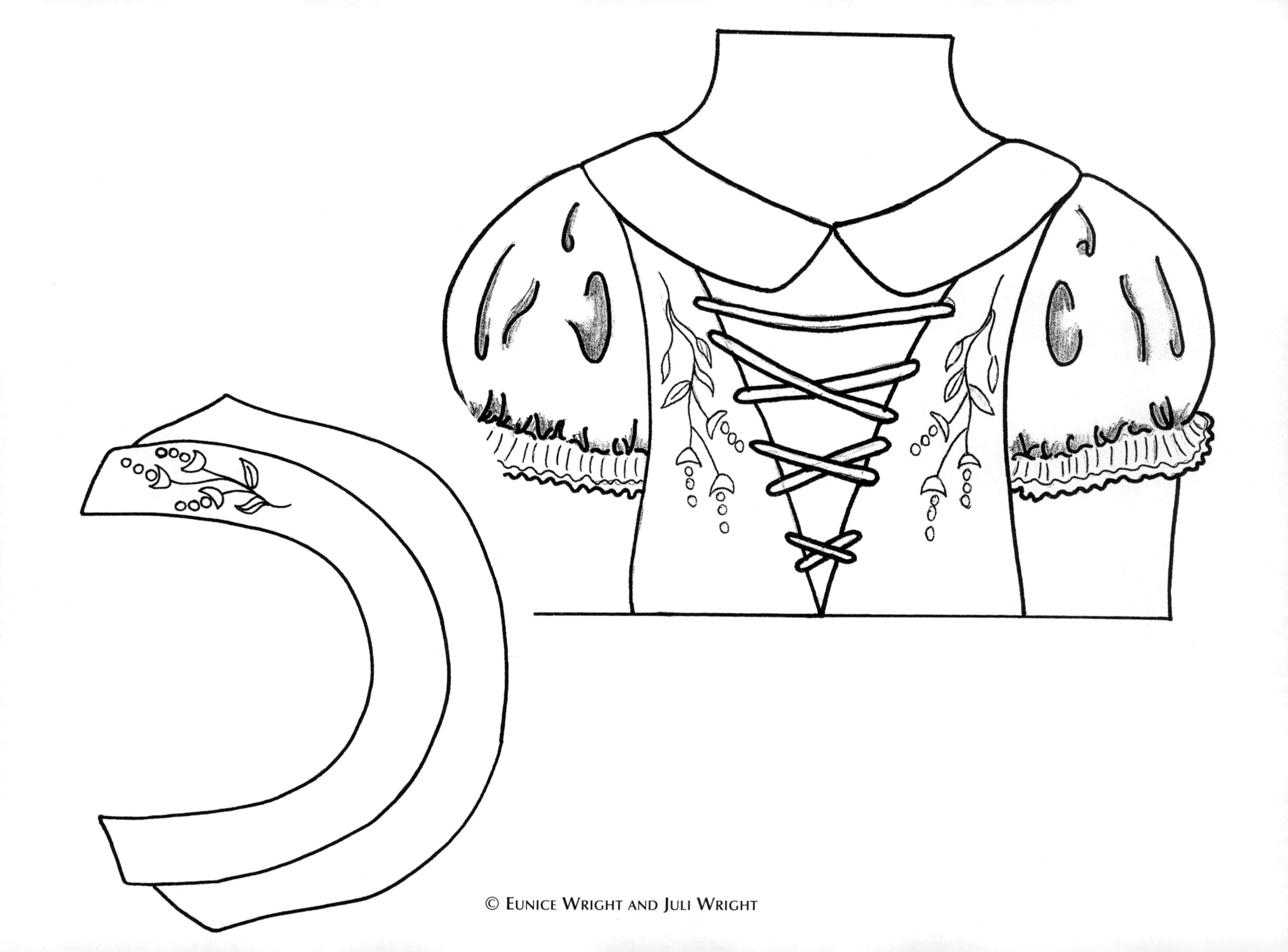

Hansel and Gretel Activities

Songs to Sing and Play

Tune: The Yellow Rose of Texas

Words by Eunice Wright

Oh, Hansel and Gretel
Lived with their father.
He loved them but stepmother,
Said they were a bother.

She made them leave their home,
In the forest they must go.
They left some of the bread crumbs
Along the path so they would know.

But soon they were so lost,
As they wandered down the lane.
Then they happened upon a little house,
Made of gingerbread, sugar and candy cane.

The little old lady who lived there,
Was really an evil witch,
Who loved to eat little children,
Into gingerbread she would switch.

When it was time to eat them,
Gretel tested the oven's heat,
She pushed the wicked witch in,
Then Hansel she did meet.

They found their way back home,
Stepmother no longer had a care.
Father was overjoyed to see them.
Hansel and Gretel lived happily there.

Tune: Little Bunny Foo Foo

Words by Eunice Wright

Hansel and Gretel, so lost in the forest,
The mean stepmother didn't want them to stay.
Hansel and Gretel, walking thru the forest,
Dropping bread crumbs all along the way.

Hansel and Gretel, eating the gingerbread house,
They were so hungry, that they couldn't stop.

(Spoken) *Out came the mean old witch,
And this is what she said:

"Hansel and Gretel, come into my house.
There's lots of candy and good things to eat."

Hansel and Gretel were locked inside the witch's house,
They kept trying to fool her, before she ate them up.

(Spoken) *Along came the mean old witch,
And this is what she said:

"Hansel, stick your finger out, of the bars of your cage.
I want to see if you are getting fat."

"Gretel, my dear, check the hot oven,
I want to bake a little boy pie."

Gretel pretended she couldn't check the oven,
The witch went to show her, and Gretel shoved her in. (gasp!)

(Spoken) *Hansel, you are free now,
Let's go home to father! (cheer!)

(Spoken) *The moral of this story is: Witch today, Gingerbread tomorrow!

Tune: Three Blind Mice

Words by Eunice Wright

Hansel and Gretel,
Hansel and Gretel.
Lost in the forest,
Lost in the forest.
They both had bread crumbs to mark the way,
They found a witch who made them stay,
Pushed her into the oven, and they got away,
Oh, Hansel and Gretel.

Tune: 10 Little Indians

Adapted by Eunice Wright

1 little, 2 little, 3 little children...
Eating ginger bread houses.

Poems and Nursery Rhymes

Hansel and Gretel

By Eunice Wright

Hansel and Gretel, poor children were they.
They had a stepmother who didn't want them to stay.

Father sent them away with a sad heavy heart.
With bread crumbs to find their way back to the start.

But soon they were lost, and so hungry, too.
Happily they found a ginger bread house to chew.

A witch who lived there, locked Hansel away.
She wanted to eat him, and insisted he stay.

When time to heat the oven, Gretel didn't know how.
So when the witch showed her, Gretel pushed her in. Wow!

At last they were free, to find their way home.
Their father sent stepmother packing her comb.

Games and Group Activities

Gingerbread House

Build a gingerbread house from gingerbread or cardboard. (See the gingerbread boy [#10] puppet section for additional activities.)

Gingerbread Children (Count Down)

By Eunice Wright

5 gingerbread children, or maybe there were more.
1 was frosted with pink, then there were four.
4 gingerbread children, on a plate for me.
1 was eaten quickly, then there were three.
3 gingerbread children, I will share with you.
If you eat one, then there will be two.
2 gingerbread children, brown like the sun,
1 ran away, then there was one.
1 gingerbread child, from five to one,
All were shared with my family, now there are none.

Books

Hansel and Gretel, by Cynthia Rylant (Hyperion, 2008). *Ages 4–8. Large picture book, large illustrations.*

Hansel and Gretel, by James Marshall (Walker, 2013). *Illustrations are not drawn to real life.*

Hansel and Gretel, by Rachel Isadora (Putnam, 2009).

Hansel and Gretel, by Will Moses (Philomel, 2006).

Hansel and Gretel, retold by Rika Lesser (Dutton, 1984). *Caldecott Award winner. Long text, large beautiful illustrations.*

Movies and Television

Cannon Movie Tales: *Hansel and Gretel* (1987).

Hansel and Gretel Fairy Tale Bedtime Story, by bedtime fairytales.

"Hansel and Gretel," Read Me a Story, episode 113. YouTube.

Looney Tunes (Bugs Bunny and Witch Hazel).

Shelley Duvall's Faerie Tale Theatre, "Hansel and Gretel" (TV episode #8, Season 2, 1983).

3c. Witch

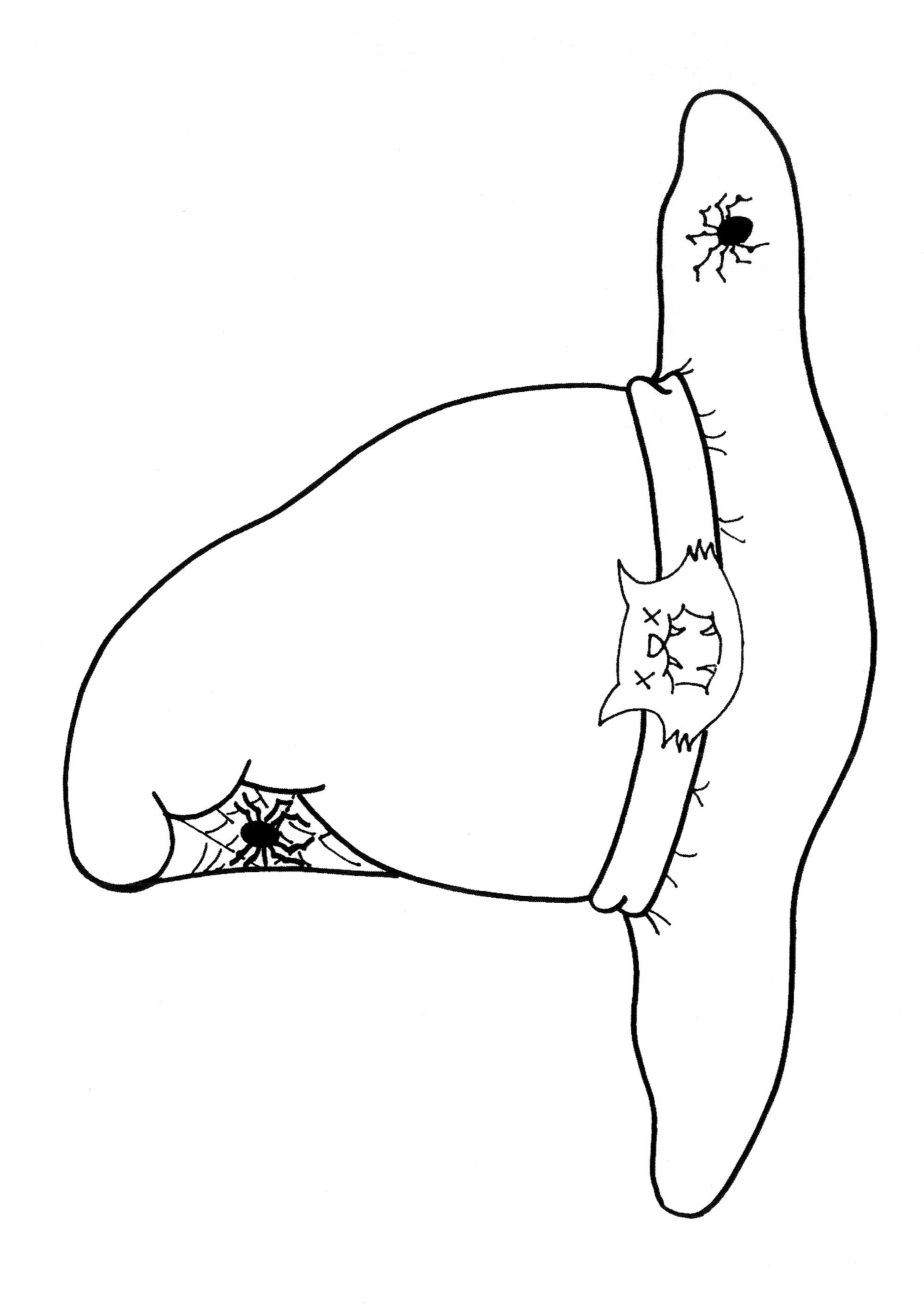

Witch Activities

Songs to Sing and Play

Tune: Three Blind Mice

Words by Eunice Wright

Three Old Witches,
Three Old Witches,
See how they fly,
See how they fly,
They all make potions and bring spells to life,
They stir their brew and poison the knife,
Did you ever see such a sight in your life,
As Three old witches.
Three old witches.

Tune: One Little, Two Little, 3 Little Indians

Words by Eunice Wright

One Little, Two Little, Three Little Witches...
Out on Halloween night.

Tune: There Was an Old Lady Who Swallowed a Fly

Words by Eunice Wright

"I know an old ***Witch*** who swallowed a ***spider***..."

Tune: This Is the Way We Wash Our Clothes

Words by Eunice Wright

This is the way we ride a broom *(cast a spell, eat a spider, make a potion)*

Tune: The Farmer in the Dell

Words by Eunice and Juli Wright

The Witch takes a... (spider, toad, newt, bat wing, etc.)
Alternate activity: The witch takes a _____ (draw a name or object from the witch's hat, then sing the verse).

Tune: A Hunting (Haunting) We Will Go

Words by Eunice Wright

Let children make up rhyming words & actions.

Oh, a haunting we will go, a haunting we will go,
We'll catch a witch and watch her twitch, and then we'll let her go.

Alternate verses:
We'll cast a spell and watch her swell, and then we'll let her go.
We'll take her cat, and put him in a hat, and then we'll let him go.
We'll take her broom and sweep the room, and then we'll put it back.
We'll take her potion and add some lotion, and then we'll put some on.
We'll eat her candy house and send her a dandy mouse, and then we'll all go home.

Tune: I'm a Little Teapot

Words by Juli, Chris and Eunice Wright

I'm a little witch, short and fat.
Here is my broom, here is my hat.
I'll cast a spell, with my cat—
Zip, zap, poof—now you're a rat!

Other Songs

"The Boogie Woogie Man," Marla Lewis (SongsforTeaching.com).
"The Boogie Woogie Pumpkin Man," The Piano Lady, Wendy Rollin (2014). Album: *Seasonal Songs in Motion*, by the Learning Station
"Halloween Night," *I Have a Song for You, Vol. 2*, by Janeen Brady, pp. 12–13, Brite Music Enterprises.
KidsMusic.co.uk (free Halloween music for kids).
"On Halloween Night," Joe Scruggs. Using Joe Scruggs' music in the classroo,

Hellojoe.com (1999–2014 Shadow Play Records and Video).

"Ride with a Witch," by Joan Lisonbee Sowards (Joansowards.com, 1989).

Songs for All Seasons (album) by Geof Johnson (2003).

"Witches' Brew," Hap Palmer (Activity Records, Inc.) SongsforTeaching.com, HapPalmer.com.

More ideas can be found online at:

- *Suite101: Halloween Songs for Children: Make New Songs from Familiar Tunes.*
- www.LearningStationMusic.com.
- BusSongs.com

Poems and Nursery Rhymes

Is She a Witch?

By Eunice Wright

My neighbor might be a witch,
She has a funny, weird little twitch.

Her house has candy cane gates,
A gingerbread door there awaits.

The windows are frosted and pink,
She passes me by with a wink.

In her window sits a black cat,
She wears a pointy black hat.

There are a few warts on her face,
She can vanish without a trace.

Her hair is long and black,
There's a lopsided hump on her back.

Strange things happen when she's near,
Could she really be a witch—or just a sweet old dear?

Hink, Minx

Aunt Kitty's Stories, *by various authors, 1870. Adapted by Juli Wright*

Hink, minx! The old witch winks.
The broom begins to fly.
There's nobody at home but a jumping toad,
A spider, a bat, and I.

An Old Witch

By Juli Wright

There was an old witch,
Who had a little itch.
She tossed a black cat
Right into her magic hat
To catch the rat,
Why did she do that?
I cannot tell,
I think she's going to cast a spell.

The Wicked Witch

By Juli Wright

The wicked witch,
With a tall black hat,
Turns all good children,
Into a spider or bat.

The Witch's Spell

Childhood's Favorites and Fairy Stories: The Young Folks Treasury, *Volume 1, ed. Jennie Ellis Burdick, 1919. Adapted by Juli Wright.*

A little Spider's scalt herself,
And the Flea weeps;
The little door creaks with the pain,
And the broom sweeps;
The little cart runs on by itself,
And the cauldron churns;
The little frogs begin to leap—
Now it is my turn! "Hocus Pocus!"

The Hare

Songs of Childhood, *by Walter De La Mare, 1902.*

In the black furrow of a field
I saw an old witch-hare this night;
And she cocked her lissome ear,
And she eyed the moon so bright,
And she nibbled o' the green;

And I whispered "Whsst! witch-hare,"
Away like a ghostie o'er the field
She fled, and left the moonlight there.

I Saw Three Witches

Songs of Childhood, by Walter De La Mare, 1902.

I saw three witches
That bowed down like barley,
And took to their brooms 'neath a louring sky,
And, mounting a storm-cloud,
Aloft on its margin,
Stood black in the silver as up they did fly.

I saw three witches
That mocked the poor sparrows
They carried in cages of wicker along,
Till a hawk from his eyrie
Swooped down like an arrow,
And smote on the cages, and ended their song.

I saw three witches
That sailed in a shallop,
All turning their heads with a truculent smile,
Till a bank of green osiers
Concealed their grim faces,
Though I heard them lamenting for many a mile.

I saw three witches
Asleep in a valley,
Their heads in a row, like stones in a flood,
Till the moon, creeping upward,
Looked white through the valley,
And turned them to bushes in bright scarlet bud.

5 Little Witches (Count Down)

By Eunice Wright

5 little witches ran out the door,
1 tripped and fell, then there were four.
4 little witches, flying over the tree.
1 fell off the broom, then there were three.
3 little witches, finding tricks to do,
1 lost her wand, then there were two.
2 little witches, now their spells are done,
1 said, "Hocus, Pocus," then there was one.
1 little witch, asleep in the sun,
She'll wake at midnight, for some Halloween fun.

The Witches' ABC's

By Juli and Glen Wright

A is for Abracadabra
B is for Bat wings
C is for Cat (*or* crystal ball)
D is for dead man's toe
E is for eye of newt
F is for frog legs
G is for gingerbread (*or* graveyard)
H is for hat (*or* Hocus Pocus)
I is for Incantation
J is for jack-o-lantern
K is for knob
L is for light's out!
M is for moon
N is for night time
O is for old owl
P is for potion
Q is for quick
R is for RUN!
S is for spider
T is for toad
U is for underground
V is for vulture
W is for witch
X is for X-spell
Y is for YOU!
Z is for Zap!

Games and Group Activities

Witch's Hat

Decorate the witch's hat for the Witch puppet after reading the book *There Was an Old Witch* and singing the song.

Hokey Pokey

Sing and do the actions to the "Hokey Pokey," adjusting the words and actions as needed. "You put your right hand in the witch's hat, cauldron, haunted house," etc. (See X-Ray [#42] activities for bones and skeletons.)

"You put your right hand in *the cauldron*, and you stir it all around. You put your right foot in the *haunted house*, and you tip toe all about. You put your left hand in the *witch's hat*, and you pull a spider out."

Witch's Brew

To the tune of "The Farmer in the Dell": Sing the following while adding pretend ingredients to the witch's caldron or hat, or make a "magic brew" and decorate cupcakes to share with the children.

The witch makes a potion (mix Kool-Aid punch, sing while stirring)
The witch adds a spider (add clean plastic spiders that float)
The witch adds cat hair (cotton candy, string licorice)
The witch adds dragon's teeth (candy corn)
The witch stirs and mutters (each child stirs his/her glass)
We all taste the brew—YUK! (drink the punch and eat the cupcake)

Alternate activities and verses: Make puppets for this song and do appropriate actions while singing. Make a witch, cat, newt, frog, and a troll.

The witch on Halloween, the witch on Halloween,
Heigh ho, the dair-y-oh, the witch on Halloween.
The witch takes a cat...
The cat takes a newt...
The newt takes a frog...
The frog takes a troll...
The troll says, "Who's crossing my bridge!"...
They all scream and run...

Books

Excuse Me ... Are You a Witch? by Emily Horn (Charlesbridge, 2003). *Great illustrations, cute story.*

The Little Green Witch, by Barbara McGrath (Charlesbridge, 2005). *The Little Red Hen is now the Little Green Witch. Great story to read at Halloween, ties in with the Little Red Hen and work cooperation. Simple story and illustrations.*

Little Witch Learns to Read, by Deborah Hautzig (Random House, 2003).

The Little Witch's Book of Games, by Linda Glovach (Prentice-Hall, 1974). *Variations of 30 indoor and outdoor children's games for all seasons. Excellent source of ideas for those boring days or Halloween parties. It also has several games about animals, dragons, and a magician. Recommended!*

Room on the Broom, by Julia Donaldson (Puffin, 2003). *With song.*

Spells to Grow Up By, Lantern Fish—Internet. *A book of TPR activities for young children. The kids decide what they want to be when they grow up, and then they cast a spell so that their wishes come true. See also* The Book of Potions *for more magical activities. A very cute online book that children will enjoy at Halloween.*

Teeny Witch and the Perfect Valentine, by Liz Matthews (Troll Associates, 1991). *A beginning reader, 2nd grade +, has a long text. Other books: Teeny Witch Goes to School, TW and the Great Halloween Ride, TW and Christmas Magic, TW and the Tricky Easter Bunny, TW Goes on Vacation, TW and the Terrible Twins, TW Goes to the Library.*

There Was an Old Witch, by Howard Reeves

(Turtleback, 2000). *In this cumulative story, an old witch collects a bat, a scratching cat, a howling creature, and other creepy crawly things to adorn her Halloween hat.*

A Very Brave Witch, by Allison McGhee (Simon & Schuster, 2006). *A cute and humorous short story, with good illustrations.*

The Witch Casts a Spell, by Suzanne Williams (Dial, 2002). *Collage-type illustrations and simple story line follows "The Farmer in the Dell." A great book for Halloween. The story can be sung to "The Farmer in the Dell."*

The Witch Who Was Afraid of Witches, by Alice Low (HarperCollins, 2000).

Movies and Television

Bewitched (TV series, SceenGems, 1964).

Bugs Bunny goes trick or treating at Witch Witch Hazel's house (Warner Brother's Looney Tunes animation—also several other animations)

Casper Meets Wendy (20th Century—Fox, 2002).

The Good Witch (Hallmark TV series, 2015).

Hocus Pocus (Disney, 1993).

Nightmare Before Christmas (Tim Burton, 1993).

Sabrina, the Teenage Witch (TV series; Paramount, 1996).

Snow White (Disney, 1937).

The Sword in the Stone (Disney, 1963).

Twitches (Disney, 2005). (Scholastic Press Book Series).

Wendy, the Good Little Witch (Harvey Comics, 1960).

The Witches (Jim Henson, Warner Bros., 1990).

The Wizard of Oz (Metro-Goldwyn-Mayer, 1939).

4. Heidi

Heidi, a Swiss orphan, is sent to live with her crotchety grandfather who lives high in the Alps tending goats. A sweet-natured girl with a sunny disposition, she eventually wins the love of her grandfather and the nearby inhabitants.

4a. Heidi

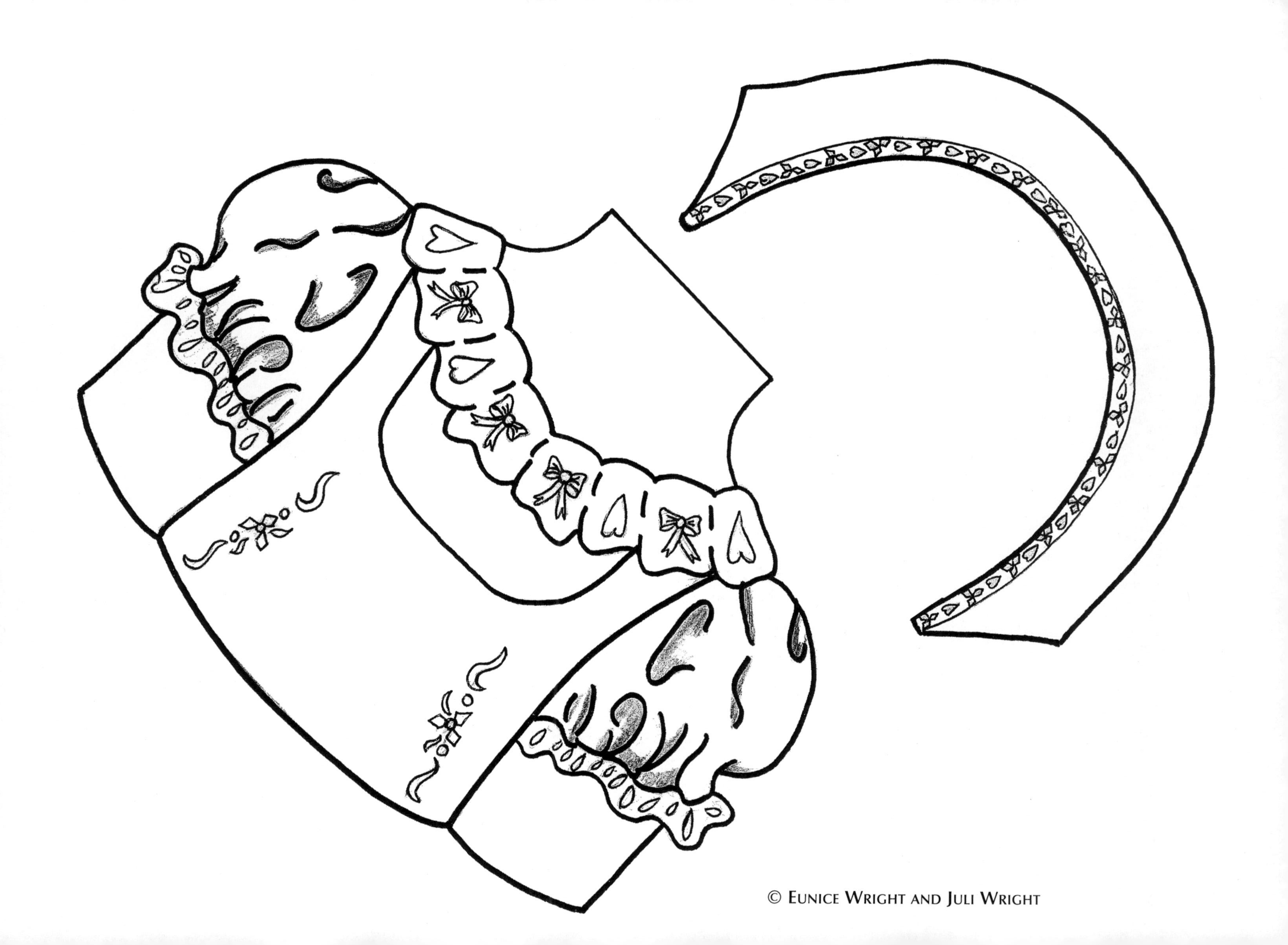

4b. Goats

See Middle-Sized Billy Goat (#14b) for puppet pattern and Goat activities.

4c. Grandfather

See Grandfather (#51) for puppet pattern and Grandfather activities.

Heidi Activities

See The Three Billy Goats Gruff (#14) for additional music and activities.

Songs to Sing and Play

Tune: Row, Row, Row Your Boat

Words by Eunice Wright

Heidi, Heidi, you're so cute!
You tend the goats all day.
High on the mountain where you live,
With Grandfather you play.

Heidi, Heidi, you're so sweet,
To the village you go to stay.
The little girl who cannot walk,
You leave to crawl away.

Heidi, Heidi, the girl who crawls,
Has the courage to walk at last.
Into her father's arms she goes,
And all are happy at last.

Tune: B-I-N-G-O

Traditional

There was a girl lived on a mountain,
And Heidi was her name-o.
H-E-I-D-I!...

Tune: Mary Had a Little Lamb

Words by Eunice and Juli Wright

Heidi had a little goat, little goat, little goat.
Heidi had a little goat, its coat was brown as dirt.
And everywhere that Heidi went, Heidi went, Heidi went,
And everywhere that Heidi went, the goat would eat a shirt.

Alternate verses:
Let children make up more rhymes.

Heidi had a little goat ... its coat was black as night.
And everywhere that Heidi went ... the goat was such a sight.
It followed her up the mountainside ... from morning until night.

Tune: 10 Little Indians

1 little, 2 little, 3 little goats...
All were Heidi's friends.

Song to play

"I'll Walk with You," by Carol Lynn Pearson. LDS, 1987.

Poems and Nursery Rhymes

Heidi

By Eunice Wright

Heidi was sweet; Heidi was cute,
Her hair in a braid, she played on a flute.

Heidi had chores; Heidi played notes.
Up on the mountain, she herded the goats.

Heidi had a friend; a girl who couldn't walk.
Down in the village, the two girls would talk.

Sad to leave her mountain, Heidi went right back.
Her grandfather was kind; so her friend didn't lack.

Heidi took her friend, right up the mountainside.
There she learned to walk, with Heidi by her side.

Games and Group Activities

Five Hungry Goats (Count Down)

By Eunice Wright

Five hungry goats, standing by the door.
One ate a tin can, then there were four.
Four hungry goats, playing under a tree.
One found a girl friend, then there were three.
Three hungry goats, wondering what to do.
One found an old shoe, then there were two.
Two hungry goats, having so much fun.
One ate a red shirt, then there was one.
One hungry goat, alone in the sun.
Went to flag down a train, then there were none.

Books

Heidi, Level 3 reader (Dorling Kindersley).

Heidi, by Johanna Spyri, translated by Helen Dole. *Young Heidi is forced to live with her grandfather who resides in a cottage high in the Alps of Switzerland. Heidi and her grandfather have a happy life together but her life changes when she is sent to the village to care for a sick girl. Originally published in 1880; many versions exist.*

The Story of Heidi (Picture Book Classics Series) by Susanna Davidson (2007).

Movies and Television

Heidi, a 1937 motion picture which starred Shirley Temple in the lead role.

Heidi, a 1952 Swiss film version in Swiss German (filmed on location in Switzerland), directed by Luigi Comencini, starring Elsbeth Sigmund. This was followed by a sequel, *Heidi and Peter*, in 1955, directed by Franz Schnyder, also starring Sigmund.

Heidi (1959), music by Clay Warnick, adapted by William Friedberg with Neil Simon.

Heidi, a 1968 television movie that starred Jennifer Edwards with Maximillian Schell and Michael Redgrave.

Heidi, Girl of the Alps, a 1974 Japanese anime series directed by Isao Takahata, dubbed into various languages.

Heidi, a 1974 BBC adaptation starring Emma Blake.

Heidi (1978). A 26-episode Swiss/German television series, starring Katia Polletin as the young heroine. It was dubbed into various languages, including English.

Heidi, a two-part television miniseries from 1993, starring Noley Thornton as Heidi. Co-stars included Jane Seymour as Miss Rottenmeier, Jason Robards as Grandfather and Lexi Randall as Clara.

Heidi (1995), animated film, 49 minutes, based on classic songs, "Start with a Smile."

Heidi, a 1996 animated film.

Heidi, a 2005 animated film.

Heidi, a 2005 live action film directed by Paul Marcus.

Heidi Four Paws, a comedic 2008 adaptation of the story of Heidi, featuring talking dogs in the acting roles, with the voice of Angela Lansbury.

Heidi's Song, a 1982 animated musical feature film, produced by Hanna-Barbera.

5. Little Red Riding Hood

Little Red Riding Hood walks through the forest carrying a basket of goodies for her sick grandmother. She meets a seemingly friendly wolf, who then rushes ahead of the girl, eats up her grandmother and poses as the old woman to gain Little Red Riding Hood's trust so he can eat her up, too.

5a. Little Red Riding Hood

Use Heidi (#4a) for face.

5b. Grandmother

Use Grandmother (#50) for face.

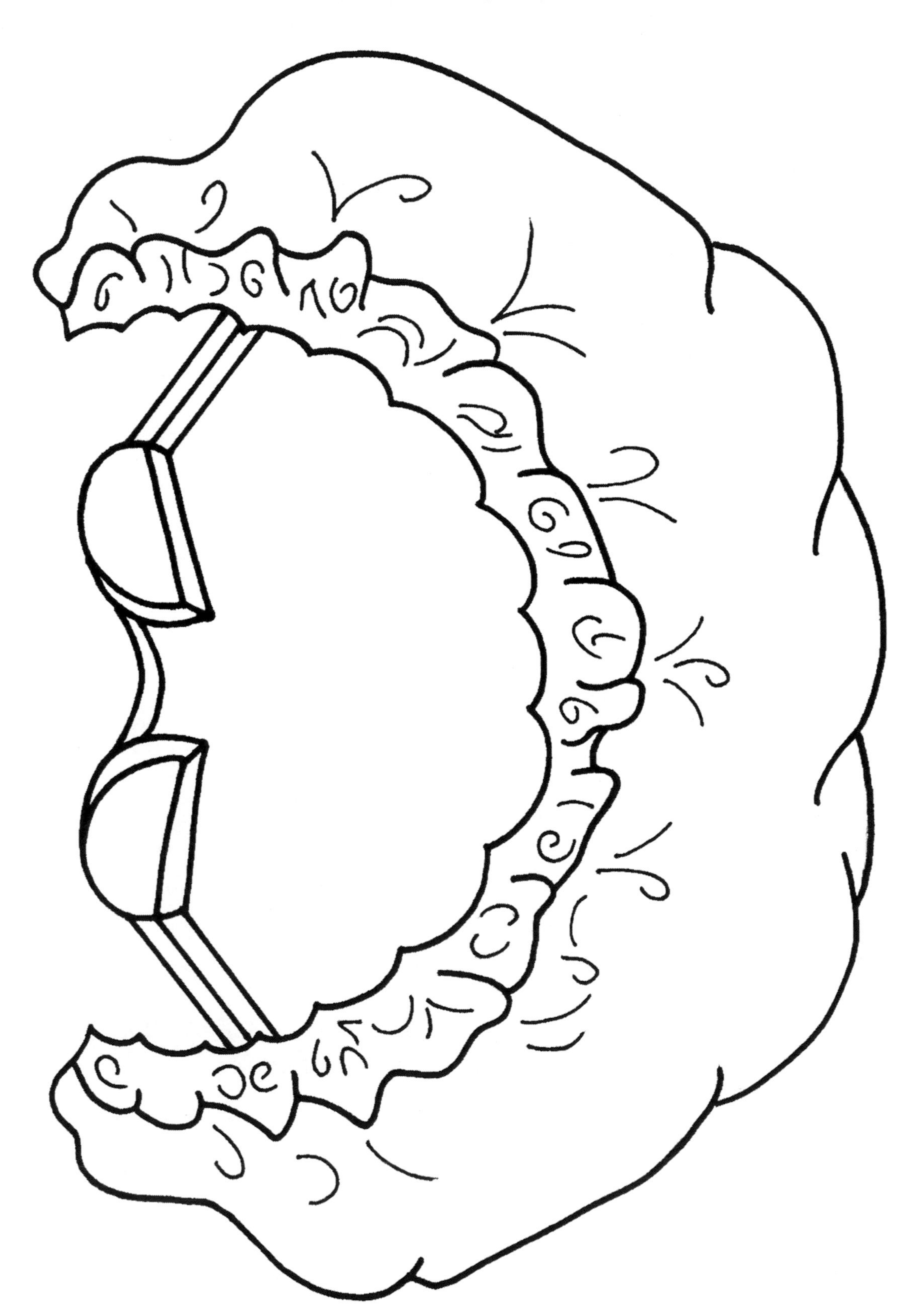

Little Red Riding Hood Activities

Songs to Sing and Play

Where, Oh Where Has Little Red Gone?

Words by Eunice Wright

To the tune of "Where, Oh Where Has My Little Dog Gone?"

Where, oh where has little red gone?
Oh where, oh where can she be?
With her Grandma's treats and a red cape and hood,
Oh where, oh where can she be?

She left home to go down the forest path,
To grandmother's house she did go.
But the wolf found out, and the plan was changed.
So the wolf got to grandma's house first.

Where, oh where has dear grandma gone?
Oh where, oh where can she be?
She heard the wolf's voice and then hid in the closet,
When the wolf came in to the house.

Where, oh where can the wolf be right now?
He wants to trick Little Red.
He put on grandma's nightgown, spectacles and cap,
And crawled in the bed to wait.

When Little Red came to grandma's house,
The wolf invited her in.
His ears were too big, and his nose way too long,
And my, what BIG teeth he had!

Then Little Red saw it was really the wolf,
So she loudly called for help.
The woodsman came, chased the wolf away.
Then Little Red and her grandmother were safe.

Tune: Over the River and Through the Woods

Words by Eunice Wright

Over the bridge and through the woods,
Red Riding Hood did go.
She took a treat, for grandmother sweet,
Who was feeling ill, you know—

While on her way, a wolf came to say,
"Where is it that you go?
Go pick some flowers, to fill her hours,"
(While straight to her house I go!)

When the wolf got there, he gave grandma a scare,
So the closet, she hid within.
The wolf climbed in bed, and covered his head,
And waited for Red to come in—

When Red saw the wolf, she said, "How strange!
You're not my grandma, I say.
What great big eyes, now don't tell me lies,
Your sharp teeth give you away."

"The better to eat you with," growled the wolf,
As he threw the covers high.
Red screamed loud, and left a dust cloud,
As she ran for help from near by—

The woodcutter came, made short work of the wolf,
And grandmother was set free.
"Time for a treat, let's sit down and eat,
And celebrate our safety."

Tune: Oh, Do You Know the Muffin Man?

Words by Eunice Wright

Oh, do you know Red Riding Hood?
Red Riding Hood, Red Riding Hood?
Oh, do you know Red Riding Hood,
Who visited her grandmother?

Oh, do you know Red Riding Hood?
Red Riding Hood, Red Riding Hood?

Oh, do you know Red Riding Hood,
Who... *(this could be a class discussion on stranger-danger, or a sequencing activity)*
Wore a red hood? (identification and clothing description)
Took a treat to grandmother? (visited a shut-in)
Picked flowers on the way? (cheer up, fragrant, colorful)
Talked to a stranger (wolf)?
Identified the home intruder? (the wolf)
Ran for her life? (scream and run safety rule)
Who was saved by the woodcutter? (first responder, good neighbor, friend, etc.)

Who Has the Color Red? (Tune: Are You Sleeping?)

Words by Eunice Wright; adapt song lyrics as needed

Who has red shoes, who has red shoes?
Please stand up, please stand up.
Clap your hands, turn around,
Then sit down, then sit down.

Who has red clothes, who has red clothes?...
(or red pants, ribbon, barrette, socks, shirt, belt, etc.)
(change actions as desired)

Which animal/bird has a red color? *(or any color you name)*
(or which animal has horns, etc.)...
Please stand up, please stand up.
Make the animal sound, make the animal sound,
Then sit down, then sit down.

Adapt the verses, change the actions, animals, colors, etc. as desired.

Let's Spell Red (Tune: The Wheels on the Bus)

Words by Eunice Wright

Let's spell red: "R-E-D,
R-E-D, R-E-D."
Let's spell red:
"R-E-D.
On our paper today."

Let's find red:
R-E-D, R-E-D, R-E-D.
Let's find red:
R-E-D.
All around the room.

Other Songs

Fairy Tale Favorites 2: More Story Time Songs for Children, including: "Rapunzel," "Brave Little Tailor," "Emperor's New Clothes," "Rip Van Winkle," "Rumpelstiltskin," "Sleeping Beauty" and more.

Shauna Tominey's *Fairy Tale Favorites: Story Time Songs for Children.* Album track listing:

1. "Three Pigs" [use also for #15 puppets]
2. "Three Billy Goats Gruff" [use also for #14 puppets]
3. "Little Red Riding Hood" [use also for #5 puppets]
4. "Gingerbread Man" [use also for #10 puppets]
5. "Little Red Hen" [use also for #12 puppets]
6. "Cinderella"
7. "Goldilocks and the Three Bears" [use also for #2 puppets]
8. "Tortoise and the Hare" [use also for #16 puppets]
9. "Frog Prince" [use also for #9 puppets]
10. "Hansel and Gretel" [use also for #3 puppets]
11. "Jack and the Beanstalk"
12. "Elves and the Shoemaker"

Poems and Nursery Rhymes

Little Red Riding-Hood

The Children's Book of Poetry, *illustrated by Henry T. Coates, 1879.*

The Little Red Riding-Hood—such was the name
Of a nice little girl who lived ages ago;
But listen, I pray you, and then how she came
Such a title to get you shall speedily know.

She lived in a village not far from a wood,
And her parents were all the relations she had,
Except her old grandmother, gentle and good,
Who to pet her and please her was always most glad.

Her grandmother made her a riding-hood, which
She was always to wear at such times as she could;
'Twas made of red cloth, so the poor and the rich
Used to call the child Little Red Riding-Hood.

Her mother, one day, said, "Your granny is ill;
Go and see her—be sure not to loiter along;
Your basket, with cheese-cakes and butter I'll fill—
Now, be sure not to gossip, for that's very wrong.

"If met by a stranger, be cautious, my child;
Do not hold conversation—just curtsey and say,
'I'm sent on an errand.' Do not be beguiled
By strange folks and smooth words
From your straight path to stray."

Not far had she gone through the wood, when she met
With a wolf, who most civilly bade her good-day;
He talked so politely, he made her forget
She was not to converse with strange folks on the way.

"To see your dear granny you're going?" said he;
"I have known her some years, so a visit I'll pay;
If what you have told me is true, I shall see";
And the wolf then ran off without further delay.

The maiden forgot her fond mother's advice;
As some pretty wild flowers she gathered with glee,
To take to her granny—she said, "'Twill be nice.
If I take them to granny—how pleased she will be!"

The wolf hastened on to the grandmother's cot;
"Who is there?" cried the dame. "'Tis your grandchild," he said.
"Pull the bobbin!" said she; soon entrance he got,
And devoured the poor helpless dame in her bed.

He scarcely had finished his horrible feast,
When the Little Red Riding-Hood came to the door.
She tapped very gently; the ravenous beast
Cried out, "Oh, I'm so hoarse! Oh, my throat is so sore!"

Then Little Red Riding-Hood said, "Granny dear,
It is I who am knocking, so please let me in."
"Pull the bobbin," the wolf said; "I am glad you are here—
You bring me a supper," he said with a grin.

When Riding-Hood entered the wolf said, "I'm weak;
I have pain in my limbs, and much pain in my head;
Be quiet, dear grandchild; don't ask me to speak,
But undress yourself quickly and come into bed."

She quickly undressed, and she got into bed,
But she could not refrain from expressing her fears.
"Oh, grandmother dear!" the maid timidly said;

"I have never before seen such very large ears!"

"The better to hear you," the wolf then replied;
But Red Riding-Hood heard what he said with surprise,
And, trembling with fear, "Oh my! Granny!" she cried,
"You have very large teeth and what great flashing eyes!"

"The better to see you! The better to bite!
I am not your old granny, I'll soon let you see—
I ate her to-day, and I'll eat you to-night;
By and by you shall make a nice supper for me."

But just as he said so the door open flew,
And in rushed some brave men, who had heard all that passed;
The bloodthirsty wolf then they speedily slew,
And saved Little Red Riding-Hood's life at the last.

Games and Group Activities

Little Red Riding Hood

In *One Person Puppet Plays* by Denise Wright (Libraries Unlimited, 1990), there is a script for the Little Red Riding Hood story (p. 52). This is a good play for one person to perform!

Ten RED Cherries, Gingerbread Cookies, Gummy Bears, Apples, etc.

By Eunice Wright

Use 10 red bird puppets (page 103) or other red items. Insert child's name in the second blank. Change words as necessary.

Ten red _____,
all of them mine.
_____ came over to play,
And now there are nine.

Nine red _____,
sitting on a plate.(flying around)
_____ came and ate one, (caught one)
And now there are eight.

Eight red _____,
Looking up to heaven.
_____ wanted one,
And now there are seven.

Seven red _____,
All in a mix.
_____ took one,
And now there are six.

Six red _____,
Right next to a hive.
_____ flew around, (ran around)
And now there are five.

Five red _____,
Sitting by the door.
In came _____,
And now there are four.

Four red _____,
Hanging from a tree. (sitting in)
_____ picked one,
And now there are three.

Three red _____,
In a bowl of blue, (a sky of)
_____ took one,
And now there are two.

Two red _____,
The waiting now is done.
_____ ate some, (sang like some)
And now there is one.

One little _____,
He is the hero.
_____ ate that one, (fed that bird)
And now there is zero.

Five Rosy Apples

By Eunice Wright

Five rosy apples on the tree by the door,
One tumbled off a twig and then there were four.

Four rosy apples, very plain to see,
The farmer's wife took one and then there were three.
Three rosy apples, underneath the sky so blue,
Susie came and ate one, then there were two.
Two rosy apples, hanging in the sun,
Billy ate the big one, then there was one.
One rosy apple, soon it will be done.
The farmer ate it for his lunch, and now there are none.

Other items can be substituted.

Books

Auntie Tiger, by Laurence Yep (Harper, 2009). *Colorful pictures, silly story. The tiger eats the little girl as in Little Red Riding Hood.*

Honestly, Red Riding Hood Was Rotten! The Story of Little REd Riding Hood as Told by the Wolf (The Other Side of the Story), by Trisha S. Shaskan (picture window, 2011).

Little Red Cowboy Hat, by Susan Lowell (Square Fish, 2000).

Little Red Riding Hood, by Candice Ransom (Brighter Child, 2001).

Little Red Riding Hood, by Jerry Pinkney (Little Brown, 2007). *A sweet little girl meets a hungry wolf in the forest while on her way to visit her grandmother.*

Little Red Riding Hood, by Trina Schart Hyman (Holiday House, 1987).

Little Red Riding Hood, retold by Harriet Ziefert (Puffin, 2000).

Little Red Riding Hood: A Newfangled Prairie Tale, by Lisa Campbell Ernst (Simon & Schuster, 1998).

Lon Po Po: A Red-Riding Hood Story from China, by Ed Young (Puffin, 1996). *Young's elegant paintings for this adventure-filled folktale won the Caldecott Medal.*

Petite Rouge: A Cajun Red Riding Hood, by Mike Artell (Dial, 2001).

Pretty Salma: A Little Red Riding Hood Story from Africa, by Niki Daly (Clarion, 2007).

Red Riding Hood, retold by James Marshall (Puffin, 1993).

Tortuga in Trouble, by Ann Paul (Holiday House, 2009). *A bilingual twist of Little Red Riding Hood. Good illustrations, okay for early childhood.*

The Wolf's Story: What Really Happened to Little Red Riding Hood, by Toby Forward (Candlewick, 2005).

Movies and Television

Cannon Movie Tales: *Red Riding Hood* (1989).

Hoodwinked! Animated, 2005.

Looney Tunes (Tweety, Bugs Bunny, Sylvester, wolf).

Shelley Duvall's Faerie Tale Theatre: "Little Red Riding Hood" (season 2, episode #7, 1983, 56 min.).

5c. Wolf

Grandma's hat and spectacles (p. 87) fit over the wolf's head.

Wolf Activities

Songs to Sing and Play

Here Comes the Wolf (Tune: Three Blind Mice)

Words by Eunice Wright

Here comes the wolf,
Here comes the wolf,
See how he runs,
See how he runs,
He ran after the pigs, you see.
He wanted them over for a cup of tea.
The pigs ran home just as fast as can be,
Oh, here comes the wolf.

Here run the pigs,
Here run the pigs,
From house to house,
From house to house,
The wolf blew and blew the straw house away.
He blew and blew the stick house away.
But he couldn't blow the brick house away.
Oh, here climbs the wolf.

Here sit the pigs,
Here sit the pigs,
Inside the house of bricks,
Inside the house of bricks,
When safe inside where the wolf couldn't be,
The pigs made a fire for a cup of tea.
The wolf climbed up to the chim-n-ey,
And, down came the wolf.
"Eeeeeeyowww!"

Who's Afraid of the Big Bad Wolf?

This is a popular song written by Frank Churchill with additional lyrics by Ann Ronell. (See Disney's animated story of the *Three Little Pigs.*)

Poems and Nursery Rhymes

The Terrible, Evil, Sinister, Loathsome Wolf

Words by Eunice and Juli Wright

He's a terrible wolf.
He always wants to leap!
He will growl and creep,
His clothes are in a heap.
He's a despicable, scroung-ie, slinking dust-heap!

He's a evil wolf.
He has a squinty eye,
He sneaks around to spy,
He hopes someone will die.
He has a rotten apple heart, with a wormy rotten core!

He's a sinister wolf.
He has rotten meat in his cheek.
He preys upon the weak.
It's a free meal that he will seek.
He has a character so hateful, you would never even want a peek!

He's a loathsome wolf.
His tail is in a twist.
The food that's on his list,
Is a strange menu, he will insist.
His dinner menu consists of ham hocks and lamb chops—which he can't resist!

Books

Betsy Who Cried Wolf, by Gail Carson Levine (HarperCollins, 2005). *Age Level: K+. A humorous story of "The Boy Who Cried 'Wolf.'" A smart young shepherd finds that there is more than one way to keep a wolf from eating her sheep.* She also wrote *Betsy Red Hoodie* (H.C., 2010).

Beware of the Storybook Wolves, by Lauren Child (Hodder and Stoughton, 2013). *Age Level: K+. When two wolves escape from his fairy tale book and threaten to eat him, Herb enlists the help of Cinderella's fairy godmother.*

The Boy Who Cried Wolf, by B. G. Hennessy (Simon & Schuster, 2006). *Age Level: Preschool +. A boy tending sheep on a mountainside thinks it a joke to cry "wolf" and watch the people come running. But one day a wolf is really there, and no one answers his call.*

The Boy Who Cried Wolf, by Jenny Giles (Rigby, 1998).

The Boy Who Cried "Wolf!" See script for puppet play in *One Person Puppet Plays* by Denise Wright (Libraries Unlimited, 1990), page 27. Recommended!

The Eyes of Gray Wolf, by Johnathan London (Chronicle, 1993).

Good Little Wolf, by Kristina Andres (North-South, 2008). *Is he really a good wolf?*

Mind Your Manners, B. B. Wolf, by Judy Sierra (Knopf, 2007). *When wolf is invited to the library for storybook tea, will he be able to mind his manners?*

There's a Wolf at the Door, Five Classic Tales, by Zoe B. Alley (Roaring Book Press, 2008). *Five well-known tales, all starring the Wolf; graphic style art work, satirical humor. For older children. This is a very large book.*

What's the Time, Grandma Wolf? by Ken Brown (Peachtree, 2015). *Age Level: Toddler and up. A group of little animals creep closer and closer to Grandma Wolf as she prepares to fix dinner.*

Where's the Big Bad Wolf? By Eileen Christelow (Clarion, 2002). *An almost graphic-novel style of complicated illustration; a detective hunts for the wolf. Long text, humorous, for older children.*

Winston the Book Wolf, by Marni McGee (Walker, 2006). *Winston likes to eat books.*

Wolf! by Becky Bloom (Scholastic, 1999). *Age Level: Preschool and up. A wolf learns to read in order to impress the group of farmyard animals. Note: Artfelt has a "Wolf!" felt puppet set to go along with this book.*

The Wolf and the Seven Kids, by the Brothers Grimm (Troll Associates, 1979). *A cute story about a wolf that tries to trick the seven little goats while their mother is away, and gobbles them up whole. They are cut free from his tummy by mother goat who replaces them with heavy stones.*

The Wolf Is Coming! by Elizabeth MacDonald (Dutton, 1998). *Age Level: Toddler and up. A father rabbit runs through the farmyard looking for a place to hide from the wolf, which creates enough commotion to protect all the animals on the farm.*

The Wolf Who Cried Boy, by Bob Hartman (Puffin, 2004). *Age Level: Preschool and up. Little Wolf is tired of eating lamb-burgers and sloppy does and tricks his parents into thinking there is a boy in the woods. Will they all miss a chance for a real feast?*

Wolf, Wolf, by Gerald Rose (MacMillan, 1988).

The Wolf's Chicken Stew, by Keiko Kasza (Puffin, 1996). *Age Level: Preschool and up. A hungry wolf's attempts to fatten a chicken for his stewpot. Note: Artfelt has a "The Wolf's Chicken Stew" felt puppet set to go along with this book.*

Wolves, by Emily Gravett (Simon & Schuster, 2006).

Wolves, by Gail Gibbons (Holiday House, 1995).

Wolves, by Laura Evert (Cooper Square, 2000). *Our Wild World series, NorthWord Press.*

Old Wolf Tales

"The Dog and the Wolf"
"Wolf and the Kid"
"The Wolf and the Lamb"
"The Wolf and the Shepherds"
"The Wolf in Sheep's Clothing"
"The Wolves and the Sheep"
"Wolves and the Sheepdogs"

Aesop's Fables

"The Ass and the Wolf."
"The Dogs against Wolves."
"A Gullible Wolf Is Scared Away."
"The Kid and the Wolf."
"The Lion, the Wolf, and the Fox."
"The Nurse and the Wolf."
"The Wolf and His Shadow."
"The Wolf and the Crane."
"Wolf and the Dog."
"The Wolf and the Goat."
"The Wolf and the Kid."
"The Wolf and the Lion."
"The Wolf Fails to Deceive the Horse."
"The Wolf in Sheep's Clothing."

Movies and Television

Balto 1, 2, 3 (Amblin Entertainment, 1995, 2002, 2004).
Cry of the Wild (Bill Mason, 1973).
The Journey of Natty Gann (Disney, 1985).
The Jungle Book (Disney, 1967).
Little House on the Prairie: The Wolves (1997).
Little Red Riding Hood (7 Arts International, 2006).
Never Cry Wolf (Disney, 1983).
Night of the Wolf (Animal Planet, 2002).
Peter and the Wolf (Break Thru Films, 2006).
White Fang, 1 and 2 (Disney, 1991, 1994).
The Wilderness Family, Part 2 (Sterling Home Video, 1978).

6. Peter and the Wolf

Peter, a young Russian boy wandering away from his home, warns a duck and bird to avoid his cat, who is stalking them. Told by his grandfather to stay close to home because wolves could be nearby, Peter defies the instructions and uses his wiles to catch a wolf, which has eaten the duck. The original is a 1936 symphony by Sergei Prokofiev.

6a. Peter

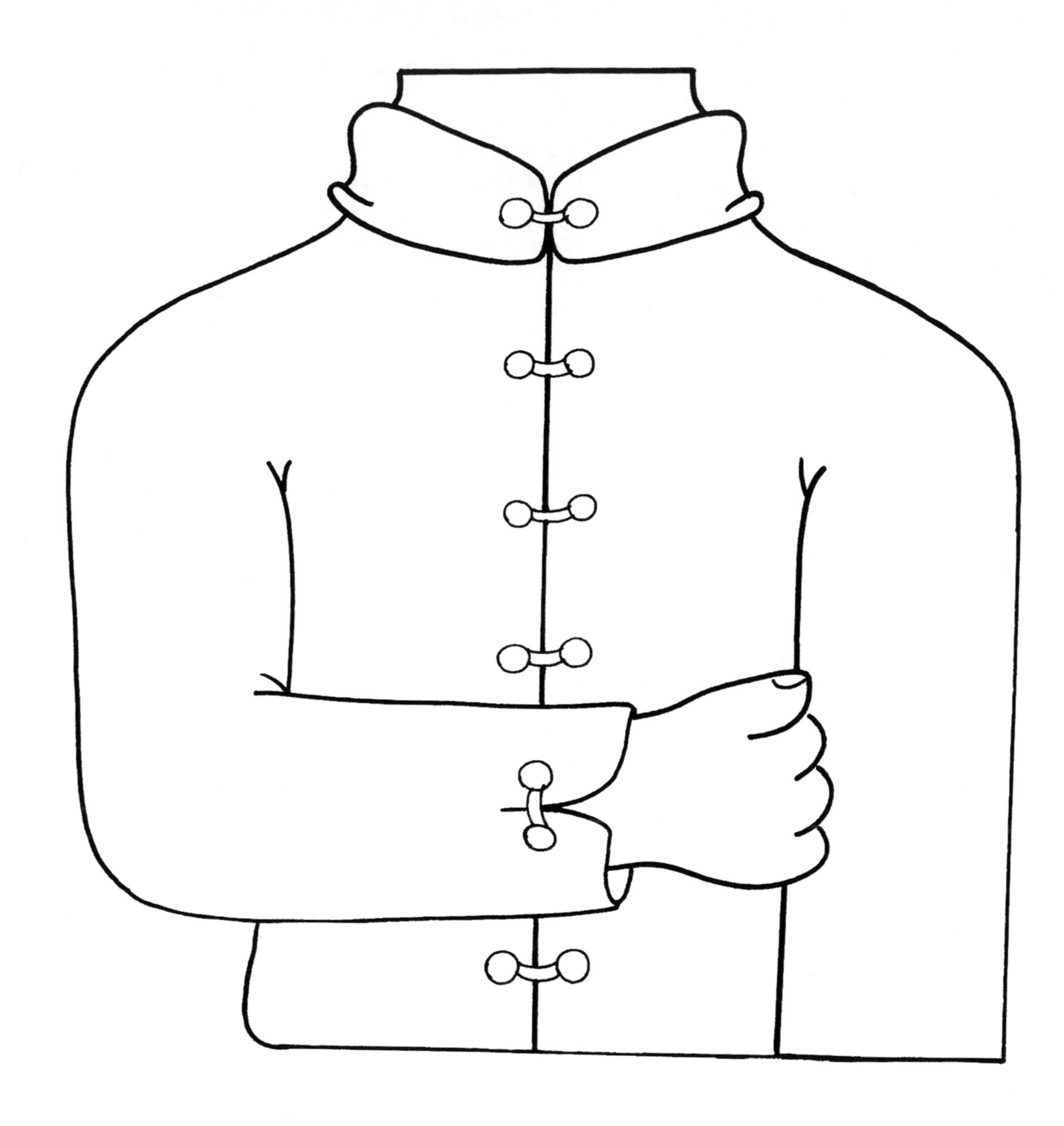

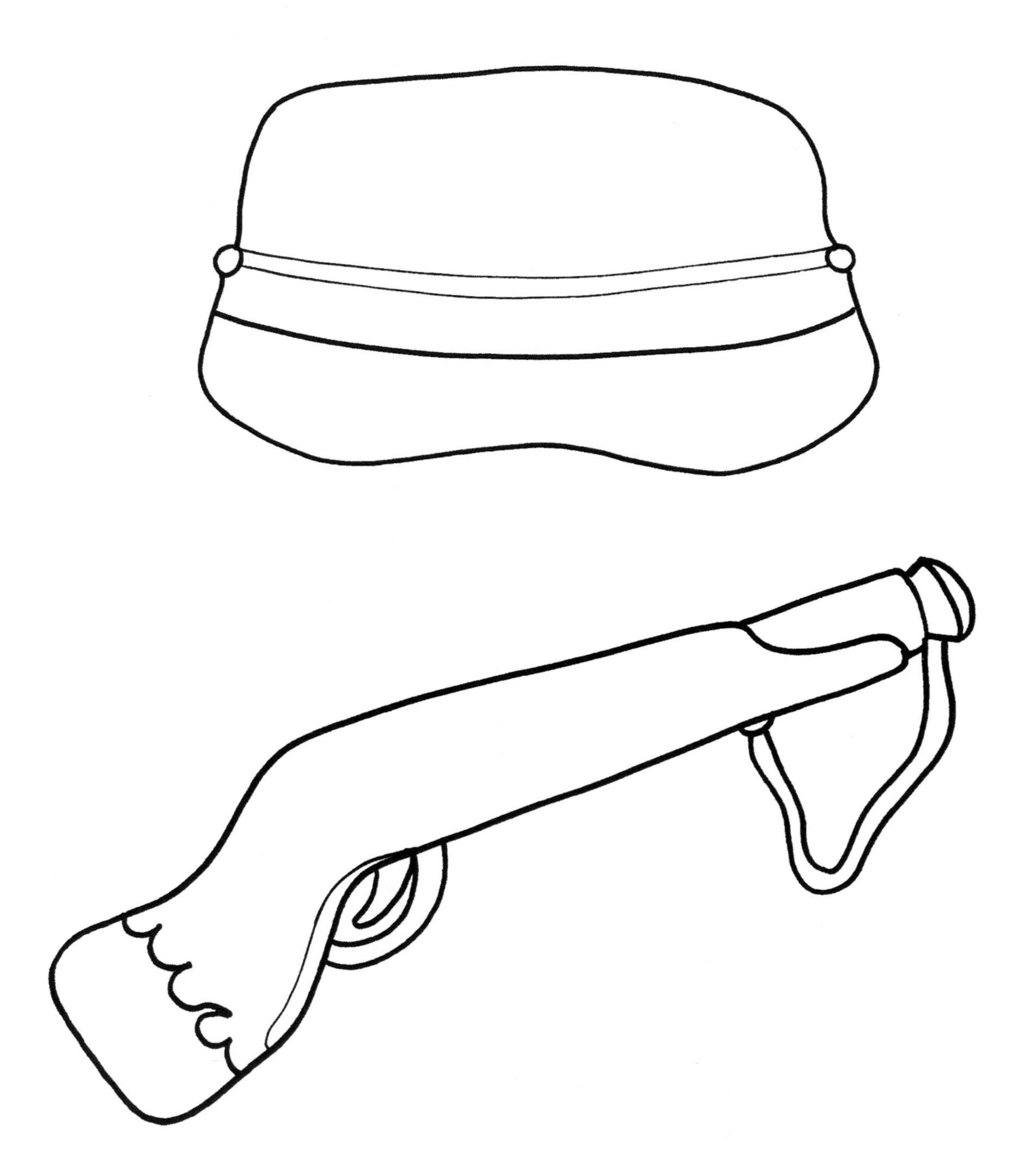

Peter and the Wolf Activities

Songs to Sing and Play

Tune: Three Blind Mice

Words by Eunice Wright

Three brave friends,
The bird, duck and cat.
See how they plan,
To catch the wolf.

They all helped Peter with his trap,
The duck was slow and met mishap,
The bird and cat with Peter sat,
Up high and safe,
In the tree.

Tune: Did You Ever See a Lassie?

Words by Juli Wright

Did you ever see a wolf,
A wolf, asked Peter?
Did you ever see a wolf,
Go this way and that?

Did you ever see a laddie,
A laddie, asked the wolf?
Did you ever see a laddie
Go this way and that?

Tune: This Is the Way We Wash Our Clothes

Words by Juli Wright

This is the way we catch a wolf,
catch a wolf, catch a wolf.
This is the way we catch a wolf,
So early in the morning.

This is the way we set the trap...
This is the way we hunt the wolf...
This is the way the wolf creeps 'round...

Books

Peter and the Wolf, by Ian Beck (Athenium, 1995). *Cute illustrations, typical story, easy to read. Musical instruments are shown throughout the book. There is a special section on the instruments used by the orchestra. Play the recording and talk about what is happening as each instrument plays. Use the music and the book for a puppet show.*

Movies and Television

Peter and the Wolf, Animated. (Disney, 1996).

Peter and the Wolf. Animated, Suzie Templeton (Break Thru Films, 2006). The film itself may be a bit dark for smaller children, but may enthrall older kids.

Peter and the Wolf. An animated version of the fairy tale of the Russian boy Peter and his hunt for a raiding wolf. 15 min. (Disney, 1946).

Peter and the Wolf. Kirstie Alley, Lloyd Bridges. "The Musical World of Peter and the Wolf": An educational introduction to the symphony for kids. (Animated, Sony Pictures, 2003).

6b. Wolf

See Wolf (#5c) for puppet pattern and Wolf activities.

6c. Duck

See Ducky Lucky (#1c) for puppet pattern and Duck activities.

6d. Bird

Bird Activities

Songs to Sing and Play

Tune: The Wheels on the Bus

Words by Eunice Wright

The birds in the tree say, "Chirp, chirp, chirp,
Chirp, chirp, chirp. Chirp, chirp, chirp."
The birds in the tree say, "Chirp, chirp, chirp,
All summer long.

The eggs in the nest go, "Crack, crack, crack..."
The babies in the nest say, "Peep, peep, peep...

Red Bird, Red Bird, What Do You See?

Words by Eunice Wright; adapted from Brown Bear, Brown Bear *(by Bill Martin)*

(*Red* Bird, *red* bird), "what do you see?
I see a (*blue* bird) looking at me."

Or vary the activity by using the names, homes or qualities of birds (songbird, owl, quail, chicks, ducks; diving, singing, hopping, swooping, marshland, mountain top, forest, claws, desert, water, webbed-feet, talons, fancy tail feathers, bill, beak, talking, tame, etc.).

Tune: 10 Little Indians

Words by Eunice Wright

1 little 2 little 3 little birds
4 little 5 little 6 little birds
7 little 8 little 9 little birds
10 little birds in a tree.

Tune: Mary Had a Little Lamb

Words by Eunice and Juli Wright

Birds have wings and love to fly.... They fly from tree to tree.
Birds have feathers on their wings.... They are colorful.
Birds have beaks to help them sing.... And eat some seeds.
Birds build nests and lay their eggs.... And hatch them in the spring.
Birds sing songs and sleep at night.... And wake us in the morning.

Kookaburra

By Marion Sinclair (1932)

"Kookaburra sits in the old gum tree, eating all the gum drops he can see...."

Tune: The Farmer in the Dell

Words by Eunice Wright

What kind of *egg* (bird, nest, home, birdsong, feather) are you?
What kind of *egg* are you?
Heigh ho, the dairy-oh,
What kind of *egg* are you?

Five Little Chickadees

Songs and Games for Little Ones, *by Harriet S. Jenks, 1887.*

1. Five little chickadees, peeping at the door,
One flew away, and then there were four.

Chorus:
Chickadee, chickadee, happy and gay,
Chickadee, chickadee, fly away!

2. Four little chickadees, sitting on a tree,
One flew away, and then there were three.

Chorus

3. Three little chickadees, Looking at you;
One flew away, and then there were two.

Chorus

4. Two little chickadees, Sitting in the sun;
One flew away, and then there was one.

Chorus

5. One little chickadee, Left all alone;
He flew away, and then there were none.

Chorus

Up, Up, in the Sky

Songs and Games for Little Ones, *by Harriet S. Jenks and Gertrude Walker, 1887. With sheet music.*

Up, up in the sky the little birds fly, down, down in the nest the little birds rest.
With a wing on the left, and a wing on the right, we'll let the dear birdies sleep all thro' the night.

Other Songs

"Birds in the Tree," by Glenna T. Holbrook, 1977, page 241. Deseret Book Co.
"In the Leafy Treetops," Anon. Arr. copyright 1989, page 240. Deseret Book Co.
"Be Happy!" by Alice Jean Cleator, copyright 1914, page 265. Deseret Book Co.
"Feed the Birds," by Richard M. and Robert B. Sherman (Walt Disney Music Co., 1964).
"Hey, Mrs. Bird," by Zach Burba. Music Movement and Magination's *Cool Creatures.*
"The Eagle and the Hawk," sung by John Denver (You Tube).
"Hummingbird," by Seals and Crofts (Summer Breeze, 1972).

Poems and Nursery Rhymes

Sing a Song of Sixpence

The Real Mother Goose, *by Jessie Willcox Smith, 1918.*

Sing a song of sixpence a pocket full of rye,
Four and twenty blackbirds baked in a pie.
When the pie was opened the birds began to sing,
Wasn't that a dainty dish to set before the king?

The king was in his counting house counting out his money,
The queen was in the parlor eating bread and honey
The maid was in the garden hanging out the clothes,
When down came a blackbird and pecked off her nose!

Little Robin Red Breast

Harry's Ladder to Learning, with Two Hundred and Thirty Illustrations, *by David Bogue and Joseph Cundall, 1850.*

Little Robin Red-breast sat upon a tree,
Up went Pussy-cat, and down went he;
Down came Pussy-cat, and away Robin ran:
Says little Robin Red-breast, "Catch me if you can."

Little Robin Red-breast hopp'd upon a wall,
Pussy-cat jump'd after him, and almost got a fall.
Little Robin chirp'd and sang, and what did Pussy say?
Pussy-cat said, "Mew," and Robin flew away.

The Robin

The Children's Book of Poetry, *by Henry T. Coats, 1879.*

There came to my window
One morning in spring
A sweet little robin,
She came here to sing.
The tune that she sang
It was prettier far,
Than any I've heard
On the flute or guitar.

Her wings she was spreading
To soar far away,
Then resting a moment
Seemed sweetly to say,
"Oh happy, how happy
The world seems to be,
Awake, dearest, child,
And be happy with me."

If I Were a Bird

By Eunice Wright

If I were a bird,
I'd fly so high
And dance about
Up in the sky.

I'd dive and float—
See all I could see.

Then rest my wings
In the branch of a tree.

Five Little Songbirds (Count Down)

By Eunice Wright

5 little songbirds, singing by the door,
1 flew away, then there were four.
4 little songbirds, Up in a tree,
1 flew away, then there were three.
3 little songbirds, under the sky so blue,
1 flew away, then there were two.
2 little songbirds, sitting in the sun.
1 flew away, then there was one.
One little songbird, having lots of fun,
He flew away, then there were none.

Five Little Blue Birds (Count Down)

By Eunice Wright

Five little blue birds, singing by my door.
One found a juicy worm, then there were four.
Four little blue birds, playing in a tree.
One found a girlfriend, then there were three.
Three little blue birds, wondering what to do.
One found a bird house, then there were two.
Two little blue birds, having so much fun.
One went to hunt for food, then there was one.
One little blue bird, alone in the sun.
Decided to take a nap, then there were none.

The Little Bird

The Real Mother Goose, *by Blanche Fisher Wright, 1916.*

Once I saw a little bird
Come hop, hop, hop;
So I cried: "Little bird,
Will you stop, stop, stop?"

And was going to the window
To say: "How do you do?"
But he shook his little tail
And far away he flew.

Two Little Black Birds

The Home Book of Verse, *Vol. 1 (of 4). Author: Various. By Burton Egbert Stevenson, 1912*

There were two blackbirds sitting on a hill,
The one named Jack, the other named Jill;
Fly away, Jack! Fly away, Jill!
Come again, Jack! Come again, Jill!

Five Little Birds

By Eunice Wright; adapted from Five Little Monkeys Teasing Mr. Crocodile

Five little birds, sitting on a fence,
Teasing Mr. Cat, "Can't catch me!"
Along came Mr. Cat, quiet as can be...
Then ... snap!
Four little birds, sitting on a fence...
(repeat, subtracting a bird each time)

Who Killed Cock Robin?

The Real Mother Goose, *by Blanche Fisher Wright, 1916.*

Who killed Cock Robin?
I, said the Sparrow,
with my bow and arrow,
I killed Cock Robin.

Who saw him die?
I, said the Fly,
with my little eye,
I saw him die.

Who caught his blood?
I, said the Fish,
with my little dish,
I caught his blood.

Who'll make the shroud?
I, said the Beetle,
with my thread and needle,
I'll make the shroud.

Who'll dig his grave?
I, said the Owl,
with my pick and shovel,
I'll dig his grave.

Who'll be the parson?
I, said the Rook,

with my little book,
I'll be the parson.

Who'll be the clerk?
I, said the Lark,
if it's not in the dark,
I'll be the clerk.

Who'll carry the link?
I, said the Linnet,
I'll fetch it in a minute,
I'll carry the link.

Who'll be chief mourner?
I, said the Dove,
I mourn for my love,
I'll be chief mourner.

Who'll carry the coffin?
I, said the Kite,
if it's not through the night,
I'll carry the coffin.

Who'll bear the pall?
We, said the Wren,
both the cock and the hen,
We'll bear the pall.

Who'll sing a psalm?
I, said the Thrush,
as she sat on a bush,
I'll sing a psalm.

Who'll toll the bell?
I said the bull,
because I can pull,
I'll toll the bell.

All the birds of the air
fell a-sighing and a-sobbing,
when they heard the bell toll
for poor Cock Robin.

A Beetle on a Broomstraw

The Peter Patter Book of Nursery Rhymes, *by Leroy F. Jackson. Printed in 1918.*

A robin and a wren, as they walked along one night,
Saw a big brown beetle on a broomstraw.
Said the robin to the wren: "What a pretty, pretty sight—
That big brown beetle on a broomstraw!"
So they got their plates and knives,
Their children and their wives,
And gobbled up the beetle on the broomstraw.

The Robin

The Real Mother Goose, *by Blanche Fisher Wright 1916.*

The north wind doth blow,
And we shall have snow,
And what will poor robin do then,
Poor thing?

He'll sit in a barn,
And keep himself warm,
And hide his head under his wing,
Poor thing!

Birds of a Feather

The Real Mother Goose, *by Blanche Fisher Wright 1916.*

Birds of a feather flock together,
And so will pigs and swine;
Rats and mice will have their choice,
And so will I have mine.

Eight Colored Birds (Count Down)

By Eunice Wright

Make 8 different colored bird puppets for this activity.

Eight little birdies, flying up to heaven,
The orange one flew away, and then there were seven.

Seven little birdies, flying through the sticks,
The black one flew away, and then there were six.

Six little birdies, flying around the hive,
The purple one flew away, and then there were five.

Five little birdies, flying around the door,
The blue one flew away, and then there were four.

Four little birdies sitting in a tree,
The yellow one flew away, and then there were three.

Three little birdies didn't know what to do,
So the red one flew away, and then there were two.

Two little birdies sitting in the sun,
The Brown one flew away, and there was one.

One little birdie, napping in the sun,
The green one flew away, and then there was none.

Later on that very day,
Eight little birdies came back to play.

Jenny Wren

The Real Mother Goose, *by Blanche Fisher Wright, 1916.*

As little Jenny Wren
Was sitting by her shed.
She waggled with her tail,
And nodded with her head.
She waggled with her tail,
And nodded with her head,
As little Jenny Wren
Was sitting by the shed.

Little Jenny Wren

The Real Mother Goose, *by Blanche Fisher Wright, 1916.*

Little Jenny Wren fell sick,
Upon a time;
In came Robin Redbreast
And brought her cake and wine.
"Eat well of my cake, Jenny,
Drink well of my wine."
"Thank you, Robin, kindly,
You shall be mine."
Jenny she got well,
And stood upon her feet,
And told Robin plainly
She loved him not a bit.
Robin being angry,
Hopped upon a twig,
Saying, "Out upon you! Fie upon you!
Bold-faced jig!"

Pretty Jenny Wren

The Baby's Opera, *by Walter Crane, 1877.*

1. 'Twas on a merry time,
When Jenny Wren was young,
So neatly as she danced,
And so sweetly as she sung,
Robin Redbreast lost his heart,
He was a gallant bird,
He doffed his cap to Jenny Wren,
Requesting to be heard.

2. "My dearest Jenny Wren,
If you will but be mine,
You shall dine on cherry pie,
And drink nice currant wine;
I'll dress you like a gold-finch,
Or like a peacock gay,
So if you'll have me, Jenny, dear,
Let us appoint the day."

3. Jenny blushed behind her fan
And thus declared her mind—
"So let it be to-morrow, Rob,
I'll take your offer kind;
Cherry pie is very good,
And so is currant wine,
But I will wear my plain brown gown,
And never dress too fine."

4. Robin Redbreast got up early,
All at the break of day,
He flew to Jenny Wren's house,
And sang a roundelay;
He sang of Robin Redbreast,
And pretty Jenny Wren,
And when he came unto the end,
He then began again.

Mary's Canary

The Little Mother Goose, *by Jesse Wilcox Smith, 1918.*

Mary had a pretty bird—
Feathers bright and yellow,

Slender legs, upon my word,
He was a pretty fellow—
The sweetest notes he always sung,
Which much delighted Mary;
And near the cage she'd ever sit,
To hear her own canary.

The Dove and the Wren

The Real Mother Goose, *by Blanche Fisher Wright, 1916.*

The dove says coo, coo, what shall I do?
I can scarce maintain two.
Pooh, pooh! says the wren, I've got ten,
And keep them all like gentlemen.

The Bird Scarer

The Real Mother Goose, *by Blanche Fisher Wright, 1916.*

Away, birds, away!
Take a little and leave a little,
And do not come again;
For if you do,
I will shoot you through,
And there will be an end of you.

The Singing Lesson

Jean Ingelow (1820–1897)

A nightingale made a mistake;
She sang a few notes out of tune;
Her heart was ready to break,
And she hid away from the moon.
She wrung her claws, poor thing!
But was far too proud to weep;
She tucked her head under her wing,
And pretended to be asleep.

A lark, arm in arm with a thrush,
Came sauntering up to the place;
The nightingale felt herself blush,
Though feathers hid her face.
She knew they had heard her song,
She felt them snicker and sneer;
She thought that life was too long,
And wished she could skip a year.

"Oh, Nightingale," cooed a dove—
"Oh, Nightingale, what's the use?
You bird of beauty and love,
Why behave like a goose?
Don't skulk away from our sight,
Like a common, contemptible fowl;
You bird of joy and delight,
Why behave like an owl?

"Only think of all you have done,
Only think of all you can do;
A false note is really fun
From such a bird as you!
Lift up your proud little crest,
Open your musical beak;
Other birds have to do their best—
You need only to speak."

The nightingale shyly took
Her head from under her wing,
And, giving the dove a look,
Straightway began to sing.
There was never a bird could pass;
The night was divinely calm,
And the people stood on the grass
To hear that wonderful psalm.

The nightingale did not care;
She only sang to the skies;
Her song ascended there,
And there she fixed her eyes.
The people that stood below
She knew but little about;
And this tale has a moral, I know,
If you'll try to find it out.

Heigh-Ho, the Carrion Crow

The Real Mother Goose, *from Blanche Fisher Wright, 1916.*

A carrion crow sat on an oak,
Watching a tailor shape his coat;

Wife, bring me my old bent bow,
That I may shoot yon carrion crow;

The tailor shot, and he missed his mark,
And shot the miller's sow right through the heart;

Wife! Oh wife! bring brandy in a spoon,
For our old sow is in a swoon.

What Does Little Birdie Say?

The Home Book of Verse, *Vol. 1 (of 4). Author: Various Editors. Burton Egbert Stevenson 1912, from "Sea Dreams" by Alfred Tennyson (1809–1892).*

What does little birdie say
In her nest at peep of day?
Let me fly, says little birdie,
Mother, let me fly away.
Birdie, rest a little longer,
Till the little wings are stronger.
So she rests a little longer,
Then she flies away.

What does little baby say,
In her bed at peep of day?
Baby says, like little birdie,
Let me rise and fly away.
Baby, sleep a little longer,
Till the little limbs are stronger,
If she sleeps a little longer,
Baby too shall fly away.

The Building of the Nest

The Home Book of Verse, *Vol. 1 (of 4). Author: Various. Editor: Burton Egbert Stevenson 1912, from "Sea Dreams" by Margaret Sangster (1838–1912).*

They'll come again to the apple tree—
Robin and all the rest—
When the orchard branches are fair to see,
In the snow of the blossoms dressed;
And the prettiest thing in the world will be
The building of the nest.

Weaving it well, so round and trim,
Hollowing it with care,—
Nothing too far away for him,
Nothing for her too fair,—
Hanging it safe on the topmost limb,
Their castle in the air.

Ah! mother bird, you'll have weary days
When the eggs are under your breast,
And shadow may darken the dancing rays
When the wee ones leave the nest;
But they'll find their wings in a glad amaze.
And God will see to the rest.

So come to the trees with all your train
When the apple blossoms blow;
Through the April shimmer of sun and rain,
Go flying to and fro;
And sing to our hearts as we watch again
Your fairy building grow.

The Sparrows

Finger Plays for Nursery and Kindergarten, *by Emilie Poulsson, 1893. Sheet music and finger-play actions.*

1. "Little brown sparrows,
Flying around,
Up in the tree-tops,
Down on the ground,
Come to my window,
Dear sparrows, come!
See! I will give you
Many a crumb."

2. "Here is some water,
Sparkling and clear;
Come, little sparrows,
Drink without fear.
If you are tired,
Here is a nest;
Wouldn't you like to
Come here and rest?"

3. All the brown sparrows
Flutter away,
Chirping and singing,
We cannot stay;
For in the tree-tops,
Mong the gray boughs,
There is the sparrows'
Snug little house."

Fly, Little Birds

Holiday Songs and Every Day Songs and Games, *by Emilie Poulsson, 1901. With sheet music and some finger plays.*

Fly, little birds, fly east and west,
Seeking a place to build your nest.

Tall trees are standing side by side;
Will you among their branches hide?

Fly, little birds, fly high and low,
Fly to the pretty place we show,
Here in the niche of the garden wall;
Doesn't this suit you best of all?

Fly, little birds, fly 'round and 'round,
Fly to the bushes and trees and ground,
Gathering tiny bits and shreds,
Grasses and lint and straws and thread.

Fly, little birds, fly through the air,
Chirping and singing everywhere;
Then, in the place that you like best,
Busily weave your cosy nest.

The Bird's Nest

Holiday Songs and Every Day Songs and Games, *by Emilie Poulsson, 1901. With sheet music and some finger plays.*

In the branches of a tree,
Birds are singing cheerily,
For their pretty nest is made,
Pearly eggs within it laid.

Mother bird with brooding wing,
Warms the eggs, the precious things,
Till the baby birds awake,
Through the pearly egg shells break.

Then they call, "Peep, mother dear!"
"Peep!" she answers, "Mother's here!"
While the father bird above
Sings his song of happy love.

A Little Woodpecker Am I

Songs and Games for Little Ones, *by Harriet S. Jenks and Gertrude Walker, 1887. With sheet music. Adapted by Walker and Jenks.*

A little woodpecker am I,
And you may always know
When from the tree I'm seeking food,
For tap, tap, tap, I go.

Hopping Birds

Songs and Games for Little Ones, *by Harriet S. Jenks and Gertrude Walker, 1887. With sheet music.*

These little birdies in their nest go hop,
hop, hop, hop, hop!
They try to do their very best to hop, hop,
hop, hop, hop!

Hop, hop, come birdies all
Hop, hop, hop, hop, come birdies all,
Over the way to make us a call;
Hop, hop, hop, hop, back to your nests,
Tuck your heads under your wings, and
rest.

Bird Song

A Book for Kids, *by Clarence Michael James Dennis, 1921.*

I am friendly with the sparrow
Though his mind is rather narrow
And his manners—well, the less we say
the better.
But as day begins to peep,
When I hear his cheery "Cheep"
I am ready to admit I am his debtor

I delight in red-browed finches
And all birds of scanty inches.
Willie wagtail is a pleasant bird, and
coy.
All the babblers, chats and wrens,
Tits and robins, and their hens,
Are my very special friends, and bring
me joy.

Nonsense Books

By Edward Lear, 1894.

There was a Young Lady whose bonnet
Came untied when the birds sat upon it;
But she said, "I don't care! all the birds
in the air
Are welcome to sit on my bonnet!"

The Illustrated Alphabet of Birds

Published by Wm. Crosby and H.P. Nichols, 1851.

THE BLUE BIRD.
B is a Blue Bird.
In early spring,
How sweet his songs
Through the forest ring.

THE DUCK.
D is a Duck.
Of the canvas back sort,
To shoot at a flock
Is considered fine sport.

THE GOOSE.
G is a Goose;
His feathers we take
And put them in sacking
Our beds to make.

THE HUMMING BIRD.
H is a Humming Bird,
Sporting mid flowers
And brightly enjoying
The sunny hours.

THE JAY.
J is a Jay,
With his blue and white coat,
With a crest on his head,
And a ring round his throat.

THE KING BIRD.
K is a King Bird,
Pugnacious and bold:
A hero in fight,
And a terrible scold.

THE LARK.
L is a Lark,
A sociable bird;
His song in the meadow
Is frequently heard.

THE OWL.
O is an Owl,
Who hides through the day;
And comes out at night,
To seek for his prey.

THE QUAIL.
Q is a Quail,
Who hides in a tree,
And whistles "Bob-White"
With lively glee.

THE ROBIN.
R is the Robin,
So kind and so good,
Who covered with leaves,
The poor babes in the wood.

THE TURKEY.
T is a Turkey,
A fine dashing beau,
By his fuming and strutting,
His pride you may know.

THE VULTURE.
V is a Vulture,
Who feeds on the dead,
When the dark battle-field,
With corpses is spread.

THE YELLOW BIRD.
Y is a Yellow Bird,
With feathers so bright,
Who sings all the day,
And sleeps all the night.

A Rule for Birds' Nesters

The Home Book of Verse, *Vol. 1 (of 4). Author: Various. Editor: Burton Egbert Stevenson, 1912.*

The robin and the red-breast,
The sparrow and the wren;
If ye take out o' their nest,
Ye'll never thrive again!

The robin and the red-breast,
The martin and the swallow;
If ye touch one o' their eggs,
Bad luck will surely follow!

Child Songs of Cheer by Evaleen Stein, 1918

Includes:

A Robin's Bath
The Bluebird

The Rash Little Sparrow
The First Red Bird
The Wren House
The Bird's Bath
Wherefore Wings
The Little Nest
The Red Bird
Lost!

Games and Group Activities

Colors

As you sing "Red Bird, Red Bird, What Do You See?" together, use different colored bird puppets, and add a new bird color, letting the children choose the correct color bird puppet during the song.

Matching Games

1. Let children decorate their eggs (paper or real eggs) after looking in the bird books for examples, and match them to the mother bird (examples: robin—blue egg, cardinal—lavender speckled egg, mourning dove—white egg, goldfinch—pale blue egg, sparrow—brown egg). Allaboutbirds.org.

2. Bring a clock to class with the bird song chimes for the hour. Look at the bird making the song and try to imitate it. Then look for that bird outside.

Musical Nests

Put three or four hula hoops or rope circles around the room for the nests. Play music ("Old MacDonald") while the students walk around the nests. Stop the music, and the children run to get into their nests. Place a large number sign on the floor in the middle of each nest that will be the limit of the number of children in each nest. Or the teacher can hold up a sign with a number on it, so the children will learn number recognition. That will be the number of children who can get into each nest.

Bird Catcher

Games for the Playground, Home, School and Gymnasium, *by Jessie H. Bancroft, 1922, p. 52.*

10 to 60 players.
Large room; playground.

Two opposite corners are marked off at one end of the playground or room, one to serve as a nest for the birds and the other as a cage. A mother bird is chosen, who takes her place in the nest. Two other players take the part of bird catchers and stand midway between nest and cage. If played in the schoolroom, the remaining players sit in their seats; if on a playground, they stand beyond a line at the farther end of the ground that is called the forest. All of these players should be named for birds, several players taking the name of each bird. The naming of the players will be facilitated by doing it in groups. If in the classroom, each row may choose its name, after which the players should all change places, so that all of the robins or orioles will not fly from the same locality.

The teacher calls the name of a bird, whereupon all of the players who bear that name run from the forest to the nest, but the bird catchers try to intercept them. Should a bird be caught by the bird catcher, it is put in the cage, but a bird is safe from the bird catchers if it once reaches the nest and the mother bird. The players should be taught to make the chase interesting by dodging in various directions, instead of running in a simple, straight line to the nest.

The distance of the bird catchers from the nest may be determined with a little experience. It may be necessary to place a handicap upon them to avoid the too easy capture of the birds.

Books

Albert, by Donna Jo Napoli (HMH, 2005). *A beautifully illustrated picture book about red cardinals that make a nest in an outstretched hand. Great for a bird unit.*

Are You My Mother? by P.D. Eastman (Random House, 1998).
The Baby Beebee Bird, by Diane Redfield Massie (HarperCollins, 2003).
The Beak Book, by Pamela Chanko (Scholastic, 1998).
The Bears' Nature Guide, by Stan and Jan Berenstain (Random House, 1975, pp. 30–33).
Beautiful Blackbird, by Ashley Bryan (Atheneum, 2003).
The Best Nest, by P.D. Eastman (Random House, 1968). *Tired of their nest, Mr. and Mrs. Bird search for a new one.*
Birds, by Jane Werner Watson (Simon & Schuster, 1958). A Little Golden Book.
Brian Wildsmith's Birds, by Brian Wildsmith (Franklin Watts, 1967). Also *The Apple Bird* (Oxford, 1987).
Don't Let the Pigeon Stay Up Late, by Mo Willems (Hyperion, 2006). *Even birds want to stay up late at night.*
Dougal Looks for Birds, by Martha Stiles (Four Winds, 1972).
The Early Bird, by Richard Scarry (Random House, 2013).
Egg in the Hole Book, by Richard Scarry (Golden Book, 2011).
Egg to Chick, by Millicent Selsam (HarperCollins, 1987).
Elsie's Bird, by Jane Yolen (Philomen, 2010).
Feathers for Lunch, by Lois Ehlert (HMH, 1996).
Feathers Like a Rainbow, an Amazon Indian Tale, by Flora (HarperCollins, 1989).
The Firebird, retold by Selina Hastings (or the version by Demi) (Cambridge, 1993; Holt, 1994).
Flap Your Wings, by P.D. Eastman (Random House, 2000).
Fly, Homer, Fly, by Bill Peet (Turtleback, 1979).
Hi, Mr. Robin, by Alvin Tresselt (William Morrow, 1968).
Hosie's Aviary, by Tobias and Leonard Baskin (Viking Press, 1979).
How to Go About Laying an Egg, by Bernard Waber (StarWalk Kids Media, 2014).
Inch by Inch, by Leo Lionni (HarperCollins, 1995). *A clever inchworm escapes from a hungry bird. Demonstrates measurement.*
Look for a Bird, by Edith Thacher Hurd Harper & Row, 1977).
My Spring Robin, by Anne Rockwell (Aladdin, 2015).
A Nest Full of Eggs, by Priscilla Jenkins (HarperCollins, 1995).
Nuts to Nightingale, Sweet Pickles Series, by Jacquelyn Reinach (Holt, 1978).
Outside and Inside Birds, by Sandra Markle (Atheneum, 1994).
The Pinkish, Purplish, Bluish Egg, by Bill Peet (Sandpiper Series Books, HMH, 1984).
Recipes for the Birds, by Irene and Ed Cosgrove (Doubleday, 1974).
The Red Horse and the Bluebird, by Sandy Rabinowitz (HarperCollins, 1975).
The Restless Robin, by Marjorie Flack (Houghton Mifflin, 1937).
Round Robin, by Jack Kent (Prentice Hall, 1982).
The Royal Raven, by Hans Wilhelm (Scholastic, 1996).
Sammy, the Crow Who Remembered, by Elizabeth Hazelton (Scribner, 1969).
Scarebird, by Sid Fleischman (Greenwillow Books, 1988).
Stork Spills the Beans, Sweet Pickles Series, by Richard Hefter (Holt, 1977).
A Year of Birds, by Ashley Wolff (Dodd, Mead, 1984).

Movies and Television

Aladdin (lago, parrot) (Buena Vista, 1992).
Bambi (owl, birds) (Disney, 1942).
Cinderella (birds) (Disney, 1950).
Condorman (Disney, 1981).
Ever After (20th Century–Fox, 1998).
Finding Nemo (pelicans, seagulls) (Pixar, 2003).

Fly Away Home (geese) (Columbia Pictures, 1996).
For the Birds (animated) (Pixar short film, 2001).
Happy Feet (penguins) 1 and 2 (Warner Bros, 2006, 2011).
Harry Potter and the Order of the Phoenix (Fawkes), owl (Hedwig) (Warner Bros., 2007).
Home Alone 2: Lost in New York (bird lady) (Fox, 1992).
Jack and the Beanstalk (animated).
Jonathan Livingston Seagull (Hall Bartzet, 1973).
Kes (a pet falcon) (Woodfall Film, 1969).
Lady Hawk (20th Century—Fox, 1985).
The Lion King (Zazu) (Disney, 1994).
Little House on the Prairie (Jenny and the carrier pigeons, a crow that talks).
The Little Mermaid (Scuttle, seagull) (Disney, 1989).
Looney Tunes (Dodo birds, Tweety bird as a carrier pigeon, roadrunner)
Mary Poppins ("Feed the Birds") (Disney, 1964).
Nanny McPhee 2 (black bird that talks, Mr. Edelweiss) (Universal, 2010).
Paulie (Paramount, 1998).
Pigeon (Orange Ball, YouTube).
The Pigeoneers (commentary on pigeons in World War II) (Alessandro Croseri Productions, 2012).
Prince of Persia (ostrich) (Disney, 2010).
The Rescuers Down Under 1 and 2 (Disney, 1990)
Rio 1 and 2 (20th Century—Fox, 2011, 2014).
Sleeping Beauty (Disney, 1959).
Snow White (Disney, 1937).
The Sword in the Stone, animated. (Young Arthur turns into a fish, then into a bird. The Owl gives advice.) (Disney, 1963).
Up (Kevin) (Disney, 2009).
Valiant, (animated) (pigeons in World War II) (Disney, 2005).

6e. Cat

Cat/Kitten Activities

Songs to Sing and Play

Three Little Kittens

New Nursery Songs for All Good Children, *1843, "A Cat's Tale, with Additions," by Eliza Lee Follen.*

Three little kittens,
They lost their mittens,
And they began to cry,
"Oh, mother dear,
We sadly fear,
Our mittens we have lost."

"What! Lost your mittens
You naughty kittens!
Then you shall have no pie.
"Meow, Meow, Meow
No, you shall have no pie.

The three little kittens,
They found their mittens,
And they began to cry,
"Oh, mother dear,
See hear, see hear,
Our mittens we have found"

"Put on your mittens,
You silly kittens,
And you shall have some pie."
"Purr, purr, purr,
Oh, let us have some pie."

The three little kittens
Put on their mittens
And soon ate up the pie;
"Oh, Mother dear,
We greatly fear
Our mittens we have soiled."

"What! Soiled your mittens,
You naughty kittens!"
Then they began to sigh,
"Meow, meow, meow,"
Then they began to sigh.

The three little kittens
They washed their mittens,
And hung them out to dry;
"Oh, mother dear,
Do you not hear?
Our mittens we have washed."

"What! Washed your mittens,
Then you're good kittens,
But I smell a rat close by."
"Meow, meow, meow,
We smell a rat close by."

I Had a Rooster

Performed by Pete Seeger. Continue to add animals and their sounds.

"I had a kitty, my kitty pleased me...
I fed my kitty 'neath the greenberry tree..."

Pussy-cat

The Baby's Opera, *by Walter Crane, 1877. Has Sheet music.*

Pussy-cat high, Pussy-cat low,
Pussy-cat was a fine teaser of tow.

2. Pussy-cat she came into the barn,
With her bag-pipes under her arm.

3. And then she told a tale to me,
How Mousey had married a humble bee.

4. Then was I ever so glad,
That Mousey had married so clever a lad.

Once There Was a Little Kitty

Songs and Games for Little Ones, *by Harriet S. Jenks and Gertrude Walker, 1887. (Sheet music)*

Once there was a little kitty white as the snow;
In the barn she used to frolic, long time ago.
In the barn a little mousie ran to and fro;
and she heard the kitty coming, long time ago.
Two black eyes had little kitty, black as a crow
and they spied the little mousie, long time ago.
Four soft paws had little kitty, soft as the snow,
and they caught the little mousie, long time ago.

Nine pearl teeth had little kitty, all in a row,
and they bit the little mousie, long time ago.
When the teeth bit little mousie, Mouse cried out "Oh!"
and she got away from kitty, long time ago.

Kitty White

Songs and Games for Little Ones, *by Harriet S. Jenks and Gertrude Walker, 1887. (With sheet music)*

Kitty white so slyly comes,
To catch the mousie gray,
But mousie hears her softly creep,
and quickly runs away!

Kitty Cat and the Mouse

Songs and Games for Little Ones, *by Harriet S. Jenks and Gertrude Walker, 1887. (With sheet music)*

Kitty cat, I hear a mouse! Pitty, pat, run through the house!
Kitty, hurry, kitty run, Quick, or you will lose the fun!
Kitty hears, and slyly creeps, Now she listens, now she leaps!
Ah, too late, you can not win it, There's the hole, the mouse is in it!
Eep! Eep! Eep! The baby mice their mother greet.
Well for them, my kitty cat, that she heard your pitty pat!

Our Kittens

Child Songs of Cheer, *by Evaleen Stein, 1918.*

Our kittens have the softest fur,
And the sweetest little purr,
And such little velvet paws
With such cunning little claws,
And blue eyes, just like the sky!
(Must they turn green, by and by?)
Two are striped like tigers, three
Are as black as black can be,
And they run so fast and play
With their tails, and are so gay,
Is it not a pity that
Each must grow into a cat?

Other Songs

"Alley Cat," performed by Bent Fabric, 1962.
"The Cat Came Back," by Harry S. Miller, 1893.
"Cat's in the Cradle," by Harry Chapin, 1974.
"The Italian Pussycat," sung by Lou Monte, 1963.
"Kitten in the Sun," *I Have a Song for You About Animals*, by Janeen Brady (Brite Music Enterprises, 1980), page 8.
"The Siamese Cat Song," by Peggy Lee and Sonny Burke (Walt Disney Music, 1987).
"What's New Pussycat?" sung by Tom Jones, 1965. Written by Burt Bacharach and Hal David.

Poems and Nursery Rhymes

Bought Me a Cat

Folk Rhymes, *by Thomas W. Talley (1922) (Title: Bought me a wife)*

Bought me a cat and the cat pleased me,
I fed my cat under yonder tree.
Cat goes fiddle-i-fee.

Bought me a hen and the hen pleased me,
I fed my hen under yonder tree.
Hen goes chimmy-chuck, chimmy-chuck,
Cat goes fiddle-i-fee.

Bought me a duck and the duck pleased me,
I fed my duck under yonder tree.
Duck goes quack, quack,
Hen goes chimmy-chuck, chimmy-chuck,
Cat goes fiddle-i-fee.

Bought me a goose and the goose pleased me
I fed my goose under yonder tree.
Goose goes hissy, hissy,
Duck goes quack, quack,
Hen goes chimmy-chuck, chimmy-chuck,
Cat goes fiddle-i-fee.

Bought me a sheep and the sheep pleased me,
I fed my sheep under yonder tree.
Sheep goes baa, baa,

Goose goes hissy, hissy,
Duck goes quack, quack,
Hen goes chimmy-chuck, chimmy-chuck,
Cat goes fiddle-i-fee.

Bought me a pig and the pig pleased me,
I fed my pig under yonder tree.
Pig goes oink, oink,
Sheep goes baa, baa,
Goose goes hissy, hissy,
Duck goes quack, quack,
Hen goes chimmy-chuck, chimmy-chuck,
Cat goes fiddle-i-fee.

Bought me a cow and the cow pleased me,
I fed my cow under yonder tree.
Cow goes moo, moo,
Pig goes oink, oink,
Sheep goes baa, baa,
Goose goes hissy, hissy,
Duck goes quack, quack,
Hen goes chimmy-chuck, chimmy-chuck,
Cat goes fiddle-i-fee.

Bought me a horse and the horse pleased me,
I fed my horse under yonder tree.
Horse goes neigh, neigh,
Cow goes moo, moo,
Pig goes oink, oink,
Sheep goes baa, baa,
Goose goes hissy, hissy,
Duck goes quack, quack,
Hen goes chimmy-chuck, chimmy-chuck,
Cat goes fiddle-i-fee.

Bought me a dog and the dog pleased me,
I fed my dog under yonder tree.
Dog goes bow-wow, bow-wow,
Horse goes neigh, neigh,
Cow goes moo, moo,
Pig goes oink, oink,
Sheep goes baa, baa,
Goose goes hissy, hissy,
Duck goes quack, quack,
Hen goes chimmy-chuck, chimmy-chuck,
Cat goes fiddle-i-fee.

I Love Little Pussy

The Home Book of Verse, *Vol. 1 (of 4). Author: Various. Editor: Burton Egbert Stevenson 1912, by Jane Taylor (1783–1824).*

I like little Pussy, her coat is so warm;
And if I don't hurt her she'll do me no harm.
So I'll not pull her tail, nor drive her away,
But Pussy and I very gently will play.

She shall sit by my side, and I'll give her some food;
And she'll love me because I am gentle and good.
I'll pat little Pussy and then she will purr,
And thus show her thanks for my kindness to her.

I'll not pinch her ears, nor tread on her paw,
Lest I should provoke her to use her sharp claw;
I never will vex her, nor make her displeased,
For Pussy can't bear to be worried or teased.

A Riddle: As I Was Going to St. Ives

The Home Book of Verse, *Vol. 1 (of 4). Author: Various. Editor: Burton Egbert Stevenson, 1912.*

As I was going to St. Ives,
I met a man with seven wives,
Every wife had seven sacks,
Every sack had seven cats,
Every cat had seven kits—
Kits, cats, sacks, and wives,
How many were going to St. Ives?
(*Answer: only one—"I"*)

The Crooked Man

The Real Mother Goose, *by Blanche Fisher Wright, 1916.*

There was a crooked man,
He walked a crooked mile,
He found a crooked sixpence
Beside a crooked stile.
He bought a crooked cat

Which caught a crooked mouse,
And they all live together
In a little crooked house.

Pussy Cat

Finger Play Reader Part 2, *by John W. Davis, 1909.*

Pussy-cat high, Pussy-cat low, Pussy-cat was a fine teaser of tow.
Pussy-cat she came into the barn, With her bag-pipes under her arm.
And then she told a tale to me, How Mousey had married a humble bee.
Then was I ever so glad, That Mousey had married so clever a lad.

Pussy Cat, Pussy Cat

Harry's Ladder to Learning, with Two Hundred and Thirty Illustrations, *by David Bogue and Joseph Cundall, 1850.*

Pussy-cat, pussy-cat, where have you been?
I've been to London to see the queen.
Pussy-cat, pussy-cat, what did you there?
I frightened a little mouse under the chair.

Dame Trot and Her Cat

The Real Mother Goose, *by Blanche Fisher Wright, 1916.*

Dame Trot and her cat
Led a peaceable life,
When they were not troubled
With other folks' strife.
When Dame had her dinner
Pussy would wait,
And was sure to receive
A nice piece from her plate.

Ding Dong Bell

The Real Mother Goose, *by Blanche Fisher Wright, 1916.*

Ding, dong, bell,
Pussy's in the well!
Who put her in?
Little Tommy Lin.
Who pulled her out?
Little Johnny Stout.
What a naughty boy was that,
To try to drown poor pussy-cat.
Who never did him any harm,
But killed the mice in his father's barn!

The Kilkenny Cats

The Real Mother Goose, *by Blanche Fisher Wright, 1916.*

There were once two cats of Kilkenny.
Each thought there was one cat too many;
So they fought and they fit,
And they scratched and they bit,
Till, excepting their nails,
And the tips of their tails,
Instead of two cats, there weren't any.

My Kitten

Harry's Ladder to Learning, with Two Hundred and Thirty Illustrations, *by David Bogue and Joseph Cundall, 1850.*

Hey, my kitten, my kitten,
And hey, my kitten, my deary,
Such a sweet pet as this
Was neither far nor neary.

Hey Diddle Diddle

Harry's Ladder to Learning, with Two Hundred and Thirty Illustrations, *by David Bogue and Joseph Cundall, 1850.*

Hey diddle diddle,
The cat and the fiddle,
The cow jumped over the moon,
The little dog laughed to see such sport,
And the dish ran away with the spoon, the spoon,
The dish ran away with the spoon.

Mrs. Pussy's Dinner

Finger Plays for Nursery and Kindergarten, *by Emilie Poulsson, 1893. Sheet music and finger-play actions.*

1. Mrs. Pussy, sleek and fat,
With her kittens four,

Went to sleep upon the mat
By the kitchen door.

2. Mrs. Pussy heard a noise—
Up she jumped in glee:
"Kittens, maybe that's a mouse!
Let us go and see!"

3. Creeping, creeping, creeping on,
Silently they stole;
But the little mouse had gone
Back within its hole.

4. "Well," said Mrs. Pussy then,
"To the barn we'll go;
We shall find the swallows there
Flying to and fro."

5. So the cat and kittens four
Tried their very best;
But the swallows flying fast
Safely reached the nest!

6. Home went hungry Mrs. Puss
And her kittens four;
Found their dinner on a plate
By the kitchen door.

7. As they gathered round the plate,
They agreed 'twas nice
That it could not run away
Like the birds and mice!

Bridle Up the Rat

Folk Rhymes Wise and Otherwise, *Thomas W. Talley, 1922; adapted by Juli Wright*

Bridle up the rat,
Saddle your cat,
and give me my riding hat.

In comes the cat,
Out goes the rat,
Down I go with my riding hat.

How the Cat Was Belled

The Jingle Book, *by Carolyn Wells, 1901.*

A fable told by La Fontaine,
Two centuries or more ago,
Describes some rats who would arraign
A cat, their direst foe,
Who killed so many rats
And caused the deepest woe,
This Catiline of cats.

The poor rats were at their wits' end
Their homes and families to defend;
And as a last resort
They took the case to court.

It seems they called a caucus wise
Of rats of every age and size,
And then their dean,
With sapient mien,
A very Solon of a rat,
Said it was best to bell the cat.

The quaint old tale goes on to tell
How this plan would have worked quite well,
But, somehow, flaws
Appeared, because
No one would hang the bell.

Though there the ancient fable ends,
Later report the tale extends,
No longer is the truth withheld;
Developments appear,
And so you have it here.
For the first time
Set down in rhyme
Just how that cat was belled.

The council, as 'twas getting late,
Was just about to separate,
When suddenly a rat arose
Who said he could a plan propose
Which would, he thought, succeed
And meet their urgent need.

Now as this rat was very small,
And had no dignity at all,
Although his plan was well advised,
We really need not be surprised
That all the rats of riper years
Expressed the gravest doubts and fears;

Till suddenly
He said, said he,
If you will leave it all to me,
I will avow

Three days from now
That you shall all be free."

The solemn council then adjourned.
Each rat to home and fireside turned;
But each shook his wise head
And to his neighbor said:
"It is a dangerous job, in truth,
Though it seems naught to headstrong youth."

Now young Sir Rat we next behold,
With manner brave and visage bold,
Go marching down
To London town,
Where wondrous things are sold.

We see him stop
At a large shop,
And with the bland clerk's courteous aid
This was the purchase that he made:
A bicycle of finest make,
With modern gear and patent brake,
Pedometer, pneumatic tire,
And spokes that looked like silver wire,
A lantern bright
To shine at night,
Enamel finish, nickel plate,
And all improvements up to date.
Said sly Sir Rat: "It suits me well,
Especially that sweet-toned bell."

The shades of night were falling fast
When Sir Rat turned toward home at last.
The neighbors watched him as he passed
And said: "What is that queer-shaped thing?
Surely that can't be made to ring."
Sir Rat went on, nor stayed
To hear the jests they made;
And just outside the old cat's gate
He stopped and boldly braved his fate,
For if that cat
Should smell a rat
How quickly he'd come out and catch him,
And with what gusto he'd dispatch him!
Sir Rat, against the picket-fence
Leaned the machine, then hurried hence,
And hid himself with glee,
And waited breathlessly
To see what that
Cantankerous cat
Would say, when in the twilight dim
He saw that brightly shining rim.

Sir Rat, though hidden quite,
And safely out of sight,
Had scarcely time to wink his eye,
When Mr. Cat came sauntering by.

"Ha! Ha!" said he,
"What's this I see,
A bicycle! and just my size!
Well, this, indeed, is a surprise!
I'll confiscate
This treasure great;
How quickly I'll fly o'er the ground
When I pursue my hunting round!"

He mounted it with eager haste,
It suited well his sporting taste;
He guided it at will,
And used the brake with skill,
He grasped the handle-bars, and then—
You see it was his custom when
He did a thing, to do it well—
Of course he used the clear-toned bell!

Victory now! the deed is done!
No longer at the set of sun
The rats fly shrieking to their nests,
They saunter round with merry jests
And ne'er a thought of fear,
Knowing full well
They'll hear the bell
When Mr. Cat draws near.

And young Sir Rat who did the deed,
Whose cleverness relieved their need,
His wondrous enterprise
Was lauded to the skies.
And everywhere his name
Was hailed with shouts of fame.
In difficulties, oft we see
Modern improvements frequently
Will prove a happy remedy.

The Funny Kittens

The Jingle Book, *by Carolyn Wells, 1901.*

Once there were some silly kittens,
And they knitted woolly mittens
To bestow upon the freezing Hottentots.
But the Hottentots refused them,
Saying that they never used them
Unless crocheted of red with yellow spots.

So the silly little kittens
Took their blue and white striped mittens
To a Bear who lived within a hollow tree;
The Bear responded sadly,
I would wear your mittens gladly,
But I fear they are too gay for such as me."

Then the kittens, almost weeping,
Came to where a Cow lay sleeping,
And they woke her with this piteous request,
Won't you wear our mittens furry?"
Said the Cow, "My dears, don't worry;
I will put them on as soon as I am dressed."

Then the Cow put on her bonnet
With a wreath of roses on it,
And a beautiful mantilla fringed with white;
And she donned the pretty mittens,
While the silly little kittens
Clapped their paws in admiration at the sight.

The Shadow Kitten

The Kitten's Garden of Verses, *by Oliver Herford, 1911.*

There's a funny little kitten that tries to look like me,
But though I'm round and fluffy, he's as flat as flat can be;

And when I try to mew to him he never makes a sound,
And when I jump into the air he never leaves the ground.

He has a way of growing, I don't understand at all.
Sometimes he's very little and sometimes he's very tall.
And once when in the garden when the sun came up at dawn
He grew so big I think he stretched half-way across the lawn.

Games and Group Activities

Puss in the Corner

Games for Everybody, *by May C. Hofmann, 1905, Dodge Publishing Co. (Games for Children)*

All the children except one stand in corners, or in any specified area if there are not enough corners to go around. The one who is out stands in the middle to represent "Puss." The players then beckon to each other one at a time saying, "Here, puss, pussy" and run and change places with the one who is called.

Puss tries to get one of the vacant places. If she succeeds, the child who is left out is "Puss," until she manages to obtain a place.

Books

Amelia's Nine Lives, by Lorna Balian (Humbug, 1994).

Bandit, by Karen Rostoker-Gruber (Two Lions, 2008). *Moving can be stressful for anyone, but Bandit, the family cat, is totally confused.*

Cat Heaven, by Cynthia Rylant (Blue Sky Press, 1997).

Cats, by Gail Gibbons (Holiday House, 1996).

Cats, Cats, Cats, by Leslea Newmann (Simon & Schuster, 2001). *A humorous rhyming story for preschool children. Crowded illustrations.*

Cats Do, Dogs Don't, by Norma Simon (Whitman, 1986).

Clifford's Kitten, by Norman Bridwel (Cartwheel, 1992).

Dewey: There's a Cat in the Library! by Vicki Myron (Little Brown, 2009). *Fantastic large illustrations, cute story based on true events. Preschool age; librarians will love it.*

Fish for Supper, by Morgan Matthews (Troll, 1986).
Five Little Kittens, by Nancy Jewell (Clarion, 1999).
Frankenstein's Cat, by Curtis Jobling (Scholastic, 2002).
Ginger, by Charlotte Voake (series; Candlewick, 2000).
Have You Seen My Cat? by Eric Carle (Simon, 2012).
Hero Cat, by Eileen Spinelli (Cavendish, 2006). *A short story with very nice large illustrations; good for preschool age. Mother cat rescues her baby kittens from a burning building.*
Hi, Cat! by Ezra Jack Keats (Viking, 1999).
I Had a Rooster: A Traditional Folk Song, by Pete and Laura Vaccaro Seeger (DK Pub, 2001).
Kat Kong, by Dav Pilkey (HMH, 2003). *Hilarious story with collage-style illustrations.*
Katie Loves the Kittens, by John Himmelman (Henry Holt, 2008). *Three new kittens at home are almost too much to handle. And being a dog gets Katie into trouble.*
The Kid's Cat Book, by Tomie De Paola (Holiday, 1979).
The Kitten Book, by Jan Pfloog (series; Golden Books, 1999). *The story of kittens discovering snow for the first time.*
The Kitten in the Pumpkin Patch, by Richard Shaw (Warne, 1973).
A Kitten Tale, by Eric Rohmann (Alfred A. Knopf, 2008).
Kittens Are Like That by Jan Pfloog (Random House Picturebooks, 1976).
Kitty Cat, Kitty Cat, Are You Waking Up? by Bill Martin, Jr. (Two Lions, 2011).
The Little Cat and the Greedy Old Woman, by Joan Rankin (McElderry, 1995).
Mama Cat Has Three Kittens, by Denise Fleming (Square Fish, 2002).
Millions of Cats, by Wanda Gag Coward (Putnam, 1977). *The little old man sets out to find a cat for the little old woman and comes home with more than enough pets.*
My Cat Loves to Hide in Boxes, by Eve Sutton (Penguin, 1973).
Rocky the Cat Who Barks, by Donna Jo Napoli (Dutton, 2002).
The Summer Cat, by Linda Benson (series; 7 Trails, 2014).
Tabby: A Story in Pictures, by Aliki Brandenberg (HarperCollins, 1995).
Three Little Kittens, by Jerry Pinkney (Dial, 2010).
Three Little Kittens, by Paul Galdone (HMH, 1988). *Ages 3–8. Match the pairs of mittens.*
Three Little Kittens, by Mother Goose, illustrated by Milo Winter (Laughing Elephant, 2009).
Where Does My Cat Sleep? by Norma Simon (Whitman, 1982).
Wish Come True Cat, by Ragnhild Scamell (Barron's, 2001). *Good illustrations, medium text length and difficulty; good preschool book.*
Won-Ton: A Cat Tale Told in Haiku, by Lee Wardlaw (Holt, 2011).

Movies and Television

The Adventures of Puss in Boots (Dreamworks, 2015).
The Aristocats (Disney, 1970).
The Cat from Outer Space (Disney, 1978).
The Cat in the Hat (Animated, CBS Television, Dr. Seuss, 1971).
Cats and Dogs 1 and *2* (Warner Bros., 2001, 2010).
Garfield (20th Century—Fox, 2004).
Homeward Bound (Disney, 1993).
The Incredible Journey (Disney, 1993).
Oliver and Company (Disney, 1988).
Puss in Boots (Cannon Movie Tales, TV Series, 1988).
The Sylvester & Tweety Mysteries (TV series, 1995–2001).
That Darn Cat! (DIsney, 1965).
Tom and Jerry: The Movie (Hanna & Barbera, Miramax, 1992).

7. Peter Rabbit; Peter Cottontail

Peter Rabbit, unhappy with his ordinary-sounding name, changes it to Peter Cottontail. His friends make fun of him, so he decides to go back to his original name. Peter Rabbit is also the main character of a Beatrix Potter book, in which the naughty rabbit sneaks into a garden and is almost caught by Farmer McGregor, losing his new jacket in the process.

7a. Rabbit

Rabbit/Bunny Activities

Songs to Sing and Play

In a Cabin in the Wood

This song can be found in The Kids' Campfire Book, *by Jane Drake (1996) and* In a Cabin in a Wood, *by Darcie McNally, 1991. See Educational Children's Music from* Songs for Teaching *for more information on this song.*

"In a cabin in the wood
Little man by the window stood
Saw a rabbit hopping by..."

Variation

First Verse:
(sing in a *normal voice*)
In a cabin in the woods...

Second Verse:
(sing in a *tiny voice*)
Itty-bitty cabin in the woods...

Third Verse:
(sing in a *deep, loud voice*)
Great big cabin in the woods...

Thumper (Bambi's Friend) (tune: Are You Sleeping?)

Words by Eunice Wright

The teacher sings one line, the children repeat it.

What does Thumper say? What does Thumper say?
"If you can't say anything nice, If you can't say anything nice,
Don't say anything at all, Don't say anything at all,"
Listen to Thumper! (or Good advice!) Listen to Thumper!

Little Peter Rabbit (tune: Battle Hymn of the Republic)

Traditional. Subtract a word for each verse.

"Little Peter Rabbit had a fly upon his ear...
And he flicked it till it flew away!"

When all the words have been subtracted, hum the tune, doing the actions only.

Variations

Little Peter Rabbit had a rose (*add various objects*) upon his nose (*or other body part*),
Little Peter Rabbit had a _____ upon his _____,
Little Peter Rabbit had a _____ upon his _____;
He flicked it and it flew away.
(Continue changing animals, objects and body parts)

Little Peter Rabbit had a *banana* on his *head...*
Little Tommy Turtle had a *rock* upon his *shell...*
Little Tony Tiger had a *knot* tied in his *tail...*

Rabbit Ain't Got No Tail at All (tune: Mary Had a Little Lamb)

Sheet music: Wee Sing Silly Songs, *p. 31.*

"Rabbit ain't got no tail at all... Just a powder puff."

Little Bunny Foo Foo (Camp Song)

Peter, Mopsy, Flopsy, Foo Foo Rabbit, *by B. Potter, 1910. Alternative tune:* Eensy, Weensy Spider

1. Little bunny foo-foo,
hopping through the forest
Scooping up the field mice,
and bopping them on the head.
(Spoken) Then down came the Good Fairy, and (this is what) she said:

Little Bunny Foo-Foo,
I don't wanna see you
Scooping up the field mice,
and bopping them on the head.
(Spoken) I'll give you three chances,
and if you don't behave,
I'll turn you into a Goon!

2. Little bunny foo-foo,
hopping through the forest
Scooping up the field mice,
and bopping them on the head.
(Spoken) Then down came the Good Fairy,
and she said:

Little Bunny Foo-Foo,
I don't wanna see you
Scooping up the field mice,
and bopping them on the head.
(Spoken) I'll give you two chances,
and if you don't behave,
I'll turn you into a Goon!

3. Little bunny foo-foo,
hopping through the forest
Scooping up the field mice,
and bopping them on the head.
(Spoken) Then down came the Good Fairy,
and she said:

Little Bunny Foo-Foo,
I don't wanna see you
Scooping up the field mice,
and bopping them on the head.
(Spoken) I'll give you one more chance,
and if you don't behave,
I'll turn you into a Goon!

4. Little bunny foo-foo,
hopping through the forest
Scooping up the field mice,
and bopping them on the head.
(Spoken) Then down came the Good Fairy,
and she said:

Little Bunny Foo-Foo,
I don't wanna see you
Scooping up the field mice,
and bopping them on the head.
POOF! You're a goon!
(Spoken) And the moral of the *(this)* story is:
Hare today, goon tomorrow!

I Had a Rooster

Performed by Pete Seeger. Traditional.

"I had a bunny, my bunny pleased me.
I fed my bunny 'neath the greenberry tree..."

Continue to add other animals and their sounds.

Caught a Hare Alive

Harry's Ladder to Learning. With Two Hundred and Thirty Illustrations, *by David Bogue and Joseph Cundall, 1850.*

One, two, three, four, five,
I caught a hare alive;
Six, seven, eight, nine, ten,
And let it go again.

Peter Cottontail (tune: There Were Three Jolly Fishermen)

By Eunice Wright

There was a rabbit with a cotton tail...
cotton, cotton, tail, tail, tail...

He hopped along the bunny trail...
bunny, bunny, trail, trail, trail...

Tune: Three Blind Mice

By Eunice Wright

Peter Cotton-tail,
Peter Cotton-tail,
See how he hops,
See how he hops,
He hops down the bunny trail,
He carries a basket or a pail,
He has Easter eggs for sale,
Oh, Peter Cottontail.

Tune: Row, Row, Row Your Boat

By Eunice Wright

Hop, hop, hop all day,
Down the trail you go.
Merrily, merrily, merrily merrily,
The Easter eggs you show.

Tune: Mary Had a Little Lamb

By Eunice Wright

Peter had a cotton tail,
Cotton tail, cotton tail.

Peter had a cotton tail,
His tail was white as snow.

And everywhere that Peter went...
His tail was sure to go.

It followed him down the trail one day...
Which was the Easter trail.

Eeny, Meeny, Miney, Mo (Alternate Tunes: Baa Baa Black Sheep and Peter Peter Pumpkin Eater)

B. Fitzgibbon, words and music by F.B. Haviland Publishing Co., 1906

Eeny, Meeny, Miney, Mo
Catch a rabbit (tiger, piggy, chicken, baby, monkey, etc.) by the toe.
If he hollers, (squeals, growls, clucks, cries, chatters, etc.) let him go.
Eeny, Meeny, Miney, Mo.

Other Songs

"Here Comes Peter Cottontail," by Steve Nelson and Jack Rollins, 1949 (Disney, 1963).

"Hippity Hop," *I Have a Song for You, Vol. 3*, by Janeen Brady, page 14 (Brite Music Enterprises, 1980).

Poems and Nursery Rhymes

The Bunny

Finger play. Traditional. Loving2Learn.com.

"Once there was a bunny
And a green cabbage head..."

The Bunny. The Tunny

Animal Analogues, by Robert Williams Wood, 1887.

The superficial naturalists have often been misled,
By failing to dis-crim-inate between the tail and head:
It really is unfortunate such carelessness prevails,
Because the bunnies have their heads where Tunnies have their tails.

Ten Little Rabbits

By Eunice Wright

One little rabbit, dressed in blue,
Soon met another, then there were two.
Two little rabbits, lived by a tree,
Another came along, then there were three.
Three little rabbits, then invited more,
One came to visit, then there were four.
Four little rabbits, saw a hawk dive,
They called for help, then there were five.
Five little rabbits, hiding in the sticks,
Saw another rabbit, then there were six.
Six little rabbits met one named Kevin.
He moved in, then there were seven.
Seven little rabbits, just couldn't wait,
They called to another, then there were eight.
Eight little rabbits, waiting to dine,
They fixed a nice dinner, and soon there were nine.
Nine little rabbits, snug in their den,
Mother came home, and then there were ten.

Zip

Child Songs of Cheer, *by Evaleen Stein, 1918.*

When we went to drive the cows home
Down the lane to-day,
There was such a funny bunny
Jumped across the way!

All we saw as he ran past us,
Faster that a quail,
Was his snow-white fuzzy-wuzzy
Little cotton tail!

The Carrot and the Rabbit

The Peter Patter Book of Nursery Rhymes, *by Leroy F. Jackson, 1918.*

A carrot in the garden
And a rabbit in the wood.
Said the rabbit, "Beg your pardon,
But you're surely meant for food;
Though you've started in to harden,
You may still be very good.

The Hare. The Harrier.

Animal Analogues, *by Robert Williams Wood, 1908.*

The Harrier, harassed by the Hare,
Presents a picture of despair;
Altho' as far as I'm concerned,
I love to see the tables turned
The Harrier flies with all his might
It is a harum- scare'm flight;
I'm not surprised he does not care
To meet the fierce pursuing Hare.

Games and Group Activities

Chase the Rabbit

Games for Everybody, *by May C. Hofmann, Dodge Publishing Co., 1905.*

All the children kneel on the floor in a circle with hands on each other's shoulders.

One is chosen to be the "rabbit" and runs around outside the circle and touches one of the players, who is to chase him to his "hole."

The minute the player is touched he must run to the left, while the rabbit goes to the right, must tag the rabbit when they pass each other and try to get back to the "hole" again.

If he fails, he becomes the "rabbit," and the game goes on as before.

Dance Activity

The Bunny Hop, *by Ray Anthony and Leonard Auletti (1952).*

Books

Brown Rabbit's Shape Book, by Alan Baker (Series, Kingfisher, 1999). *Rabbit opens his square present and blows up 5 shaped balloons.*

Bruh Rabbit and the Tar Baby Girl, by Virginia Hamilton (Blue Sky Press, 2003). *If you can read this cute book with a southern Gullah accent, all the better.*

Bunches and Bunches of Bunnies, by Louise Mathews (Putnam, 1978).

Bunny Money, by Rosemary Wells (series; Puffin, 2000). *Two rabbits save money for a present.*

Busy Bunnies, by Stephen Caitlin (Troll, 1988).

The Cabbages Are Chasing the Rabbits, by Arnold Adoff (Harcourt, 1985).

A Cabin in the Woods, by Linda Stiles Fox (Createspace, 2015).

Cottontail Rabbit, by Elizabeth Schwartz (Cadmus, 1957).

The Country Bunny and the Little Gold Shoes, by DuBose Heyward (HMH, 2010).

The Favorite Uncle Remus, by Joel Chandler Harris (HMH, 1973).

Fifteen Rabbits: A Celebration of Life, by Felix Salten (Delacorte, 1976).

Good Night Moon, by Margaret Wise Brown, (Harper Collins, 1947). *The bedtime book in which a bunny bids goodnight to room and possessions. A sweet family treasure for more than 50 years.*

Gray Rabbit's 1, 2, 3, by Alan Baker (Kingfisher, 1994). *One little rabbit molds some friends out of colorful clay to count.*

Great Big Especially Beautiful Easter Egg, by James Stevenson (Greenwillow, 1983).

The Great Bunny Race, by Kathy Feczko (Troll, 1985).

I Can Count 100 Bunnies, and So Can You! by Cyndy Szekeres (Cartwheel, 1999).

I Had a Rooster: A Traditional Folk Song, by Pete Seeger (DK Pub, 2001).

In a Cabin in a Wood, by Darcie McNally and illustrated by Robin M. Koontz (Dutton, 1991).

Leo, the Lop (Tail One, Two or Three), by Stephen Cosgrove (Serendipity, 1983). Also *Gram-pa Lop* (series).

Little Bunny Foo Foo: The Real Story, by Cori Doerrfeld (Dial, 2012).

Little Bunny Foo Foo: Told and Sung by the Good Fairy, by Paul Brett Johnson (Scholastic, 2004).

The Little Rabbit by Judy Dunn (Random House, 1980).

Little Rabbit Foo Foo, by Michael Rosen (Aladdin, 1993).
Little White Rabbit, by Kevin Henkes (Greenwillow, 2011).
Marshmallow, by Claire Newberry (Smithmark, 1998). *Cat and rabbit are friends at last! Long text.*
Missing Rabbit. Companion to *Room for Rabbit*, by Roni Schotter (Clarion, 2002).
Mr. Rabbit and the Lovely Present, by Charlotte Zolotow (Harper, 1962). *Peter, the naughty bunny, disobeys his mother and sneaks into Mr. McGregor's. The little rabbit with the blue jacket is a family favorite.*
One More Bunny, by Rick Walton (series; Lothrop, Lee & Shepard, 2000). *One bunny joins another at the park until there are ten.*
A Rabbit for Easter, by Carol Carrick (Greenwillow, 1979).
Rabbits Can't Dance! by Dale Binford (Gareth Stevens, 1989).
Rabbit's Pajama Party, by Stuart J. Murphy (HarperCollins, 1999). *Rabbit and three friends have a sleepover.*
Rabbits, Rabbits and More Rabbits, by Gail Gibbons (Holiday House, 2000).
The Rabbit's Tail. A story from Korea, by Suzanne C. Han (Henry Holt, 1999). *The Tiger is really the main character—a very cute and funny book, excellent illustrations. Use a dried persimmon as visual aid.*
Rest, Rabbit, Rest (Sweet Pickles Series), by Jacquelyn Reinach (Holt, 1978).
The Runaway Bunny, by Margaret Wise Brown (Harper, 1972).
Seven Little Rabbits, by John Becker (Walker, 1994).
Seven Little Rabbits, by Julie Stiegemeyer (Cavendish, 2010). *A beautifully illustrated rhyming story, great for young children.*
So Many Bunnies, by Rick Walton (Harper Festival, 2000). *A bedtime ABC and counting book.*
The Tale of Peter Rabbit, by Beatrix Potter (Warner, 1902).
That Rabbit Belongs to Emily Brown, by Cressida Cowell (Hyperion, 2007). *"That rabbit is not for sale!"*
Thunder Bunny, by Barbara Berger (Philomel Books, 2007). *Nice illustrations, short text, a magical story for preschool children.*
The Velveteen Rabbit, by Margery Williams Bianco (Troll, 1988).
What a Funny Bunny, by Patricia Whitehead (Troll, 1985).
What's the Matter, Bunny Blue? by Nicola Smee (Boxer Books, 2010). *A very simple text, nice illustrations. Six creatures help bunny find his granny.*
Zomo the Rabbit: A Trickster Tale from West Africa, by Gerald McDermott (HMH, 1996).

Movies and Television

Alice in Wonderland (movie and book), The White Rabbit. Animated (Disney, 1951; movie 2010).
Alice's Adventures in Wonderland (Cinevision, 1973).
Brer Rabbit—*Song of the South* (Disney, 1946).
Bugs Bunny (Warner Bros.).
"Thumper" in *Bambi* (Disney, 2005).
The Velveteen Rabbit (movie and book) (Amazon Digital, 2012).
Winnie, the Pooh (Rabbit) (Disney, 2011).

8. The City Mouse and the Country Mouse; Three Blind Mice

In the story of the City Mouse and the Country Mouse, the two mice visit each other's houses, where they discover many cultural differences. Each mouse is thereafter content to return to his own home. Three Blind Mice is a traditional nursery rhyme where three blind mice chase a farmer's wife. The mouse ran up the clock (Hickory Dickory Dock) is another traditional nursery rhyme.

8a. The City Mouse

8b. The Country Mouse

8c. Three Blind Mice

8a. The City Mouse

8b. The Country Mouse

8c. Blind Mice

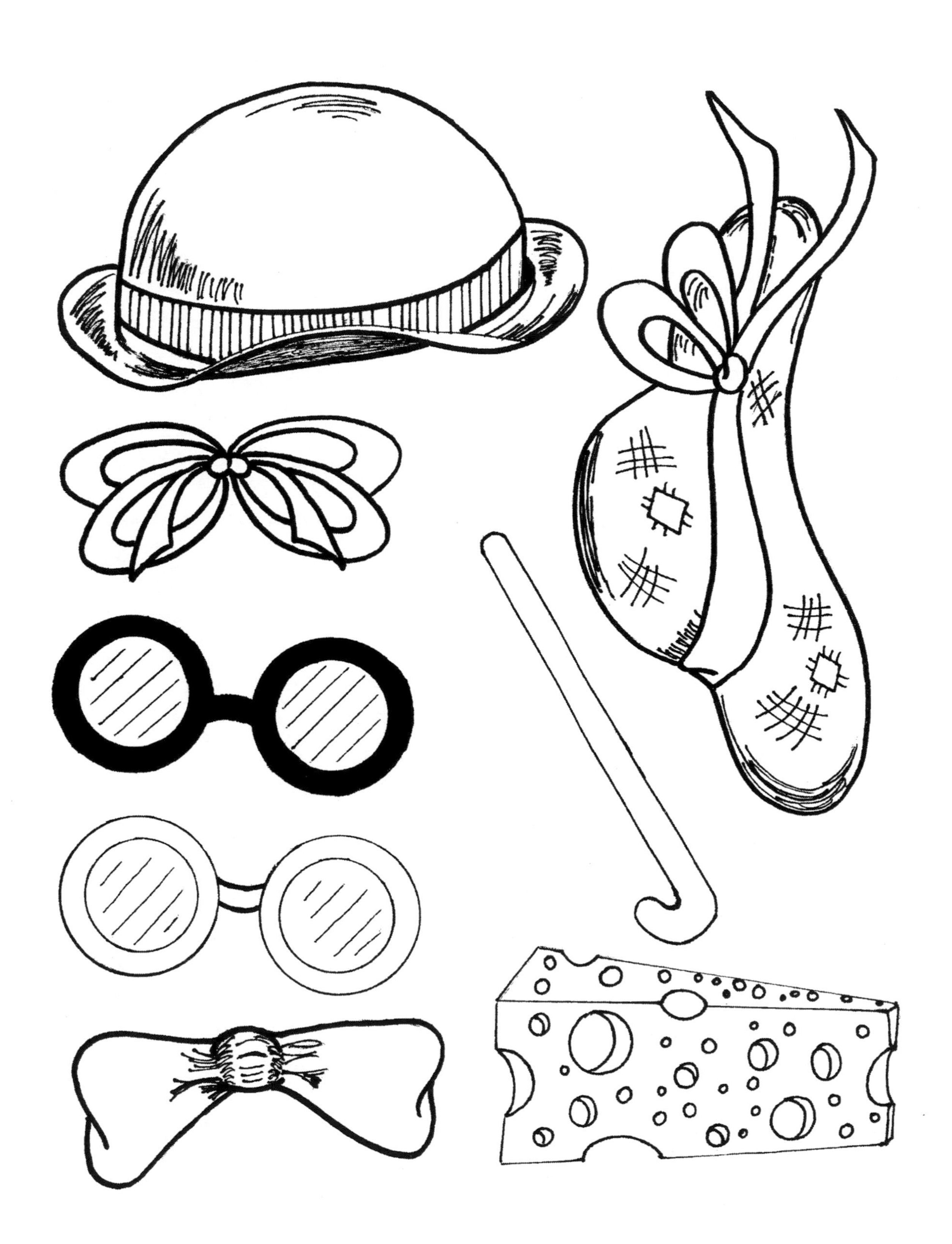

Mice Activities

Songs to Sing and Play

Tune: Itsy Bitsy Spider

Words by Eunice and Juli Wright

The Itsy Bitsy mouse crawled up the water spout,
Down came the cat and chased the mouse right out.
Out came the farm animals when they heard the cat shout,
And the Itsy Bitsy mouse went running down the spout.

Three Blind Mice

The Real Mother Goose, *by Blanche Fisher Wright, 1916.*

Three blind mice! See how they run!
They all ran after the farmer's wife,
Who cut off their tails with a carving knife.
Did you ever see such a thing in your life
As three blind mice?

Three Blind Mice

The Baby's Opera, *by Walter Crane, 1877 (sheet music). Sung in a round for 3 voices.*

Three blind mice,
Three blind mice,
Three blind mice

See how they run!
See how they run!
See how they run!

They all ran after the farmer's wife
Who cut off their tails with a carving knife
Did you ever see such a sight in your life
As three blind mice?

(Twice through and finish at pause.)

It Was a Mouse

Traditional folk song from Nova Scotia (from A Frog He Would A-Wooing Go). Also see "Frog Went A Courtin'."

It was a mouse lived in a well-a-hum,
There was a mouse lived in a well
And there he lived there very well.
And *lickedy too de fall de dey,*
Whack fall de dum.

Next come in it was a flea-a-hum,
Next come in it was a flea,
And he fetched a load of tea.

Next come in it was a fly-a-hum,
Next come in it was a fly,
He eat so much it made him die.

Next come in it was a tick-a-hum,
Next come in it was a tick,
He eat so much it made him sick.

Next come in it was a frog-a-hum,
Next come in it was a frog,
And he fetched in a load of grog.

Next come in it was a snail-a-hum,
Next come in it was a snail,
He had the bagpipes on his tail.

Next come in it was a bee-a-hum,
Next come in it was a bee,
He brought the fiddle on his knee.

Next come in it was a snake-a-hum,
Next come in it was a snake,
And he fetched in a load of cake.

The big black snake he swamped the land-a-hum,
The big black snake he swamped the land,
And he was killed by an overgrown man.

This overgrown man he went to France-a-hum,
This overgrown man he went to France,
To learn the ladies how to dance.

See related books *A Frog He Would a Wooing Go*, by Randolph Caldecott, namesake of the Caldecott Medal (Amazon Digital, 2015), and *A Frog He Would A Wooing Go*, by Henry Louis Stephens (Nabu Press, 2011).

Tune: The Wheels on the Bus

Words by Eunice Wright

The mouse in the barn
Goes squeak, squeak, squeak,
squeak, squeak, squeak,
squeak, squeak, squeak.
The mouse in the barn
Goes squeak, squeak, squeak,
All around the barn.

Tune: Mary Had a Little Lamb

(Substitute child's name & animal; white mouse, baby mouse, squeaky mouse, etc.)

Susie saw a gray mouse, gray mouse, gray mouse,
Susie saw a gray mouse,
It ran around and squeaked (ran in its hole, ate some cheese, teased the cat, etc.).

Frog Went A-Courtin'

Song based on the Aesop's fable, by Jack Hartmann.

A frog went a-courtin,'
And he did ride. Hum-hum, hum-hum.
A frog went a-courtin,'
And he did ride,
With his horse right by his side. Hum-hum, hum-hum.

He rode up to Miss Mousie's den...
Said, "Please, Miss Mousie, let me in...

"Yes, Sir Frog, I sit and spin...
Please, Mr. Froggie, won't you come in?"

The frog said, "My dear, I've come to see...
If, Miss Mousie, you'll marry me..."

"Oh, yes, Sir Frog, I'll marry you...
And we'll have children two by two..."

The frog and mouse they went to France...
And that's the end of my romance...

Many thanks to Jack Hartmann for permission to display these lyrics. www.jackhartmann.com.

Poems and Nursery Rhymes

The Mouse and the Clock

The Real Mother Goose, by Blanche Fisher Wright, 1916.

Hickory, dickory, dock!
The mouse ran up the clock;
The clock struck one,
And down he run,
Hickory, dickory, dock!

Three Little Mice

Finger Play Reader Part 2, *by John W. Davis, 1909.*

Three little mice crept out to see.
What they could find to have for tea

For they were dainty, saucy mice,
And lik'd to nibble something nice,

But pussy's eyes, so big and bright,
Soon sent them scampering off in fright.

Three Tabby Cats went forth to mouse,
And said, "Let's have a gay carouse."

For they were handsome, active cats,
And famed for catching mice and rats.

But savage dogs, disposed to bite.
These cats declined to encounter in fight.

The City Mouse and the Country Mouse

By Eunice Wright

Are you a city mouse, or a country mouse,
Or does it really matter?
Where is your house, you little mouse,
Is it the first or is it the latter?

Do you live in the city, and wish for a house,
With country peace and quiet?
Or live in the country, and wish for a house,
With much more action and riot?

Which ever you choose, you don't seem happy,
You want the opposite house.
The grass is always greener, and life is snappy,
Wanting the other "mouse-house."

The City Mouse and the Garden Mouse

The Home Book of Verse, Vol. 1 (of 4). *Author: Various. Editor: Burton Egbert Stevenson, 1912, by Christina Georgina Rossetti (1830–1894)*

The city mouse lives in a house;—
The garden mouse lives in a bower,
He's friendly with the frogs and toads,
And sees the pretty plants in flower.

The city mouse eats bread and cheese;—
The garden mouse eats what he can;
We will not grudge him seeds and stocks,
Poor little timid furry man.

5 Little Hungry Mice

Words by Eunice Wright. Based on the game "This Little Piggy Went to Market," played with a child's toes.

This little mouse went to market,
This little mouse stayed home.
This little mouse ate cheesecake,
This little mouse had none.
This little mouse went, "Squeak, squeak, squeak,"
All the way home.

Five Little Mice

Traditional Fingerplay

Five little mice came out to play
Gathering crumbs along the way.
Out came pussycat sleek and fat
Four little mice went scampering back.

Continue with: Four little mice, then three, etc.

Wee Mousie

Traditional Fingerplay. (A great one-on-one game for little ones!)

Round about, Round about
Goes the little mouse
up a bit, up a bit
build a little house
down a bit, down a bit,
Catch a wee mouse.

Round about, round about, went the wee mouse *(Circle a finger on child's hand)*.
Up the stairs, up the stairs *(quickly walk your fingers up the child's arm)*,
In the wee house *(tickle the child under the chin)*!

Tommy Mouse

The Real Mother Goose, *by Blanche Fisher Wright, 1916; adapted by Juli Wright*

Little Tommy Tittle-mouse
Lived in a little house;
He caught fishes
In other men's ditches.

Alternate:
Little Tommy mouse
Lived in a little house;
He caught fishes
To make little wishes.

The Little Mouse

The Real Mother Goose, *by Blanche Fisher Wright, 1916.*

I have seen you, little mouse,
Running all about the house,
Through the hole your little eye
In the wainscot peeping sly,
Hoping soon some crumbs to steal,
To make quite a hearty meal.

Look before you venture out,
See if pussy is about.

If she's gone, you'll quickly run
To the larder for some fun;
Round about the dishes creep,
Taking into each a peep,
To choose the daintiest that's there,
Spoiling things you do not care.

Five Little Mice and Five Little Quail

By Eunice Wright

Five little mice went out to play,
And met five quail that came their way.

The five little quail followed after their mother,
And the five little mice ran chasing one another.

White Mouse

The Only True Mother Goose Melodies, *by Munroe and Francis, 1833.*

Oh, what a sweet little white Mouse!
Oh, what a dear little bright Mouse!
With his eyes of pink,
Going winky-wink,
Oh, what a sweet little white mouse.

Some Little Mice Sat in a Barn

The Little Mother Goose, *by Jessie Willcox Smith, 1918. Use a cat puppet and 6 mice puppets.*

Some little mice sat in a barn to spin.
Pussy came by, and she popped her head in;
"Shall I come in and cut your threads off?"
"Oh no, kind sir, you will snap our heads off."

Variation:
Six little mice sat down to spin;
Pussy passed by and she peeped in.
What are you doing, my little men?
Weaving coats for gentlemen.
Shall I come in and cut off your threads?
No, no, Mistress Pussy, you'd bite off our heads.
Oh, no, I'll not; I'll help you to spin.
That may be so, but you can't come in!

The Mouse

Aunt Kitty's Stories, *by Various Authors, 1870.*

O come brother come;
I'm frightened, because
There's a mouse in the room,
It is under the drawers.

O silence, John said,
Do not make such a noise;
The mouse is afraid
Of us little boys.

It is gentle and weak,
And can never do harm;
But it gives a faint squeak
At the slightest alarm.

The Mice

Finger Plays for Nursery and Kindergarten, *by Emilie Poulsson, 1893. (Sheet music and finger play actions, p. 44.)*

Five little mice on the pantry floor,
Seeking for bread-crumbs or something more;
Five little mice on the shelf up high,
Feasting so daintily on a pie—

But the big round eyes of the wise old cat
See what the five little mice are at.

Quickly she jumps!—but the mice run away,
And hide in their snug little holes all day.

"Feasting in pantries may be very nice;
But home is the best!" say the five little mice.

Mousie

Love and Law in Child Training: A Book for Mothers, *by Emilie Poulsson, 1899.*

"Creep, mousie,
From the barn
To the housie;
Old cat
Catch the little mousie!"

Mouse and Cat

Holiday Songs and Every Day Songs and Games, *by Emilie Poulsson, 1901. (With sheet music and some finger plays.)*

Good morning, Mister Mouse;
We've nothing for you here.
You'd better run away,
for Kitty Cat is near!
Run! run! run! Run!

The Little Mice Are Creeping

By Margaret B. Morton. Songs and Games for Little Ones, *by Harriet S. Jenks and Getrude Walker, 1887. (With sheet music.) Modified by Juli Wright.*

The little mice are creeping, creeping,
The little mice are creeping through the house.
The little mice are nibbling, nibbling,
The little mice are nibbling through the house.
The little mice are sleeping, sleeping,
The little mice are sleeping through the house.
The old gray cat comes creeping, creeping,
The old gray cat comes creeping through the house.
The little mice all scamper, scamper,
The little mice all scamper through the house.

The Mouse

Chinese Mother Goose Rhymes, *by Isaac Taylor, 1900.*

He climbed up the candlestick,
The little mousey brown,
To steal and eat tallow,
And he couldn't get down.

He called for his grandma,
But his grandma was in town,
So he doubled up into a wheel
And rolled himself down.

An Old Tale

In My Nursery: A Book of Verse, *by Laura E. Richards, 1890; adapted by Juli Wright.*

He was a mouse, and she was a mouse,
And down in one hole they did dwell.

And each was as black as your Sunday hat,
And they loved one another well.

He had a tail, and she had a tail;
Both long and curling and fine.

And each said, "My love's is the finest tail
In the world, excepting mine!"

He smelt the cheese, and she smelt the cheese,
And they both pronounced it good;

And both remarked it would greatly add
To the charms of their daily food.

The Mouse

In My Nursery: A Book of Verse, *by Laura E. Richards, 1890.*

I'm only a poor little mouse, Ma'am.
I live in the wall of your house, Ma'am.
With a fragment of cheese,
And a very few peas,
I was having a little carouse, Ma'am.

No mischief at all I intend, Ma'am.
I hope you will act as my friend, Ma'am.
If my life you should take,
Many hearts it would break,
And the mischief would be without end, Ma'am.

My wife lives in there, in the crack, Ma'am,
She's waiting for me to come back, Ma'am.
She hoped I might find
A bit of a rind,
For the children their dinner do lack, Ma'am.

'Tis hard living there in the wall, Ma'am,
For plaster and mortar will pall, Ma'am,
On the minds of the young,
And when specially hung—
Ry, upon their poor father they'll fall, Ma'am.
I never was given to strife, Ma'am,—
(Don't look at that terrible knife, Ma'am!)
The noise overhead
That disturbs you in bed,
'Tis the rats, I will venture my life, Ma'am.

In your eyes I see mercy, I'm sure, Ma'am.
Oh, there's no need to open the door, Ma'am.
I'll slip through the crack,
And I'll never come back,
Oh! I'll never come back any more, Ma'am!

Games and Group Activities

Seven Blind Mice

Read the story "Seven Blind Mice" (Reading Railroad) by Ed Young (Puffin, 2002). Watch the YouTube video book. Make seven colored mice puppets and an elephant puppet and act out the story. Try blindfolding some children and let them describe the objects that they feel and try guess to what they are. See Elephant puppet activities for poem (pattern, p. 272; poem, p. 274).

Mousetrap

Students form a circle, join hands, and raise them high to make the mousetrap. A small group of children (mice) run inside and outside of the trap until the teacher calls "snap." When the children hear "snap," they close the trap by quickly lowering their arms. The mice that are trapped become part of the circle. When all the mice have been caught, new ones are chosen.

A Frog Went A-Courtin'

Choose different children to hold the "Frog" and "Mouse" puppets and act out "A Frog Went A-Courtin.'"

Cat and Mice

Games for the Playground, Home, School and Gymnasium, by Jessie H. Bancroft (1922), p. 59.

5 to 60 players. Schoolroom.

One player is chosen to be the cat, and hides behind or under the teacher's desk. After the cat hides, the teacher motions to five or six other players, who creep softly up to the desk, and when all are assembled, scratch on it with their fingers, to represent the nibbling of mice. As soon as the cat hears this, she scrambles out from under the desk and gives chase to the mice, who may save themselves only by getting back to their holes (seats). If a mouse is caught, the cat changes places with him for the next round of the game. If no mouse is caught, the same cat may continue, or the teacher may choose another (at her discretion).

A different set of mice should be chosen each time, to give all of the players an opportunity to join in the game.

This is a favorite schoolroom game for little children. They should give the cat quite a chase before returning to their seats, instead of seeking safety in the shortest and most direct way.

Cat and Mouse

Games for Everybody, by May C. Hoffmann, 1905, by Dodge Publishing Co. (Games for Children)

The children sit in two rows facing each other, with a space between. Blindfold two children, one being the "cat" and the other the "mouse."

The "cat" stands at one end of the row and the "mouse" at the other. They start in opposite directions and the "cat" tries to catch the "mouse." The children may give hints as to the direction the players are to go.

When the "mouse" is caught, he becomes "cat," and another child is chosen as "mouse."

Books

Alexander and the Wind-Up Mouse, by Leo Lionni (Dragonfly Books, 1974).

Angelina Ballerina, by Katharine Holabird (Crown Books, 1983). *A little mouse dreams of dancing her way to fame and ballerina glory.*

Baby Mouse, Queen of the World, by Jennifer Ann Holm (series; Random House, 2005). *Baby mouse faces her enemy in a dodge ball match and comes out a winner.*

Babymouse #8: Puppy Love, by Jennifer L. Holm and Matthew Holm (Random House, 2007). *Babymouse has trouble with pets, but she is sure getting a dog will be different. Graphic novel format.*

Babymouse #9: Monster Mash, by Jennifer L. Holm and Matthew Holm (Random

House, 2008). *Baby mouse and the bullies at Halloween. Graphic format.*

Complete Version of Ye Three Blind Mice, by John W. Ivimey (Warne, 1979). *Contains sheet music and story in rhyme with illustrations that can be sung to the music.*

Cottonball Colin, by Jeanne Willis (Eerdmans, 2008). *Colin is the smallest mouse child in the family, and not allowed to go outside to play because mother is too worried he might get hurt. Grandma suggests wrapping him in cotton.*

The Country Mouse and the City Mouse, by Eric Blair (Picture Window, 2004).

The Country Mouse and the City Mouse, by Laura Lydecker (Knopf, 1987).

Frederick, by Leo Lionni (Dragonfly Books, 1973).

Hickory Dickory Dock, by Keith Baker (HMH, 2007). *There's more than just the nursery rhyme in this story.*

If You Give a Mouse a Cookie, by Laura Numeroff (series; HarperCollins, 1985). *"If you give a mouse a cookie, he'll ask for a glass of milk," is the story of a child trying to please a little guest.*

The Little Mouse, the Red Ripe Strawberry and the Big Hungry Bear, by Don and Audrey Wood (Scholastic, 1984). *A little mouse learns how to protect the things he treasures, and discovers the joy in sharing.*

Little Mouse's Big Book of Fears, by Emily Gravett (Simon & Schuster, 2008).

The Mouse Before Christmas, by Michael Garland (Dutton, 1997).

Mouse Count, by Ellen Walsh (Harcourt Brace, 1991).

Mouse Match: A Chinese Folktale, by Ed Young (Silver Whistle, 1997).

Mouse Paint, by Ellen Stoll Walsh (Harcourt Brace, 1989). *Three white mice play in buckets of red, yellow and blue paint, creating new colors—and a good time—as they cross paths. Helpful for teaching mixing colors.*

Mouse Tails, by Arnold Lobel (HarperCollins, 1978). *Seven mouse boys lie awake one night and ask father to tell them a story. He tells them seven stories, one for each boy. A chapter book.*

Mouse Went Out to Get a Snack, by Lyn Rossiter McFarland (Farrar, Straus & Giroux, 2005). *Cute text. Mouse is counting food but gets too much. Short text, preschool age.*

Mrs. Brice's Mice, by Syd Hoff (HarperCollins, 1991). *Mrs. Brice has 25 mice and they all do everything together. (Great for a classroom of 25 children.)*

One Moose, 20 Mice, by Claire Beaton (Barefoot Books, 2000). *Count the animals from 1 to 20, but keep your eye on that sneaky cat!*

The Tale of Despereaux. The Deluxe Movie Storybook (Candlewick Press, 2008). *A book with fold-out pages, but difficult reading. Fun to look at!*

The Town Mouse and the Country Mouse, by Bernadette Watts (North-South Books, 1998).

The Town Mouse and the Country Mouse, by Helen Craig (Candlewick, 1995).

The Town Mouse and the Country Mouse, by Helen Ward (Templar, 2012).

The Town Mouse and the Country Mouse, by Janet Stevens (Holiday House, 1987).

The Town Mouse and the Country Mouse, by Lorinda Bryan Cauley (Picadilly Press, 1984).

The Town Mouse and the Country Mouse, by Paul Galdone (HMH, 2012).

Town Mouse, Country Mouse, by Jan Brett (G.P. Putnam's Sons, 1994). *Beautiful illustrations and story. The animals all wear clothing. Two mice couples exchange houses. The story is a little long for preschoolers, probably best for K–2.*

Town Mouse Country Mouse, by Carol Jones (Houghton, 1994). *Cute illustrations with peepholes. Text is a little long for very young children.*

Upstairs Mouse, Downstairs Mole, by Wong H. Yee (Houghton Mifflin, 2005). *Mouse and Mole are neighbors and friends, but still have a hard time getting along. A chapter book.*

Valentine Mice! by Bethany Roberts (Clarion, 1997).

Whose Mouse Are You? by Robert Kraus (Macmillan, 1970).

Movies and Television

An American Tail (Universal, 1986).

Cinderella (Disney, 2015).

Dumbo (Disney, 1941).

The Great Mouse Detective (Disney, 1986).

Little Sneezer (Tiny Toon Adventures, 1990).

Mickey Mouse (Disney, created in 1928).

Minnie Mouse (Disney, 1928).

The Mouse and His Child (Audible Book, by Russell Hoban, 2012).

Mouse Hunt (DreamWorks, 1997).

The Muppets (Disney, The Mouse Family; The Muppet Christmas Carol).

Once Upon a Forest (Hanna-Barbera, 1993).

Pinky and the Brain (TV series, Warner Bros. 1995).

Ratatouille (rats) (Disney, 2007).

Rescuers (Disney, 1997).

Rescuers Down Under (Disney, 1990).

The Secret of Nimh 1, 2 (Aurora, Don Bluth, 1982, 1998).

Speedy Gonzoles (Warner Bros., 1955).

Stuart Little 1, 2, 3 (Columbia Pictures, 1999, 2002, 2005).

The Tale of Desperaux (Universal, 2008; TV series, 2012).

Tom & Jerry (Hanna-Barbera, 1990–1994, TV series).

The Witches (Jim Henson Co., Lorimar, 1990).

9. The Frog Prince; The Princess and the Frog

Playing with her ball one day, the princess loses it in a pond. A frog offers to return it to her in exchange for coming to the castle to stay with the princess. Once she has the ball, the princess forgets her promise and runs off to the castle. The frog later appears and demands entrance. Most stories end with the princess reluctantly kissing the frog, who then turns into a prince.

9a. Frog

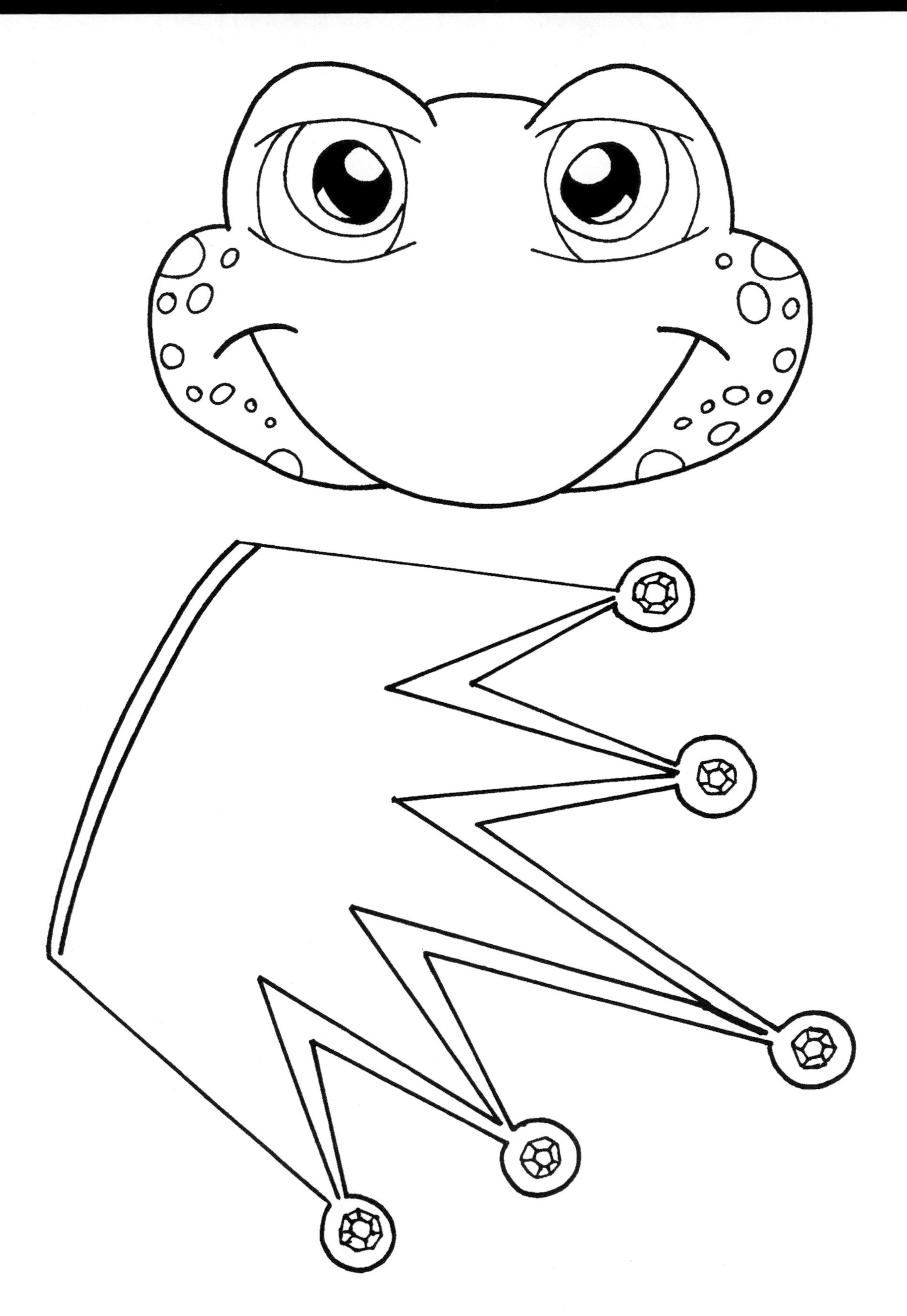

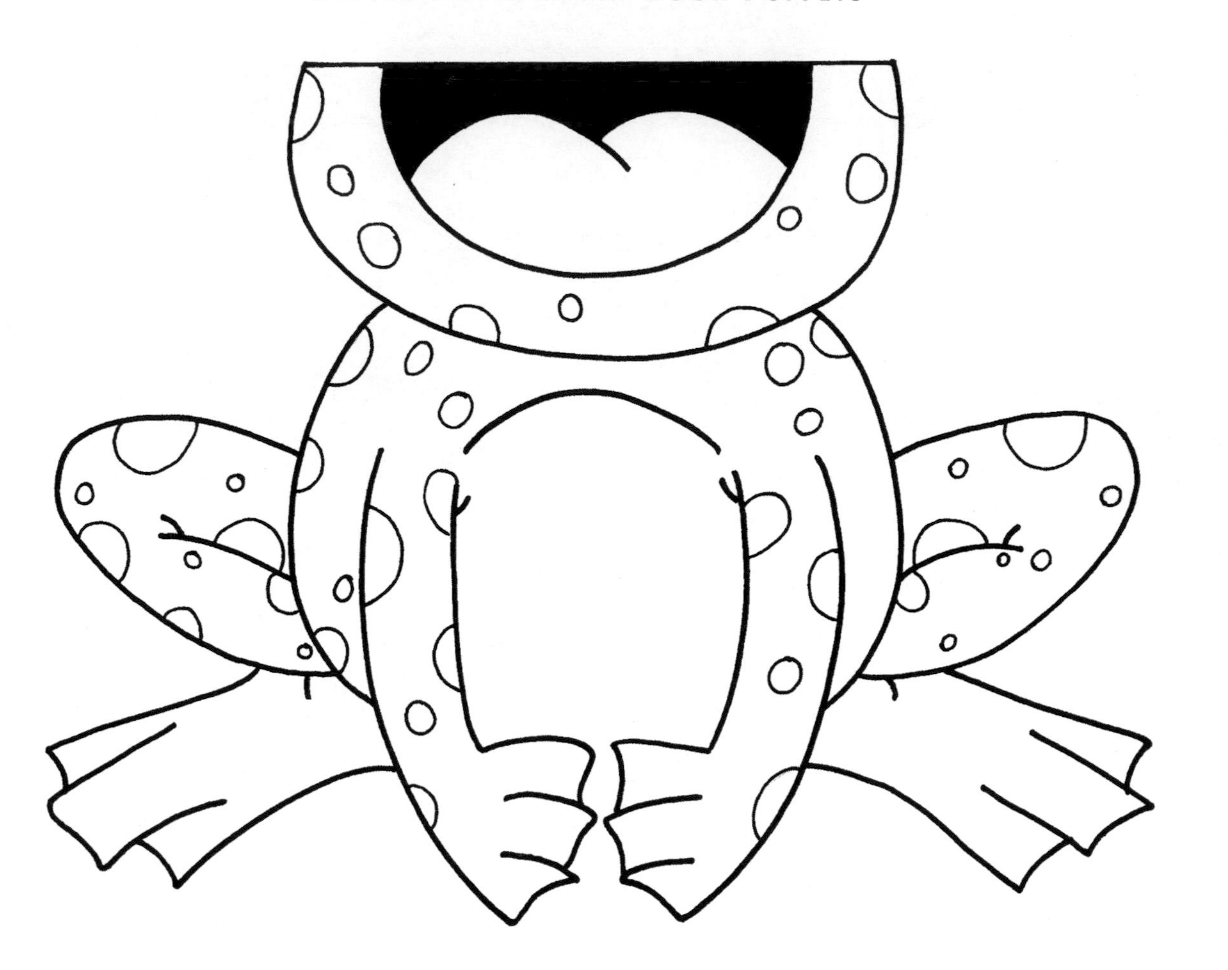

Frog Activities

Songs to Sing and Play

The Big Mouth Frog

Sung by The Lamanite Generation

"What do you feed your babies?
I feed them *big mouth* frogs!"

Flip Flop Went the Little Green Frog

Traditional camp song

Flip flop went the little green frooooog one day...
Flip flop went the little green frooooog.
Flip flop went the little green frooooog one day,
And they all went flip flop flip.

But, we all know frogs go (clap) ladedadeda (clap)
Ladedadeda (clap), Ladedadeda (clap)
We all know frogs go (clap) ladedadeda
They don't go flip flop flip.

Frog Went A-Courtin' (version 2)

Traditional English folk song (from "A Froggie Would A Wooing Go," The Baby's Opera, *by Walter Crane, 1877). (See drjean.org for music.)*

Frog went a courtin' and he did ride, uh-huh
Frog went a courtin' and he did ride, uh-huh
Frog went a courtin' and he did ride
With a sword and a pistol by his side,
uh-huh uh-huh uh-huh

He rode right up to Miss Mousie's door,
uh-huh

He rode right up to Miss Mousie's door,
uh-huh
He rode right up to Miss Mousie's door
Gave three loud raps, and a very big roar,
uh-huh uh-huh uh-huh

Said Miss Mouse, are you within, uh-huh
Said Miss Mouse, are you within, uh-huh
Said Miss Mouse, are you within
Miss Mousie said, I sit and spin, uh-huh,
uh-huh, uh-huh

Took Miss Mousie on his knee, uh-huh
Took Miss Mousie on his knee, uh-huh
Took Miss Mousie on his knee,
Said Miss Mousie, will you marry me, uh-huh,
uh-huh, uh-huh

Without my Uncle Rat's consent, uh-huh
Without my Uncle Rat's consent, uh-huh
Without my Uncle Rat's consent,
I wouldn't marry the President, uh-huh, uh-huh, uh-huh

Uncle Rat laughed, and he shook his fat
sides, uh-huh
Uncle Rat laughed, and he shook his fat
sides, uh-huh
Uncle Rat laughed, and he shook his fat
sides
To think his niece would be a bride, uh-huh,
uh-huh, uh-huh

Uncle Rat went running downtown, uh-huh
Uncle Rat went running downtown, uh-huh
Uncle Rat went running downtown
To buy his niece a wedding gown, uh-huh,
uh-huh, uh-huh

Where shall the wedding supper be, uh-huh
Where shall the wedding supper be, uh-huh
Where shall the wedding supper be
Way down yonder in the hollow tree, uh-huh,
uh-huh, uh-huh

What shall the wedding supper be, uh-huh
What shall the wedding supper be, uh-huh
What shall the wedding supper be
Fried mosquito and a black-eyed pea, uh-huh, uh-huh, uh-huh

First to come in was a flyin' moth, uh-huh...

Alternate:

A frog went a-courtin',
And he did ride. Hum-hum, hum-hum.
A frog went a-courtin',
And he did ride,
With his horse right by his side.
Hum-hum, hum-hum.

He rode up to Miss Mousie's den
Said, "Please, Miss Mousie, let me in
"Yes, Sir Frog, I sit and spin...
Please, Mr. Froggie, won't you come in?"

The frog said, "My dear, I've come to see...
If, Miss Mousie, you'll marry me..."
"Oh, yes, Sir Frog, I'll marry you...
And we'll have children two by two..."

The frog and mouse they went to France...
And that's the end of my romance...

Tune: Ten Little Indians (Frogs)

Traditional tune. Words by Eunice Wright

One Little, two little, three little frogs,
Four little, five little, six little frogs,
Seven little, eight little, nine little frogs,
Jumping up and down.

(Repeat song, changing the action words: running, hopping, skipping, dancing, sliding, crawling, swimming.)

There's a Frog on a Log

Traditional. Make up your own verses.

There's a hole in the bottom of the sea,
There's a hole in the bottom of the sea,
There's a hole, there's a hole,
There's a hole in the bottom of the sea.

There's a frog in the middle of the _______
(pond, well, lily pad, swamp, etc.).

The Frog and the Crow

Traditional English folk song, The Baby's Opera, *by Walter Crane, 1877.*

A jolly fat frog
Lived in the river swim O!
A comely black crow

Lived on the river brim O!
"Come on shore, Come on shore,"
Said the crow to the frog
And then O!
"No you'll bite me,
No you'll bite me"
Said the frog to the crow
Again O!

"O there is sweet music
On yonder green hill O!
And you shall be a dancer,
A dancer in yellow,
All in yellow, All in yellow"
Said the crow to the frog
And then O!
"All in yellow,
All in yellow"
Said the frog to the crow
And then O!

"Farewell, ye little fishes
That in the river swim O!
I'm going to be a dancer,
A dancer in yellow."
"O beware! O beware!"
Said the fish to the frog
And then O!
"I'll take care,
I'll take care,"
Said the frog to the fish
Again O!

The frog began a swimming,
A swimming to land O!
And the crow began jumping
To give him a hand O!
"Sir, you're welcome, Sir, you're welcome,"
Said the crow to the frog
And then O!
"Sir, I thank you,
Sir, I thank you,"
Said the frog to the crow
Again O!

"But where is the sweet music
On yonder green hill O?
And where are the dancers,
The dancers all in yellow?
All in yellow, All in yellow,"
Said the frog to the crow
And then O!
"Sir, they're here,
Sir, they're here,"
Said the crow to the frog—
(Swallows the frog)
GULP!

The Frog and the Mouse

Traditional folk song (from: A Froggie Would A Wooing Go), The Baby's Opera *by Walter Crane, 1877.*

There was a frog lived in a well,
Whipsee diddledee dandy dee,
There was a mouse lived in a mill,
Whipsee diddledee dandy dee.
This frog he would a-wooing ride,
With sword and buckler by his side.
With a harum scarum diddle dum darum,
Whipsee diddledee dandy dee.

He rode till he came to Mouse's Hall,
Whipsee diddledee dandy dee,
Where he most tenderly did call,
Whipsee diddledee dandy dee.
"Oh! Mistress Mouse, are you at home?
And if you are, oh pray, come down."
With a harum scarum diddle dum darum,
Whipsee diddledee dandy dee.

"My Uncle Rat is not at home;
Whipsee diddledee dandy dee,
I dare not for my life come down."
Whipsee diddledee dandy dee.
Then Uncle Rat he soon comes home,
"And who's been here since I've been gone?"
With a harum scarum diddle dum darum,
Whipsee diddledee dandy dee.

"Here's a fine young gentleman,
Whipsee diddledee dandy dee,
Who swears he'll have me if he can."
Whipsee diddledee dandy dee.
Then Uncle Rat gave his consent,
And made a handsome settlement.
With a harum scarum diddle dum darum,
Whipsee diddledee dandy dee.

Four partridge pies with season made,
Whipsee diddledee dandy dee,

Two potted larks and marmalade,
Whipsee diddledee dandy dee.
Four woodcocks and a venison pie,
I would that at that feast were I!
With a harum scarum diddle dum darum,
Whipsee diddledee dandy dee.

Moral Song

Songs for Parents, *John Farrar, 1922.*

Oh, so cool
In his deep green pool
Was a frog on a log one day!
He would blink his eyes
As he snapped at flies,
For his mother was away,
For his mother was away!

Now that naughty frog
Left his own home log
And started out to play.
He flipped and he flopped
And he never stopped
Till he reached the great blue bay,
Till he reached the great blue bay!

Alas, with a swish
Came a mighty fish,
And swallowed him where he lay.
Now it's things like this
That never miss
Little frogs who don't obey,
Little frogs who don't obey!

Spring Wish

Songs for Parents, *John Farrar, 1922.*

A frog's a very happy thing,
Cool and green in early spring,
Quick and silver through the pool,
With no thought of books or school.
Oh, I want to be a frog,
Sunning, stretching on a log,
Blinking there in splendid ease,
Swimming naked when I please,
Nosing into magic nooks,
Quiet marshes, noisy brooks.
Free! And fit for anything!
Oh, to be a frog in spring!

Other Songs

"The Bullfrog Song," DLTK (sheet music with lyrics)—*Recommended!* (DLTK-Teach.com).
"A Clever Amphibian," *I Have a Song for You* by Janeen Brady (Brite Music Enterprises, 1979), page 21.
"Froggy!" Camp Song. See *Pete's Activity Advice for Camps and All.*
"Hop Over It," by Jack Hartmann.
"It's Not Easy Bein' Green," sung by Kermit the Frog, by Joe Raposo (*The Muppet Show*).

Poems and Nursery Rhymes

Five Little Speckled Frogs

Nursery Rhyme and Traditional Tune

On the Internet there is a creative activity that can be used with this rhyme located in the Rainbow Resource Room, Counting and Number Theme.

Five little speckled frogs,
Sitting on a speckled log,
Eating some most delicious bugs ... yum, yum!
One jumped into the pool,
Where it was nice and cool.
Now there are four green speckled frogs.
"Glub, Glub."

Repeat song, subtracting a frog each time. Continue until only one frog is left (or none).

One little speckled frog.
Sitting on a speckled log,
Eating the most delicious bugs ... yum,yum.
He jumped into the pool
Where it was nice and cool.
Now there are no speckled frogs.

Mr. Bullfrog

By Eunice Wight

Mr. Bullfrog goes, "Gar-rump!"
The froggies all say, "Rivett."
But my favorite is the little toad,
Who says, "(Here), Cricket, Cricket, Cricket!"

(Mix and match sounds and frogs—pollywog, tagpole, etc.)

Froggie

Chinese Mother Goose Rhymes, *by Isaac Taylor, 1900.*

Froggie, old froggie,
Come over to me;
You'll never go back
To your home in the sea.
You're an idle old croker
As ever I saw,
And if not calling papa,
You're calling the mama.

Hippy-Hi-Hoppy

The Peter Patter Book of Nursery Rhymes, *by Leroy F. Jackson, 1918.*

Hippy-Hi-Hoppy, the big fat toad,
Greeted his friends at a turn of the road.

Said he to the snail:
"Here's a ring for your tail
If you'll go into town for my afternoon mail."

Said he to the rat:
"I have talked with the cat;
And she'll nab you so quick you won't know where you're at."

Said he to the lizard:
"I'm really no wizard,
But I'll show you a trick that will tickle your gizzard."

Said he to the lark:
"When it gets fairly dark
We'll chase the mosquitoes in Peek-a-Boo Park."

Said he to the owl:
"If it were not for your scowl
I'd like you as well as most any wild fowl."

Said he to the wren:
"You're tiny, but then
I'll marry you quick, if you'll only say when."

Five Frogs on a Lily Pad

By Eunice Wright

Five green frogs sat on a lily pad,
And paddled it 'round like a boat.
The first frog slipped and then fell off,
But quickly learned how to float.

The second frog tried to be in front,
And paddled in a hurry.
It wasn't long before he met
Something big and furry.

The third frog liked the scenic view,
And laid on his back to rest.
But soon he felt a little pressure
Right upon his chest.

"Get off, Get off!," he cried aloud,
And kicked and pushed away,
Until the fourth frog tumbled off,
And floated away in the bay.

The last little frog was left alone,
Riding the lily pad boat.
Soon a princess scooped him up,
And with a kiss, he became a goat.

Five Little Froggies

Author Unknown

Five little froggies sitting on a well
One looked up, and down he fell...

Little Frog

By Juli Wright

There's a little frog who lives in a bog,
Who sits and waits all day on a log.
He waits until his dinner is near,
And gulps it down with a giant sneer.

Frogs at School

The Children's Book of Poetry, *by George Cooper; illustrated by Henry T. Coates, 1879.*

Twenty froggies went to school
Down beside a rushy pool:
Twenty little coats of green,
Twenty vests all white and clean.
"We must be in time," said they;
"First we study, then we play;
That is how we keep the rule
When we froggies go to school."

Master Bullfrog, grave and stern,
Called the classes in their turn;
Taught them how to nobly strive,
Likewise how to leap and dive;
From his seat upon the log,
Showed them how to say "Ker-chog!"
Also how to dodge a blow
From the sticks that bad boys throw.

Twenty froggies grew up fast;
Bullfrogs they became at last;
Not one lesson they forgot;
Polished in a high degree,
As each froggie ought to be,
Now they sit on other logs,
Teaching other little frogs.

The Frog

Bad Child's Book of Beasts, *by Hilaire Belloc, 1896.*

Be kind and tender to the Frog,
And do not call him names,
As "Slimy skin," or "Polly-Wog,"
Or likewise "Ugly James,"
Or "Gap-a-grin," or "Toad-gone-wrong,"
Or "Bill Bandy-knees":
The Frog is justly sensitive
To epithets like these.
No animal will more repay
A treatment kind and fair;
At least so lonely people say
Who keep a frog (and by the way,
They are extremely rare).
Oh! My!

The Phrisky Phrog

In My Nursery: A Book of Verse, *by Laura E. Richards, 1890.*

Now list, oh! list to the piteous tale
Of the Phrisky Phrog and the Sylvan Snayle;

Of their lives and their loves, their joys and their woes,
And all about them that any one knows.

The Phrog lived down in a gruesome bog,
The Snayle in a hole in the end of a log;

And they loved each other so fond and true,
They didn't know what in the world to do.

For the Snayle declared 'twas too cold and damp
For a lady to live in a gruesome swamp;

While her lover replied, that a hole in a log
Was no possible place for a Phrisky Phrog.

"Come down! come down, my beautiful Snayle!
With your elegant horns and your tremulous tail;

Come down to my bower in the blossomy bog,
And be happy with me," said the Phrisky Phrog.

"Come up, come up, to my home so sweet,
Where there's plenty to drink, and the same to eat;

Come up where the cabbages bloom in the vale,
And be happy with me," said the Sylvan Snayle.

But he wouldn't come, and she wouldn't go,
And so they could never be married, you know;

Though they loved each other so fond and true,
They didn't know what in the world to do.

Some Fishy Nonsense

In My Nursery: A Book of Verse, *by Laura E. Richards, 1890.*

Timothy Tiggs and Tomothy Toggs,
They both went a-fishing for pollothywogs;
They both went a-fishing
Because they were wishing
To see how the creatures would turn into frogs.

Timothy Tiggs and Tomothy Toggs,
They both got stuck in the bogothybogs;
They caught a small minnow,
And said 'twas a sin oh!
That things with no legs should pretend to be frogs.

Games and Group Activities

Frog in the Middle

Games for Everybody, by May C. Hofmann. Dodge Publishing Co., 1905

The children form a ring. One, the frog, is chosen, and he stands in the middle of the circle. The children, holding hands, dance around him, saying: "Frog in the middle, jump in, jump out." As the last line is sung, the frog takes one child by the hands and pulls him to the center, exchanging places with him. The children continue dancing around and singing while the frogs jump thick and fast. The game continues until all have been frogs or are tired out.

Books

Aesop's Fables: The Happy Frogs. The frogs pray for a king.

All About Frogs, by Jim Arnosky (Scholastic Press, 2002). *Nice easy text and good illustrations.*

(Animals Animals) Frogs, by Martin Schwabacher (Benchmark Books, 2004). *Large beautiful photos, good text for older children.*

April Showers, by George Shannon (Greenwillow Books, 1995). *A group of frogs enjoy dancing in the rain so much they don't notice the snake sneaking up.*

Baby Bird's First Nest, by Frank Asch (Harcourt Brace, 1999). *Baby bird falls from mama's nest and finds a friend in Little Frog.*

The Biggest Frog in Australia, by Susan Roth (Simon & Schuster, 1996). *When a thirsty frog drinks up all the water, the other animals must think up a way to make him give it back.*

A Boy, a Dog, and a Frog, by Mercer Mayer (series; Dial, 2003).

Can You Jump Like a Frog? by Marc Brown (Dutton, 1989).

The Caterpillar and the Polliwog, by Jack Kent (Aladdin, 1985). Both creatures turn into something different.

City Dog, Country Frog, by Mo Willems.

Discovering Frogs, by Douglas Florian (Macmillan, 1986).

Down by the Cool of the Pool, by Tony Mitton.

Face to Face with Frogs, by Mark W. Moffett (National Geographic, 2008). *Beautiful photographs and a wonderful true story told by the photographer as he "shoots" frogs around the world.*

Fish Is Fish, by Leo Lionni (Pantheon Books, 1970). *Tadpole becomes a frog and fish doesn't want to be left behind.*

Five Little Speckled Frogs, illustrated by Sue Hendra (Books Are Fun, 2002). *A hands-on number board book with plastic frogs in plastic bubbles and a counting wheel to turn to the right number as you read the story.*

The Foolish Frog, by Pete Seeger.

Freddie the Frog, by Rose Greydanus (Troll, 1980).

Frog, by Susan Cooper.

Frog and Toad All Year, by Arnold Lobel (HarperCollins, 1976).

Frog and Toad Are Friends, by Arnold Lobel (HarperCollins, 1970).

Frog and Toad Together, by Arnold Lobel (HarperCollins, 1971).

A Frog in the Bog, by Karma Wilson and Joan Rankin.

The Frog in the Pond, by Wil Mara.

Frog on His Own, by Mercer Mayer (Dial, 1973).

A Frog Thing (with Audio CD), by Eric Drachman.

Frog Went A-Courtin,' by John Langstaff.

Froggie Went A-Courtin,' by Iza Trapani.

Froggy Goes to School, by Jonathan London. (Also *Froggy Bakes a Cake.*)

Frogs, by Dan Greenberg. Animal Ways (Benchmark Books, 2001). Other books in this series: *Bats, Crocodiles, Gorillas, Horses.* Lots of information, for older children. Nice photos. A reference book.

Frogs, by Gail Gibbons.

Frogs, by Nic Bishop (Scholastic, 2008). *A*

wonderful large book of photos and good text.

Frogs Jump, by Alan Brooks. *One frog jumps, 2 ducks dive, etc. Count to 12 and back again.*

Frogs Sing Songs, by Yvonne Winer (Charlesbridge, 2003). *Beautifully illustrated large pictures with a rhyming text. A frog identification guide section is at the back. Recommended for early childhood.*

From Tadpole to Frog, by Wendy Pfeffer (HarperCollins). Let's Read and Find Out Science.

Green Tree Frogs, Colorful Hiders, by Natalie Lunis (Bearport Pub., 2010). *A beautiful book with large photos and simple text.*

Green Willma, by Ted Arnold.

The Hare and the Frogs, adapted by William Stobbs (Merrimack, 1979).

Hop Jump, by Ellen Stoll Walsh (Harcourt Brace, 1993). *Bored with just hopping and jumping, frog discovers dancing.*

I Took My Frog to the Library, by Eric K. Kimmel.

If You Hopped Like a Frog, by David M. Schwartz.

In the Middle of the Puddle, by Mike Thaler (Harper and Row, 1988). *Frog and Turtle watch their puddle grow into an ocean before the sun dries it up.*

In the Small, Small Pond, by Denise Flemming (Henry Holt, 1998). *Ages 3–6, rhyming text (fish, frog, fowl). Also:* In the Tall, Tall Grass.

It's Mine! by Leo Lionni.

Jubal's Wish, by Audrey Wood (Blue Sky Press, 2000). *Jubal wishes for happiness.*

Jump! by Scott Fischer. *Many animals and creatures can jump.*

Jump, Frog, Jump! by Robert Kalan (Greenwillow Books, 1981). *A cumulative tale in which a frog tries to catch a fly without getting caught itself.*

The Lilypad, written by Eric Owen.

Marsh Music, by Marianne Berkes (Millbrook Press, 2000). *The marsh comes alive at night with frog music.*

Once There Was a Bull-frog, by Rick Walton (Gibbs Smith, 1995). *A bull-frog in the Old West loses his hop. Each page turned completes the previous one.*

One, Two, Three Jump! by Penelope Lively (McElderry Books, 1999).

The Rainy Day Puddle, by Ei Nakabayashi (Random House, 1989). *Little frog's puddle grows bigger but more crowded as more animals come to join him.*

Seven Froggies Went to School, by Kate Duke (Dutton, 1985).

Stick, by Steve Breen (Puffin, 2009). *Stick, a little frog, seems to need help...*

Tale of a Tadpole, by Karen Wallace (Dorling Kindersley Readers, 2009).

Tuesday, by David Wiesner (Clarion Books, 1991). *Frogs rise on their lily pads, float around and explore while everyone sleeps.*

Twenty Tellable Tales: Audience Participation Folktales for the Beginning Storyteller, by Margaret Read MacDonald (Wilson, 1986). *This book includes a fun story about Grandpa Parley and the frogs.*

Unusual Animals—FROGS, by Lynn M. Stone (The Rourke Corp., 1993). *Nice photos, short book, good text.*

The Wide-mouthed Frog: A Pop-up Book, by Keith Faulkner (Dial, 1996). *A wide-mouthed frog is interested in what other animals eat—until he meets a creature that eats only wide-mouthed frogs!*

Movies and Television

Kermit the Frog, character from the Muppets. Also appears on *Sesame Street.*

The Princess and the Frog (Disney, 2009, animated).

Shelley Duvall's Faerie Tale Theatre: The Tale of the Frog Prince, 1982.

9b. Princess

Princess Activities

Songs to Sing and Play

Tune: There Were 3 Jolly Fishermen

Words by Eunice Wright

There once was a princess and a frog.
There once was a princess and a frog.
Princess, Princess, Frog, Frog, Frog.
Princess, Princess, Frog, Frog, Frog.
There once was a princess and a frog.

The frog brought the golden ball...

She wouldn't kiss the frog, "No way!"
She wouldn't kiss the frog, "No way!"
"No, No, Way, Way, Way!"
"No, No, Way, Way, Way!"
She wouldn't kiss the frog, "No way!"

The frog slept on her pillow all night...
The frog sat on her dinner plate...

The King said, "Keep your promise, dear..."
The Princess said, "Fine, I will kiss the frog!"
The frog became a handsome prince...

Poems and Nursery Rhymes

The Princess and the Frog

By Eunice Wright

Once there was a princess, spoiled without a doubt;
She played with a golden ball, through the garden in and out.

One day she dropped her ball, the one made out of gold;
Into the well of water, where lived a froggie bold.

She sobbed and begged the frog, to fetch her ball right now;
But froggie made her promise first, to be his friend somehow.
She let him sleep on the royal pillow, and eat the royal dish;
And play with the royal golden ball; it was his secret wish.

The princess couldn't help it—she fell for the froggie dear;
So finally she kissed him, even though it felt so queer.

The frog was really a handsome brute, a prince under a spell;
And so they wed that very day, beside the garden well.

Books

The Adventures of the Frog Prince, by J.R. Barker.
Don't Kiss the Frog! Princess Stories with Attitude, chosen by Fiona Waters (Kingfisher, 2008).
Dragon's Breath (The Tales of the Frog Princess Series #2), by E. D. Baker.
The Frog Bride, by Antonia Barber, 2007. *A folk tale from Russia. Beautiful illustrations; story is for older children.*
A Frog Prince, by Alix Berenzy.
The Frog Prince, by Edith H. Tarcov.
The Frog Prince, by Eric Blair (Picture Window, 2004).
The Frog Prince, by Hillary Robinson and Jane Abbott.
The Frog Prince, by Jacob and William Grimm. *Spurned by the Princess after he retrieves her golden ball, the noble frog sets out to find another suitable mate.*
The Frog Prince, by Jan Ormerod.
The Frog Prince, by Kathy Jo Wargin.
The Frog Prince, by Susana Davidson.
The Frog Prince, by the Brothers Grimm, retold by Kathy-Jo Wargin, 2007. *A rich spoiled princess who doesn't want to keep her word, and is mean to the frog, still gets to marry the handsome prince.*
The Frog Prince and Other Frog Tales from Around the World, SurLaLune Fairy Tales Series, by Heidi Ann Heiner. *More than 100 stories.*
The Frog Prince Continued, by Jon Scieszka

(Viking, 1991). *Age 5+, humorous repeating story, medium to higher level, some difficult text, dark illustrations.*

The Frog Prince Fairy Tale Classics, by the Brothers Grimm (North South).

The Frog Prince's Daughters, by Wendy Palmer.

The Frog Princess, by Jan Oremod. *Best friends after 3 nights? This time it's the frog who becomes a princess.*

The Frog Princess, by Rosalind Allchin (Kids Can Press, 2001).

The Frog Who Would Be King, by Kate Walker.

Froggy's First Kiss, by Jonathan London.

Happy Ever After: The Frog Prince Hops to It, by Tony Bradman.

The Hog Prince, by Sudipta Bardhan-Quallen (Dutton, 2009). *Beautiful, large illustrations. A very cute and funny story. Preschool children will like this book.*

Hoppily Ever After, adapted by Elle D. Risco (Random House, 2009). Series: *The Princess and the Frog.*

Old, Old Fairy Tales; the Frog Prince, by Annie Anderson.

The Princess and the Frog, by Margaret Nash (Picture Window, 2004).

The Princess and the Frog, by Rachel Isadora (Greenwillow, 1989).

The Princess and the Frog, by the Brothers Grimm, retold by Will Eisner (Turnaround, 2000).

Movies and Television

Faerie Tale Theatre: The Tale of the Frog Prince, 1982.

The Princess and the Frog, Disney

The Swan Princess, Disney, 1994

10. The Gingerbread Boy

An elderly childless couple decides to make a gingerbread boy, which comes to life after coming out of the oven. With the catchphrase "Run, run, as fast as you can! You can't catch me—I'm the gingerbread man!" the gingerbread boy runs away from the old couple, a cow, a horse, a dog and a cat before finally encountering a fox, who gobbles up the gingerbread boy.

10a. Gingerbread Boy

Gingerbread Boy Activities

Songs to Sing and Play

Tune: Oh, Do You Know the Muffin Man?

Words by Eunice Wright

Oh, do you know the gingerbread boy,
The gingerbread boy, the gingerbread boy?
Oh, do you know the gingerbread boy,
Who was baked in the oven today?

Oh yes, I know the gingerbread boy...
He was very de-li-cous!

Tune: Have You Ever Seen a Lassie?

Words by Eunice Wright

Have you ever seen a gingerbread boy,
A gingerbread boy, a gingerbread boy?
Have you ever seen a gingerbread boy,
Who wasn't quickly eaten up?

With creamy frosting and a red cherry nose,
And candy dots and raisins? (Yummm....)
Have you ever seen a gingerbread boy,
Who wasn't quickly eaten up?

Tune: This Is the Way We Wash Our Clothes

Words by Eunice Wright

This is the way we make gingerbread,
Make gingerbread, make gingerbread.
This is the way we make gingerbread,
So early in the morning.

Tune: Pop! Goes the Weasel

Words by Eunice Wright

All around the kitchen table,
The woman chased the gingerbread boy.
The gingerbread boy thought 'twas all in fun—
Pop! goes the gingerbread boy!

Tune: Old MacDonald Had a Farm

Words by Eunice Wright

And on this farm he had a gingerbread boy...
With a yum, yum here...

Tune: 10 Little Indians

Words by Eunice Wright

1 little, 2 little, 3 little gingerbread boys...
All ready for us to eat!

Tune: The Wheels on the Bus

Words by Eunice Wright

The Gingerbread boy runs and runs,
Runs, and runs—runs and runs.
The Gingerbread boy runs and runs,
All around the town (farm, house, field, country-side).

Tune: Are You Sleeping?

Words by Eunice Wright

The Gingerbread boy,
The Gingerbread boy,
Ran away, ran away.
Past the little old man,
Past the little old woman,
They couldn't catch him.
They couldn't catch him.

Past the horse,
And past the cow.
Down the path,
He did go.
At the river,
He had to stop.
The Fox ate him up!
The Fox ate him up!

Tune: Are You Sleeping?

Words by Eunice Wright

Gingerbread boy,
Gingerbread boy,
Yum, yum, yum;

Yum, yum, yum.
I like gingerbread,
Fresh from the oven.
Let's eat some,
Yum, Yum, Yum.

Tune: I'm a Little Teapot

Words by Eunice Wright

I'm a little gingerbread man,
Warm and brown.
Here is my frosting,
I won't frown.

When I'm all decorated
With candy and chocolate chips,
Put me into your mouth
Right past your lips!

Tune: Down on Grandpa's Farm

Written by Robert D. Singleton/Traditional.

(See songs for teaching.com or *One Light, One Sun*—Raffi to listen to the tune.)

Alternate verse:
Down on Grandpa's Farm there is a gingerbread boy...

Tune: Oh Where, Oh Where Has My Little Dog Gone?

Words by Eunice Wright

Oh where, oh where is the gingerbread boy?
Oh where, oh where can he be?
Is he running away as fast as he can?
Oh where, oh where can he be?

Tune: Row, Row, Row Your Boat

Words by Eunice Wright

Ginger, ginger, ginger bread man,
Baking in the oven.
Merrily, Merrily, Merrily, Merrily,
He's so good to eat.

Tune: Baa, Baa, Black Sheep

Words by Eunice Wright

Gingerbread-man, Gingerbread-man, have you any sweets?
Yes sir, yes sir, 3 bags of treats.
1 bag of raisins, 1 bag of chocolate chips,
And 1 bag of frosting that sticks to your lips.

The Gingerbread Man

By Ron Brown. An instrumental version for plays and concerts is also available.

I'm a little gingerbread man, I am.
Come on and run with me.
I'm a little gingerbread man, I am.
You can run but you can't catch me.
I look so good in my
gingerbread clothes.
I'm baked so perfectly.
With my raisin eyes and
my cinnamon nose
It's no wonder everyone I see
wants to take a bite of me.
Ah-ah-ah-ah-ah!

Chorus

I'll stay all day and we can play.
I'll never move my feet.
Until the time I hear you say,
"Hey everybody, it's time to eat!"
Ah-ah-ah-ah-ah!
I'm a little gingerbread man, I am.
Come on and run with me.
I'm a little gingerbread man, I am.
You can run but you can't catch me.
I'm a little gingerbread man, I am.
You can run but you can't catch me.

The Gingerbread Girl Rap

By Jim Rule. This rap is available on Jim Rule's Let It Shine!

Poems and Nursery Rhymes

The Gingerbread Man

By Eunice Wright

A little old woman and a little old man,
Wanted to make a gingerbread man.
They stirred the dough, put it in the pan,
And then baked a little gingerbread man.

When the oven was opened to take a peak,
The gingerbread man took off with a streak.
He ran away, saying, "You can't catch me,
I'm the gingerbread man. Now let me be!"

He ran out the door and into the yard,
Past all the animals, it wasn't too hard.
The (*cow—or other animal*) thought he
looked good to eat,
And chased him around until he was beat.

The gingerbread man was fast, it is true.
But the (*horse*) was sure he could do it, too.
The gingerbread man said, "Run as fast as
you can,
You can't catch the fast gingerbread man."

The cow and the horse were way too slow,
The fast gingerbread man was raring to go.
He ran past the (*goat*) and the (*goose*), it's
true,
And only stopped at the river so blue.

There was no way to cross to the other side,
So the fox, so sly, offered him a ride.
And that was the end of the gingerbread
man,
Who was eaten by the fox as fast as *he* can.

The Gingerbread Recipe

By Eunice Wright

Take 1 bag of flour,
Add a can of spice.
Throw them in a bowl,
Boy, that smells nice!

Beat 2 chicken eggs,
And 2 from a goose.
When I cook a ginger boy,
Just turn me loose!

Add a little butter,
And a little sweet sugar.
Mix it all together,
It's better than a burger!

Roll out the dough,
So it's nice and flat.
Then you cut the Gingerbread-man,
And bake it like that!

5 Little Gingerbread Boys (Count Down)

By Eunice Wright

5 little gingerbread boys, ran away and out
the door.
1 was eaten by the cat, then there were 4.
4 little gingerbread boys, dancing 'round the
tree,
1 was eaten by the dog, then there were 3.
3 little gingerbread boys, each with an icing
shoe,
1 was eaten by the cow, then there were 2.
2 little gingerbread boys, playing in the sun,
1 was eaten by the horse, then there was 1.
1 little gingerbread boy, playing super hero,
He was eaten by a little girl/boy, now there
is zero!

Five Gingerbread Cookies (Count Down)

By Eunice Wright

Five gingerbread cookies, on the tray by the
door.
(Child's Name) ate one, then there were four.
Four little cookies, all warm and yum-my.
(Child's Name) ate the next one, then there
were three.
Three little cookies, nice and soft to chew.
(Child's Name) ate the next one, then there
were two.
Two little cookies, eat them when they're
done.
(Child's Name) ate the next one, then there
was one.
One gingerbread cookie, decided to get up
and run.
And when he was gone, then there was none.

Gingerbread Man

Poem at www.DLTK-cards.com. Recommended!

Games and Group Activities

Who Stole the (Gingerbread) Cookies from the Cookie Jar?

Oral Traditional children's chant/game

Who stole the cookies from the cookie jar (tray)?
Who, me? Yes, you!
Couldn't be! Then who?

(Child's name) stole the cookies from the cookie jar.
Who, me? Yes, you!
Couldn't be! Then who?

(Continue with as many children as desired)

Other Games

Fi Fie Fo Fum by Carol Taylor Bond. Pages 31–32 for Gingerbread boy activities.
Who Ate My Gingerbread? Online game.

Books

Cajun Gingerbread Boy, by Berthe Amoss.
Can't Catch Me!, by John and Ann Hassett (Houghton, 2006). *An ice cube escapes from the freezer and runs away, saying, "Can't catch me!" Simple story line; comical, cute illustrations. Small children will love this book. Great for puppet plays. Read this story after reading the basic gingerbread man story, and compare the two.*
Gingerbread Baby, by Jan Brett.
The Gingerbread Boy, by Scott Cook (Knopf, 1987).
The Gingerbread Boy, Paul Galdone (Seabury Press, 1975).
The Gingerbread Boy, Richard Egielski.
Gingerbread Girl, by Lisa C. Ernst (Scholastic, 2006). *A very cute book, nice illustrations, great for young children.*
The Gingerbread Man: An Old English Folktale, by John A. Rowe.
The Gingerbread Man, by Carol Jones (Houghton, 2002). *Illustrations are complicated and crowded, but the story is cute. Nursery rhyme characters are encountered by the gingerbread man—a good way to introduce or teach nursery rhymes. Recipe at end of book—great for snacks for children.*
The Gingerbread Man, by Catherine McCafferty.
The Gingerbread Man, by Eric A. Kimmel and Megan Lloyd.
The Gingerbread Man, by Jim Aylesworth (Scholastic Press, 1998). *Nice illustrations, simple story (good for retelling and for puppet plays).*
The Gingerbread Man (Easy-to-Read Folktales), by Karen Schmidt (author/illustrator), 1985.
The Gingerbread Man Loose in the School, by Laura Murray.
The Gingerbread Pirates, by Kristin Kladstrup.
Musubi Man: Hawaii's Gingerbread Man, by Sandi Takayama.

Movies and Television

The Brothers Grimm
English Talking Book—*Gingerbread Man*, 4:25, You Tube.
Fairytale: The Gingerbread Man, read by John Krasinski. 3:25, You Tube.
The Gingerbread Man (TV series, 1992). He makes friends with salt and pepper.
The Gingerbread Man Story (song by Jack Hartmann) 3:24, You Tube.
Shrek (Gingy, 2001)
The Story of the Gingerbread Man, read by Heather Padua. 4:57, You Tube.

10b. Grandma

See Grandmother (#50) for puppet pattern and Grandmother activities.

10c. Grandpa

See Grandfather (#51) for puppet pattern and Grandfather activities.

10d. Horse

COPY THE HORSE PATTERN AT 125%

COPY THE MOUTH PATTERN AT 167%

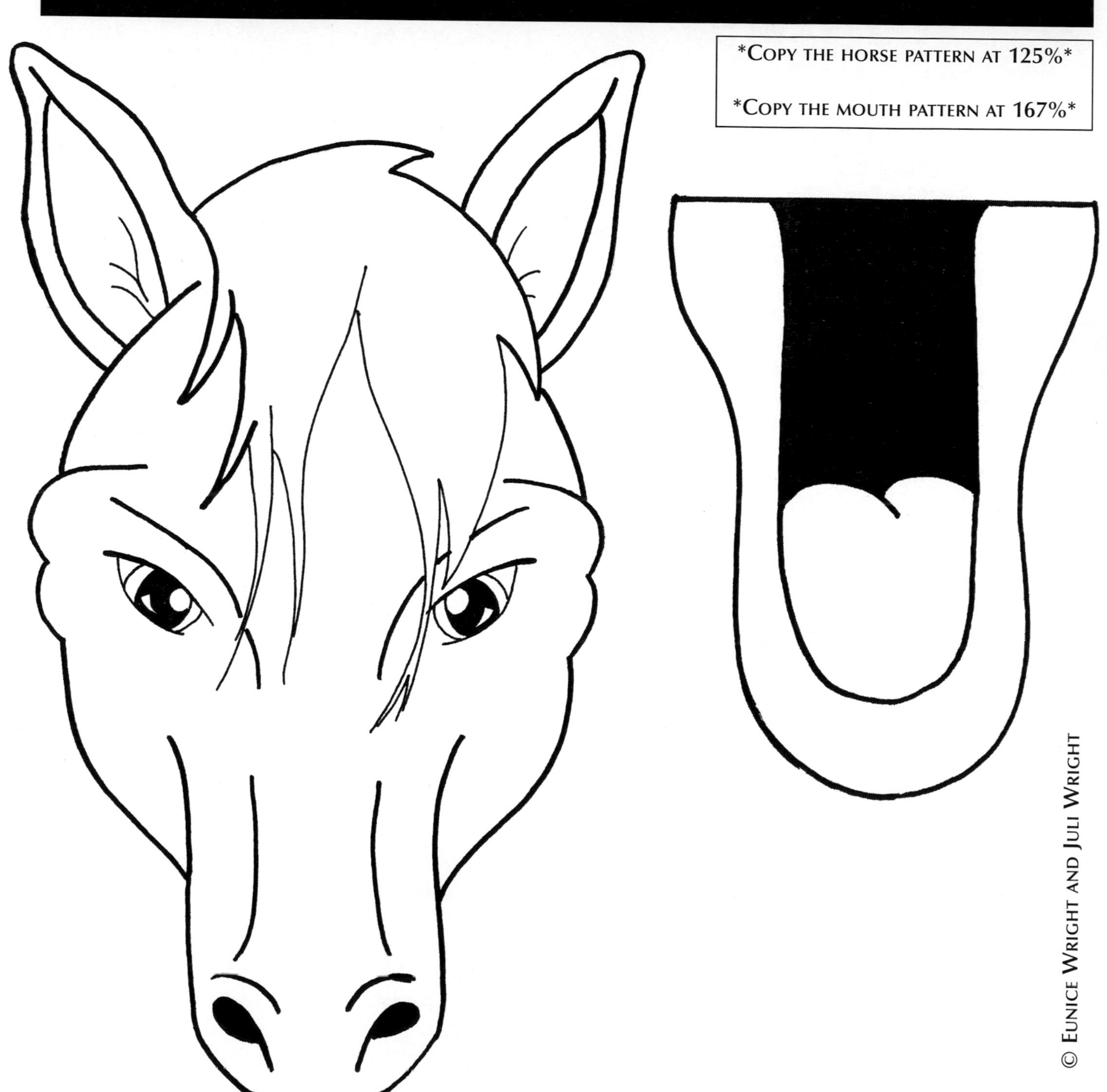

Horse Activities

Songs to Sing and Play

Bought Me a Cat

Southern traditional (see KIDiddles for more). See Cat puppet activities (#6e) for entire song.

Bought me a horse and the horse pleased me,
I fed my horse under yonder tree.
Horse goes neigh, neigh,
Cow goes moo, moo,
Pig goes oink, oink,
Sheep goes baa, baa,
Goose goes hissy, hissy,
Duck goes quack, quack,
Hen goes chimmy-chuck, chimmy-chuck,
Cat goes fiddle-i-fee.

Tune: "Mr. Ed's" Theme Song (TV series)

Original Lyrics by Jay Livingston and Ray Evans; words by Eunice Wright

Fill in blanks with appropriate words from children.

If I were a horse
A beautiful horse,
I'd like to be a (racing) horse.
I'd like to (run around the track)
And my name would be _______ (Silver Streak)

If I were a horse
A beautiful horse,
I'd like to be a (working) horse.
I'd like to (pull a wagon or cart)
And my name would be _______ (Big John)

If I were a horse
A beautiful horse,
I'd like to be a (merry-go-round) horse.
I'd like to (go up and down)
And my name would be _______ (Prancing Dan)

All the Pretty Little Horses

Traditional American folk song (First printed in On the Trail of Negro Folk Songs *by Dorothy Scarborough, 1925. Believed to be older than this first printing.)*

Hush-a-bye, don't you cry
Go to sleep my little baby
When you wake, you shall see
Coach and six-a-little horses

Blacks and bays, dapples and grays
Coach and six-a-little horses
When you wake you shall have
All the pretty little horses

Hush-a-bye, don't you cry
Go to sleep my little baby
When you wake, you shall have
All the pretty little horses

Blacks and bays, dapples and grays
All the pretty little horses
Blacks and bays, dapples and grays
All the pretty little horses

The Old Gray Mare

Adapted traditional spiritual

The old gray mare,
She ain't what she used to be
Ain't what she used to be,
Ain't what she used to be
The old gray mare,
She ain't what she used to be
Many long years ago.

Many long years ago,
Many long years ago,
The old gray mare,
She ain't what she used to be
Many long years ago.

The old gray mare,
She kicked on the whiffletree,
Kicked on the whiffletree,
Kicked on the whiffletree
The old gray mare,
She kicked on the whiffletree
Many long years ago.

Many long years ago,
Many long years ago,
The old gray mare,

She kicked on the whiffletree
Many long years ago.

Oh, the Horse Went Around (Tune: Turkey in the Straw)

1. Oh, the horse went around with his foot off the ground,...

Chorus: (spoken)
Same song, second verse,
A little bit faster and a little bit worse!

2. Oh, the horse went around with his foot off the ______.

(Chorus to be spoken after each verse)

3. Oh, the horse went around with his foot off _____ ______.

4–12. Continue leaving off a word with each verse until whole song is sung silently. End song by repeating verse 1.

Horsey, Horsey

By Paddy Roberts, 1938. A camp round—or sing each verse separately, then sing both together in harmony.

Horsey, horsey don't you stop. Just let your feet go clippetty clop...

Boom, Boom, Ain't It Great to Be Crazy?

Thought to be an oral traditional camp song. See Wee Sing Silly Songs *for tune/sheet music.*

A horse and a flea and three blind mice
Sat on a curb-stone shooting dice...

Dapple-Gray—Tune: 99 Bottles of Pop

Harry's Ladder to Learning, with Two Hundred and Thirty Illustrations, *by David Bogue and Joseph Cundall, 1850.*

I had a little pony,
His name was Dapple Gray,
I lent him to a lady,
To ride a mile away.

She whipp'd him,
She lash'd him,
She rode him
Through the mire;
I would not lend
My pony now
For all the lady's hire.

Sally, the Camel (Tune: Dem Bones)

Traditional spiritual song, by James Weldon Johnson (1871–1938)

Try singing this tune using other animals or people: Molly, the monkey has one tail; Nellie, the horse has four legs; Newton, the Newt has four legs; Tommy, the Turtle has one shell; Peter, the rabbit has two ears (or one carrot); Rapunzel the princess has long hair; Sir John, the knight has one sword; Merlin the wizard has one wand.

Sally the Camel has two humps,
Sally the Camel has two humps,
Sally the Camel has two humps,
So Ride Sally, Ride!
Boom, Boom, boom.

Sally the Camel has one hump,
Sally the Camel has one hump,
Sally the Camel has one hump,
So Ride Sally, Ride!
Boom, Boom, Boom.

Sally the Camel has no humps,
Sally the Camel has no humps,
Sally the Camel has no humps,
Now Sally ... is a *Horse!*

Tune: Oh Where, Oh Where Has My Little Dog Gone?

Words by Eunice Wright

Oh where, oh where is the horse on the farm?
Oh where, oh where can she be?
Is she running around *(change actions as needed)*
Or eating some grass?
Oh where, or where can she be?

Tune: The Wheels on the Bus

Words by Eunice Wright

The horses in the field
Go neigh, neigh, neigh,

Neigh, neigh, neigh,
Neigh, neigh, neigh.
The horses in the field
Go neigh, neigh, neigh.
All around the farm.

Tune: Mary Had a Little Lamb

Substitute child's name and kinds of horses; prancing pony, gray mare, jumping horse, pulling horse, farm horse, horse and buggy, draft horse, Arabian horse, plow horse, etc.

Susie had a racing horse, racing horse, racing horse,
Susie had a racing horse,
Its mane was flying in the wind.

She'll Be Comin' Round the Mountain

Oral Traditional predates 1890. Oldest printed version, 1927, American Sandbag. See Dr. Jean's website for a great version.

She'll be comin' round the mountain when she comes. Yeehaw! (Yeehaw!: Fist in air.)
She'll be comin' round the mountain When she comes. Yeehaw!
She'll be comin' round the mountain,
She'll be comin' round the mountain,
She'll be comin' round the mountain
When she comes. Yeehaw!

She'll be driving 6 white horses when she comes... Whoa back! (Pull back on reins.)

We'll all go out to greet (meet) her when she comes... Hi ya'll! (Wave hand.)

She'll be wearing red pajamas... Scratch, scratch! (Scratch self.)

She will have to sleep with grandma... Zzzz! Zzzz! (Close eyes and snore.)

We will all have chicken and dumplings... Yum! Yum! (Pat tummy.)

She'll Be Coming Round the Mountain, Alternate verses

Yee Haa!

She'll be coming round the mountain when she comes...
Singin' "Aye Aye Yippee Yippee Aye,"
Singin' "Aye Aye Yippee Yippee Aye,"
Singin' "Aye Aye Yippee, Aye Aye Yippee,"
"Aye Aye Yippee Yippee Aye."
She'll be driving six white horses when she comes, (Yee Haa)...
Singin' "Aye Aye Yippee Yippee Aye..."
Oh, we'll all go out to meet her when she comes ...
Singin' "Aye Aye Yippee Yippee Aye..."
She'll be wearing pink pajamas when she comes...
Singin' "Aye Aye Yippee Yippee Aye..."

Yee Haa!

Other Songs

"Magic Pony," by Jack Hartmann.
"My Little Pony," *I Have a Song for You About Animals*, by Janeen Brady, page 9.

Poems and Nursery Rhymes

This Is the Way the Ladies Ride

The Nursery Rhyme Book, *edited by Andrew Lang, 1897.*

This is the way the ladies ride,
Nimble, nimble, nimble.
This is the way the gentlemen ride,
A gallop, a trot, a gallop, a trot.
This is the way the farmers ride,
Joggety-jog, joggety-jog.
And when they come to a hedge—they jump over!
And when they come to a slippery space—
They scramble, scramble, scramble,
Tumble-down Dick!

The Farmer and the Raven

The Nursery Rhyme Book, *edited by Andrew Lang, 1897.*

A farmer went trotting upon his gray mare,
Bumpety, bumpety, bump!
With his daughter behind him so rosy and fair,

Lumpety, lumpety, lump!
A raven cried croak! and they all tumbled down,
Bumpety, bumpety, bump!
The mare broke her knees, and the farmer his crown,
Lumpety, lumpety, lump!
The mischievous raven flew laughing away,
Bumpety, bumpety, bump!
And vowed he would serve them the same the next day,
Lumpety, lumpety lump!

For Want of a Nail

The Home Book of Verse, Vol. 1 (of 4). *Author: Burton Egbert Stevenson. Various editors, 1912.*

For want of a nail, the shoe was lost;
For want of the shoe, the horse was lost;
For want of the horse, the rider was lost;
For want of the rider, the battle was lost;
For want of the battle, the kingdom was lost;
And all from the want of a horseshoe nail.

Shoe the Horse

Love and Law in Child Training: A Book for Mothers, by Emilie Poulsson, 1899.

Shoe the horse, shoe the mare,
But let the little colt go bare.

Pitty, patty, polt.
Shoe the wild colt;
Here a nail and there a nail,
Pitty, patty polt.

Here Goes My Lord

The Real Mother Goose, by Blanche Fisher Wright, 1916.

Here goes my lord
A trot, a trot, a trot, a trot,
Here goes my lady
A canter, a canter, a canter, a canter!
Here goes my young master
Jockey-hitch, jockey-hitch, jockey-hitch, jockey-hitch!
Here goes my young miss
An amble, an amble, an amble, an amble!
The footman lags behind to tipple ale and wine,
And goes gallop, a gallop, a gallop, to make up his time.

The Hobby-Horse

The Real Mother Goose, *by Blanche Fisher Wright, 1916.*

I had a little hobby-horse,
And it was dapple gray;
Its head was made of pea-straw,
Its tail was made of hay,
I sold it to an old woman
For a copper groat;
And I'll not sing my song again
Without another coat.

If Wishes Were Horses

The Real Mother Goose, *by Blanche Fisher Wright, 1916.*

If wishes were horses, beggars would ride.
If turnips were watches, I would wear one by my side.
And if "ifs" and "ands"
Were pots and pans,
There'd be no work for tinkers!

Money and the Mare

The Real Mother Goose, *by Blanche Fisher Wright, 1916.*

"Lend me thy mare to ride a mile."
"She is lamed, leaping over a stile."
"Alack, and I must keep the fair!
I'll give the money for thy mare."
"Oh, oh! Say you so?
Money will make the mare to go!"

The Runaway

Child Songs of Cheer, *by Evaleen Stein (1918).*

A frantic clatter of horses' feet!
A runaway's coming down the street!

Flurry, scurry,
Children, hurry!
Drop your playthings! Quick! don't wait!
Run and get within the gate!
Push the baby in the door,
Scramble in yourselves before
—Whoa! Whoa!
There they go!
Pell-mell rushing, snorting, quaking,
Wagon rumbling, harness breaking,
Frightened so they cannot know
Everybody's shrieking "Whoa!"
O my, don't cry!
Whiz, bang, they've galloped by!
No one hurt, but horses dashed
Round a post and wagon smashed!
Dear me! Dear me!
When a runaway we see,
Children, too, must run, oh, fast!
Run and hide as it goes past!

Bell Horses

The Real Mother Goose, *by Blanche Fisher Wright, 1916.*

Bell horses, bell horses, what time of day?
One o'clock, two o'clock, three and away.

Ride a Cock-horse to Banbury Cross

Harry's Ladder to Learning, with Two Hundred and Thirty Illustrations, *by David Bogue and Joseph Cundall, 1850.*

Ride a cock-horse to Banbury Cross,
To see an old woman ride on a white horse,
With rings on her fingers and bells on her toes,
And she shall have music wherever she goes.

Games and Group Activities

She'll Be Comin' Round the Mountain

Write key words for each verse of "She'll Be Comin' Round the Mountain" on a paper plate. (Yee haw! Whoa back! Hi ya'll! Scratch, scratch! Zzzz! Zzzz! Yum! Yum!) Have children demonstrate these.

Choose children to hold the plates up in the air in sequential order with the corresponding puppets as you sing the song.

For the puppets: "She"—use the girl/woman or princess puppet; make six white horses; make red pajamas and add to girl puppet; a grandma; a bowl with chicken and dumplings from the Little Red Hen puppet accessories.

Books

Anna's Prince, by Krista Ruepp (North South Books, 2006). *A young girl gets a horse. Great illustrations, long text, good for older children who love horses.*
Billy and Blaze; A Boy and His Horse, by C.W. Anderson (1992).
The Black Stallion, by Walter Farley (1991).
Blaze and the Grey Spotted Pony, by C.W. Anderson.
Every Cowgirl Needs a Horse, by Rebecca Janni (2010).
Everything Horse: What Kids Really Want to Know About Horses, by Marty Crisp.
Florian the Emperor's Horse, by Felix Salten.
For Horse-Crazy Girls Only: Everything You Want to Know About Horses, by Christina Wilsdon (2010).
Fritz and the Beautiful Horses, by Jan Brett (Sandpiper Books).
Girls and Their Horses, by Camela Decaire (American Girl Library, 2006).
The Horse in Harry's Room, Level 1, by Syd Hoff (1985).
Horse Show, Level 2 reader (Dorling Kindersley).
Horses, by Laura Discoll (1997).
Horses, by Margo Lundell.
Horses in the Fog, by Krista Ruepp.
Iron Horses, by Verla Kay.
The Kingfisher Illustrated Horse and Pony Encyclopedia, by Sandy Ransford (2010).
Midnight Rider, by Krista Ruepp.
Molly, the Pony: A True Story, by Pam Kaster.
My Chincoteague Pony, by Susan Jeffers (Hyperion, 2008).

My Pony, by Susan Jeffers (2008).
One Good Horse, by Ann Herbert Scott. *A boy and his dad spend the day checking on cattle and counting what they see on the ranch.*
One Horse Waiting for Me, by Patricia Mullins. *Beautiful collages for the numbers 1–12.*
Robert the Rose Horse, by Joan Heilbroner (1962).
Runaway Pony, by Krista Ruepp.
The Sea Pony, by Krista Ruepp.
Snowflake (Breyer Stablemates), by Kristin Earhart (2006).
Stormy, Misty's Foal, by Marguerite Henry. Also, *King of the Wind*.
Summer Pony, by Jean S. Doty.
Winter Pony, by Krista Ruepp.
Wonderful World of Horses, by John Green.

Movies and Television

Barbie—Magic of Pegasus
Black Beauty
The Black Stallion
Clash of the Titans (Pegasus)
Dr. Quinn, Medicine Woman
Flicka
Hercules (animated)
Hildalgo
The Horse in the Gray Flannel Suit
King of the Wild (Rated PG)
Little House on the Prairie (Laura's horse, Bunny, races against Nellie's stallion.)
The Lone Ranger
Miracle of the White Stallions, 1963. Walt Disney Prod. *World War II army saves stallions.*
Mr. Ed
Mulan (animated)
National Velvet
Racing Stripes
Roy Rogers
Spirit
Wild Hearts Can't Be Broken
Zorro

10e. Cow

See Cow (#21) for puppet pattern and Cow activities.

10f. Dog

Dog Activities

Songs to Sing and Play

Bingo

A Book of Nursery Rhymes and Songs, by Sabine Baring, 1895, "Little Bingo."

There was a farmer had a dog,
And Bingo was his name-o.
B-I-N-G-O!
B-I-N-G-O!
B-I-N-G-O!
And Bingo was his name-o!

There was a farmer had a dog,
And Bingo was his name-o.
(Clap)-I-N-G-O!
(Clap)-I-N-G-O!
(Clap)-I-N-G-O!
And Bingo was his name-o!

There was a farmer had a dog,
And Bingo was his name-o.
(Clap, clap)-N-G-O!
(Clap, clap)-N-G-O!
(Clap, clap)-N-G-O!
And Bingo was his name-o!

There was a farmer had a dog,
And Bingo was his name-o.
(Clap, clap, clap)-G-O!
(Clap, clap, clap)-G-O!
(Clap, clap, clap)-G-O!
And Bingo was his name-o!

There was a farmer had a dog,
And Bingo was his name-o.
(Clap, clap, clap, clap)-O!
(Clap, clap, clap, clap)-O!
(Clap, clap, clap, clap)-O!
And Bingo was his name-o!

There was a farmer had a dog,
And Bingo was his name-o.
(Clap, clap, clap, clap, clap)
(Clap, clap, clap, clap, clap)
(Clap, clap, clap, clap, clap)
And Bingo was his name-o!

Tune: The Wheels on the Bus

Words by Eunice Wright

The dogs on the farm
Go bark, bark, bark
Bark, bark, bark
Bark, bark, bark.
The dogs on the farm
Go bark, bark, bark
All around the farm.

Bought Me a Cat

Bought Me a Cat Folk Rhymes, *by Thomas W. Talley, (1922). (Title:* Bought Me a Wife*) This song is also found in the following books:* Fiddle-I-Fee, *by Will Hillenbrand (uses original rhyme, lots of good repetition);* Fiddle-I-Fee, *by Melissa Sweet;* Fiddle-I-Fee, *by Paul Galdone.*

Bought me a dog and the dog pleased me,
I fed my dog under yonder tree.
Dog goes bow-wow, bow-wow,
Horse goes neigh, neigh,
Cow goes moo, moo,
Pig goes oink, oink,
Sheep goes baa, baa,
Goose goes hissy, hissy,
Duck goes quack, quack,
Hen goes chimmy-chuck, chimmy-chuck,
Cat goes fiddle-i-fee.

Where, Oh Where Has My Little Dog Gone?

By Septimus Winner, 1864

Where, oh where has my little dog gone?
Where, oh where can he be?
With his tail cut short,
And his ears are long,
Oh where, oh where can he be?

Do Your Ears Hang Low?

Tune from "The Turkey in the Straw." Origin obscure. Oldest published works, "Do Your Balls Hang Low?" 1956, but pre-dates to Civil War.

Make long felt ears for the dog that can be tied in a knot or a bow. Do the actions, increasing speed each time the song is repeated.

Do your ears hang low?
Do they wobble to and fro?
Can you tie them in a knot?
Can you tie them in a bow?
Can you throw them over your
Shoulder like a Continental soldier?
Do your ears hang low?

I Had a Rooster

Oral Traditional; performed by Pete Seeger.

I had a rooster, my rooster pleased me
I fed my rooster 'neath the greenberry tree
My little rooster went cocka doodle doo
Dee doodle-ee doodle-ee doodle-ee do.

I had a dog, my dog pleased me
I fed my dog 'neath the greenberry tree
My little doggie went ruff ruff ruff
My little rooster went cocka doodle doo
Dee doodle-ee doodle-ee doodle-ee do.

This Old Man

English Folk Songs for Schools, by S. B. Gould and C. J. Sharp, 1906.

This old man, he played one ... give a dog a bone...

Other Songs

"He's a Dog," *I Have a Song for You, Vol. 3,* by Janeen Brady, page 10.
"He's a Tramp," by Peggy Lee and Sonny Burke, Walt Disney's Movie: *Lady and the Tramp.*
"How Much Is That Doggie in the Window?," 1952, by Bob Merrill. (Also see the book by Iza Trapani.)
"My Dog's Bigger Than Your Dog," by Tom Paxton.
"Who Let the Dogs Out?" Anslen Douglas, 1998.

Poems and Nursery Rhymes

The Animal Store

By Rachel Field

"The Animal Store" is from Taxis and Toadstools: Verses and Decorations. *Copyright 1926 by Doubleday. Random House Children's Books, a division of Random House, Inc. Source:* The Golden Book of Poetry *(1947).*

"If I had a hundred dollars to spend, or maybe a little bit more,..."

Our Puppies

Child Songs of Cheer, *by Evaleen Stein, 1918.*

Little ears as soft as silk,
Little teeth as white as milk,
Little noses cool and pink,
Little eyes that blink and blink,
Little bodies round and fat,
Little hearts that pit-a-pat,
Surely prettier puppies never
Were before nor can be ever!

This Little Dog

By Eunice Wright

This little dog ran out to play,
Chasing the cats and squirrels all day.

This little dog began to dig,
In the dirt and mud with the pig.

This little dog barked all night,
Guarding the farmhouse until it was light.

This little dog helped the blind,
Guiding along so very kind.

This little dog herded the sheep,
And brought them home in time to sleep.

Old Mother Hubbard

The Real Mother Goose, *by Blanche Fisher Wright, 1916.*

Old Mother Hubbard
Went to the cupboard
To get her poor dog a bone.

But when she got there
The cupboard was bare,
And so the poor dog had none.

Caesar's Song

The Real Mother Goose, *by Blanche Fisher Wright, 1916.*

Bow-wow-wow!
Whose dog art thou?
Little Tom Tinker's dog,
Bow-wow-wow!

Hark! Hark!

The Real Mother Goose, *by Blanche Fisher Wright, 1916.*

Hark, hark! the dogs do bark!
Beggars are coming to town:
Some in jags, and some in rags
And some in velvet gown.

Leg Over Leg

The Real Mother Goose, *by Blanche Fisher Wright, 1916.*

Leg over leg,
As the dog went to Dover;
When he came to a stile,
Jump, he went over.

Ten Little Puppies

By Eunice Wright

Make 10 dog puppets and 10+ other animal puppets. Subtract one puppy for each verse as the puppy meets each animal.

Ten little puppies went outside to play. (10)
One found a rabbit and chased him all day. (9)

One found a chicken and they began a dance. (8)
One saw a little cat and he began to prance. (7)

One saw a little pig playing in the dirt. (6)
One found a duck hiding in the farmer's shirt. (5)

One followed a horse carrying a heavy load. (4)
One barked at the cow running down the road. (3)

One herded sheep out behind the house.(2)
One lonely puppy found a friendly mouse. (1)

No little puppies were playing in the sun, (0)
They were all napping, their playing was all done.

Puppies, Puppies

By Juli Wright

Puppies, puppies, here and there,
Puppies dancing everywhere.

Puppies, puppies, up and down,
Puppies playing on the ground.

Puppies now are fast asleep,
Puppies do not make a peep.

The Dog and the Bumblebee

Traditional

A little dog set out one day, adventuring was he—
When what did he meet upon the way but a great big bumblebee!

"Bzz, bzz, bzz," said the bumblebee,
"Little dog—stay away from me."

The little dog laughed, "Silly fly—you can't give me a scare.
Afraid of no little bug am I—and I will bite you … there!"

"Bzz, bzz, bzz," said the bumblebee.
"I'm warning you—stay away from me."

But the little dog opened his mouth up wide—and just as you'd suppose—
"Very well," the bee replied—and stung the little dog's nose!

The little dog yelped, "Oh-oh-oh," and the bee replied, "I told you so."
So the little dog turned—and ran did he—as fast as he could go—

Now—he nevermore will bite a bee!
Absolutely NO!

Two Little Puppy Dogs

Obscure origins; oral traditional finger-play.

Two little puppy dogs
Lying in a heap,
Soft and wooly
And fast asleep.
Along came a pussycat
Creeping near, "Meow,"
She cried right in their ear.
Two little puppy dogs
After one cat,
Did you ever play tag like that?

Little Dogs

Adapted by Juli Wright, from Folk Rhymes Wise and Otherwise, *by Thomas W. Talley, 1922.*

I had a little dog; his name was Ball;
When I give him a bone, he wants it all.
I had a little dog, his name was Trot;
He held up his tail, all tied in a knot.
I had a little dog, his name was Blue;
I put him on the road, and he almost flew.
I had a little dog, his name was Mack;
I tugged his little tail, that is way on his back.

I Had a little Doggy

The Home Book of Verse, *American and English, 1580–1918, p. 46.*

I had a little Doggy that used to sit and beg;
But Doggy tumbled down the stairs and broke his little leg.
Oh! Doggy I will nurse you and try to make you well,
And you shall have a collar with a little silver bell.

Ah! Doggy, don't you think that you should very faithful be,
For having such a loving friend to comfort you as me?
And when your leg is better and you can run and play,
We'll have a scamper in the fields and see them making hay.

But, Doggy, you must promise (and mind your word you keep)
Not once to tease the little lambs, or run among the sheep:
And then the little yellow chicks that play upon the grass,
You must not even wag your tail to scare them as you pass.

Games and Group Activities

This Old Man

Add a bone for each verse of "This Old Man." Bones can be placed in a "doggie" bag or dish in front of the dog puppet. When the song is done, count the bones.

I Have a Little Dog

I have a little doggie, and he won't bite you, and he won't bite you, and he won't bite you—but he WILL bite you!! (A version of Duck, Duck, Goose)

Doggie, Doggie, Where's Your Bone?

Children sit in a circle. One child, playing the "dog," leaves the room. An adult places a "bone" (a small wooden block or object) in a child's hands. All children pretend to hold the bone in their clasped hands in front of them. When the "doggie" returns, the children all chant, "Doggie, doggie, where's your bone?" The "doggie" has 3 chances to guess who is holding the bone.

Alternate: When the bone is found, the doggie chases the child with the bone around the outside of the circle, as in Duck, Duck, Goose.

Books

Bag Full of Pups, by Dick Gackenback.
A Bath for a Beagle, by Thomas Crawford (Troll, 1970).

Big Dog ... Little Dog: A Bedtime Story, Random House Picturebacks.

The Big Little Book of Happy Sadness, Colin Thompson (Kane/Miller Book Publishers). *A three-legged dog, a boy, and his grandmother lead to what is important in life—a sense of belonging.*

Bingo! (Bunny Reads Back), by Rosemary Wells.

Biscuit Goes to School, by Alyssa S. Capucilli. *Biscuit wants to go to school, but dogs aren't allowed.*

The Blue House Dog, by Deborah Blumenthal (2010).

The Bravest Dog Ever: The True Story of Balto, by Natalie Standiford (Random House, 1989).

Cats Do, Dogs Don't, by Norma Simon and illustrated by Dora Leder.

Circle Dogs, by Kevin Henkes. *Two circle dogs with triangle ears live in a square house... (shapes).*

Copycat Dog, by Michael Pellowski (Troll, 1986).

Count on Clifford, by Norman Bridwell. *Clifford has fun counting from 1 to 10 at his birthday party.*

Dog Breath, the Horrible Trouble with Hally Tosis, by Dav Pilkey (Scholastic, 1994).

Dog Heaven, by Cynthia Rylant.

Doggies, by Sandra Boynton. *A book for very young children.*

Dogs, by Emily Gravett (Simon & Schuster, 2009). *Preschool book with very good illustrations showing different kinds of dogs. Good short text.*

Dogs, by Gail Gibbons.

Dogs, Dogs, Dogs, by Leslea Newmann (Simon & Schuster). *Crowded illustrations.*

Give the Dog a Bone, by Steven Kellogg.

Go, Dog, Go, by P.D. Eastman.

Good Dog, Carl, by Alexandra Day (Simon & Schuster, 1991, Paperback, 1998). *Lovable Rottweiler tries very hard to be good.*

Harry the Dirty Dog, by Gene Zion and illustrated by Margaret Bloy Graham (Harper, 1976).

Hope So, Too, by Jodi Hills (Tristan Pub. 2004). *A girl and a puppy.*

How Much Is That Doggie in the Window? by Iza Trapani. *A young boy longs to have a dog that he sees in the pet store window.*

Hunter and His Dog, by Brian Wildsmith.

I Swapped My Dog, by Harriet Ziefert. *A fussy farmer swaps his dog for a horse, but not satisfied, he keeps swapping animals and ends up back with his dog.*

I Want a Dog, by Dayal Kaur Khalsa

Ivan the Terrier, by Peter Catalanotto. *Ivan loves story hour, but keeps interrupting.*

Kitty Up! by E. Wojtusik (2008). *Kitty is rescued by her friend Big Dog after a day of exploring.*

Marmalade's Picnic, by Cindy Wheeler.

Maxie the Mutt, by Sharon Peters (Troll, 1988).

Move Over Rover! by Karen Beaumont. *It's raining cats and dogs, and the doghouse is getting full.*

My Big Dog, by Janet Stevens (Golden Books). *Story from a cat's viewpoint. Very busy text and illustrations. Nice story of companionship.*

My Dog Never Says Please, by Suzanne Williams.

My Dog Lyle, by Jennifer P. Goldfinger.

No Kicks for Dog (Sweet Pickles Series), by Richard Hefter.

Oh Where, Oh Where Has My Little Dog Gone? (Paperback), by Iza Trapini (Charlesbridge, 1998).

Old Yeller (Perennial Classics), by Fred Gipson.

Ollie All Over, Denis Roche. *A board book about a puppy hiding in the house.*

The Pigeon Wants a Puppy, by Mo Willems (New York: Disney Book Group). *Pigeon is begging the reader for a puppy and promising to take care of it. Then when a puppy arrives, he changes his mind and asks for a walrus.*

Please, Puppy, Please, by Spike Lee.

The Poky Little Puppy, by Janette Sebring Lowrey.

Prehistoric Pinkerton, by Steven Kellogg (Dial, 1987, Puffin Paperback, 1993). *Teething puppies can be a problem when they are in search of something to chew. The Great Dane Pinkerton seeks out a chew toy.*
Pup and Hound at Sea, by Susan Hood. *Two friends have a scary adventure on a raft.*
Puppies and Dogs (Price, Stern, Sloan, 1984).
Puppies Are Like That, Random House Picturebacks.
Ruff! Ruff! Where's Scruff? by D. Carter (2006). *Help the reader find Scruff who is hiding all around the farm.*
Snoopy's Baseball Game, by Lee Mendelson (Worlds of Wonder, 1986).
Spot Can Count, by Eric Hill (1999). *Spot and dad have fun counting farm animals from 1 to 10. Lift the flap book.*
Spot's First Picnic, by Eric Hill.
Surprise Puppy! Level 1 reader, Dorling Kindersley.
10 Dogs in the Window, by Claire Masurel. *Ten dogs patiently wait in a pet store window for new homes.*
This Old Man (Classic Book with Holes), by Pam Adams.
What a Dog! by Sharon Gordon (Troll, 1980).
Where the Red Fern Grows, by Wilson Rawls.
Where's Spot? by Eric Hill. *Lift the flaps and search the house for Spot.*
Yip! Snap! Yap! by Charles Fuge (Tricycle Press, 2000). *Let's make dog sounds. Beautiful illustrations.*
You Dirty Dog, by Stephen Caitlin (Troll, 1988).

Movies and Television

Air Bud: Spikes Back
Air Bud—World Pup
Air Buddies
All Dogs Go to Heaven
Babe
Balto
Beethoven 1, 2, 3
Beverly Hills Chihuahua
Biscuit Eater
Bolt
Cats and Dogs 1, 2
Chestnut
Chihuahua
Cop Dog
Dr. Doolittle
Eight Below
Extraordinary Dogs (TV Series/Special), documentary
Far from Home: The Adventures of Yellow Dog, 1995.
Fieval Goes West
Firehouse Dog
Fluke
The Fox and the Hound
Frank (Bulldog)
Franken-Dog
Gold Retrievers
Golden Christmas
The Great Dog Detective, 1986 Disney movie.
Hachi—A Dog's Tale
Homeward Bound 1 and 2
Homeward Bound—The Incredible Journey
Hotel for Dogs (Recommended!)
The Incredible Journey
Iron Will
K-9
Lady and the Tramp
Lassie
Marmaduke (2010, Great Dane, PG)
Miracle Dogs
Miracle Dogs Too
My Dog Skip
Napoleon
Old Yeller
Oliver and Company
101 Dalmatians
Pluto
The Retrievers (Golden Retrievers in action.)
Rin Tin
Santa Paws, 2009
Scooby Doo
The Shaggy D.A.
The Shaggy Dog

The Shaggy Dog, remake with Tim Allen.
Shiloh, by Phyllis Reynolds Naylor.
Snoopy
Snow Dogs
Under Dog
Up (Dug, the talking dog). Pixar
Where the Red Fern Grows
Wishbone
Wonder Dog (animation)

10g. Cat

See Cat (#6e) for puppet pattern and Cat activities.

10h. Fox

See Foxy Loxy (#1g) for puppet pattern and Fox activities.

11. The Lion and the Mouse

This Aesop's fable has a mouse waking up a lion, who decides to eat the mouse in retaliation. The mouse convinces the lion to let him go. Later, when the lion is netted by hunters, the mouse, remembering the lion's earlier kindness, frees him by chewing through the cords.

11a. Lion

Lion Activities

Songs to Sing and Play

Little Scrawny Lion (Tune: Little Peter Rabbit Had a Fly Upon His Nose)

Words by Eunice Wright

(See book: The Tawny Scrawny Lion*, by Kathryn Jackson)*

Little Scrawny Lion had a bee upon his nose,
Little Scrawny Lion had a bee upon his nose,
Little Scrawny Lion had a bee upon his nose,
He flicked it and it flew away.

Little Scrawny Lion had a tall giraffe for lunch,
Little Scrawny Lion had a tall giraffe for lunch,
Little Scrawny Lion had a tall giraffe for lunch,
They both ate chocolate cake for dessert.

Little Scrawny Lion had a thirst for zebra tea,
Little Scrawny Lion had a thirst for zebra tea,
Little Scrawny Lion had a thirst for zebra tea,
So zebra brought his tea over at three.

Little Scrawny Lion chased a gazelle up the hill,
Little Scrawny Lion chased a gazelle up the hill,
Little Scrawny Lion chased a gazelle up the hill,
But the gazelle won the race to the top.

Little Scrawny Lion found a nice little cave,
Little Scrawny Lion found a nice little cave,
Little Scrawny Lion found a nice little cave,
And then he took a nice long nap.
(Snore—ZZZzzz...)

Tune: Brown Bear, Brown Bear, What Do You See? (Bill Martin, Jr.)

Words by Eunice Wright

Yellow lion, yellow lion, why do you roar?
I roar to scare the Zebras next door.

Zebra, Zebra, why do you run?
I run from Tigers when they come.

Tigers, tigers, who do you eat?
I eat elephants, but not any meat.

Elephants, elephants, why water do you spray?
We like the cool water, and play, play, play.

Brown monkey, brown monkey, what do you see?
I see children looking at me.

(Everyone giggle and cup hands around eyes as if looking around.)

Other Songs

"Hakuna Matata," 1994, Wonderland Music Company, Inc (BMI). From the Walt Disney Records album *Rhythm of the Pride Lands*.

"The Lion and the Mouse," Song based on the Aesop's Fable, by Jack Hartmann © Jack Hartmann & Hop 2 It Music.

"The Truth About Lions," *I Have a Song for You About Animals*, by Janeen Brady, page 30.

Poems and Nursery Rhymes

The Lion and the Mouse (Aesop's Fable)

By Eunice Wright

The mighty, fright-y lion
Had no need to fear.
His roar shook the jungle,
A roar to easily hear.

Along came a mouse,
Which the lion easily caught.
"Please let me go, because someday,
I may help you out a lot."

The mighty king of beasts,
Reluctantly let go.
"Too tiny a morsel—
Besides ... you never know."

While walking along one day,
He fell into a trap.
The net held him tight,
He could not make it snap.

He roared for some help,
For a strong and friendly hand.
But no big creature came,
Just a mouse in the sand.

"Let me help you, sir,"
The tiny mouse did say.
"Ha, Ho, what can you do?
Too small in every way!"

But the tiny mouse began to chew,
Through ropes holding so tight.
The lion watched with interest,
As mouse chewed with all his might.

The ropes began to loosen,
And the lion wiggled free.
"Many thanks, my friend," the lion said.
A good lesson let this be."

The Lion and the Mouse

The Home Book of Verse, *Vol. 1 (of 4) Author: Various; Editor: Burton Egbert Stevenson 1912, by Jeffreys Taylor (1792–1853)*

A lion with the heat oppressed,
One day composed himself to rest:
But while he dozed as he intended,
A mouse, his royal back ascended;
Nor thought of harm, as Aesop tells,
Mistaking him for someone else;
And travelled over him, and round him,
And might have left him as she found him
Had she not—tremble when you hear—
Tried to explore the monarch's ear!
Who straightway woke, with wrath immense,
And shook his head to cast her thence.
"You rascal, what are you about?"
Said he, when he had turned her out,
"I'll teach you soon," the lion said,
"To make a mouse-hole in my head!"
So saying, he prepared his foot
To crush the trembling tiny brute;
But she (the mouse) with tearful eye,
Implored the lion's clemency,
Who thought it best at last to give
His little prisoner a reprieve.

'Twas nearly twelve months after this,
The lion chanced his way to miss;
When pressing forward, heedless yet,
He got entangled in a net.
With dreadful rage, he stamped and tore,
And straight commenced a lordly roar;
When the poor mouse, who heard the noise,
Attended, for she knew his voice.
Then what the lion's utmost strength
Could not effect, she did at length;
With patient labor she applied
Her teeth, the network to divide;
And so at last forth issued he,
A lion, by a mouse set free.

Few are so small or weak, I guess,
But may assist us in distress,
Nor shall we ever, if we're wise,
The meanest, or the least despise.

The Lion

*By Hilaire Belloc, 1896 (*Bad Child's Book of Beasts*)*

The Lion, the Lion, he dwells in the waste,
He has a big head and a very small waist;
But his shoulders are stark, and his jaws
they are grim,
And a good little child will not play with him.

Wild Beasts

Child Songs of Cheer, *by Evaleen Stein, 1918.*

I will be a lion
And you shall be a bear,
And each of us will have a den
Beneath a nursery chair;
And you must growl and growl and growl,
And I will roar and roar,
And then—why, then—you'll growl again,
And I will roar some more!

The Lion and the Unicorn

The Real Mother Goose, *by Blanche Fisher Wright, 1916.*

The lion and the unicorn
Were fighting for the crown
The lion beat the unicorn
All around the town.

Some gave them white bread,
And some gave them brown;
Some gave them plum cake
And drummed them out of town.

The Lion

The Kitten's Garden of Verses, *by Oliver Herford, 1911.*

The Lion does not move at all, Winter or Summer, Spring or Fall,
He does not even stretch or yawn, But lies in silence on the lawn.
He must be lazy it is plain, For there is moss upon his mane,
And what is more, a pair of Daws Have built a nest between his paws.
Oh, Lazy Lion, big and brown, This is no time for lying down!
The Sun is shining, can't you see? Oh, please wake up and play with me.

The Lion

A Book of Nursery Songs and Rhymes, *by Sabine Baring-Gould. Nursery Songs.* The Whale, *adapted by Juli Wright.*

The lion, the lion, and now we must sing
The forest's pride and the jungles king,
He is a cat and a mighty thing,
Roaring so loud in the jungle ring.

Down to the water hole he sometimes will go,
Then up to the pride lands, just for show.
And when he is done, then off goes he,
Running in the jungle, mighty and free.

In the forest where a tree stands bold,
A lion is the pride, as I've been told,
And there he will sport his mighty glee,
With very sharp claws, he climbs a tree.
'Tis a dangerous thing to catch a lion,
He'll bite and hurt you, without even try'n,
And when he's done, then off goes he,
Running in the forest, mighty and free.

Books

Library Lion, by Michelle Knudsen. *One day, a lion came to the library.*
The Lion and the Mouse, adaptation by Carol Jones (Random House, 1998).
The Lion and the Mouse, by Ed Young (Doubleday, 1980).
The Lion and the Mouse, by Gail Herman (Random House, 1988).
The Lion and the Mouse, by Gerald Rose (Macmillan, 1988).
The Lion and the Mouse, by Jerry Pinkney. *Cute illustrations.*
The Lion and the Mouse, by Mark White (Picture Window, 2004).
The Lion and the Mouse, by Tom Lynch.
The Lion and the Mouse, retold by Bernadette Watts (North South, 2000).
Lion Is Down in the Dumps (Sweet Pickles Series), by Richard Hefter.
The Lion's Share, by Matthew McElligott. *A tale of halving cake and eating it, too. Long text, humorous, not preschool age, elementary math for older children.*
Mouse and Lion, by Rand Burkert.
Roar! A Noisy Counting Book, by Pamela Edwards. *One lonely lion cub sets out to find some friends with a not-so-friendly ROAR!*
Tawny Scrawny Lion, by Kathryn Jackson.
We're Going on a Lion Hunt, by Margery Cuyler, Illustrated by Joe Mathieu (Marshall Cavendish, 2008). *The teacher takes her students on an imaginary safari.*

Movies and Television

The Addams Family (Kitty). TV series
Animals Are Beautiful People
Big Cats: the Dark Side (Nat. Geo. W. 190)

Dr. Doolittle (lion has a toothache)
The Gods Must Be Crazy!
The Greatest Show on Earth
Hatari
Indiana Jones and the Last Crusade (the circus train)
Jumanji
The Lion King
Madagascar
Tarzan

11b. Mouse

See Mouse (#8) for puppet pattern and Mouse activities.

12. The Little Red Hen

The Little Red Hen finds a grain of wheat and decides to plant it. She asks for help from the farmyard animals, including a cat, a dog and a pig. All refuse to help during the different stages of turning the wheat into flour. When it comes time to share in the bounty of fresh bread, though, the farmyard animals are all too willing to help eat the bread. Since they didn't help before, the Little Red Hen and her chicks enjoy the bread by themselves.

12a. Little Red Hen

COPY THE PATTERN OF THE CHICKEN BODY AT 118%

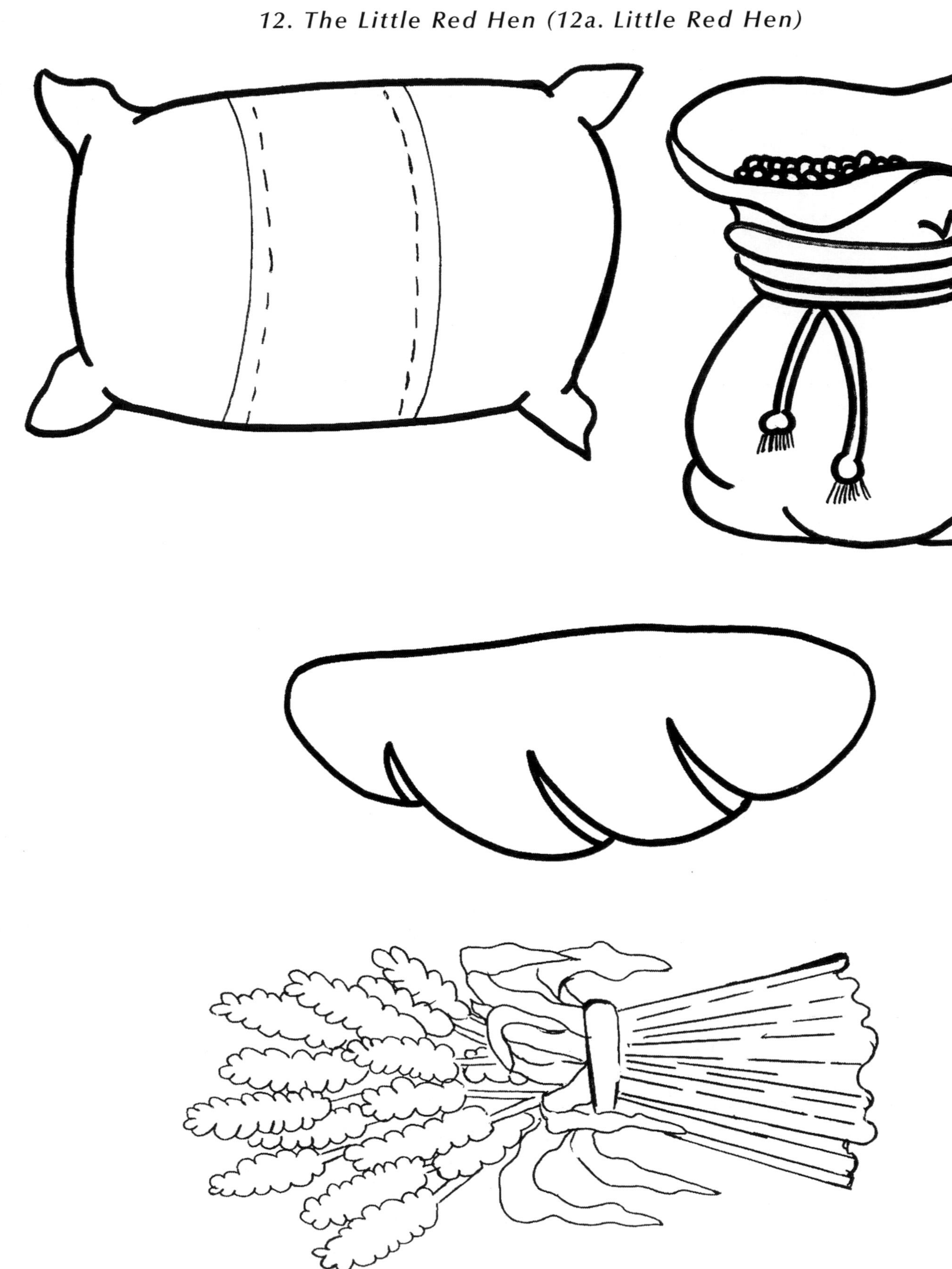

Hen Activities

See also activities under Henny Penny (#1d).

Songs to Sing and Play

Tune: The Wheels on the Bus

Words by Eunice Wright

The little red hen had some grains of wheat,
Grains of wheat, grains of wheat.
The little red hen had some grains of wheat,
"Who will help me plant this wheat?"

"Not I," said the dog, "Not I," said the cat,
"Not I," said the pig, "No, none of that!"
"We'll sit and watch you do the work,
For we are tired today."

Spoken: "Then I'll do it myself!"

"It is time to cut the wheat,
Cut the wheat, Cut the wheat,
It is time to cut the wheat,
Who will help me cut the wheat?"

"Not I," said the dog, "Not I," said the cat,
"Not I," said the pig, "No, none of that!"
"We'll sit and watch you do the work,
For we are tired today."

Spoken: "Then I'll do it myself!"

"It is time to grind the wheat,
Grind the wheat, grind the wheat,
It is time to grind the wheat,
Who will help me grind the wheat?"

"Not I," said the dog, "Not I," said the cat,
"Not I," said the pig, "No, none of that!"
"We'll sit and watch you do the work,
For we are tired today."

Spoken: "Then I'll do it myself!"

"It is time to make the bread,
Make the bread, make the bread.
It is time to make the bread,
Who will help me make the bread?"

"Not I," said the dog, "Not I," said the cat,
"Not I," said the pig, "No, none of that!"
"We'll sit and watch you do the work,
For we are tired today."

Spoken: "Then I'll do it myself!"

"It is time to eat the bread,
Eat the bread, eat the bread.
It is time to eat the bread,
Who will help me eat the bread?"

"I will," said the dog, "I will," said the cat,
"I will," said the pig, "Yes, all of that!"
"We'll sit and eat the bread you made,
For we are hungry today."

Spoken: "I'll eat it myself!"

"You didn't help me plant the wheat,
Cut the wheat, or grind the wheat.
You didn't help me make the bread,
You will not help me eat the bread!"

Spoken: So—she ate it herself!

Tune: Down on Grandpa's Farm

Written by Robert D. Singleton/Traditional. See songs for teaching.com or One Light, One Sun*—Raffi to listen to the tune.*

Down on Grandpa's farm there is a little red hen.
Down on Grandpa's farm there is a little red hen.
The hen, she makes a sound like this: "Cluck, Cluck."
The hen, she makes a sound like this: "Cluck, Cluck."
Down on Grandpa's farm there is a little red hen.

Bought Me a Cat

Folk Rhymes, *by Thomas W. Talley (1922) (Title: Bought Me a Wife)*

Bought me a hen and the hen pleased me,
I fed my hen under yonder tree.
Hen goes chimmy-chuck, chimmy-chuck,
Cat goes fiddle-i-fee.

Tune: the Wheels on the Bus

Words by Eunice Wright

The hens on the farm
Go cluck, cluck, cluck
Cluck, cluck, cluck
Cluck, cluck, cluck
The hens on the farm
Go cluck, cluck, cluck
All around the farm.

Oh, the Little Red Hen

Copyright by Ron Brown

Oh, the Little Red Hen
Was asking all her friends
"Who will help me plant my grain?"

"Not I," said the dog.
"Not I," said the cat.
"Not I," said the little mouse.

So the Little Red Hen
With no help from her friends
Planted it by herself.

Oh, the Little Red Hen
Was asking all her friends
"Who will cut and grind my wheat?"

"Not I," said the dog.
"Not I," said the cat.
"Not I," said the little mouse.

So the Little Red Hen
With no help from her friends
Cut and ground it by herself.

Oh, the Little Red Hen
Was asking all her friends
"Who will help me bake my bread?"

"Not I," said the dog.
"Not I," said the cat.
"Not I," said the little mouse.

So the Little Red Hen
With no help from her friends
Ate it by herself.

So the Little Red Hen
With no help from her friends
Simply ate it by herself.
Yum! Yum!

This song is available on Intelli-Tunes' Storybook Friends.

Atilla the Hen

Sung by Big Bird on *The Sesame Street Fairy Tale Album*, to the tune of "Sweet Betsy from Pike."

Tune: 10 Little Indians

Words by Eunice Wright

1 little, 2 little, 3 little hens...
Scratching in the yard.

Alternate verse:
1 little, 2 little, 3 little animals...
Who wouldn't help the red hen.

Poems and Nursery Rhymes

The Little Red Hen (My Mother)

By Juli Wright

My Little Red Hen works hard and long,
And all day long she sings a song.
She doesn't worry about time to play,
She works hard the whole long day.

Making Bread

Finger Plays for Nursery and Kindergarten, *by Emilie Poulsson, 1893. Sheet music and finger-play actions.*

1. "The farmer and the miller
Have work'd," the mother (Red Hen) said,
And got the flour ready,
So I will make the bread."
She scooped from out the barrel
The flour white as snow,
And in her sieve she put it
And shook it to and fro.

2. Then in the pan of flour
A little salt she threw;
A cup of yeast she added,
And poured in water, too.
To mix them all together
She stirred with busy might,
Then covered it and left it
Until the bread was light.

3. More flour then she sifted
And kneaded well the dough,
And in the waiting oven
The loaves of bread did go.
The mother (Red Hen) watched the baking,
And turned the loaves, each one,
Until at last, rejoicing,
She said, "My bread is done!"
("Let's eat!" And they ate every last crumb!)

Little Red Hen

Folk Rhymes Wise and Otherwise, *by Thomas W. Talley, 1922; adapted by Juli Wright*

My little red hen,
Never lived in a pen.
With her little white foot,
Built her nest in berry root.

She laid more eggs,
And had longer legs
Than any hen on the farm;
Berries and eggs were her charm.

The Easter Hen

In My Nursery: A Book of Verse, *by Laura E. Richards, 1890.*

Oh! children, have you ever seen
The little Easter Hen,
Who comes to lay her pretty eggs,
Then runs away again?

She only comes on Easter Day;
And when that day is o'er,
Till next year brings it round again,
You will not see her more.

Her eggs are not like common eggs,
But all of colors bright:
Blue, purple, red, with spots and stripes,
And scarcely one that's white.

She lays them in no special place,—
On this side, now on that.
And last year, only think! she laid
One right in Johnny's hat.

But naughty boys and girls get none:
So, children, don't forget!
And be as good as good can be—
It is not Easter yet!

Games and Group Activities

"Duck, Duck, Goose" (Dog, Cat, Pig & Red Hen)

I have a little dog, and he won't help me...
I have a little cat, and he won't help me...
I have a little pig, and he won't help me...
Then I'll do it myself! (*or:* But the Little Red Hen WILL help!)

Chase the Hen

The Red Hen (teacher or child) drops the handkerchief in the lap of (or behind) a child and runs around the outside of the circle, being chased by the child with the handkerchief, back to the original place where the hanky was dropped, before being caught by the "Hen."

Books

The Little Red Elf, by Barbara Barbieri McTGrath (Charlesbridge, 2009). *A reindeer, penguin, hare and a little elf follow the "Little Red Hen" story. Great to read at Christmas time, a simple and comical story, but has unrealistic illustrations.*
The Little Red Hen, by Alan Garner.
The Little Red Hen, by Bryon Barton.
The Little Red Hen, by Candice Ransom.
The Little Red Hen, by Carol Ottolenghi.
The Little Red Hen, by Heather Forest (August House, 2006). *Great illustrations, simple story.*

The Little Red Hen, by Jacob Grimm.
The Little Red Hen, by Jerry Pinkney.
The Little Red Hen, by Paul Galdone.
The Little Red Hen, by Trina Schart Hyman.
The Little Red Hen (Little Golden Books), by Diane Muldrow.
The Little Red Hen, retold by Susanna Davidson.
The Little Red Hen; Help Yourself, Little Red Hen, by Alvin Granowski.
The Little Red Hen Makes a Pizza, by Philemon Sturges.
The Little Red Hen Makes Soup, by Rozanne Lanczak Williams (2003).
The Little Red Pen, by Susan S. Crummel.
The Sesame Street Players Present the Little Red Hen, by Emily P. Kingsley.
With Love, the Little Red Hen, by Alma Flor Ada.

12b. Baby Chicks

See Chicken Little (#1a) for puppet pattern and Chicken activities.

12c. Cat

See Cat (#6e) for puppet pattern and Cat activities.

12d. Dog

See Dog (#10f) for puppet pattern and Dog activities.

12e. Pig

See Pig (#15a) for puppet pattern and Pig activities.

13. The Swan Princess

An enchanted princess is a swan by day and only holds her true form by night. True love is needed to break the evil sorcerer's spell.

13a. Princess

Use Princess (#9b), Sister (#48) or any girl puppet pattern.

13b. Swan

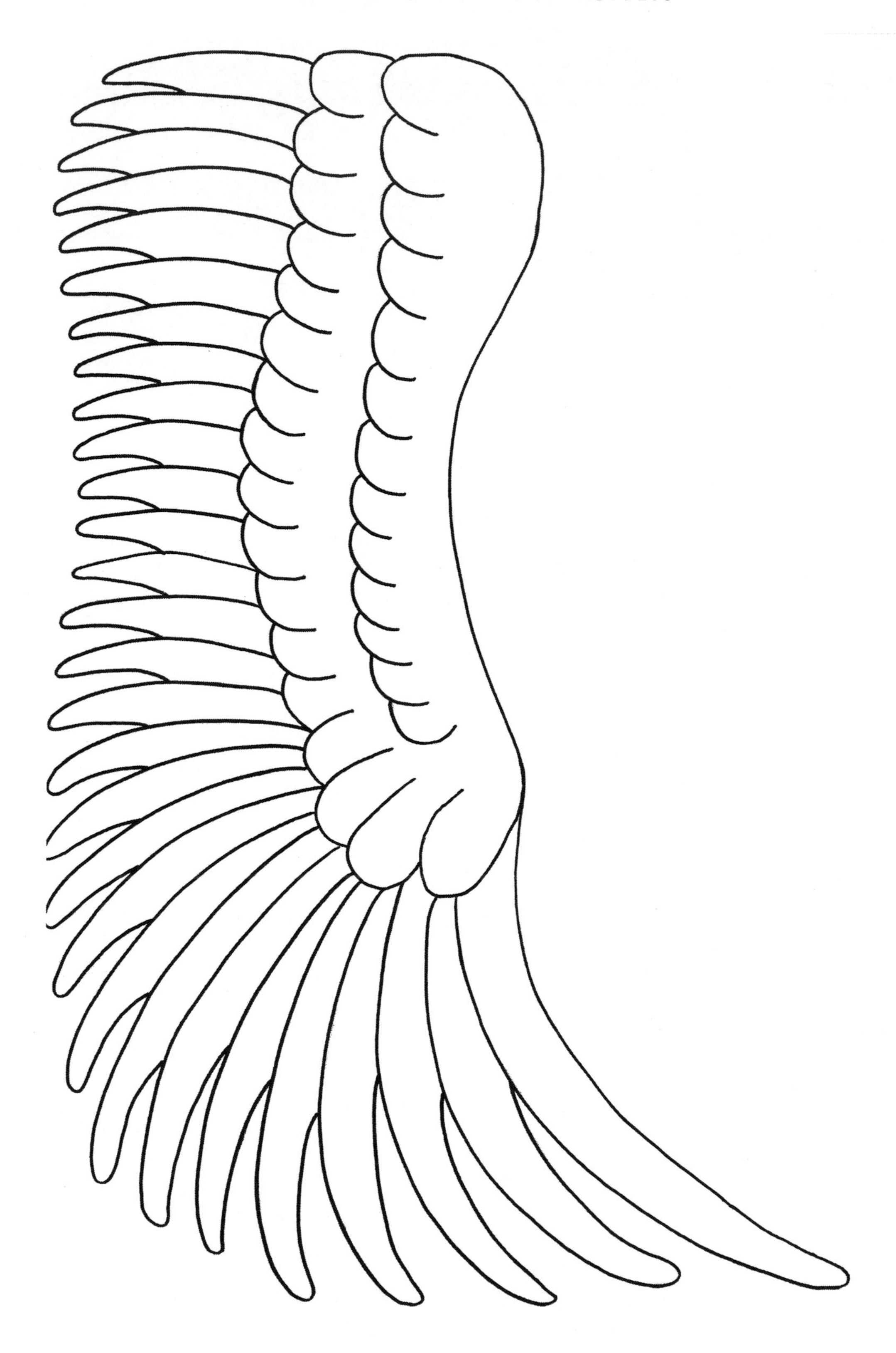

The swan is very large; you may have to use larger paper (11 × 17) to make it work at a reasonable size. Also, see instructions for creating a stick or rod puppet in the Games and Group Activities section of the Ugly Duckling chapter (17).

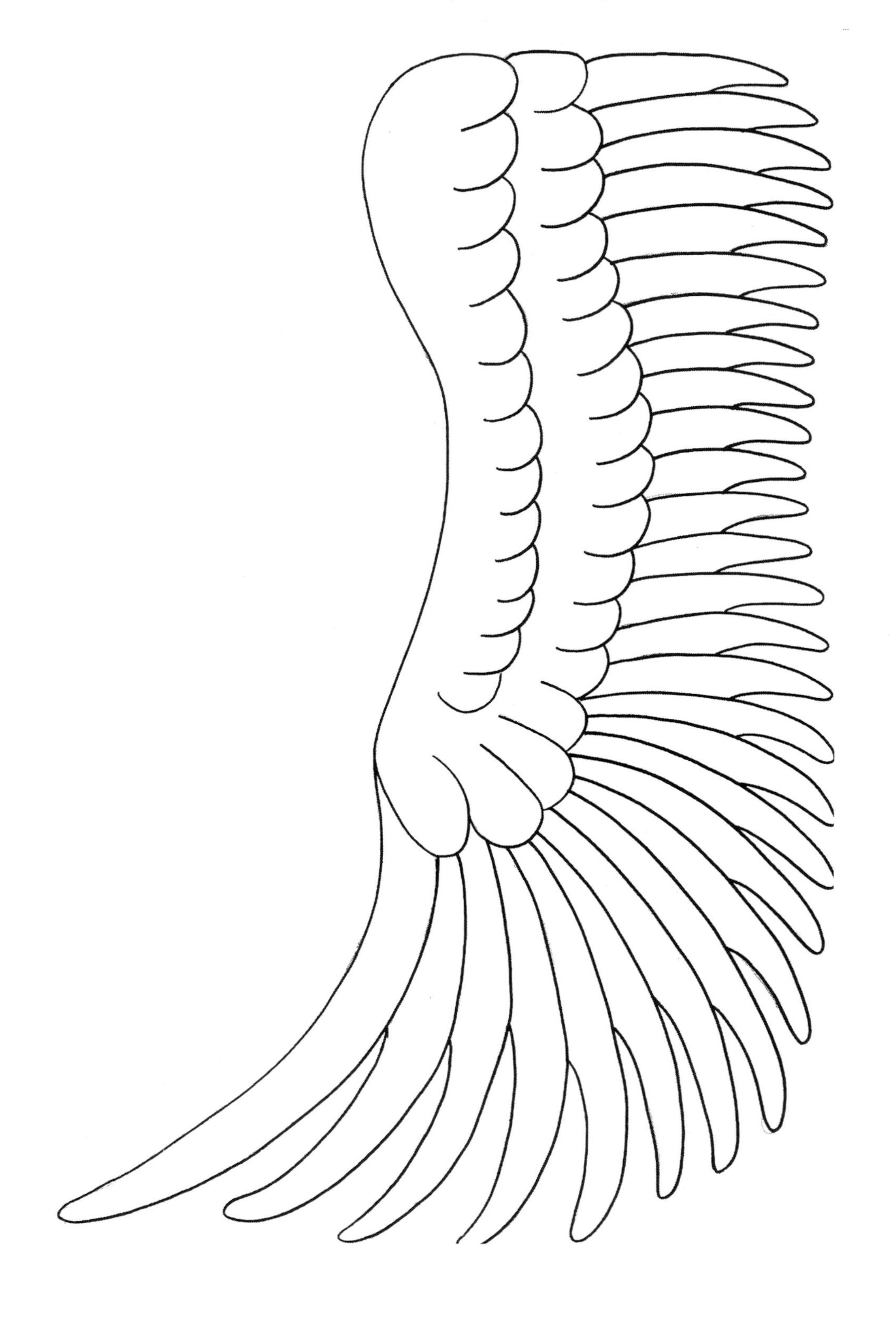

The Swan Princess Activities

Songs to Sing and Play

Tune: Three Blind Mice

Words by Eunice Wright

See the beautiful swan,
See the beautiful swan
See how she swims
See how she swims
She swims through the water from dusk to light,
Hoping the prince will do what's right,
To break the spell and free her tonight,
See the beautiful Swan.

Tune: Mary Had a Little Lamb

Words by Eunice Wright

Once there was a princess, a princess, a princess.
Once there was a princess, a pretty, pretty girl.
She had a spell cast on her, on her, on her.
She had a spell cast on her, and turned into a swan.
When the moonlight touched the lake, touched the lake, touched the lake.
When the moonlight touched the lake, she was in human form.
The prince came and saved her, saved her, saved her.
The prince came and saved her, happily they wed.

Poems and Nursery Rhymes

Swan

The Real Mother Goose, by Blanche Fisher Wright, 1916.

Swan, swan, over the sea;
Swim, swan, swim!
Swan, swan, back again;
Well swum, swan!

The Swan

By Evaleen Stein (1863–1923)

Stately swan, so proud and white
Glistening in the morning light,
Come and tell me is it true
That a snow-white swan like you,
Guided by bright golden chains
In his beak for bridle reins,
Once upon a time from far
Fabled lands where fairies are
Brought a magic boat wherein
Rode the brave knight Lohengrin?

Stately swan, so proud and white
Glistening in the morning light,
If you only wore a gold
Harness, like that swan of old,
And if trailing in your wake
Sailing on the silver lake
Was a boat of magic and
You could float to fairy-land,
Then I'd jump in and begin
Traveling like Lohengrin!

Books

The Green Fairy Book; The Magic Swan. Whoever touches the Swan is held fast.
Illustrated Fairy Tales Usborne Book, author/illus. Leslie Sims. Includes: "Sleeping Beauty," "The Emperor and the Nightingale," "Beauty and the Beast," "The Dragon Painter," "The Frog Prince, the Elves and the Shoemaker," "Little Red Riding Hood," "Cinderella," "The Swan Princess," "The Emperor's New Clothes."
The Princess and the Swan, by C.J. Grant.
Princess Sarah, and the Silver Swan, by Vivian French.
Swan Lake, by Lisbeth Zwerger.
Swan Lake, by Peter Tchaikovsky.
Swan Princess (Barbie Series), by Pamela Duarte.
Swan Princess, by A.L. Singer.
Swan Princess, by Francine Hughes.

The Swan Princess, by Rosie Dickins, illus. by Jenny Press.
Swan Princess with Charm, by M.J. Carr.
The Yellow Fairy Book: "The Six Swans." *Six brothers are turned into swans.*

Movies and Television

Barbie of Swan Lake, 2003.
The Swan Princess, Disney, 1994.
The Swan Princess, Disney (Escape from Castle Mountain)
The Swan Princess Christmas, 2012.
The Swan Princess: The Mystery of the Enchanted Treasure, 1998.

14. The Three Billy Goats Gruff

A troll lives under a bridge, eating anyone who dares to cross the bridge. The Three Billy Goats Gruff want to pass over to the other side of the river to a grassy meadow, but are each in turn stopped by the troll. The first two, the small goat and the medium-sized goat, convince the troll to wait for a bigger goat, as that would make for a better meal. The biggest goat, though, is big enough to kick the troll into the river, where he doesn't bother anyone again.

14a. Smallest Billy Goat

14b. Medium Billy Goat

14c. Biggest Billy Goat

14d. Troll

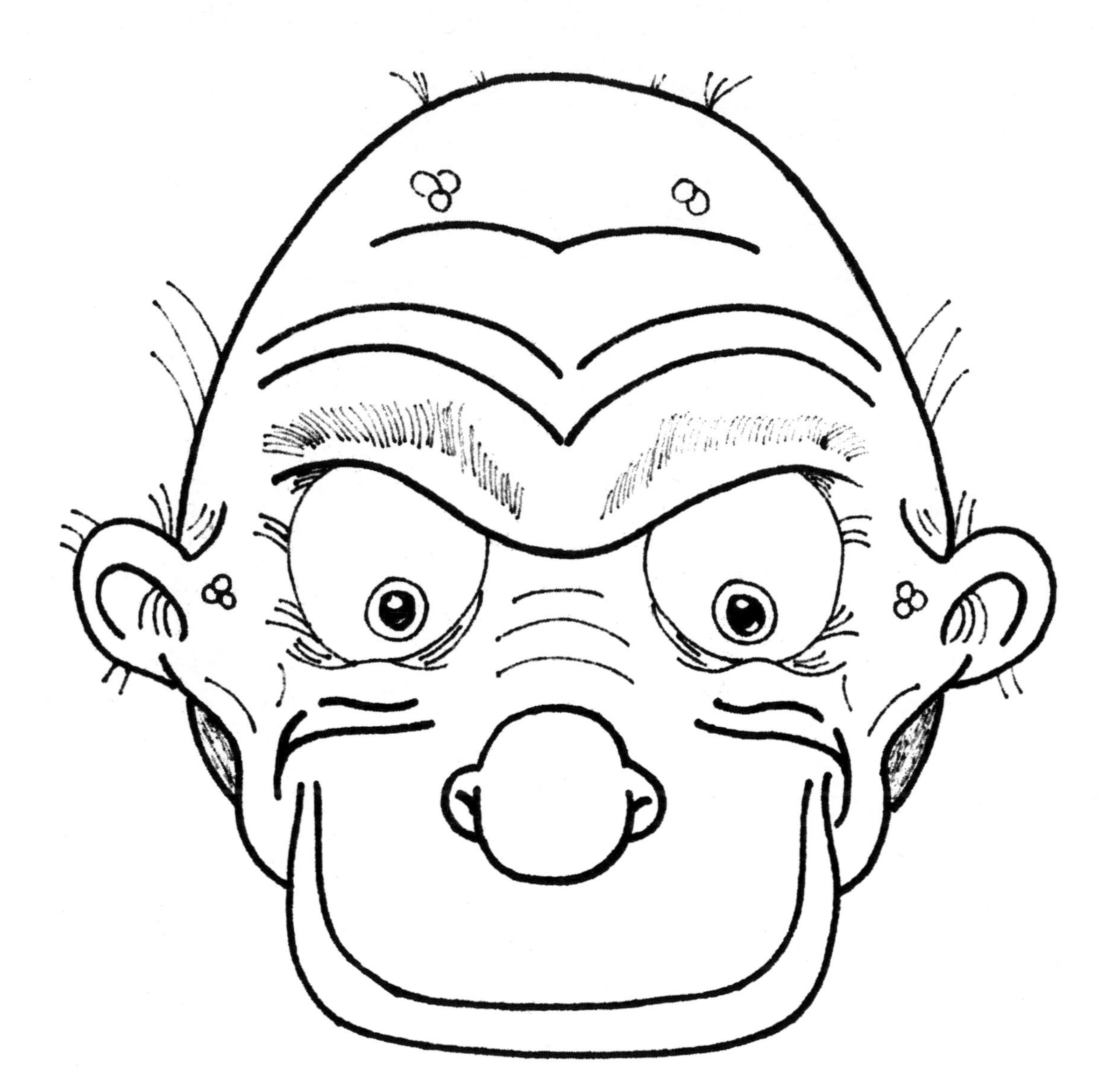

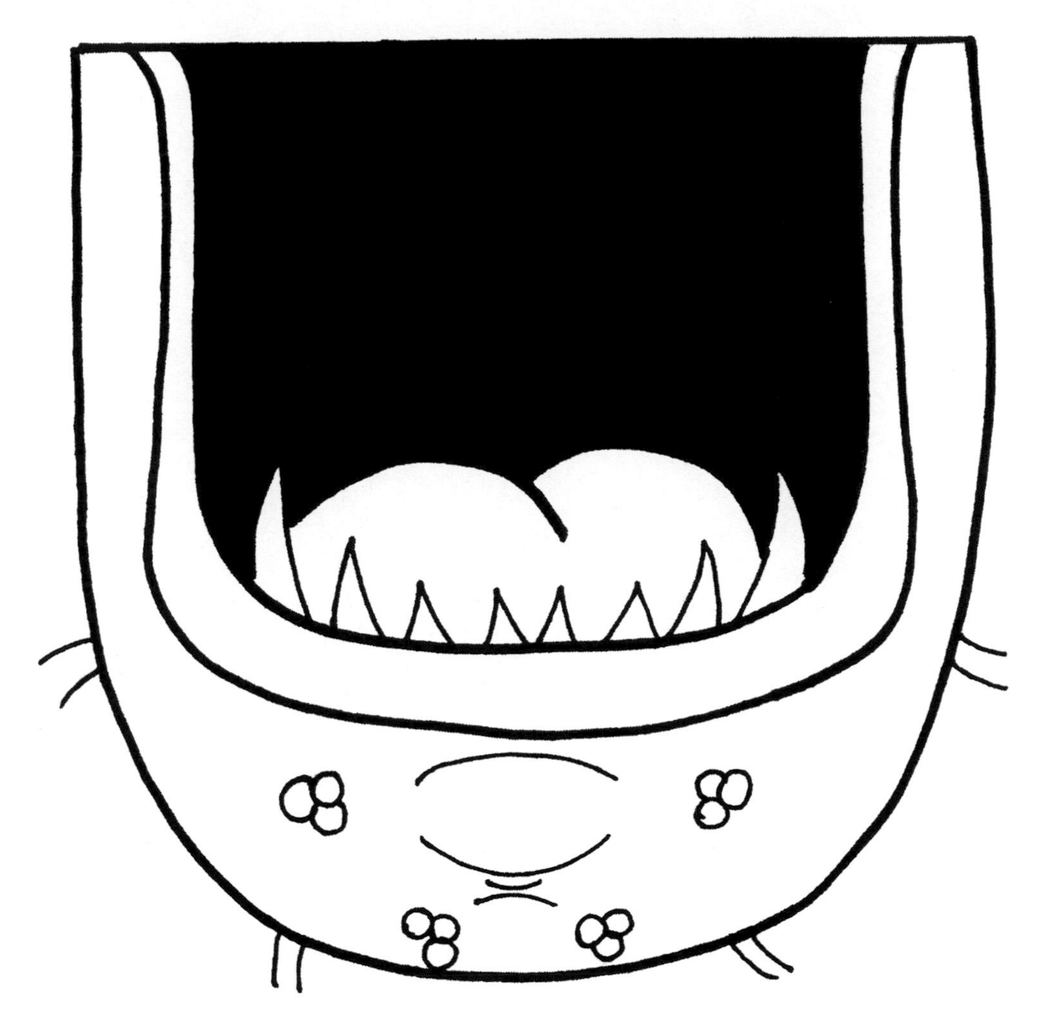

The Three Billy Goats Gruff Activities

See Heidi (#4b) for additional goat music and activities.

Songs to Sing and Play

Bill Grogan's Goat

*Oral traditional campfire echo song. Earliest printed version, 1904 (*The Tale of a Shirt*). Also, Will Hayes song, "O Grady's Goat," published 1890, in* Shoemaker's Best Selections, *by Silas Nef.*

There was a man (There was a man)
Now please take note (Now please take note)
There was a man (There was a man)
Who had a goat (Who had a goat)

He loved that goat (He loved that goat)
Indeed he did (Indeed he did)
He loved that goat (He loved that goat)
Just like a kid (Just like a kid)

One day that goat (One day that goat)
Felt frisk and fine (Felt frisk and fine)
Ate three red shirts (Ate three red shirts)
Right off the line (Right off the line)

The man, he grabbed (The man, he grabbed)
Him by the back (Him by the back)
And tied him to (And tied him to)
A railroad track (A railroad track)

Now, when that train (Now, when that train)
Hove into sight (Hove into sight)
That goat grew pale (That goat grew pale)
And green with fright (And green with fright)

He heaved a sigh (He heaved a sigh)
As if in pain (As if in pain)
Coughed up those shirts (Coughed up those shirts)
And flagged the train! (And flagged the train!)

The Billy Goat

Frank C. Brown Collection of North Carolina Folklore, *Vol. 3, 1913.*

A billy goat was feeling fine,
Ate six red shirts from off the line.
Sal took a stick and broke Bill's back
And tied him to the railroad track.

'Long came a freight just six hours late.
It was too bad, made poor Bill mad.
Bill gave a shriek of roar (fear?) and pain,
Coughed up the shirts and flagged the train.

A Goat Idyl

Modern Medical Science, *Vol. 16, Number 6, Dec. 1903, p. 364.*

Dr. Johnson, a friend of mine,
Hung three red shirts upon a line.
Now, what else do you think our doctor did
But buy a goat for his only kid?

One day this goat, while roaming round,
Spied those red shirts and ate them down.
The doctor was mad, and cursed and swore
That he would have the old goat's gore.

So he led him to the railroad track,
And tied him there upon his back,
Leaving him in this sorry plight,
Just as a freight train hove in sight.

"Say au revoir, but not good-bye!"
This goat was far too cute to die.
He strove with all his might and main—
Coughed up those shirts and flagged the train!

Tune: Oh Where, Oh Where Has My Little Dog Gone?

Words by Eunice Wright

Oh where, oh where are the goats today?
Oh where, oh where can they be?
Are they eating tin cans
Or the clothes on the line?
Oh where, oh where can they be?

Tune: 3 Blind Mice

Words by Eunice Wright

3 Billy Goats Gruff.
3 Billy Goats Gruff.
See how they tramp.
See how they tramp.
They all went over the bridge, one day,
The troll said, "You really must stay and play."
The biggest Billy goat got his own way.
3 Billy Goats Gruff. (*or* Good-bye Troll!)
3 Billy Goats Gruff.

Tune: Who Did Swallow Jonah? (Echo Song)

Words by Eunice Wright; Who Did Swallow Jonah? *by Barton, 1899, p. 40.*

1. Who's that? Who's that?
Who's that? Who's that?
Who's that tramping over my bridge?

(Repeat above 2 more times, moving up & down a few musical steps each time.)

Who's that tramping over,
Who's that tramping over,
Who's that tramping over my-bridge?
(*or* "They really must pay the toll.")

2. It is I, it is I, Littlest Billy Goat, goat, goat, goat ...
Wait for my big brother ... goat.

(repeat verse 1)

3. It is I, it is I, Middle-sized Billy Goat, goat, goat, goat.
Wait for my big brother ... goat.

(repeat verse 1)

4. It is I, it is I, Great Big Billy Goat, goat, goat, goat.
Great Big Billy Goat... Goodbye, troll!

Tune: 10 Little Indians

Words by Eunice Wright

1 little, 2 little, 3 little billy goats ... all went out to play (*or* all went over the bridge).

The 3 Billy Goats Gruff

By Jack Hartmann (Hop 2 it Music).

Find it at www.jackhartmann.com.

Poems and Nursery Rhymes

Five Billy Goats (Count Down)

By Eunice Wright

Five billy goats, running out the door,
One ate a tin can, then there were four.
Four billy goats, running 'round the tree,
One found a troll, then there were three.
Three billy goats, chewing on a shoe,
One followed a train, then there were two.
Two billy goats, all began to run,
One ate a red shirt, then there was none.

Sheep and Goat

Folk Rhymes Wise and Otherwise, *by Thomas W. Talley, 1922; adapted by Juli Wright.*

A sheep and goat were going to the pasture;
Says the goat to the sheep: "Can't you walk a little faster?"
The Sheep did reply, "I can't, I am a little too full."
The goat said: "You can with my horns in your wool."
But the goat fell down and skinned his shin
And the sheep split his lip with a wide broad grin.

The Grandiloquent Goat

The Jingle Book, *by Carolyn Wells, 1901.*

A very grandiloquent Goat
Sat down to a gay table d'hôte;
He ate all the corks,
The knives and the forks,
Remarking: "On these things I dote."

Then, before his repast he began,
While pausing the menu to scan,
He said: "Corn, if you please,
And tomatoes and peas,
I'd like to have served in the can."

Books

Awful Ogre's Awful Day, by Jack Prelutsky (Scholastic, 2001). *A collection of poems for older children.*

Favorite Tales of Monsters and Trolls, Random House Picturebacks.

Go Away, Big Green Monster, by Ed Emberley.

Huck Runs Amuck! by Sean Taylor (Dial, 2011).

Just a Friendly Old Troll; The Three Billy Goats Gruff, by Alvin Granowsky.

The Little Goat, Random House Picture books.

The Monster at the End of This Book, by Jon Stone. *Grover tries to prevent the reader from turning pages. A very cute book; highly recommended.*

My Monster Mama Loves Me So, by Laura Leuck.

Nature's Children, GOATS, by Ann Weil (Grolier, 1997). *Beautiful photos, informative text.*

There Was an Old Monster! by Rebecca Emberley.

There's a Nightmare in My Closet, by Mercer Mayer (Dial, 1968).

The Three Billy-Goats Gruff, by Ellen Appleby.

The Three Billy Goats Gruff, by Stephen Carpenter.

The Three Billy Goats Gruff, by Steven Kellogg.

The Three Billy Goats Gruff (Easy-to-read Folktales), by Paul Galdone.

The Three Billy Goats Gruff, retold and illustrated by Janet Stevens (Harcourt Brace, 1987). *Parents' Choice Award. Beautiful illustrations and story. This would be a great story to turn into a puppet play.*

The Three Cabritos, by Eric A. Kimmel (Marshall Cavendish Children, 2007). *Three goats belonging to a band want to go over the bridge to the fiesta in Mexico. They charm the "troll" with their music. Very cute illustrations, and Hispanic children will enjoy this version.*

Where the Wild Things Are, by Maurice Sendak (Harper Collins, 1963). *Max, who goes to bed with no supper, has a dream filled with scary, wild things. Luckily, he takes control of the beasts and wakes up safe and sound in his bed.*

The Wolf and the Seven Kids, by the Brothers Grimm (Troll Associates, 1979). *A cute story about a wolf that tries to trick the seven little goats while mother is away, gobbles them up whole, and then are cut free from his tummy by mother goat who replaces them with heavy stones.*

Movies and Television

Aesop's Fables Animated Stories, "Fox and the Goat"

The Black Caldron (animated)

The Chronicles of Narnia

Dark Crystal

Ella Enchanted (blue trolls)

Fainting Goats (National Geographic)

Happy Never After (animated)

Harry Potter (A troll in the dungeon)

Hercules (animated)

Hoodwinked

The Hunchback of Notre Dame

Labyrinth

Legend (for older children)

Little House on the Prairie—The TV series. Laura has a goat that drinks Mr. Edwards' homemade brew.

Little Monsters

The Little Troll Prince (animated)

Merlin (TV series)

Monsters, Inc.

Monsters vs. Aliens

The Never Ending Story (Rock creatures)

Oz, Return to Oz

Percy and the Lightning Thief

Princess and the Goblin (Walt Disney—Walden Media)

Quest for Camelot (animated)

Shrek (animated)

The Sound of Music—Song: "The Lonely Goatherd" (by Rogers and Hammerstein)

Spiderwick Chronicles

A Troll in Central Park (animated)

Willow (for older children)

15. The Three Little Pigs

Three pigs each build a house—a straw house, a stick house and a brick house. A wolf, wanting a good meal, "huffs and puffs" and blows down first the straw house and then the stick house. The pigs living in those two houses flee to the brick house of the third pig, where despite the wolf's best efforts they are safe. (The wolf pattern is on pages 93–94.)

15a. Pigs

Straw
House

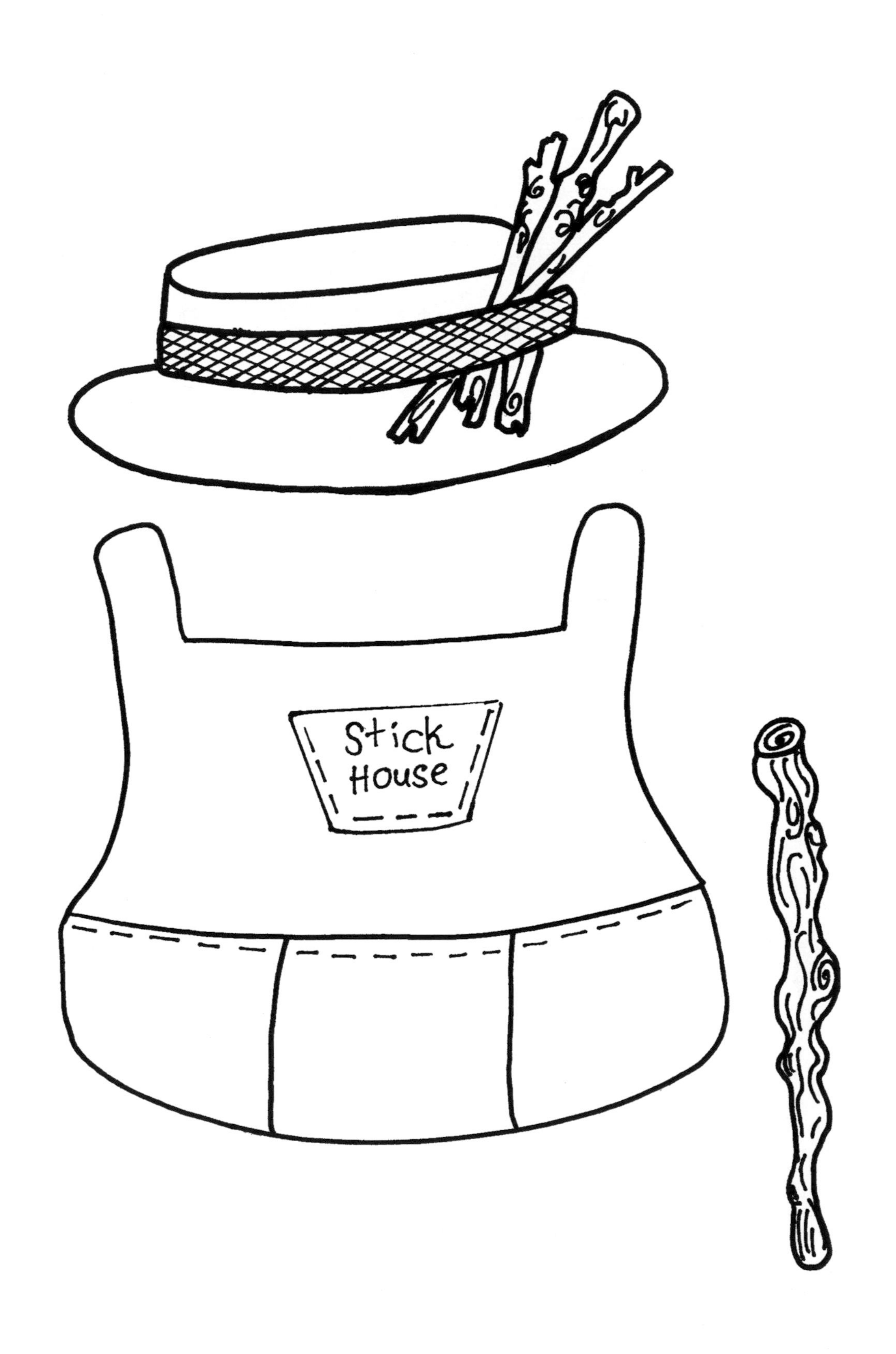
Stick
House

Brick
House

Pig Activities

Songs to Sing and Play

Tune: Oh, Where, Oh Where, Has My Little Dog Gone?

Words by Eunice Wright

Oh where, oh where are the three pigs today?
Oh where, oh where can they be?
Are they building a house
Made of straw, sticks or bricks?
Oh where, oh where can they be?

Each one ran inside the house he built,
Each time the wolf came around.
The wolf blew and blew
'Till the straw house came down,
Then away ran the first little pig

Soon inside his brother's house of sticks,
The two pigs huddled in fear.
Soon the wolf came 'round,
And blew and blew it down,
Then away ran the two little pigs.

Safe inside their brother's house of bricks they hid,
Then quickly heated the pot.
The wolf came 'round,
But couldn't blow it down,
So up on the roof he went.

The wolf thought it smart to find a new way inside,
He slid down the chimney with ease,
Landing right in the pot
Of water so hot,
He ran screaming, "OWWWEEEeeee OOOoooowww!

The Three Little Pigs Song (tune: This Is the Way We Wash Our Clothes)

Words by Eunice Wright

This is the story of three little pigs,
Three little pigs, three little pigs,
This is the story of three little pigs,
Who left home to seek their fortunes.

The first little pig built a house of straw
A house of straw, a house of straw,
The first little pig built a house of straw,
A quick and easy house.

The second little pig built a house of sticks,
A house of sticks, a house of sticks.
The second little pig built a house of sticks,
A quick and easy house.

The third little pig built a house of brick,
A house of brick, a house of brick,
The third little pig built a house of brick,
A sturdy, wind-proof house.

The wolf wanted a piglet snack,
To eat them up, and gobble them down.
The wolf came to the house of straw,
And blew and blew it down.

The first little pig did run and run,
To his brother's house, his brother's house.
The first little pig did run and run,
Quick inside the house of sticks.

The wolf wanted a piglet snack,
To eat them up, and gobble them down.
The wolf came to the house of sticks,
And blew and blew it down.

The two little pigs did run and run,
To their brother's house, their brothers house.
The two little pigs did run and run,
Safe inside the house of bricks.

The wolf came to the house of bricks,
He blew and blew, and blew and blew.
The wolf came to the house of bricks,
But he could not blow it down.

The wolf climbed up on the roof so high,
The chimney was the only way in.
He slid right down and into the pot
The three little pigs had heated up.

The wolf jumped out and yelped and ran,
And to this day has never been seen.
The three little pigs lived happily,
Inside the house of bricks.

A Hunting We Will Go

Traditional, by Thomas Arne, 1777. Make up more rhyming verses.

A hunting we will go, a hunting we will go,
Heigh ho, the dairy-o, a hunting we will go!
A hunting we will go, a hunting we will go,
We'll catch a pig and dance a little jig,
And then we'll let him go!

Bought me a Cat

Folk Rhymes, *by Thomas W. Talley (1922)*

Bought me a pig and the pig pleased me,
I fed my pig under yonder tree.
Dog goes bow-wow, bow-wow,
Horse goes neigh, neigh,
Cow goes moo, moo,
Pig goes oink, oink,
Sheep goes baa, baa,
Goose goes hissy, hissy,
Duck goes quack, quack,
Hen goes chimmy-chuck, chimmy-chuck,
Cat goes fiddle-i-fee.

Down on Grandpa's Farm

By Joseph K. Phillips, born 1960

(See songs for teaching.com or Raffi @CD Universe to listen to this song.)

"Down on Grandpa's farm there is fat pink pig.
The pig, he makes a sound like this: "Oink, Oink."

This Little Piggy (tune: Are You Sleeping?)

Echo song. The Home Book of Verse, *Vol. 1. Author: Various. Editor: Burton Egbert Stevenson, 1912.*

1. This little pig went to market;
This little pig stayed at home;
This little pig got roast beef;
This little pig got none;
This little pig cried wee, wee, all the way home.

ECHO:
This little piggy, this little piggy
Went to market, went to market.
This little piggy, this little piggy
He stayed home, he stayed home.

This little piggy, this little piggy
Had roast beef, had roast beef.
This little piggy, this little piggy
He had none, he had none.

This little piggy, this little piggy
Cried, "Wee, wee, wee; wee, wee, wee."
This little piggy, this little piggy
Cried all the way home, cried all the way home.

The Three Little Pigs

By Ron Brown. An instrumental version for plays and concerts is also available.

We're three little pigs,
Sitting in our houses,
The best houses around.
We're three little pigs,
Sitting safe and sound
In our houses made of
Straw and sticks and bricks.

But then one very bad day,
A big bad wolf came to town
And he blew (whew!),
Blew (whew!),
Blew (whew!),
Blew (whew!),
The stick and straw houses down!

We're three little pigs
Sitting in our house,
So glad it's made of bricks!

Many thanks to Ron Brown for permission to display these lyrics. intelli-tunes.com.

Old MacDonald Had a Farm

And on this farm he had some pigs...

The Farmer in the Dell

The Farmer takes a pig...

Little Peter Pig (tune: Little Peter Rabbit)

Little Peter Pig had a worm upon his nose,...
He flicked it and it crawled away.
Little Peter Pig had a dish upon his head,...
He licked it and it soon was clean.
Little Peter Pig had a wart upon his toe,...
He stomped it in the mud all day.

Make up more verses as a group—the funnier the better. Add accessories to the puppet: gummy worm, plastic dish, clay or bubble gum wart, etc.

Other Songs

"Counting Piggy Tails" by Jack Hartmann.
"Little Pigs Groove" by Jack Hartmann.
"Pigs Ka-Ligs." *Sing-a-Long Tunes for Tots*, by Baughman & Park, 1971, pp. 20–21.
"The Three Little Pigs Blues." M. Lewis & Greg Scelsa, Little House Music/Gregorian Chance Music (ASCAP), 1991 Youngheart Music. From the album *Playing Favorites*. Narration of story and singing of chorus. This is a very cute song, great for a puppet play.
"The Three Little Pigs Rap" by Rule.
"Who's Afraid of the Big Bad Wolf?" See Disney's *The Three Little Pigs* for music.
"Whose Tail Is Curly?" *I Have a Song for You About Animals*, Vol. 3, by Janeen Brady, Brite Music, 1979, pp. 16–17.

Poems and Nursery Rhymes

This Little Pig

Harry's Ladder to Learning, with Two Hundred and Thirty Illustrations, *by David Bogue and Joseph Cundall, 1850.*

Make 5 different pig puppets.
1. This little pig went to market;
2. This little pig stayed at home;
3. This little pig had roast meat;
4. This little pig had none;
5. This little pig said, "Wee, wee, wee,
I can't find my way home!"

Tom, Tom the Piper's Son

The Real Mother Goose, *by Blanche Fisher Wright, 1916.*

Tom, Tom the Piper's son,
Stole a pig, and away he run!
The pig was eat, and Tom was beat,
And Tom went crying down the street.

Five Little Pigs *(Make 5 different pig puppets)*

By Eunice Wright

Five Little Pigs lived on a farm.
The first one said, "My, it's getting warm!"
The second one said, "I want to eat!"
The third one said, "Let's find a treat!"
The fourth one said, "I see the farmer's wife!"
The fifth one said, "Run for your life!"
And the five little pigs Ran, squealing out of sight.

A Long-tailed Pig

The Nursery Rhyme Book, *by Edward Lang, 1897.*

A long-tailed pig, or a short-tailed pig,
Or a pig without ever a tail,
A sow-pig, or a boar-pig,
Or a pig with a curly tail.

The Old Woman and Her Pig

English Fairy Tales, *by Joseph Jacobs, 1890. Also found in other Mother Goose books.*

An old woman was sweeping her house, and she found a sixpence.
"What shall I do with this sixpence?" she said.
"I know. I will go to market and buy a little pig."
So she went to the market and she bought a little pig.
On the way home, they came to a stile.
But the pig would not go over the stile.

She went a little farther, and she met a dog.
So she said to the dog, "Dog, dog, bite pig!"

Pig won't go over the stile, And I shan't get home tonight."
But the dog would not.

She went a little farther, and she met a stick.
So she said to the stick, "Stick, stick, beat dog!
Dog won't bite pig, Pig won't go over stile,
And I shan't get home tonight."
But the stick would not.

She went a little farther, and she met a fire.
So she said to the fire, "Fire, fire, burn stick!"
Stick won't beat dog, Dog won't bite pig,
Pig won't go over stile, and I shan't get home tonight."
But the fire would not.

She went a little farther, and she met some water.
So she said to the water, "Water, water, quench fire!
Fire won't burn stick, Stick won't beat dog,
Dog won't bite pig, Pig won't go over stile,
And I shan't get home tonight."
But the water would not.

She went a little farther, and she met an ox.
So she said to the ox, "Ox, ox, drink water!
Water won't quench fire, Fire won't burn stick,
Stick won't beat dog, Dog won't bite pig,
Pig won't go over stile, and I shan't get home tonight."
But the ox would not.

She went a little farther, and she met a butcher.
So she said to the butcher, "Butcher, butcher, kill ox!
Ox won't drink water, Water won't quench fire,
Fire won't burn stick, Stick won't beat dog,
Dog won't bite pig, Pig won't go over stile,
And I shan't get home tonight."
But the butcher would not.

She went a little farther, and she met a rope.
So she said to the rope, "Rope, rope, hang butcher!
Butcher won't kill ox, Ox won't drink water,
Water won't quench fire, Fire won't burn stick,
Stick won't beat dog, Dog won't bite pig,
Pig won't go over stile, and I shan't get home tonight."
But the rope would not.

She went a little farther, and she met a rat.
So she said to the rat, "Rat, Rat, gnaw rope!
Rope won't hang butcher, Butcher won't kill ox,
Ox won't drink water, Water won't quench fire,
Fire won't burn stick, Stick won't beat dog,
Dog won't bite pig, Pig won't go over stile,
And I shan't get home tonight."
But the rat would not.

She went a little farther, and she met a cat.
So she said to the cat, "Cat, cat, kill rat!
Rat won't gnaw rope, Rope won't hang butcher,
Butcher won't kill ox, Ox won't drink water,
Water won't quench fire, Fire won't burn stick,
Stick won't beat dog, Dog won't bite pig,
Pig won't go over stile, and I shan't get home tonight."

And the cat said to her,
"If you will go over to the cow in the next field and fetch me a saucer of milk, I will kill the rat."
So the old woman went over to the cow in the next field.
And the cow said to her,
"If you will go over to the haystack and fetch me a handful of hay, I will give you milk."
So the old woman went over to the haystack to fetch a handful of hay for the cow.
After the cow had eaten the hay, she gave the old women the milk.
The old woman went back to the cat with the

milk in a saucer. As soon as the cat had lapped up the milk—
The cat began to kill the rat—
The rat began to gnaw the rope—
The rope began to hang the butcher—
The butcher began to kill the ox—
The ox began to drink to water—
The water began to quench the fire—
The fire began to burn the stick—
The stick began to beat the dog—
The dog began to bite the pig—
The pig jumped over the stile—
And the old woman got home that night!

Five Little Piggies

Traditional finger-play. Make a mother pig puppet and five little pigs.

"It's time for my piggies to go to bed."
Great big mother piggy said.
"So I will count them first to see
All my piggies came back to me.
Little piggy, two little piggies, three little piggies dear
Little piggies, five little piggies,
They're all here!"

10 Little Pigs

Author Unknown

"This little pig found a hole in the fence,
This little pig jumped through..."

To Market, to Market

The Real Mother Goose, *by Blanche Fisher Wright, 1916.*

To market, to market, to buy a fat pig,
Home again, home again, jig-gi-ty jig.

To market, to market, to buy a fat hog;
Home a-gain, home a-gain, Jig-ge-ty jog.

The Flying Pig

The Real Mother Goose, by Blanche Fisher Wright, 1916.

Dickory, dickory, dare,
The pig flew up in the air;
The man in brown soon brought him down,
Dickory, dickory, dare.

If a Pig Wore a Wig

Sing-Song: A Nursery Rhyme Book, *by Christina Georgina Rossetti, 1872.*

If a pig wore a wig,
What could we say?
Treat him as a gentleman,
And say, "Good day."

If his tail chanced to fail,
What could we do?—
Send him to the tailoress
To get one new.

Barber

The Real Mother Goose, *by Blanche Fisher Wright, 1916; adapted by Juli Wright.*

Barber, barber, shave a pig.
How many hairs will make a wig?
Four and twenty; that's enough.
Give the barber all his stuff.

A Pig

The Real Mother Goose, *by Blanche Fisher Wright, 1916.*

As I went to Bonner,
I met a pig
Without a wig
Upon my word and honor.

There Was an Old Woman Who Had a Little Pig

One version: The Book of Drills: A Series of Entertainments, *by Mary Barnard Horne, 1896.*

There was an old woman who had a little pig,
He didn't cost much, 'cause he wasn't very big.

This old woman kept the pig in the barn,
The cutest little thing she had on the farm.

But that little pig did a heap of harm,
He made little tracks all around the barn.

(More verses and different versions available.)

The Pigs

Finger Plays for Nursery and Kindergarten, *by Emilie Poulsson, 1893.*

Sheet music and fingerplay actions.

1. Piggie Wig and Piggie Wee,
Hungry pigs as pigs could be,
For their dinner had to wait
Down behind the barnyard gate.

2. Piggie Wig and Piggie Wee
Climbed the barnyard gate to see,
Peeping through the gate so high,
But no dinner could they spy.

3. Piggie Wig and Piggie Wee
Got down sad as pigs could be;
But the gate soon opened wide
And they scampered forth outside.

4. Piggie Wig and Piggie Wee,
What was their delight to see
Dinner ready not far off—
Such a full and tempting trough!

5. Piggie Wig and Piggie Wee,
Greedy pigs as pigs could be,
For their dinner ran pell-mell;
In the trough both piggies fell.

There Was a Lady Loved a Swine

The Baby's Opera, *by Walter Crane, 1877. Has Sheet music.*

1. There was a lady loved a swine,
"Honey!" said she;
"Pig-hog, wilt thou be mine?"
"Hunc!" said he.

2. "I'll build thee a silver sty,
Honey!" said she;
"And in it thou shalt lie!"
"Hunc!" said he.

3. "Pinned with a silver pin,
Honey!" said she;
"That thou mayest go out and in,"
"Hunc!" said he.

4. "Will thou have me now,
Honey?" said she;
"Speak, or my heart will break,"
"Hunc!" said he.

Oh, There Once Was a Sow

Mother Goose Rhymes, *by Watty Piper, 1922.*

Oh, there once was a sow who had three little pigs,
Three little piggies had she.
The old sow always went oink, oink, oink,
And the piggies went wee, wee, wee, wee.

Now, one day one of the three little pigs
To the other two piggies said he,
"Why don't we always go oink, oink, oink?
It's so childish to go wee, wee, wee, wee."

These three piggies grew skinny and limp
Skinny they well should be
For they always would try to go oink, oink, oink,
And they wouldn't go wee wee wee wee.

Now these three piggies they up and they died
A very sad sight to see
So don't ever try to go oink, oink, oink,
When you ought to go wee, wee, wee, wee.

Sow = a female pig (boar is a male pig)
Piglet = baby pig (piggie is a child's word for baby pig)

The Three Little Pigs

Children's Rhymes, Children's Games, Children's Songs, Children's Stories, a Book for Bairns and Big Folk. *Author: Robert Ford, 1904, p. 137.*

A jolly old sow once lived in a sty, and three little piggies had she;
And she waddled about saying, "grumph! grumph! grumph!"
While the little ones said "wee! wee!"

And she waddled about saying, "grumph! grumph! grumph!"
While the little ones said "wee! wee!"

"My dear little piggies," said one of the brats,
"My dear little brothers," said he,
"Let us all for the future say, 'grumph! grumph! grumph!'
'Tis so childish to say, 'wee! wee!'"

Let us all, etc.

These three little piggies grew skinny and lean,
And lean they might very well be,
For somehow they couldn't say "grumph! grumph! grumph!"
And they wouldn't say "wee! wee!"

For somehow, etc.

So after a time these little pigs died,
They all died of fe-lo-de-see,
From trying too hard to say "grumph! grumph! grumph!"
When they only could say "wee! wee!"

From trying, etc.

A moral there is to this little song, A moral that's easy to see:
Don't try when you're young to say "grumph! grumph! grumph!"
When you only can say "wee! wee!"
Don't try when you're young to say "grumph! grumph! grumph!"
When you only can say "wee! wee!"

Precocious Piggy

Childhood's Favorites and Fairy Stories the Young Folks Treasury, *Volume 1. By Thomas Hood. Editor: Jennie Ellis Burdick, 1919.*

Where are you going to, you little pig?
"I'm leaving my Mother, I'm growing so big!"
So big, young pig, so young, so big!
What, leaving your Mother, you foolish young pig?
Where are you going to, you little pig?
"I've got a new spade, and I'm going to dig!"
To dig, little pig! A little pig dig!

Well, I never saw a pig with a spade that could dig!
Where are you going to, you little pig?
"Why, I'm going to have a nice ride in a gig!"
In a gig, little pig! What, a pig in a gig!
Well, I never yet saw a pig ride in a gig!
Where are you going to, you little pig?
"Well, I'm going to the Queen's Head to have a nice swig!"
A swig, little pig! A pig have a swig!

What, a pig at the Queen's Head having a swig!
Where are you going to, you little pig?
"Why, I'm going to the Ball to dance a fine jig!"
A jig, little pig! A pig dance a jig!
Well, I never before saw a pig dance a jig!
Where are you going to, you little pig?
"I'm going to the fair to run a fine rig!"
A rig, little pig! A pig run a rig!

Well, I never before saw a pig run a rig!
Where are you going to, you little pig?
"I'm going to the Barber's to buy me a wig!"
A wig, little pig! A pig in a wig!
Why, whoever before saw a pig in a wig!

My Uncle Jehoshaphat

In My Nursery: A Book of Verse, *by Laura E. Richards, 1890.*

My Uncle Jehoshaphat had a pig,—
A pig of high degree;
And he always wore a brown scratch wig,
Most beautiful for to see.

My Uncle Jehoshaphat loved this pig,
And the piggywig he loved him;
And they both jumped into the lake one day,
To see which best could swim.

My Uncle Jehoshaphat he swam up,
And the piggywig he swam down;
And so they both did win the prize,
Which the same was a velvet gown.

My Uncle Jehoshaphat wore one half,
And the piggywig wore the other;
And they both rode to town on the brindled calf,
To carry it home to its mother.

Games and Group Activities

Pass the Pigs

This game is made by Winning Moves and is a version of the dice game Pig. Players compete by rolling their pigs against other players and keeping score.

Pin the Tail on the Pig

Make or find a poster of a tailless pig to hang on the wall. Create separate tails for the pig. Each player is blindfolded and tries to attach the tail to the pig in the correct spot. Whoever gets closest is the winner.

Books

Alaska's Three Pigs, by Arlene Laverde (Paws IV—Alaska children's books). *The classic story of the little pigs is retold Alaskan style, as the pigs camp, fish, ski, and build homes. A great book to teach children some details of Alaska.*

The Boy Who Cried Wolf, by Jenny Giles (Rigby, 1998). *Artfelt has "The Three Little Pigs" felt board set.*

Emmett's Pig, by Mary Stolz. *Emmett wants a pig, but lives in the city in a little apartment.*

How Big Is a Pig? by Claire Beaton. *A plump pig explores the barnyard and all the animal opposites he finds there in a quest to answer the question.*

If You Give a Pig a Pancake, by Laura Numeroff and Felicia Bond (1998).

The Little Red Hen has a pig in the story. *See the Little Red Hen (#12) activities in this book.*

The Little Red Hen, by Carol Ottolenghi. *The Pig doesn't want to help.*

The Little Red Hen, by Jon Scieszka, illustrated by Lane Smith. *Pig won't help.*

Mercy Watson to the Rescue, by Kate DiCamillo. *Pig climbs into bed with the family, the bed breaks, and trouble begins.*

Mrs. Pig Gets Cross and Other Stories, by Mary Rayner (Dutton, 1986). *A beginning reader for second to third grade children.*

Oink, by Arthur Geisert (Houghton, 1991).

The Old Woman and Her Pig, adapted by Eric A. Kimmel (Holiday House, 1992). *This is the nursery rhyme story of the old woman who bought a pig that wouldn't go over the stile, so she couldn't get home tonight. Comical illustrations, everything seems to have a face. Some vocabulary may be difficult for the very young.*

Pig Thinks Pink (Sweet Pickles Series), by Richard Hefter.

Piggy in the Puddle, by Charlotte Pomerantz.

Pigs, by Gail Gibbons.

Pigs Aplenty, Pigs Galore! Written and illustrated by David McPhail. *How would you like to have pigs as house guests? How will the man handle this?*

Pigs in Pajamas, by Maggie Smith (2012). *Ages 3+.*

Pigs, Pigs, Pigs, by Leslea Newmann (Simon & Schuster). *Crowded illustrations.*

Pigs Say Oink, Random House Picturebooks.

The Princess and the Pig, by Jonathan Emmett (2011).

Princess Pig, by Eileen Spinelli. *Cute story of farm animals and a pig who thinks she is a princess. Wonderful illustrations. Recommended.*

A Show of Hands: Using Puppets with Young Children, by Ingrid Crepeau and Ann Richard. *On p. 114 there is a puppet play script and instructions to help teachers involve children in a non-conventional tale of the three little pigs.*

Small Pig, by Arnold Lobel (1988).

Storytime Puppet Zoo, Simple Puppet Patterns and Plays, by Marilyn Lohnes. *On p. 29 this book has a puppet play script and visual aids for the Three Pig houses and the pot the wolf falls into.*

Ten Dirty Pigs/Ten Clean Pigs, by Carol Roth. *This bathtime counting book is great for bath time, as pigs from 1 to 10 splash up in the tub.*

The Three Little Cajun Pigs, by Berthe Amoss. *That mean ol' alligator wants to gobble up the three little Cajun pigs. Help the pigs escape by moving the alligator through the pages until he gets what he deserves!*

Three Little Cajun Pigs, by Mike Artell.

Three Little Hawaiian Pigs and the Magic Shark, by Donivee M. Laird. *The three little pigs story is set in Hawaii with a shark in the mean role of the big bad wolf.*

The Three Horrid Little Pigs, by Liz Pichon.

The Three Little Javelinas, by Susan Lowell, illustrated by Jim Harris. *The traditional story of the three little pigs moves to the southwest, where the big bad wolf becomes a coyote, and the three little pigs are javelinas building their homes from tumbleweed, saguaro cactus and adobe.*

Three Little Pigs, by Marie-Louise Gay.

Three Little Pigs, by Milo Winter. *A pig-shaped book. Green Tiger.*

The Three Little Pigs, by Patricia Seibert.

The Three Little Pigs, by Paul Galdone (Houghton, 1998). *A well told story, great for a puppet play.*

The Three Little Pigs, by Steven Kellogg.

The Three Little Pigs (Reading Railroad Books), by James Marshall.

The Three Little Pigs and the Fox: An Appalachian Tale, by William H. Hooks. *After the three older pigs leave home, it's time for little sister to leave. And she has learned everything she needs to know from her Mama. She'll make her way in the world just fine, even with a tricky old fox around.*

The Three Little Wolves and the Big Bad Pig, by Eugene Trivizas. *It's time for the three little wolves to go out into the world and build themselves a house, and their mother warns them to beware of the big bad pig.*

The Three Pigs, by David Wiesner. *The three pigs story begins in the usual way, going to build houses of straw, sticks, and bricks. But all that changes ... and they land in the realm of imagination.*

To Market, to Market, by Anne Miranda.

The True Story of the 3 Little Pigs, by Jon Scieszka. *The wolf gives his own outlandish version of what really happened when he met the three little pigs.*

Wait! No Paint! by Bruce Whatley (illustrator). *All the three little pigs want to do is move out of their crowded home (where 73 other little pigs live) and build their own little houses.*

Movies and Television

Babe

Charlotte's Web

Dr. Doolittle

The Lion King (Boar)

Miss Piggy (The Muppets)

Nanny McFee 2 (dancing pigs)

Porky Pig

The Three Little Pigs (Disney)

"Three Little Pigs," John Branyan—You Tube, Shakespeare version.

15b. Wolf

See Wolf (#5c) for puppet pattern and Wolf activities.

16. The Tortoise and the Hare

The Hare challenges the Tortoise to a race. The Hare, being quick, is confident that he will win the race, so wanders off the track and takes a nap. The Tortoise, slow but steady, ends up winning the race.

16a. Tortoise

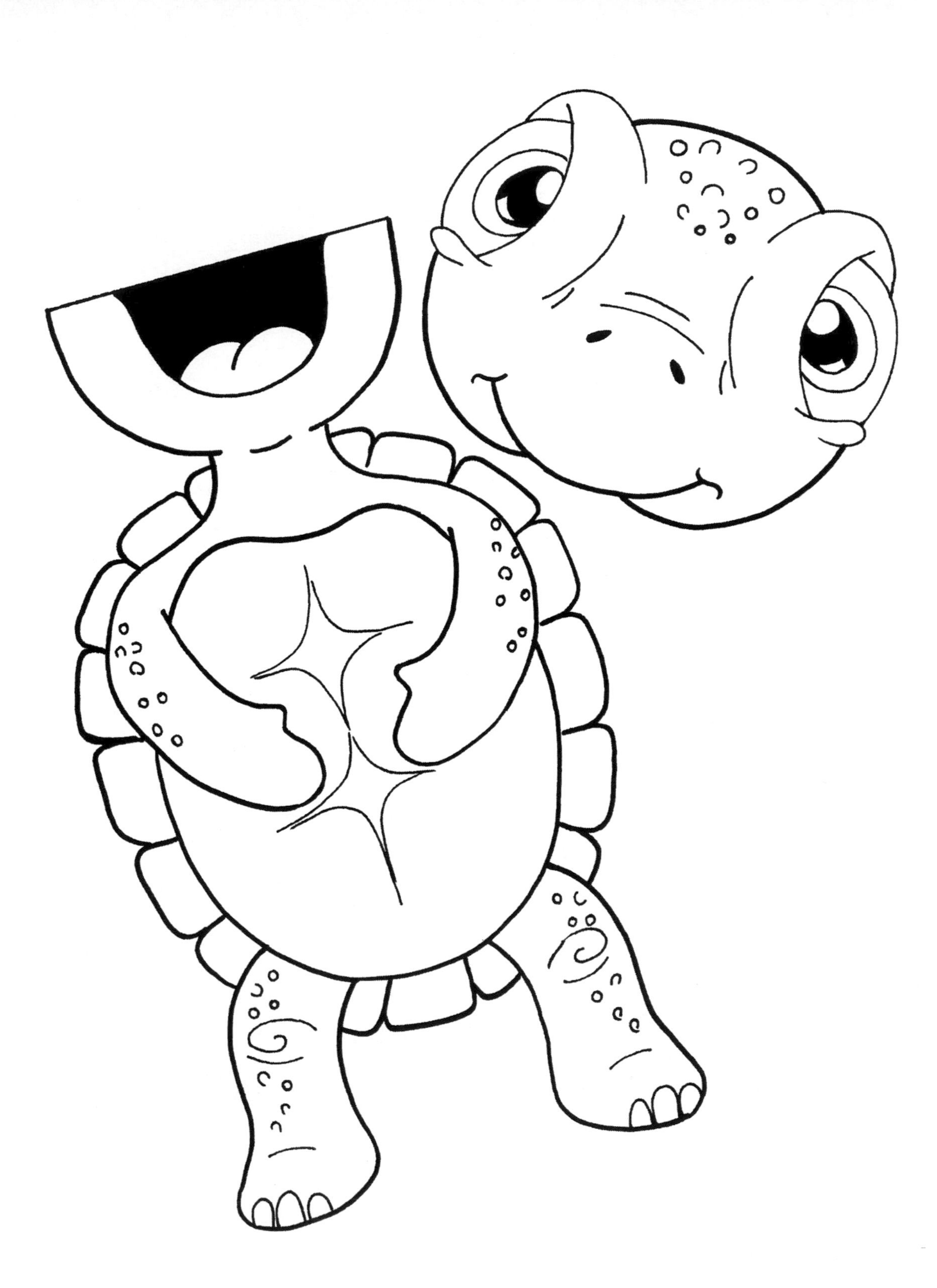

Tortoise/Turtle Activities

Songs to Sing and Play

Little Green Turtle (tune: Little Peter Rabbit Had a Fly Upon his Nose)

Words by Eunice Wright

Little green turtle had a leaf upon his nose,
Little green turtle had a leaf upon his nose,
Little green turtle had a leaf upon his nose;
He flicked it and it blew away.

Alternate: (Make up more verses)
Little Tommy Turtle had a fish upon his back,
Little Tommy Turtle had a fish upon his back,
Little Tommy Turtle had a fish upon his back,
He flicked it and it swam away.

Tune: I'm Bringing Home a Baby Bumble Bee

Words by Eunice Wright

I'm bringing home a little baby turtle,
Won't my mommy want to call her "Myrtle,"
I'm bringing home a little baby turtle,
Oh, she's slippery!!

I'm hiding my little baby turtle,
Won't my sister have to jump a hurdle!...

I'm feeding my little baby turtle,
My aunt May might even pop her girdle!...

I'm hugging my little baby turtle,
Won't my little baby brother want to gurgle...

Tune: Did You Ever See a Lassie?

Words by Eunice Wright

Did you ever see a turtle, a turtle, a turtle?
Did you ever see a turtle,
Swim this way and that?

Swim this way, and that way,
And this way, and that?
Did you ever see a turtle,
Swim this way and that?

Other actions: dive, float, crawl, eat, snap, hide, etc.

Tune: Fish and Chips and Vinegar (Tune: One Bottle of Pop)

Words by Eunice Wright; based on a folk and traditional campfire song

Fish and turtles by the stream,
By the stream, by the stream.
Fish and turtles by the stream,
Flip, flop, splash, snap!

Sally, the Camel

Sing the song using other animals: Molly, the monkey has one tail; Nellie, the horse has four legs; Newton, the Newt has four legs; Tommy, the Turtle has 1 shell.

Tiny Tim (tune: Miss Lucy Had a Baby or Miss Susie or Miss Molly/Polly)

Jump rope chant

There was a little turtle,
His name was tiny Tim
I put him in the bathtub to see if he could swim.
He drank up all the water,
He ate up all the soap,
And now he's sick in bed,
With bubbles in his throat.

Bubble, bubble, bubble,
Bubble, bubble, bubble,
Bubble, bubble, bubble,
Bubble, bubble, pop!

Poems and Nursery Rhymes

The Little Turtle

The Golden Whales of California and Other Rhymes, *1920, by Vachel Lindsay.*

There was a little turtle,
He lived in a box

He swam in a puddle,
He climbed on the rocks.
He snapped at a mosquito,
He snapped at a flea,
He snapped at a minnow,
And he snapped at me.

He caught the mosquito,
He caught the flea,
He caught the minnow,
But he didn't catch ME!

Mr. Turtle

By Eunice Wright

Mr. Turtle, so green and round,
You move so slowly along the ground.
Your house is right upon your back,
When you move, you don't need to pack.

Turtles (Count Up)

By Eunice Wright

One little turtle in an ocean of blue,
He found a friend, then there were two.
Two little turtles in the deep blue sea,
Along came another, then there were three.
Three little turtles hunting for some more,
They found another, and then there were four.
Four little turtles all swim and dive,
Along came mother turtle, then there were five.

Books

All About Turtle, by Jim Arnosky.
The Big Storm: A Very Soggy Counting Book, by Nancy Tafuri, Caldecott Honor Artist (Simon & Schuster, 2009). *For young readers and preschool children; beautiful illustrations of animals. This cute story might lead to a discussion of different animals, storms and weather.*
A Children's Treasury of Poems, illus. by Linda Bleck.
Devin and Goliath, by Mary Blount Christian.
A Family of Poems. Selected by Caroline Kennedy, p. 48.
The Foolish Tortoise, by Richard Buckley.
Franklin and the Tooth Fairy, by Paulette Bourgeois (Scholastic, 1996). *The animals talk, wear clothing, and all want something from the tooth fairy.*
Franklin in the Dark, by Paulette Bourgeois.
The Hare and the Tortoise, by Brian Wildsmith.
The Hare and the Tortoise, by Carol Jones (Houghton, 1996). *Crowded illustrations, cute story.*
The Hare and the Tortoise, by Caroline Castle (Dial, 1985).
The Hare and the Tortoise, by Gerald Rose (Macmillan, 1988).
The Hare and the Tortoise, by Helen Ward (Millbrook, 1999).
The Hare and the Tortoise, by Paul Galdone (Whittlesey House, 1962).
How the Turtle Got His Shell, adapted by Sandra Robbins.
How the Turtle Got His Shell, by Justine Fontes.
Hurry Up, Franklin, by Paulette Bourgeois.
Jack Gets a Clue #2: The Case of the Tortoise in Trouble, by Nancy Krulik.
Minn of the Mississippi, by Holling C. Holling.
No, No, No, Little Turtles! by Sally Doherty. Wobblies (Backpack Books, 2007). *Ages 4–6.*
Old Turtle, by Douglas Wood.
One Tiny Turtle, by Nicola Davies (Read and Wonder.)
Poems of Early Childhood. Vol. 1 (pub. by Field Enterprises Educational Corp.), p. 96, by various artists.
Rabbit Ears, by Amber Stewart (Bloomsbury, 2006). *Beautiful illustrations, a cute story about growing up. Great for preschool age children.*
The Race, by Caroline Repchuk (Chronicle Books, 2002). *A cute rhyming story of the famous race between the tortoise and the hare, modernized with cars and ships. Nice illustrations, ideal for discus-*

sion with small children. This could easily lead to a puppet show to develop the story further.

Sea Turtles, by Gail Gibbons.

Sea Turtles, Our Wild World series (North-Word Press).

A Silly Snowy Day, by Michael Coleman.

Small Gods, by Terry Pratchett.

The Tortoise and the Hare, by Janet Stevens (Reading Rainbow Books. Holiday, 1994). *Cute book; the animals wear clothing. A comical story.*

The Tortoise and the Hare, by Mark White (Picture Window, 2004).

The Tortoise and the Hare: Friends at the End, by Alvin Granowsky.

The Tortoise or the Hare, by Toni Morrison.

Tortuga in Trouble, by Ann Paul (Holiday House, 2009). *A bilingual twist of Little Red Riding Hood. Good illustrations; okay for early childhood.*

Turtle Girl, by Carole Crowe (Boyd's Mill Press, 2008). *Wonderful illustrations; the story of sea turtles. Good preschool introduction to sea turtles.*

Turtle Splash! Countdown at the Pond, by Cathryn Falwell (HarperCollins, 2008). *Ages 3–8. Ten tired turtles rest on a log, until one by one they slip into the mud of the river for a nap.*

Turtle Tale, by Frank Asch.

Turtle Throws a Tantrum, by Richard Hefter. (Sweet Pickles Series.)

What's in the Pond? by Anne Hunter (Houghton Mifflin, 1999). *Age 4–8. Tadpole, turtle and others.*

When Turtle Grew Feathers, by Tim Tingle (August House, 2007). *A Choctaw Indian variation of Aesop's Fable, with rhymes, good illustrations and some good humor.*

Whose Hat Is It? by Valeri Gorbachev. *When someone's hat blows off in the wind, Turtle tries to find its owner.*

Yertle the Turtle, by Dr. Seuss.

Movies and Television

Finding Nemo

Nature: Voyage of the Lonely Turtle

Teenage Mutant Ninja Turtles

Turtle Dance

Turtle: The Incredible Journey

A Turtle's Tale: Sammy's Adventures (recommended!)

16b. Hare

See Rabbit (#7a) for pattern and Rabbit activities.

17. The Ugly Duckling

A duckling hatches with his cute nest-mates, but he looks very different from them. Some say he is ugly and make fun of him. After a while, though, he grows into a beautiful swan.

17a. Duck

See Ducky Lucky (#1c) for puppet pattern and Duck activities.

17b. Swan

See Swan (#13b) for puppet pattern and Swan activities.

The Ugly Duckling and Swan Activities

Songs to Sing and Play

Tune: Here We Sit Like Birds in the Wilderness (Tune: The Old Gray Mare)

Camp song; words by Eunice Wright

Here we sit like lovely swans on the lake,
Lovely swans on the lake,
Lovely swans on the lake.
Here we sit like lovely swans on the lake,
Swimming gracefully.

Tune: Row, Row, Row Your Boat

Words by Eunice Wright

Glide, glide, glide along.
Swimming gracefully.
Silently swans swim along,
All majestically.
Swim, swim, swim along,
Gliding gracefully.
With your neck bent like an "S,"
All so elegantly.

Tune: Old Folks at Home

By Stephen Foster, 1851; adapted by Eunice Wright

1. Way down upon the Swan's River,
Far, far away.
That's where my heart is turning ever
That's where the old ducks stay.
All up and down the whole creation,
Sadly I swim.
Still longing for the swan's company,
And for the old ducks at home.

Chorus:
All the world is sad and dreary everywhere I roam.
Oh duckies, how my heart grows weary,
Far from the old ducks at home.

2. All 'round the little farm I wandered,
When I was young.
Then many happy days I squandered,
Many the songs I sung.
When I was playing with my brother,
Happy was I.
Oh, take me to my kind old mother,
There let me live and die.

(Chorus)

3. One little duck among the bushes,
One that I love.
Still sadly to my mem'ry rushes,
No matter where I rove.
When shall I see the bees a humming,
All 'round the comb.
When shall I hear the banjo strumming,
Down by my good old home.

(Chorus)

The Ugly Duckling Blues (A Song to Encourage Acceptance)

By Susan Harrison

This song is available on Susan Harrison's *Once Upon a Rhyme.*

Tune: Oh, My Darling Clementine

Words by Eunice and Juli Wright

In the country, on the farm,
An ugly duckling was born.
He was teased and scorned forever,
Dreadful sorry, ugly duck!

Drove she ducklings to the water,
Every morning just at nine.
But the others pushed ugly duckling
Down into the foaming brine.

Ugly duckling heard the teasing,
And he hid his head in shame.
He was sad and so lonely,
Dreadful sorry, ugly duck.

Hiding quietly, in the bushes,
Day after day he stayed away.
Until one day he up and left there,
And decided to swim away.

Light he was and like a fairy,
Gracefully swimming around the lake.
Hearing voices without teasing,
Now he heard no words that ache.

The others saw him, so surprised,
And in the early morning dawn,
There before them was a beauty,
A happy grown up, beautiful swan.

Down on Grandpa's Farm

Same song as in Goosey Loosey (#1b).

See songs for teaching.com or Raffi @CD Universe to listen to this song.

Alternate verses:

Down on Grandpa's farm there is: a little white duck, a lonely little duck, an ugly duckling, a beautiful swan, etc.

Poems and Nursery Rhymes

Ten Beautiful Swans (Count up)

By Eunice Wright

One beautiful swan, under the sky so blue,
Soon met another, then there were two.
Two beautiful swans, majestic to see,
Another came along, then there were three.
Three beautiful swans; they invited more.
One came to visit, then there were four.
Four beautiful swans, going down to dive,
They called for others, then there were five.
Five beautiful swans, swimming through the sticks,
They saw another swan, then there were six.
Six beautiful swans, met one named Kevin.
He moved in, then there were seven.
Seven beautiful swans, just couldn't wait,
They called to another, then there were eight.
Eight beautiful swans, waiting to dine,
Found plenty of food, and soon there were nine.
Nine beautiful swans, met one named "Jen."
She joined in, and then there were ten.

Black and White

By Juli Wright

As white as snow
It's beauty we know.
The slender neck
Seems to beck.
Graceful, like a prayer
No other can compare
To the white swan
Flying through the dawn.

As black as coal
Not an evil soul.
Wing tips tinged with white
And feathers black as night.
A rare and beautiful sight,
Like the fading twilight.
The black swan's duet
Flying into the sunset.

The Swan

Child Songs of Cheer, *by Evaleen Stein, 1918.*

Stately swan, so proud and white
Glistening in the morning light,
Come and tell me is it true
That a snow-white swan like you,
Guided by bright golden chains
In his beak for bridle reins,
Once upon a time from far
Fabled lands where fairies are
Brought a magic boat wherein
Rode the brave knight Lohengrin?

Stately swan, so proud and white
Glistening in the morning light,
If you only wore a gold
Harness, like that swan of old,
And if trailing in your wake
Sailing on the silver lake
Was a boat of magic and
You could float to fairy-land,
Then I'd jump in and begin
Traveling like Lohengrin!

The Swans

All Round the Year, *by Edith Nesbit, Saretta Nesbit (AKA Caris Brooke), 1888.*

The swans along the water glide,
Unfettered and yet side by side—
So should true lovers ever be,
Together ever—ever free.
A chain upon the white swan's neck,
What were it good for—save to break?
And swans who wear and break a chain
Swim never side by side again.

Games and Group Activities

Swan stick puppet

Any of the paper sack puppet patterns can easily be converted into a stick puppet or a rod puppet by gluing the head and mouth together into one piece, and then gluing the one piece onto the top of a paint or craft stick. The bigger, flat paint stirring sticks or a yardstick seem to work the best for the swan. This author prefers to leave the mouth unglued and just put glue around the top of the puppet so the mouth opening can be partly seen.

The swan puppet can be converted into a stick and rod puppet to accommodate the wing span and make the wings move a little. Attach the head and body onto the top of the yard-stick, and attach pieces of a coat hanger wire or wooden dowels to the wings with wide tape.

You will need a helper to make the puppet work. One person can hold the head and body stick, and the other person can hold the dowels or wires taped to the back of the wings. Move the wings *gently* as if they are flying in the air, while *gently* and slightly moving the head and body stick up and down. Try to give the impression of a live animal with gentle movements while the swan talks or sings.

Any of the other puppets with arms and/or wings (e.g., The Little Red Hen) can also be converted in this way to use the rods to move the arms and wings. The head and mouth can still be glued onto the paper sack, so the mouth can "speak."

Books

Animal Ark (Swan in the Swim), by Lucy Daniels.
Ballerina Swan, by Allegra Kent.
The Goose and the Swan, by Anne-Louise DePalo.
Little Swan, by Jonathan London.
Princess of the Wild Swans, by Diane Zahler.
The Silver Swan, by Michael Morpurgo (2000).
Spirit of the Swan, by Mary Lundeberg.
Sunflower and the Swan, by Ruth Read.
Swan Harbor: A Nature Counting Book, by Laura Rankin (2003).
Swan Lake, by Margot Fonteyn.
Swan Song, by J. Patrick Lewis (2003).
The Trumpet of the Swan, by E.B. White.
The Trumpet of the Swan, by Fred Marcellino (2000).

The Trumpet of the Swan: Louie the Hero, by Lin Oliver (2002).

The Ugly Duckling, adapted and illus. by Jerry Pinkney (Morrow Junior Books, 1999). *Beautiful illustrations and story, but many words, long sentences, advanced vocabulary; for older children. Caldecott Honor Book.*

The Ugly Duckling, by Hans Christian Andersen. Adapted by Susan Blackaby, illustrated by Charlene DeLage.

The Ugly Duckling, by Hans Christian Andersen, Pirkko Vainio (North-South, 2009). *Beautiful illustrations, long story; best for older children if reading the story aloud.*

The Ugly Duckling, by Harriet Ziefert.

The Ugly Duckling, by Kevin Crossley-Holland (Knopf, 2001). *Fair illustrations, long text; for older children.*

The Ugly Duckling, retold and illus. by Rachel Isadora (G.P. Putnam's Sons). *Set in Africa. Collage illustrations; easy to read story for young children.*

The Wild Swans, by Susan Jeffers (Dutton, 2008). *Hans Christian Anderson's story of the wicked queen who turns all the princes into swans. Beautiful illustrations, but the text is too long for young children.*

Movies and Television

Barbie of Swan Lake (2003)

Garfield and Friends (episode of the Ugly Duckling starring Wade the Cowardly Duck; animated)

Hans Christian Anderson, starring Danny Kaye, 1952. A wonderful movie with songs for many fairy tales! It has a very cute song for *The Ugly Duckling*. Highly recommended!

The Swan Princess, "Escape Castle Mountain" (Animated)

The Swan Princess, "The Mystery of the Enchanted Treasure" (Animated)

The Ugly Duckling (Animated, 1997)

The Ugly Duckling (Crayola)

The Ugly Duckling (Disney), "A Silly Symphony" (1939)

The Ugly Duckling and Me (Comedy animation from France)

18. Wolf in Sheep's Clothing; The Boy Who Cried "Wolf"

The Wolf in Sheep's Clothing is a cautionary tale about being fooled by outward appearances: A wolf disguised as a sheep infiltrates a herd of sheep and is able to eat all the sheep he wants. The Boy Who Cried "Wolf" is a story of a shepherd boy who thinks it's funny to trick the villagers by falsely claiming a wolf is in with the sheep. He does this one too many times, and when a wolf does appear, the villagers don't believe him and he loses many sheep.

18a. Wolf in Sheep's Clothing

Use Wolf puppet pattern (#5c) for body, adding the sheep's clothing on top. Use Lamb (#30) for flock of sheep.

COPY THE PATTERN OF THE SHEEP'S BODY AT 125%

18b. Shepherd Boy

See Brother (#47) for puppet pattern and Brother (Boy) activities. The cane from Three Blind Mice (#8c) can be used as a shepherd's crook.

Wolf in Sheep's Clothing and The Boy Who Cried "Wolf" Activities

Songs to Sing and Play

Tune: 5 and 20 Blackbirds (Sing a Song of Sixpence)

Words by Eunice Wright

Sing a song of pity for an undercover spy,
When along came a wolf who had just begun to cry.
"I haven't any wool suit to wear to work today,
Please sell me some wool and I'll be on my way."

All dressed up in a new wool suit, the wolf looked very cute.
He danced a merry jig while playing on a flute.
He invited all to join in as he gave a graceful leap,
Wasn't that a crazy thing to do before the sheep?

Sing a song of sixpence a pocket full of rye,
Four and twenty wool socks were baked in a pie.
When the pie was opened, the sheep began to sing,
Wasn't that a silly dish for the wolf to bring?

The shepherd was in his camper counting out his money,
The lambs were in the fenced corral eating bread and honey.
The sheep were in the field grazing all the day,
When along came a wolf who just wanted to play!

Tune: This Is the Way We Wash Our Clothes

Words by Juli Wright

This is the way he tends the sheep, tends the sheep, tends the sheep...
This is the way he cries, "Wolf, Wolf!"
This is the way the villagers run...
This is the way he learns a lesson...

Other Songs

"Wolf in Sheep's Clothing" by This Providence.
"A Wolf in Sheep's Clothing" by Face to Face, a punk rock band from Victorville, California.

Poems and Nursery Rhymes

The Sneaky Wolf in Sheep's Clothing

By Eunice Wright

Sneaky wolf, sneaky wolf,
You think you're so smart!
You try to trick others,
By dressing their part.

You may look like a sheep,
All dressed up in wool.
But the way you act,
Is not really cool.

The sheep see right through
The disguise you wear.
The shepherd will chase you,
So come if you dare!

Tricky Wolf

By Juli Wright

A wolf found great difficulty getting near the sheep,
He wished the shepherd and his dogs would finally go to sleep.

One day while the shepherd was out a-sheering,
The wolf was not too far off a-peering.

The wool the wolf did gather to make a sheep disguise,
Thinking that no one would see through his lies.

The wolf strolled down closely to the sheep,
But the shepherd's dogs were not asleep.

They made the wolf leave quickly with a giant leap,
They ran barking and chasing away that old creep.

Never Cry "Wolf"

By Eunice Wright

Never Cry "Wolf!"
When there isn't one.
You'll be sorry, by and by.
For when a lie is done,
Then more will come,
And soon you will see why;

When you call for help,
And you cry out bold,
No one will believe it.
Because the lies you told
Are what people will hold
As the truth—every little bit.

The Boy and the Wolf

The Home Book of Verse, Vol. 1 (of 4). *Author: Various. Editor: Burton Egbert Stevenson 1912, by John Hookham Frere (1769–1846)*

A little Boy was set to keep
A little flock of goats or sheep;
He thought the task too solitary,
And took a strange perverse vagary:

To call the people out of fun,
To see them leave their work and run,

He cried and screamed with all his might,—
"Wolf! wolf!" in a pretended fright.

Some people, working at a distance,
Came running in to his assistance.

They searched the fields and bushes round,
The Wolf was nowhere to be found.

The Boy, delighted with his game,
A few days after did the same,
And once again the people came.

The trick was many times repeated,
At last they found that they were cheated.

One day the Wolf appeared in sight,
The Boy was in a real fright,

He cried, "Wolf! wolf!"—the neighbors heard,
But not a single creature stirred.

"We need not go from our employ,—
'Tis nothing but that idle boy."

The little Boy cried out again,
"Help, help! the Wolf!" he cried in vain.

At last his master came to beat him.
He came too late, the Wolf had eat him.

This shows the bad effect of lying,
And likewise of continual crying.

If I had heard you scream and roar,
For nothing, twenty times before,

Although you might have broke your arm,
Or met with any serious harm,
Your cries could give me no alarm;

They would not make me move the faster,
Nor apprehend the least disaster;

I should be sorry when I came,
But you yourself would be to blame.

The Boy Who Loved to Lie

Childhood's Favorites and Fairy Stories The Young Folks Treasury, Volume 1. Copyright 1919. Author: Various. Editor: Jennie Ellis Burdick, The Boy Who Never Told a Lie; adapted by Juli Wright

Once there was a little boy,
With curly hair and pleasant eye—
While he was tending his little sheep
He thought he would tell a little lie.
At the end of the day, he went off to the village,
Wanting some fun, he began to cry,
"Wolf, Wolf, Wolf"—"Help or we'll die!"

The villagers, leaving their work undone,
Looked for a wolf they couldn't spy.
The little boy laughed, it was for fun.
The villagers knew, he had told a lie."
Villagers swore never again to come.
The boy thought no harm was done.
Ha, Ha, He, He—

One day, while tending his sheep
The boy say a wolf pass by,
Quickly he ran to tell the truth,
For this was really not a lie,
But when he came to the village,
And shouted and did cry,
"Wolf, wolf, wolf"—

The villagers thinking it was a lie.
And thought the boy uncouth,
So nobody came to help,
Because he never told the truth,
If only he hadn't told a lie,
He wouldn't of died in his youth.
"Boo-ho, Boo-ho, Sob!"

Books

A Big Fat Enormous Lie, by Marjorie Weinman.
The Boy Who Cried Wolf, by B.J. Hennessy. *The traditional story of telling a lie when there is no real wolf.*
The Boy Who Cried, "Wolf!" by Jenny Giles.
The Boy Who Cried, "Wolf!" by Lee Wildish.
The Boy Who Cried Wolf, retold by Eric Blair (Picture Window, 2004).
Don't Squeal Unless It's a Big Deal, by Jeanie Franz Ransom.
Julie of the Wolves. A young Eskimo girl joins a pack of wolves to survive.
Never Cry Wolf, by Farley Mowat (1963). *This was made into a movie in 1983. The true story of life among Arctic wolves. Older grades.*
Ruthie and the (Not So) Big Teeny Tiny Lie, by Laura Rankin.
Sam Tells Stories, by Thierry Robberecht.
There's a Wolf at the Door, by Zoe Alley.
Wolf Brother, by Michelle Paver (2006).
The Wolf in Sheep's Clothing, retold by Mark White (Picture Window, 2004).
The Wolf Who Cried Boy, by Bob Hartman.
Wolves in Sheep's Clothing, by Clark Jensen (2009).

Movies and Television

The Boy Who Cried Wolf (short film)
Call of the Wild
Dances with Wolves (adults)
The Muppets—*The Boy Who Cried Wolf*
Never Cry Wolf
Peter and the Wolf
The Three Little Pigs
Wilderness Family

Additional Activities

Songs to Sing and Play

Fairy Tale Favorites: Story-time Songs for Children

CD by Shauna Tominey. Track listing:

1. Three Pigs
2. Three Billy Goats Gruff
3. Little Red Riding Hood
4. Gingerbread Man
5. Little Red Hen
6. Cinderella
7. Goldilocks and the Three Bears
8. Tortoise and the Hare
9. Frog Prince
10. Hansel and Gretel
11. Jack and the Beanstalk
12. Elves and the Shoemaker

Children love listening to songs and stories and singing along with their favorites! This CD is perfect for storytime, group singing and puppet plays, dramatizing, relaxing naptime, and long car rides. These songs are great for classrooms, libraries or home story times, learning activities, and just for fun.

Also: *Fairy Tale Favorites 2: More Storytime Songs for Children*, including:

Rapunzel
Brave Little Tailor
Emperor's New Clothes
Rip Van Winkle
Rumpelstiltskin
Sleeping Beauty

Poems and Nursery Rhymes

Nursery Rhyme: What If?

The Book of Knowledge, Vol. 7 *(some verses are missing), 1910.*

If the old woman who lived in a shoe
Had lived in a cottage instead,
Her children could have played at hide-and-seek,
And needn't have been sent to bed.

If Little Bo-Peep hadn't lost her sheep,
She wouldn't have had to find them,
If Little Boy Blue had not any sheep,
He wouldn't have had to mind them.

If the goose that laid the golden eggs
Had not been killed that day,
She'd still be laying golden eggs
As hard as she could lay.

In fact, if we could imagine things,
How different they would be!
But as we can't, we'll let them stay
Just as they are, you see.

Puppet Play Ideas

The Boy Who Cried, "Wolf!" (boy, wolf, townspeople, sheep)
Cinderella (princess, stepsisters and mother, prince/man, king, queen, crown)
The Fox and the Hound (fox, dog, men, horses)
The Goose That Laid the Golden Egg (see goose puppet section, Peter Cottontail's egg)

Jack and the Beanstalk (see goose puppet activities—Jack, goose, mother, troll, cow)
Johnny Appleseed (man, Little Red Hen's sack of seeds, pan or dish for hat)
Little Black Sambo (tigers, black boy with removable clothes and accessories, mother)
The Princess and the Pea (princess, crown, man/prince)
Rapunzel (Use princess [with braided yarn for long hair], prince/man, crown from Frog Prince, witch)
Rip Van Winkle (grandfather with beard that grows)
Robin Hood (princess, man, merry men, sheriff)
Sleeping Beauty (princess, witch, prince/man, crown from Frog Prince)
Snow White (princess, witch, man, crown)
The Wolf and the Seven Little Kids (goats, wolf)

Movies and Television

The Boy Who Couldn't Get the Shivers
Cinderella, Disney Animated
Ella Enchanted
Frog Prince, Jim Henson
Happily Ever After
Jack and the Beanstalk, 1952, Abbott and Costello
Jack and the Beanstalk, Disney Animated.
Johnny Appleseed, Animated
Pinocchio
The Princess and the Pea, the Muppets
Rapunzel
Rumpelstiltskin, Jim Henson's the Storyteller
Sapsarrow, Jim Henson's The Storyteller
Sleeping Beauty, Disney Animated
Tangled, Disney Animated

Shelley Duvall's Faerie Tale Theatre

Little Red Riding Hood (episode #7, season 2, 1983).
Hansel and Gretel (episode #8, season 2, 1983).
Goldilocks and the 3 bears (episode #9, Season 3, 1983, 48 min.)
The Princess and the Pea (episode #10 Season 3, 1984, 51 min.)
Pinocchio (episode #11, Season 3, 1984, 51 min.)
Thumbelina (episode #12, Season 3, 1984, 51 min.)
Snow-white and the Seven Dwarfs (episode #13, Season 3, 1984, 53 min.)
Beauty and the Beast (episode #14, Season 3, 1984).
The Boy Who Left Home to Find out About the Shivers (episode #15, Season 3, 1984, 52 min.)
The Three Little Pigs (episode #16, Season 4, 1985, 52 min.)
The Snow Queen (episode #17, Season 4, 1985).
The Pied Piper of Hamelin (episode #18, Season 4, 1983, 4 min.)
Cinderella (episode #20, Season 4, 1985, 54 min.)
Puss in Boots (episode #21, Season 4, 1985, 52 min.)
The Emperor's New Clothes (episode #22, Season 5, 1985, 54 min.)
Aladdin and His Wonderful Lamp (episode #23, Season 5, 1986, 48 min.)
The Princess Who Had Never Laughed (episode #24, Season 5, 1986, 52 min.)
Rip Van Winkle (episode #25, Season 6, 1987, 49 min.)
The Little Mermaid (episode #26, Season 6, 1987, 51 min.)
The Dancing Princesses (episode #27, Season 6 1987, 51 min.)

Cannon Movie Tales

Beauty and the Beast
Rumpelstiltskin
The Frog Princesses
Red Riding Hood
The Frog Prince

Snow White
Hansel and Gretel
Cinderella

Books

Nursery Rhyme Books

Hey, Diddle Diddle, by Tiger Tales and Hannah Wood (2012).
Hickory, Dickory, Dock: And Other Favorite Nursery Rhymes, illus. by Sanja Rescek (2006).
This Little Piggy: And Other Favorite Action Rhymes, by Hannah Wood (2010).
Twinkle, Twinkle Little Star and Other Favorite Bedtime Rhymes, by Sanja Rescek (2006).

Additional Fairytales & Fables Books

Aesop's Fables, by Jerry Pinkney.
The Bremen Town Musicians, by Hsin-Shih-Lai.
Cinderella—That Awful Cinderella: A Classic Tale, by Alvin Granowsky.
The Elves and the Shoemaker, by Jacob Grimm.
Fables, by Arnold Lobel.
Giants Have Feelings, Too (Jack and the Beanstalk), by Alvin Granowsky.
Jack and the Beanstalk, by Carol Ottolenghi.
Jack and the Beanstalk, by Steven Kellogg.
Jack and the Beanstalk (Classic Fairy Tale Collection), by John Cech.
Johnny Appleseed, by Steven Kellogg.
Johnny Appleseed, My Story, by David L. Harrison (Step into Reading, level 3).
King Midas and the Golden Touch, by Charlotte Craft.
Mike Fink, by Steven Kellogg.
My First Picture Book, by Joseph Martin Kronheim. Includes *My First Alphabet, The Little Old Woman Who Lived in a Shoe, The Babes in the Wood, Little Bo-Peep, The History of Five Little Pigs, The History of Old Mother Goose and Her Son Jack.*
Paul Bunyan, by Steven Kellogg.
Pecos Bill, by Steven Kellogg.
The Princess and the Pea (Classic Fairy Tale Collection), by John Cech.
The Princess and the Pea (Easy-to-read, Puffin), by Harriet Ziefert.
Puss in Boots, by Charles Perrault.
Rapunzel (Caldecott Medal Book), by Paul O. Zelinsky.
Rip Van Winkle; Wake Up, Rip Van Winkle, by Alvin Granowsky.
Robin Hood: The Sheriff Speaks, a Classic Tale, by Alvin Granowsky.
Rumpelstiltskin: A Deal Is a Deal, a Classic Tale, by Alvin Granowsky.
Rumplestiltskin, by Paul Galdone.
Rumplestiltskin, by Paul O. Zelinsky.
Sleeping Beauty, by Mahlon F. Craft.
Sleeping Ugly, by Jane Yolen.
Snow White, the Unfairest of Them All, by Alvin Granowsky.
The Tales of Mother Goose, as First Collected by Charles Perrault (1696).

Old-Time Stories

By Charles Perrault. Includes the following:

"The Sleeping Beauty in the Wood"
"Puss in Boots"
"Little Tom Thumb"
"The Fairies"
"Ricky of the Tuft"
"Cinderella"
"Little Red Riding Hood"
"Blue Beard"
"Beauty and the Beast"
"The Friendly Frog"
"Princess Rosette"

My Book of Favorite Fairy Tales

By Edric Vredenburg. Includes the following:

"The Old, Old Stories"
"The Goose Girl"
"Little Snow-White"
"Cinderella"
"Princess Goldenhair"

"Little Red Riding Hood"
"The White Fawn"
"Hansel and Gretel"
"Snow-White and Rose-Red"
"The Sleeping Beauty"
"Prince Cheri"
"The White Cat"
"Bluebeard"
"Beauty and the Beast"
"Tufty Riquet"
"Thumbling"

Children's Hour With Red Riding Hood and Other Stories

Edited by Watty Piper (1922). Includes the following:

"Little Red Riding Hood"
"The Goose-Girl"
"Babes in the Wood"
"The Sleeping Beauty"
"Snowdrop and the Seven Little Dwarfs"

Grimm's Fairy Stories

By Jacob Grimm and Wilhelm Grimm. Contents:

"The Goose-Girl"
"The Little Brother and Sister"
"Hansel and Gretel"
"Oh, If I Could but Shiver!"
"Dummling and the Three Feathers"
"Little Snow-White"
"Catherine and Frederick"
"The Valiant Little Tailor"
"Little Red Cap"
"The Golden Goose"
"Bearskin"
"Cinderella"
"Faithful John"
"The Water of Life"
"Thumbling"
"Briar Rose"
"The Six Swans"
"Rapunzel"
"Mother Holle"
"The Frog Prince"
"The Travels of Tom Thumb"
"Snow-White and Rose-Red"
"The Three Little Men in the Wood"
"Rumpelstiltskin"
"Little One-Eye, Two-Eye and Three-Eyes"

Illustrated Fairy Tales Usborne Book

Author/illus. Leslie Sims. Includes:

"Sleeping Beauty"
"The Emperor and the Nightingale"
"Beauty and the Beast"
"The Dragon Painter"
"The Frog Prince, the Elves and the Shoemaker"
"Little Red Riding Hood"
"Cinderella"
"The Swan Princess"
"The Emperor's New Clothes"

19. A—Alligator

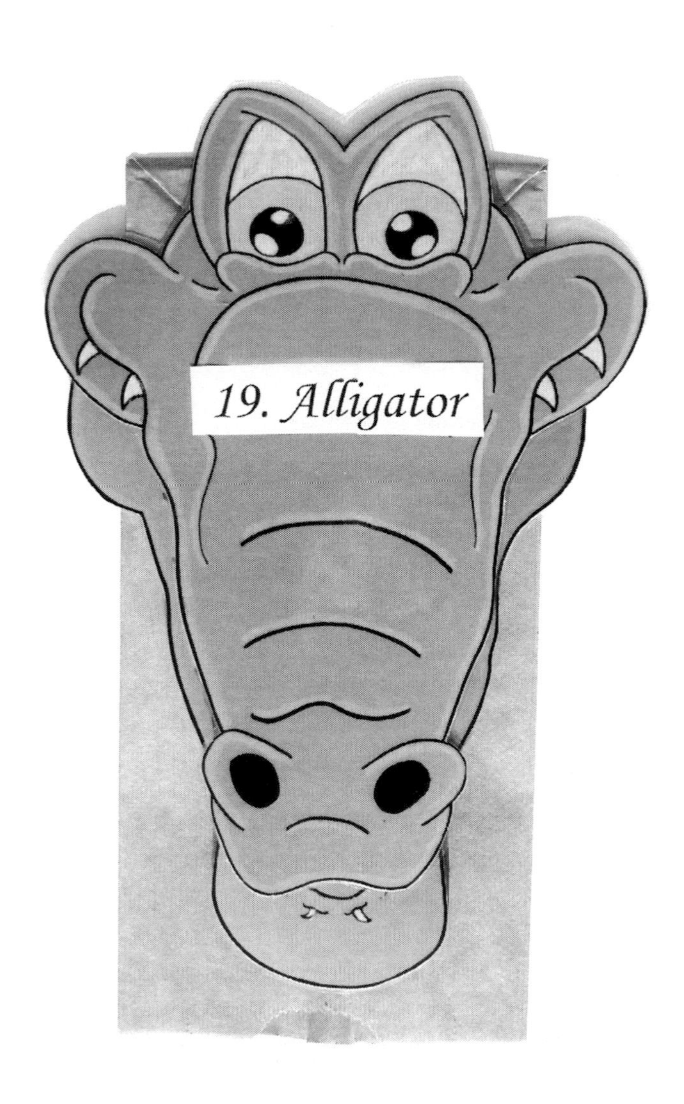

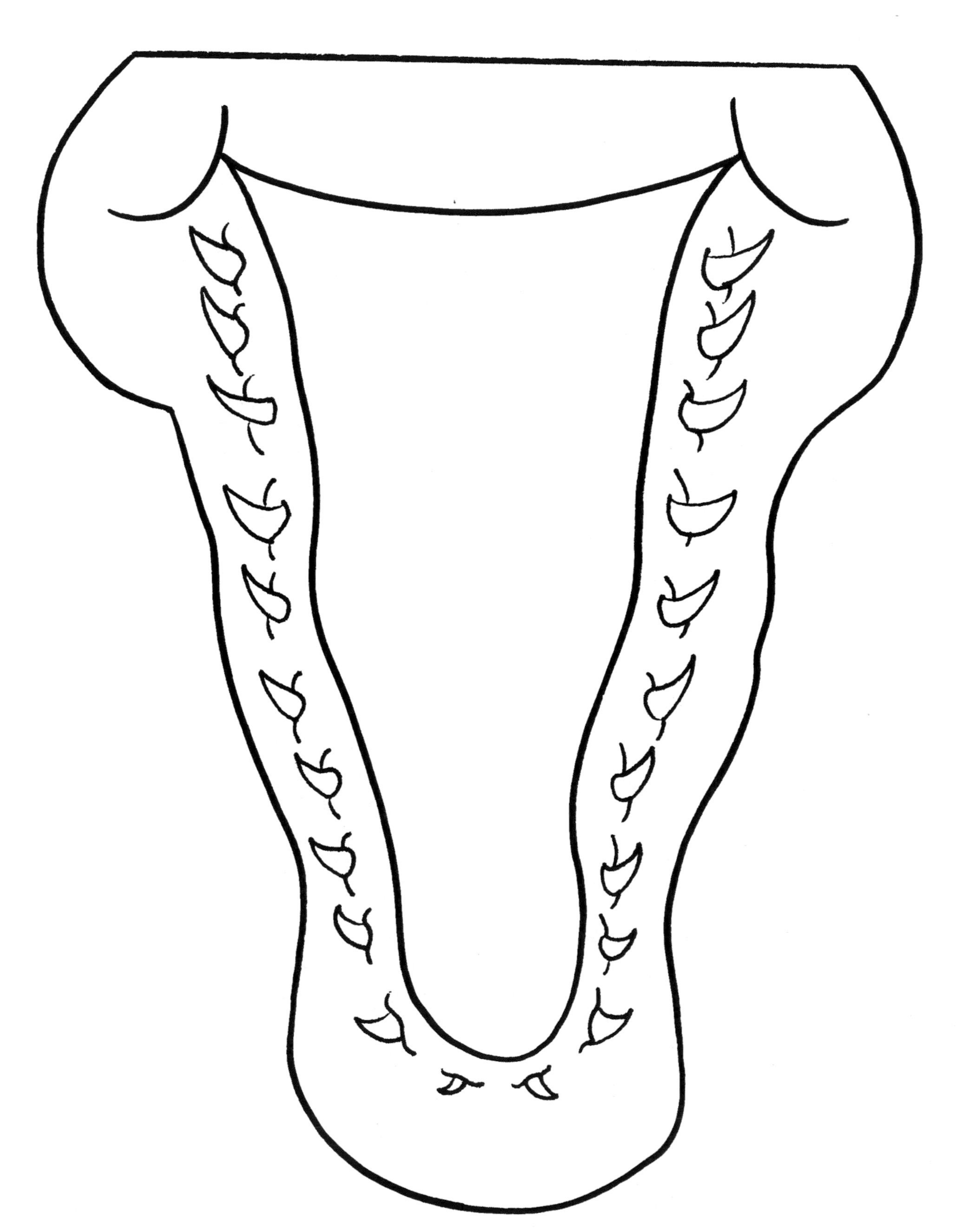

Alligator and Crocodile Activities

Songs to Sing and Play

If You Should Meet an Elephant

"If you should meet a crocodile on a summer's day..."

Merry Little Fishes

Adapted by Juli Wright; Finger Play Reader (see book for sheet music)

Merry little fishes
In the river at play,
Floating in the shallows,
Darting swift away.

Along came the Alligator,
As quiet as can be
"Happy little fishes,
Come and play with me.

"Yes, yes, yes!" said the fishes.
"That sounds like fun."
The alligator smiled,
And away they all run.

The Crocodile

Traditional, obscure origins

She sailed away on a sunny summer day,
On the back of a crocodile.
"You see," said she, "he's as tame as tame can be,
I'll ride him down the Nile."

The crock winked his eye as she bade them all goodbye,
Wearing a happy smile—
At the end of the ride, the lady was inside,
And the smile was on the crocodile!

Never Smile at a Crocodile, *by Jack Lawrence, music by Frank Churchill, 1952, Walt Disney Music Company.*

Poems and Nursery Rhymes

Alligator, Alligator (Teddy Bear Jump Rope Chant)

By Eunice Wright

Alligator, alligator, you're so long and green.
Alligator, alligator, your teeth look so mean.
Alligator, alligator, crawl away.
Alligator, alligator, come another day.

The Monkeys and the Crocodile, or Teasing Mr. Alligator/Crocodile

Originated from In My Nursery, A Book of Verse, *by Laura E. Richards, 1890. (See grandparents.com, and KingCountyLibrarySystem to watch this performed.)*

Clap hands loudly on the word, "Snap!"

Three little monkeys
Swinging in a tree
Teasing Mister Alligator,
Can't catch me, can't catch me.
Along comes Mister Alligator,
Quiet as can be
And SNAPS that monkey
Right out of that tree!

Two little monkeys...

One little monkey
Swinging in a tree
Teasing Mister Alligator,
Can't catch me, can't catch me
Along comes Mister Alligator,
Quiet as can be
And SNAPS that monkey
Right out of that tree!

Alternate endings:

Quiet as can be ... Snap! Missed me!
And SNAP! No more monkeys swinging in a tree!
But here's Mr. Alligator/Crocodile, full as can be!

Alligator on a Log

By Eunice Wright

Once there was an alligator hiding in a bog.
Along came a little green speckled frog.

Up jumped the alligator, who mis-stepped on a log, ("Oooops!")
Splash! in the mud, and away hopped the frog.

How Doth the Little Crocodile

By Lewis Carroll (songs from Alice In Wonderland and Through the Looking Glass, *1921).*

How doth the little crocodile
Improve his shining tail,
And pour the waters of the Nile
On every golden scale!

How cheerfully he seems to grin,
How neatly spreads his claws,
And welcomes little fishes in
With gently smiling jaws!

Five Dancing Alligators (Count Up)

By Eunice Wright

One little alligator, dancing on his toes,
Up and down the music goes.
Two little alligators, both politely bow,
Holding hands tightly, one yells, "OW!"
Three little alligators, dancing the fox trot,
Three is a crowd, so I think not!
Four little alligators, doing the limbo crawl,
One whacked his head & started to bawl.
Five little alligators, having fun at last,
Dancing, singing, and twirling around fast.

Mr. Alligator

By Juli Wright

Mr. Alligator, fat and long,
With a big wide grin,
Began to sing a happy song,
"Come in! Come for a little swim."

Mr. Alligator heard a monkey say,
"We think it's safer in the tree."
His reply, "It's hot! The water today,
Is nice and cool, come and see!"

The monkeys were so very hot
A cool swim sounded nice.
The wisest of them said, "Do Not!
You'd better think it twice."

Soon the monkeys began to come
One, two, with a splash!
Into the water quickly went some,
And out again, in a flash.

Sneaky, sneaky the alligator came
With a big old grin,
No more monkeys, what a shame,
If only they hadn't jumped in.

The moral of this story is really lame
Stay at home or you're insane!

The Monkeys and the Crocodile

In My Nursery: A Book of Verse, *by Laura E. Richards, 1890.*

Heads up, tails up,
Little do they care.
Swinging up, swinging down,
Swinging far and near:
"Poor Uncle Crocodile,
Aren't you hungry, dear?"

Four little monkeys
Sitting in the tree;
Heads down, tails down,
Dreary as can be.
Weeping loud, weeping low,
Crying to each other:
"Wicked Uncle Crocodile,
To gobble up our brother!"

Books

Alligator Alphabet, by Stella Blackstone and Stephanie Bauer.
Alligator Arrived with Apples, by Crescent Dragonwagon. A Thanksgiving story.
Alligator Baby, by Robert Munsch and Michael Martchenko.
Alligator Shoes, by Arthur Dorros.
Alligators All Around, by Maurice Sendak.
Bill and Pete to Rescue (Picture Puffins), by Tomie DePaola.
Catch That Crocodile! by Anushka Ravishankar and Pulak Biswas.
Counting Crocodiles, by Judy Sierra. *One very*

clever monkey and some not-so-bright crocodiles. A preschool picture book.

Crocks! by David Greenberg and Lynn Munsinger.

Crocodile! Crocodile! Stories Told Around the World, by Barbara Baumgartner (Dorling Kindersley, 1994). This book has a special section on making stick puppets and presenting puppet plays. Very different but very cute illustrations; good stories. These can be easily adapted for puppet plays.

Crocodile Listens, by April Sayre (Greenwillow Books, 2001). Large illustrations showing mother crocodile raising baby crocodiles. A nice story to be told to young children by an adult with dramatic vocal "sound effects."

Doodle Bites: A Tilly and Friends Book, by Polly Dunbar.

The Enormous Crocodile, by Roald Dahl.

An Extraordinary Egg, by Leo Lionni (Knopf).

Feliciana Feydra LeRoux: A Cajun Tall Tale, by Tynia Thomassie and Cat Smith.

Funny, Funny Lyle (Lyle the Crocodile), by Bernard Waber.

Gator Gumbo: A Spicy-Hot Tale, by Candace Fleming and Sally Anne Lambert.

The Gift of the Crocodile: A Cinderella Story, by Judy Sierra and Reynold Ruffins.

The Hunterman and the Crocodile: A West African Folktale, by Baba Wague Diakite.

I Am a Little Alligator: Mini (Barron's Little Animal Miniatures), by Francois Crozat.

I, Crocodile, by Fred Marcellin.

I'd Really Like to Eat a Child, by Sylviane Donnio. A young hungry crocodile is tired of eating bananas and wants to eat a child, but bites off more than he can chew.

The Lady with the Alligator Purse, by Nadine Bernard Westcott.

Lovable Lyle (Lyle the Crocodile), by Bernard Waber.

Lyle and the Birthday Party (Lyle the Crocodile), by Bernard Waber.

Lyle Finds His Mother (Lyle the Crocodile), by Bernard Waber.

Lyle, Lyle Crocodile (Read Along Book and CD), by Bernard Waber.

Mama Don't Allow, by Thacher Hurd.

The Monkey and the Crocodile, Seabury Press (1969).

No Biting, Louise, by Margie Palatini and Matthew Reinhart.

No Laughing, No Smiling, No Giggling, by James Stevenson.

On the Go with Mr. and Mrs. Green, by Keith Baker.

Snappy Heads Andy Alligator (Snappy Fun), by Sarah Albee and Jo Brown. Board book.

There's a Crocodile Under My Bed, by Ingrid and Dieter Schubert (1980). Cute story with a moral. Has a long text, fair illustrations.

There's an Alligator Under My Bed, by Mercer Mayer.

The Three Little Gators, by Helen Ketteman.

Uncle Wiggily and the Alligator, by Howard R. Garis (Whitman Publishing Company, 1953).

What Time Is It, Mr. Crocodile? by Judy Sierra (Harcourt, 2004). Five monkeys tease Mr. Crocodile until they become friends in the end. A nice preschool story; good illustrations.

Who Stole Alligator's Shoe? (Sweet Pickles Series), by Jacquelyn Reinach.

Zack's Alligator (An I Can Read Book), by Shirley Mozelle and James Watts.

Zack's Alligator Goes to School, by Shirley Mozelle and James Watts.

Movies and Television

Animal Planet

Animals Are Beautiful People

Crocodile Dundee 1 & 2

Crocodile Hunter

Frog Prince

Hook

Jewel of the Nile

Lady and the Tramp

National Geographic

Peter Pan

Rescuers 1

20. B—Beaver

Beaver Activities

Songs to Sing and Play

Tune: This Is the Way We...

Words by Eunice Wright

This is the way we... (build a dam, cut down a tree, swim under water)

Tune: Did You Ever See a Lassie?

Words by Eunice Wright

Did you ever see a groundhog,
A groundhog, a groundhog,
Did you ever see a groundhog,
Who saw his shad-ow?

Tune: Row, Row, Row Your Boat

Words by Eunice Wright

Chew, chew, chew the tree,
Chew it right in two.
I'll make a dam that you can see,
My flat wide tail helps too.

Chew, chew, chew the tree,
Big teeth help you chew.
I'll make a pond that you can see.
That is what I do.

Chew, chew, chew the tree,
Chewing is so fun.
I teach my family to work like me.
Our work is never done.

Poems and Nursery Rhymes

A Beaver's Work

Words by Eunice Wright

A beaver's work is never done,
He works all day in the hot, hot sun.
Two large teeth and a tail flat and wide,
Help him swim and build and hide.

Two Little Beavers

Mother Goose Rhymes, *edited by Watty Piper, 1922.*

Two little beavers lived in a dam,
One named Sue, the other named Sam.
Come to me, Sue; come to me, Sam.
Go again, Sue; go again, Sam.

Funny Furry Little Beaver

By Juli Wright

Funny furry little beaver
Chewing, chewing he can't go wrong.
Funny furry little beaver,
Working, working all day long
To build himself a little dam.
Then he'll sing the beaver song.

"I'm a furry little beaver,
And the thing I do
As a furry little beaver
Is chew, chew, chew.
I love to chew and that's no lie;
If you were a beaver,
Then you would chew too."

Books

Born to Be Wild, Little Beavers, by Christian Marie (GarethStevens Pub., 2006). *Nice photos and text.*
Busy Little Beaver, by Dawn Bentley (Little Sound Prints, 2003). *Beginning Reader, easy text, nice illustrations; mostly facts, no story.*
A Garden for Groundhog, by Lorna Balian.
Go to Sleep, Groundhog! by Judy Cox (Holiday House, 2004). *Long text about Groundhog Day.*
A Gopher in the Garden, and Other Animal Poems, by Jack Prelutsky (Macmillan, 1966). *A nice collection of poems for almost every need.*
Gretchen Groundhog, It's Your Day! by Abby Levine.
Groundhog Day! by Gail Gibbons.
Groundhog Day (Rookie Read-About Holidays), by Michelle A. Becker.

The Groundhog Day Book of Facts and Fun, by Wendie C. Old.
Groundhog Gets a Say, by Pamela C. Swallow.
Groundhog Stays Up Late, by Margery Cuyler.
The Life Cycle of a Beaver, a Bobbie Kalman Book (Crabtree, 2007). *Very nice photos and text.*
Punxsutawney Phyllis, by Susana Leonard Hill.
Substitute Groundhog, by Pat Miller.
Ten Grouchy Groundhogs, by Kathryn Heling.
Turtle's Race with Beaver, by Joseph and James Bruchac.

Movies and Television

Be Polite, Merry Melodies, Looney Tunes (1:45)
Best Friends Sneak Peak, Looney Tunes (2:22)
Gopher Broke, You Tube short clip.
A Ham in a Roll, Looney Tune (6:49)
Lady and the Tramp (the beaver chews on wood to make a dam).
2 Gophers from Texas, Looney Tunes, 1948 (6:58)

21. C—Cow

Cow Activities

Songs to Sing and Play

Tune: Skip to My Lou (Version 1)

Traditional children's song; Popular Folk Games, *1907.*

Chorus:
Skip, skip, skip to my Lou,
Skip, skip, skip to my Lou,
Skip, skip, skip to my Lou,
Skip to my Lou, my darlin'.

Fly's in the buttermilk, shoo, fly, shoo,
Fly's in the buttermilk, shoo, fly, shoo,
Fly's in the buttermilk, shoo, fly, shoo,
Skip to my Lou, my darlin'.

Chorus

Cow's in the cornfield, what'll I do?
Cow's in the cornfield, what'll I do?
Cow's in the cornfield, what'll I do?
Skip to my Lou, my darlin'.

Chorus

There's a little red wagon, paint it blue
There's a little red wagon, paint it blue
There's a little red wagon, paint it blue
Skip to my Lou, my darlin'.

Chorus

Purple Cow

The Lark, *by Frank Gelett Burgess, 1895.*

I never saw a purple cow.
I never hope to see one.
But I can tell you anyhow
I'd rather see than be one.

I never saw a _____ (purple tiger)
I never hope to see one,
But I can tell you anyhow,
I'd rather see a _____ (tame) one.

Tune: Brown Bear, Brown Bear

Book by Bill Martin, Jr., Holt, 1983.

Brown cow, brown cow, what do you see? I see a _____ looking at me.

Mrs. O'Leary's Cow

Music by Theodore August Metz, lyrics by Joe Hayden, 1896. Also called "Old Mother Leary" and "There'll Be a Hot Time in the Old Town Tonight."

Late one night
When we were all in bed
Old Mother Leary
Left a lantern in the shed

And when the cow kicked it over,
She winked her eye and said,
"There'll be a hot time
In the old town tonight."

Spoken:
"FIRE, FIRE, FIRE!"

Expanded version, most familiar in Chicago:

Five nights ago,
When we were all in bed
Old Mrs. Leary left the lantern in the shed
And when the cow kicked it over,
She winked her eye and said
It'll be a hot time, in the old town tonight!
FIRE FIRE FIRE!

Four nights ago,
When we were all in bed
Old Mrs. Leary left the lantern in the shed
And when the cow kicked it over,
She winked her eye and said
It'll be a hot time, in the old town tonight!
FIRE FIRE FIRE!

Three nights ago,
When we were all in bed
Old Mrs. Leary left the lantern in the shed
And when the cow kicked it over,
She winked her eye and said
It'll be a hot time, in the old town tonight!
FIRE FIRE FIRE!

Two nights ago,
When we were all in bed
Old Mrs. Leary left the lantern in the shed
And when the cow kicked it over,
She winked her eye and said
It'll be a hot time, in the old town tonight!
FIRE FIRE FIRE

One night ago,
When we were all in bed
Old Mrs. Leary left the lantern in the shed
And when the cow kicked it over,
She winked her eye and said
It'll be a hot time, in the old town tonight!
FIRE FIRE FIRE!

Note—other "rounds" or verses can be concluded with:

Water, water, water!
Jump, lady, jump!
Save my child, save my child!

Down on Grandpa's Farm

Traditional; see songs for teaching.com to listen to this song.

...there is a big brown cow.

Tune: 10 Little Indians

Words by Eunice Wright

One little, two little, three little cows...
All inside the barn.

Tune: The Wheels on the Bus

Words by Eunice Wright

The cows on the farm
Go moo, moo, moo,
Moo, moo, moo,
Moo, moo, moo.
The cows on the farm
Go moo, moo, moo,
All around the farm. (Or down on the farm, out in the barn, etc.)

Bought Me a Cat

Southern Traditional

Bought me a cow and the cow pleased me,
I fed my cow under yonder tree.
Cow goes moo, moo,
Pig goes oink, oink,
Sheep goes baa, baa,
Goose goes hissy, hissy,
Duck goes quack, quack,
Hen goes chimmy-chuck, chimmy-chuck,
Cat goes fiddle-i-fee.

I Had a Rooster

Traditional

I had a rooster, my rooster pleased me
I fed my rooster 'neath the greenberry tree
My little rooster went cocka doodle doo
Dee doodle-ee doodle-ee doodle-ee do.

I had a cow, my cow pleased me
I fed my cow 'neath the greenberry tree
My big old bossy cow went moo
My little kitty went meow
My little doggie went ruff ruff ruff
My little rooster went cocka doodle doo
Dee doodle-ee doodle-ee doodle-ee do.

Tune: Go In and Out the Window (or Go Round and Round the Village)

Words by Eunice Wright

The cow goes round the field,
The cow goes round the field,
The cow goes round the field,
As she has done before.

The cow goes in the barn,
The cow goes in the barn,
The cow goes in the barn,
As she has done before.

She gives us milk to drink,
She gives us milk to drink,
She gives us milk to drink,
As she has done before.

Other Songs

The Clever Cow

"The Clever Cow," I Have a Song for You, *by Janeen Brady, page 15, Vol. 3. Brite Music Enterprises, 1980.*

Poems and Nursery Rhymes

Hey Diddle Diddle

Harry's Ladder to Learning, with Two Hundred and Thirty Illustrations, *by David Bogue and Joseph Cundall, 1850.*

Hey diddle diddle, the cat and the fiddle,
The cow jumped over the moon,
The little dog laughed to see such a sport,
And the dish ran after the spoon.

Cushy Cow

The Real Mother Goose, *by Blanche Fisher Wright, 1916.*

Cushy cow, bonny, let down thy milk,
And I will give thee a gown of silk;
A gown of silk and a silver tee,
If thou wilt let down thy milk to me.

Pretty Cow

By Anne Taylor, 1883

Thank you, pretty cow, that made
Pleasant milk to soak my bread,
Every day and every night,
Warm, and fresh, and sweet, and white.

Do not chew the hemlock rank,
Growing on the weedy bank;
But the yellow cowslips eat;
They perhaps will make it sweet.

Where the purple violet grows,
Where the bubbling water flows,
Where the grass is fresh and fine,
Pretty cow, go there to dine.

Frightened by a Cow

Aunt Kitty's Stories, *1870*

A very young lady,
With Susan, the maid,
Who carried the baby,
Were one day afraid.

They saw a cow feeding,
Quite harmless and still,
Yet screamed without heeding
The man at the mill.

Who seeing their flutter,
Said, "Cows do no harm,
But give you good butter
And milk from the farm."

"So don't have the folly
Of running at sight
Of a gentle old Mooly,
In terror and fright."

There Was a Piper Had a Cow

Aunt Kitty's Stories, *1870.*

There was a piper had a cow,
And he had naught to give her,
He pull'd out his pipes and play'd her a tune,
And bade the cow consider.

The cow considered very well,
And gave the piper a penny,
And bade him play the other tune,
"Corn rigs are bonny."

The Cow

A Child's Garden of Verses, *by Robert Louis Stevenson, 1916.*

The friendly cow all red and white, I love with all my heart:
She gives me cream with all her might, to eat with apple-tart.
She wanders lowing here and there, and yet she cannot stray,
All in the pleasant open air, the pleasant light of day.

And blown by all the winds that pass and
wet with all the showers,
She walks among the meadow grass and eats
the meadow flowers.

The Moo Cow Moo

Poems Teachers Ask For, *Book 1, by various authors, 1922. Poem by Edmund Vance Cooke.*

My papa held me up to the moo cow moo
So close I could almost touch,
And I fed him a couple of times or so,
And I wasn't a fraid-cat, much.
But if my papa goes in the house,
And my mamma she goes in too,
I keep still like a little mouse
For the moo cow moo might moo.

The moo cow's tail is a piece of rope
All raveled out where it grows;
And it's just like feeling a piece of soap
All over the moo cow's nose.
And the moo cow moo has lots of fun
Just switching his tail about,
But if he opens his mouth, why then I run,
For that's where the moo comes out.

The moo cow moo has deers on his head,
And his eyes stick out of their place,
And the nose of the moo cow moo is
spread
All over the moo cow's face.
And his feet are nothing but fingernails,
And his mamma don't keep them cut,
And he gives folks milk in water pails,
When he don't keep his handles shut.

But if you or I pull his handles, why
The moo cow moo says it hurts,
But the hired man sits down close by
And squirts, and squirts, and squirts.

Our Cow

A Book for Kids, *by Clarence Michael James Dennis, 1921.*

Down by the sliprails stands our cow
Chewing, chewing, chewing,
She does not care what folks out there
In the great, big world are doing.
She sees the small cloud-shadows pass
And green grass shining under.
If she does think, what does she think
About it all, I wonder?

She sees the swallows skimming by
Above the sweet young clover,
The light reeds swaying in the wind
And tall trees bending over.
Far down the track she hears the crack
Of bullock-whips, and raving
Of angry men where, in the sun,
Her fellow-beasts are slaving.

Girls, we are told, can scratch and scold,
And boys will fight and wrangle,
And big, grown men, just now and then,
Fret o'er some fingle-fangle,
Vexing the earth with grief or mirth,
Longing, rejoicing, rueing—
But by the sliprails stands our cow,
Chewing.

The Spotted Heifers

A Book for Kids, *by Clarence Michael James Dennis, 1921.*

Mr. Jeremiah Jeffers
Owned a pair of spotted heifers [a kind of
cow]
These he sold for two pounds ten
To Mr. Robert Raymond Wren

Who reared them in the lucerne paddocks
Owned by Mr. Martin Maddox,
And sold them, when they grew to cows,
To Mr. Donald David Dowse.

A grazier, Mr. Egbert Innes,
Bought them then for twenty guineas,
Milked the cows, and sold the milk
To Mr. Stephen Evan Silk.

Who rents a butter factory
From Mr. Laurence Lampard-Lee.
Here, once a week, come for his butter
The grocer, Mr. Roland Rutter,

Who keeps a shop in Sunny Street
Next door to Mr. Peter Peat.
He every afternoon at two
Sent his fair daughter, Lucy Loo,

To Mr. Rutter's shop to buy
Such things as were not priced too
high,
Especially a shilling tin
Of "Fuller's Food for Folk Too Thin."

This food was bought for Lucy Loo—
A girl of charming manners, who
Was much too pale and much too
slight
To be a very pleasant sight.

When Lucy Loo beheld the butter
Stocked by Mr. Roland Rutter,
She said, "I'll have a pound of that."
She had it, and thenceforth grew fat.

We now go back to Mr. Jeffers,
Who sold the pair of spotted heifers.
He had a son, James Edgar John,
A handsome lad to gaze upon,

Who had now reached that time of life
When young men feel they need a wife;
But no young girl about the place
Exactly had the kind of face

That seemed to suit James Edgar
John—
A saddening thing to think upon,
For he grew sad and sick of life
Because he could not find a wife.

One day young James was passing by
(A look of sorrow in his eye)
The shop of Mr. Roland Rutter,
When Lucy Loo came out with butter.

At once James Edgar John said,
"That
Is just the girl for me! She's fat."
He offered her his heart and hand
And prospects of his father's land.

The Reverend Saul Sylvester Slight
Performed the simple marriage rite.
The happy couple went their way,
And lived and loved unto this day.

Events cannot be far foreseen;
And all this joy might not have been
If Mr. Jeremiah Jeffers
Had kept his pair of spotted heifers.

The Cow

Chinese Mother Goose Rhymes, by Isaac Taylor, 1900.

"There's a cow on the mountain."
The old saying goes,
On her legs are four feet;
On her feet are eight toes;
Her tail is behind
On the end of her back,
And her head is in front
On the end of her neck.

The Cow. The Cowry

Animal Analogues, by Robert Williams Wood, 1908.

The Cowry seems to be, somehow,
A sort of mouth-piece for the cow:
A speaking likeness one might say,
Which I've endeavored to portray.

Games and Group Activities

The Purple Cow

Make up your own verses to the Purple Cow following the pattern in the song. Color the puppets accordingly).

Books

And the Dish Ran Away with the Spoon, by Janet Stevens. *A large book with beautiful illustrations, long text. Great for K+, introduces nursery rhymes in a whole new way.*

Click, Clack, Moo, Cows That Type, by Doreen Cronin. *Very cute story. Great for young children.*

The Cow That Laid an Egg, by Andy Cutbill

(HarperCollins, 2006). *Cute story, good book for young children.*

One Cow, Moo, Moo! by David Bennett. *A young boy watches the barnyard animals from 1 cow to 10 mice go racing by. What are they running from?*

Open the Barn Door, Find a Cow, by Christopher Santorro (Random House, 1993).

22. D—Dolphin

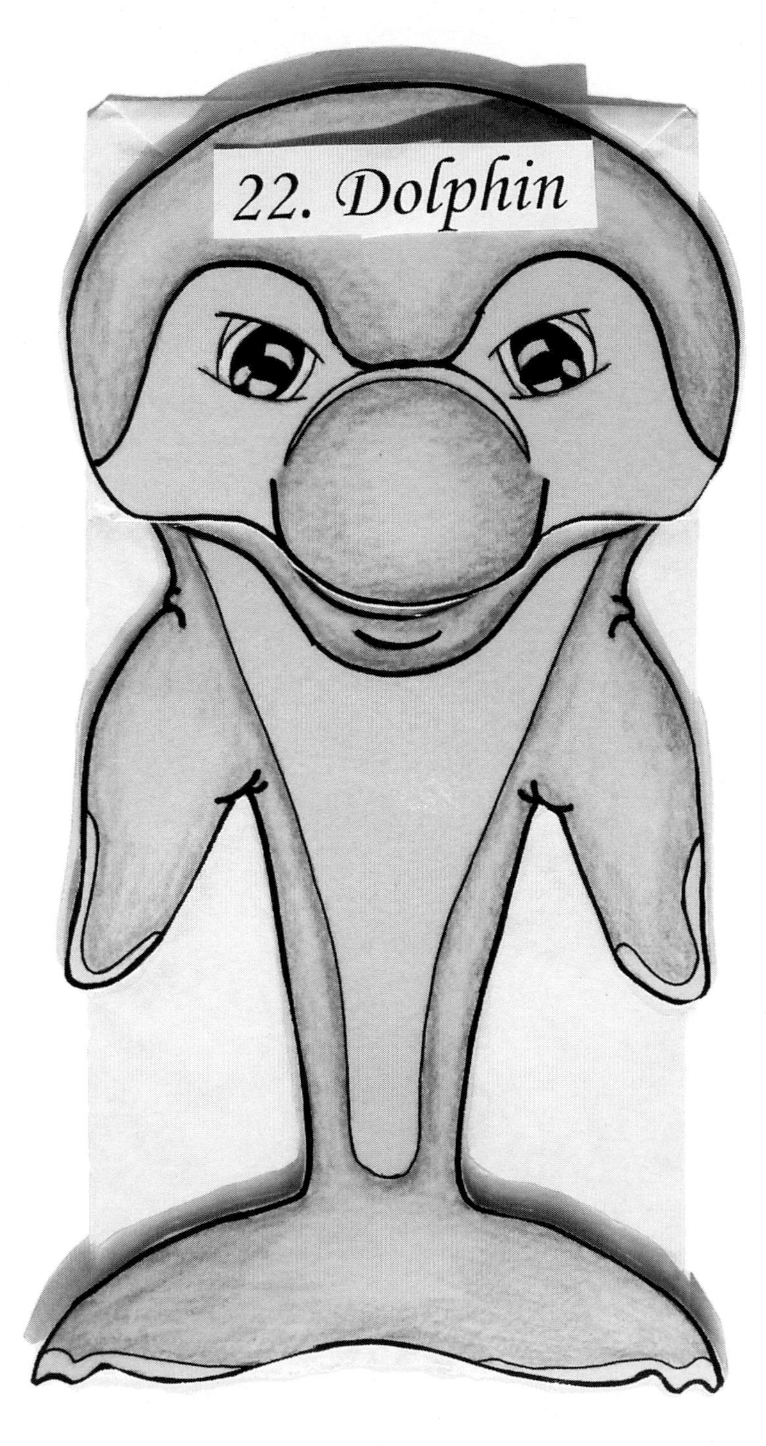

Copy the dolphin head pattern at 133%

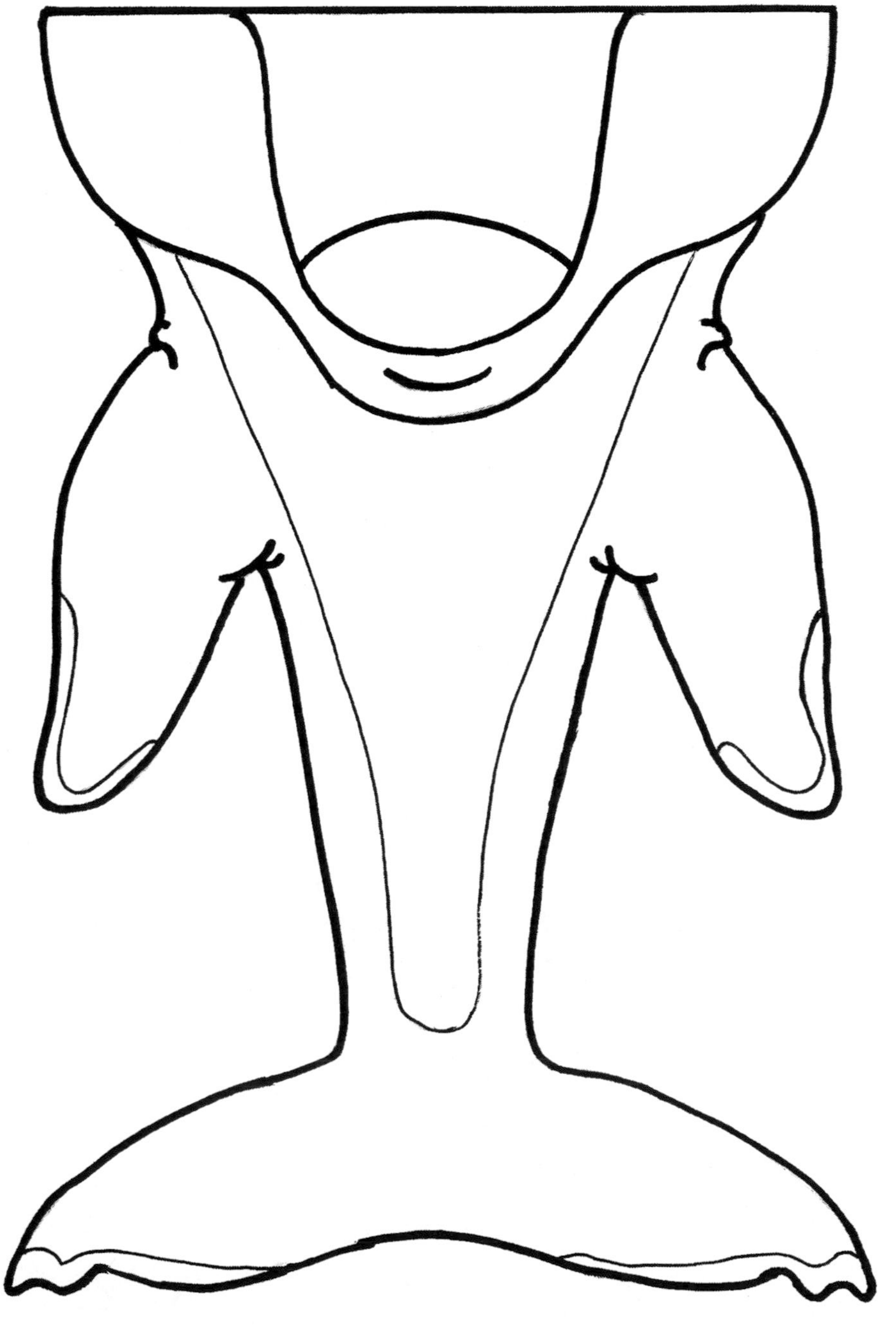

Dolphin Activities

Songs to Sing and Play

Tune: Row, Row, Row Your Boat

Words by Eunice Wright

Dolphin, dolphin, jump up high.
When you jump through hoops,
You will always make a splash,
Swimming loop-de-loops.

One, Two, Three, Four, Five

Mother Goose's Melody, *1765*

One, two, three, four, five,
I caught a fish alive.
Six, seven, eight, nine, ten,
I let him go again!

Why did I let him go?
Because he bit my finger so.
Which finger did he bite?
The little one on the right.

Tune: 10 Little Indians

Words by Eunice Wright

One little, two little, three little dolphins...
Swimming all together.

Tune: Have You Ever Seen a Lassie?

Words by Eunice Wright

Have you ever seen a dolphin, a dolphin, a dolphin?
Have you ever seen a dolphin, swim this way and that?...

Tune: The Old Gray Mare

Words by Eunice Wright

Here we sit like birds in the wilderness
Birds in the wilderness
Birds in the wilderness
Here we sit like birds in the wilderness
Waiting for our food.

Here we jump like dolphins in the water...
Swimming in our pool.

Fishes (Dolphins) at Play

Holiday Songs and Every Day Songs and Games, *by Emilie Poulsson, 1901. With sheet music and some finger plays. Adapted by Juli Wright.*

In the rippling water, clear and cool and bright,
Shiny little fishes (dolphins) frolic with delight,
Swimming through the ripples, diving down below,
Rising now and sinking oh! how fast they go!
Now they chase each other, now they dash away,
Thus the little fishes (dolphins) in the water play.

The Fish Riddle

Songs from Alice in Wonderland *and* Through the Looking Glass, *by Lewis Carroll, 1921.*

1. "First, the fish must be caught."
That is easy: a baby, I think, could have caught it.
"Next, the fish must be bought."
That is easy: a penny, I think, would have bought it.
"Now, cook me the fish!"
That is easy, and will not take more than a minute.
"Let it lie in a dish!"
That is easy, because it already is in it!

2. "Bring it here! Let me sup!"
It is easy to set such a dish on the table.
"Take the dish-cover up!"
Ah, that is so hard that I fear I'm unable!
For it holds it like glue—
Holds the lid to the dish, while it lies in the middle:
Which is easiest to do,
Undish-cover the fish, or dish-cover the riddle?

The Message to the Fish

Songs from Alice in Wonderland *and* Through The Looking Glass, *by Lewis Carroll, 1921.*

In winter, when the fields are white,
I sing this song for your delight—

In spring, when woods are getting green,
I'll try and tell you what I mean.

In summer, when the days are long,
Perhaps you'll understand the song:

In autumn, when the leaves are brown,
Take pen and ink, and write it down.

I sent a message to the fish:
I told them "This is what I wish."

The little fishes of the sea
They sent an answer back to me.

The little fishes' answer was
"We cannot do it, sir, because—"

I sent to them again to say
"It will be better to obey."

The fishes answered, with a grin,
"Why, what a temper you are in!"

I told them once, I told them twice:
They would not listen to advice.

I took a kettle large and new,
Fit for the deed I had to do.

My heart went hop, my heart went thump;
I filled the kettle at the pump.

Then some one came to me, and said,
"The little fishes are in bed."

I said to him, I said it plain,
"Then you must wake them up again."

I said it very loud and clear;
I went and shouted in his ear.

But he was very stiff and proud;
He said, "You needn't shout so loud!"

And he was very proud and stiff;
He said, "I'd go and wake them, if—"

I took a corkscrew from the shelf:
I went to wake them up myself.

And when I found the door was locked,
I pulled and pushed, and kicked and knocked.

And when I found the door was shut,
I tried to turn the handle, but—

Other Songs

"I Wish I Were a Fish," *I Have a Song for You*, Vol. 3, by Janeen Brady, page 19.
"A Seahorse Merry-Go-Round," *I Have a Song for You*, Vol. 3, by Janeen Brady, page 20.
"Five Little Fish," by Jack Hartmann.

Poems and Nursery Rhymes

As Soon as I Could Bait My Hook

Mother Goose Rhymes, *edited by Watty Piper, 1922.*

As soon as I could bait my hook,
I dropped the line into the brook,
A trout soon saw and quickly caught it;
I pulled, and pulled, and out I brought it;
My first brook trout!
I then was small,
But felt that instant 6 feet tall.

3 Little Dolphins

By Juli Wright

Once upon a time, in a far away place,
Three little dolphins liked to race.
Through the waves they liked to dash,
Slipping and sliding, they made a splash!

The Dolphin

Words by Eunice Wright

The dolphin jumps
Up high, then dives.
He swims so fast,
And can save some lives.

They say the dolphin
Brings good luck.
So when he comes,
You're a lucky duck!

Six Little Salmon

The Peter Patter Book of Nursery Rhymes, *by Leroy F. Jackson, 1918; adapted by Juli Wright.*

I sing a funny song from away out west,
Of six little dolphins with their hats on;
How they all left home—but I forget the
rest—
The six little dolphins with their hats on.

A Fish Out of Water

By Eunice Wright

Once there was a little fish
Who swam around inside his dish.
"Will I ever, ever get free to go,
While I'm swimming to and fro?
I want to see what's outside the dish!"
He said, determined to see his wish.
He jumped up high into the air,
And did a somersault right up there.
He landed on the table top,
He danced a jig, he could not stop.
He slid around and then jumped down.
He acted funny like a clown.
"I'm so happy, here I'll stay."
And that's where you'll find him to this day.

Five Little Fish

By Eunice Wright

Five little fish, swimming in a lake,
This one said, "Oh, for goodness sake."
This one said, "I see a yummy treat."
This one said, "We'd better not eat!"
This one said, "Let's take a good look."
This one said, "See, it's on a hook."
Then the five little fish quickly swam away,
And they didn't get caught, at least not that
day.

Wynken, Blynken, and Nod

The Home Book of Verse, *Vol. 1 (of 4), Author: Eugene Field (1850–1895). Editor: Burton Egbert Stevenson, 1912.*

Wynken, Blynken, and Nod one night
Sailed off in a wooden shoe,—
Sailed on a river of crystal light
Into a sea of dew.
"Where are you going, and what do you
wish?"
The old moon asked the three.
"We have come to fish for the herring fish
That live in this beautiful sea;
Nets of silver and gold have we!"
Said Wynken,
Blynken,
And Nod.

The old moon laughed and sang a song,
As they rocked in the wooden shoe;
And the wind that sped them all night long
Ruffled the waves of dew.
The little stars were the herring fish
That lived in that beautiful sea—
"Now cast your nets wherever you wish,—
Never afeard are we!"
So cried the stars to the fishermen three,
Wynken,
Blynken,
And Nod.

All night long their nets they threw
To the stars in the twinkling foam,—
Then down from the skies came the wooden
shoe,
Bringing the fishermen home:
'Twas all so pretty a sail, it seemed
As if it could not be;
And some folk thought 'twas a dream they'd
dreamed
Of sailing that beautiful sea;
But I shall name you the fishermen three:
Wynken,
Blynken,
And Nod.

Wynken and Blynken are two little eyes,
And Nod is a little head,
And the wooden shoe that sailed the skies
Is a wee one's trundle-bed;
So shut your eyes while Mother sings
Of wonderful sights that be,
And you shall see the beautiful things
As you rock in the misty sea

Where the old shoe rocked the fishermen
three:—
Wynken,
Blynken,
And Nod.

The Dolphin

Animal Analogues, *by Robert Williams Wood, 1887; adapted by Eunice Wright.*

The dolphin is a kind of fish!
I'm sure that none of us would wish
To have him scuttle round the house,
Like puss, when she espies a mouse:

When you secure your house-hold pet,
Be very sure you do not get
The dolphin, or there may be
Dom-es-tic in-felis-ity.

The Musical Carp (Dolphin)

The Jingle Book, *by Carolyn Wells, 1901; words adapted by Eunice Wright.*

There once was a dolphin sharp,
Who wanted to play on a harp,
But to his chagrin
So short was his fin
That he couldn't reach up to C sharp.

Books

Amazing Dolphins! I Can Read! level 2, Wildlife Conservation Society, by Sarah L. Thompson (Harper Collins, 2006). *Good colorful photos, easy read text. Recommended.*

Arion and the Dolphins, by Lonzo Andersen.

Artie, the Smartie. Small fish can make a difference when they're smart.

Bottlenose Dolphins, by John F. Prevost (ABDO Pub., 1995). *Colorful photos, text for older children.*

Bottlenose Dolphins, Whales and Dolphins, an Imagination Library Series (Gareth Stevens Pub., 2001). *Nice colorful photos, good information. Good resource list. Elementary age.*

The Curious Little Dolphin, by Ariane Hottin.

Diving Dolphin, by Karen Wallace (Dorling Kindersley Book, 2001). *Beginning reader, level 1. Nice colorful photos and simple text.*

Do Dolphins Really Smile? by Laura Driscoll (Grosset & Dunlap, 2006). *A very cute beginning reader book, nice illustrations, and good information about training dolphins ... or are they training us?*

Dolphin Talk: Whistles, Clicks, and Clapping Jaws, by Wendy Pfeffer (HarperCollins, 2003). *Nice colorful illustrations; good information. This basic introduction compares humans and dolphins.*

Dolphins, by Casey Horton (Benchmark Books, 1996).

Dolphins, by Donna Bailey.

Dolphins, by Elizabeth Laskey (Heinemann Library, 2003). *Colorful photos, informative text. Upper elementary age.*

Dolphins, by Julia Bogel (Creative Publishing Int., 2001). *Informative text, colorful photos. Upper grades.*

Dolphins, by Seymour Simon (Smithsonian/Collins, 2009). *Large colorful photos; text is interesting, but not for young children.*

Dolphins, by the Cousteau Society.

Dolphins and Porpoises, by Beth Brust (Wildlife Education Ltd., 1999).

Dolphins at Daybreak, by Mary Pope Osborne (Random House).

Dolphins: Our Friends in the Sea, by Judith E. Rinard (National Geographic). *Full of information and facts.*

Dolphins, Seals, and Other Sea Mammals, by Mary Jo Rhodes and David Hall (Scholastic, 2007).

Encantado: Pink Dolphin of the Amazon, by Sy Montgomery (Houghton, 2002). *Colorful photos, large book, interesting narrative tale of expedition by author; for older children and adults.*

Extreme Rescue: Dolphin Mission, by Erica David.

Face to Face with Dolphins, by Flip and

Linda Nicklin (National Geographic, 2007). *Nice photos and information, told by the photographer team.*

Falling for a Dolphin, by Heathcote Williams (Jonathan Cape).

Follow That Fun! Studying Dolphin Behavior. Turnstone Ocean Pilot Book series, by Amy Samuels (Raintree).

Friendly Dolphins, by Allen Fowler.

Island of the Blue Dolphins, by Scott O'Dell.

Meeting Dolphins: My Adventures in the Sea, by Kathleen Dudzinski (National Geographic Society, 2000).

Our Wild World Series: Dolphins, by Julia Vogel (NorthWord Press, 2001). *Informative, for older children, colorful photos.*

Secret at Dolphin Bay, Dorling Kindersley Reader, Level 1.

The Sierra Club Handbook of Whales and Dolphins (Sierra Club Books, 1983).

Undersea Encounters. A very interesting book, easy reading with colorful photos. It covers a lot of sea life.

Whales and Dolphins, by Caroline Bingham (DK Pub., 2003).

Whales and Dolphins (series), by Victor Gentle and Janet Perry (Gareth Stevens).

Whales and Dolphins in Question (Smithsonian Institution, 2002).

Whales, Dolphins and Porpoises, by Doug Perrine.

Whales, Dolphins and Porpoises, by Mark Carwardine (Dorling Kindersley).

Whales, Dolphins and Porpoises (Time Life Books, 1998).

Whales of the World, by June Bebsens.

Wild About Dolphins, by Nicola Davies (Candlewick Press, 2001). *An interesting story told by an 18-year-old girl who loves dolphins and tries to find them. Colorful photos, interesting facts and identification charts.*

Winter's Tale: How One Little Dolphin Learned to Swim Again, by Juliana Hatkoff.

Movies and Television

Bedknobs and Broomsticks. Dancing under the sea with animated creatures.

Dolphin Tale 1 and 2

Dolphins (Image Entertainment). Nonfiction.

Dolphins: The Dark Side (National Geographic. W-G)

Dolphins: The Wild Side (National Geographic). Nonfiction.

Dolphins with Robin Williams (PBS Home Video). Nonfiction.

Finding Nemo

Flipper (MGM). TV series, 20th Century—Fox, 2007. Recommended!

The Incredible Mr. Limpet (World War II). A very cute movie. Recommended.

The Little Mermaid

The Sword in the Stone (Disney). Animated. Young Arthur turns into a fish.

23. E—Elephant

Elephant Activities

Songs to Sing and Play

One Elephant Went Out to Play

"One elephant went out to play, upon a spider's web one day..."
Two elephants went out to play...

Continue as each child or puppet is chosen and added to group.

Tune: 1 Little, 2 Little, 3 Little Indians

Words by Eunice Wright

1 little, 2 little, 3 little elephants...
All walking in the ring. (Or "All living at the zoo, all dressed in gray, all doing tricks.")

If You Should Meet an Elephant

See DLTK Internet site for sheet music and tune.

"If you should meet an elephant on a summer's day.
What would you do? What would you say?..."

Tune: 16 Tons

Words by Eunice Wright

Sixteen tons and this is what you get—
An elephant, rhino and hippo set.
The zookeeper says, "I can't pay for you yet!
I'm another year older and deeper in debt!"

Tune: The Old Gray Mare (Here We Sit Like Birds in the Wilderness)

Words by Eunice Wright

Here we sit like birds in the wilderness
Birds in the wilderness
Birds in the wilderness
Here we sit like birds in the wilderness
Waiting for our food.

Here we sit like elephants in the zoo...
Eating our peanuts.

Other Songs

"Baby Elephant Walk" is a tune written in 1961 by composer Henry Mancini for the 1962 release of the movie Hatari!
Pink elephants on parade. *Dumbo*, Walt Disney. Music by Ned Washington, music by Oliver Wallace.
"An Elephant Never Forgets," Kelly and the Apemen. Council Rock Music, Dominion Entertainment, Inc. From the KIDTEL Records album, *Songs from the Jungle*. 4:51.
"A Riddle," *I Have a Song for You*, Vol. 3, by Janeen Brady, p. 42.
"Jack's Miss Mary Mack," by Jack Hartmann. See the elephants jump the fence.

Poems and Nursery Rhymes

The Elephant's Trunk

By Eunice Wright

The elephant has a long trunk for a nose,
And back and forth is the way it goes.
He wears a gray saggy, baggy suit,
And trumpets loudly with his giant flute.

His trunk comes in handy when it's time for a swim,
He doesn't hesitate, but jumps right in.
Like a snorkel, his nose held high above water,
Can also be his shower when he feels hotter.

His trunk is strong and can lift heavy loads,
He gives rides to people in all sorts of modes.
His favorite snack is some peanuts to eat,
And his circus tricks keep you in your seat.

Five Big Elephants (Count Down)

By Eunice Wright

Five big elephants, trumpeting by my door.
One found some peanuts to eat, then there were four.
Four big elephants, playing under a tree.

One found a girl friend, then there were three.
Three big elephants, wondering what to do.
One found a log to lift, then there were two.
Two big elephants, having so much fun.
One went to hunt for food, then there was one.
One big elephant, alone in the sun.
Decided to take a nap, then there were none.

The Elephant

Bad Child's Book of Beasts, *by Hilaire Belloc, 1896.*

When people call this beast to mind,
They marvel more and more
At such a *little* tail behind,
So *large* a trunk before.

Eletelephony

Laura Richards, 1850–1943

Once there was an elephant,
Who tried to use the telephant—
No! No! I mean an elephone
Who tried to use the telephone—
(Dear me! I am not certain quite
That even now I've got it right.)

Howe'er it was, he got his trunk
Entangled in the telephunk;
The more he tried to get it free,
The louder buzzed the telephee—
(I fear I'd better drop the song
Of elephop and telephong!)

The Eel. The Elephant.

Animal Analogues, *by Robert Williams Wood, 1887.*

The marked aversion which we feel,
When in the presence of the eel,
Makes many view with consternation,
The elephant's front ele-vation.
Such folly must be clearly due
To their peculiar point of view.

Six Men of Indostan (The Blind Men and the Elephant)

An Argosy of Fables, *selected and edited by Frederic Taber Cooper, 1921; by John Godfrey Saxe.*

It was six men of Indostan to learning much inclined
Who went to see the Elephant (though all of them were blind),
That each by observation might satisfy his mind.

The first approached the elephant and, happening to fall
Against his broad and sturdy side, at once began to bawl:
"God bless me!—but the elephant Is very like a wall!"

The second, feeling of the tusk, cried "Ho! What have we here
So very round and smooth and sharp? To me 'tis mighty clear
This wonder of an elephant is very like a spear!"

The third approached the animal. And, happening to take
The squirming trunk within his hands. Thus boldly up and spake:—
"I see," quoth he, "the elephant is very like a snake!"

The fourth reached out his eager hand, and felt about the knee;
"What most this wondrous beast is like. Is mighty plain," quoth he;
"'tis clear enough the elephant is very like a tree!"

The fifth who chanced to touch the ear, said, "E'en the blindest man
Can tell what this resembles most; deny the fact who can,
This marvel of an elephant is very like a fan!"

The sixth no sooner had begun about the beast to grope,
Than seizing on the swinging tail that fell within his scope,

"I see," quoth he, "the elephant is very like a rope!"

And so the men of Indostan disputed loud and long.
Each in his own opinion exceeding stiff and strong,
Though each was partly in the right and all were in the wrong!

MORAL

So, oft in theologic wars the disputants, I ween,
Rail on in utter ignorance of what each other mean
And prate about an elephant not one of them has seen!

A Famous Case

By Theodore C. Williams, Boys and Girls Bookshelf *(Vol. 2 of 17). Folklore, fables, and fairy tales. 1920.*

Two honey-bees half came to blows
About the lily and the rose,
Which might the sweeter be;
And as the elephant passed by,
The bees decided to apply
To this wise referee.

The elephant, with serious thought,
Ordered the flowers to be brought,
And smelt and smelt away.
Then, swallowing both, declared his mind:
No trace of perfume can I find,
But both resemble hay."

MORAL:

Dispute is wrong. But foolish bees,
Who will contend for points like these,
Should not suppose good taste in roses
Depends on elephantine noses.

The Three Little Chickens and the Elephant

In My Nursery: A Book of Verse, *by Laura E. Richards, 1890.*

Little chickens, one, two, three,
They went out to take their tea,
Brisk and gay as gay could be,
Cackle wackle wackle!

Feathers brushed all smooth and neat,
Yellow stockings on their feet,
Tails and tuftings all complete,
Cackle wackle wackle!

"Very seldom," said the three,
"Like of us the world can see,
Beautiful exceedingly,
Cackle wackle wackle!

Such our form and such our face,
Such our Cochin China grace,
We must win in beauty's race,
Cackle wackle wackle!"

Met an elephant large and wise,
Looked at them with both his eyes:
Caused these chickens great surprise,
Cackle wackle wackle!

"Why," they said, "do you suppose
Elephant doesn't look out of his nose,
So very conveniently it grows?
Cackle wackle wackle!

"Elephant with nose so long,
Sing on now a lovely song,
As we gayly trip along,
Cackle wackle wackle!

Sing of us and sing of you,
Sing of corn and barley too,
Beauteous beast with eyes of blue,
Cackle wackle wackle!"

Elephant sang so loud and sweet,
Chickens fell before his feet;
For his love they did entreat,
Cackle wackle wackle.

"Well-a-day! and woe is me!
Would we all might elephants be!
Then he'd marry us, one, two, three,
Cackle wackle wackle!"

Little chickens, one, two, three,
When you're walking out to tea,
Don't make love to all you see,
Cackle wackle wackle!

Elephants have lovely eyes,
But to woo them is not wise,
For they are not quite your size!
Cackle wackle wackle!

Books

Babar Learns to Cook, Random House Picturebacks.

Babar Saves the Day, Random House Picturebacks.

Bashi, Elephant Baby, by Theresa Radcliffe.

The Blind Men and the Elephant, by Karen Backstein.

Elephant Eats the Profits (Sweet Pickles Series), by Jacquelyn Reinach.

Elephants Never Forget! by Anushka Rairshankar (Houghton, 2007). *Cute rhyming short story, fair illustrations.*

Horton Hatches the Egg, by Dr. Seuss.

Just a Little Bit, by Ann Tompert. *Elephant and mouse need help to balance the seesaw just a little bit. (Measurement)*

Little Elephant and Friends, by Kath Jewitt.

Meet Babar and His Family, Random House Picturebacks.

No Matter What, by Emma Dudd.

The Saggy Baggy Elephant, by Kathryn and Byron Jackson (Golden, 1947). *Being different is never easy for young children. The elephant doesn't seem to fit in.*

Seven Blind Mice (Reading Railroad), by Ed Young.

Splash! by Flora McDonnell (Candlewick Press, 2003). *Board book. Good rhyming and repeating text; preschool age.*

The Story of Babar, by Jean de Brunhof (Random House, 1966). *Babar, the Elephant King.*

Twenty One Elephants and Still Standing, by April Prince. *A true story of 21 elephants on the Brooklyn Bridge. Not for very young children. Beautiful illustrations.*

What Elephant? by Genevieve Cote. *No one believes there is an elephant in the house.*

Which Way, Hugo? by Morgan Matthews (Troll Associates, 1986). *A very cute, easy reader book for beginning readers and preschool children. Nice illustrations.*

Movies and Television

Abbott and Costello—Africa Screams
Babar
The Blue Elephant (animated)
Born to Be Wild: Baby Animals, 2012, IMAX
Dumbo
The Dumbo Drop
Echo: An Elephant to Remember, by Nature PBS, 2010
Echo and Other Elephants, 2008
The Elephant Kingdom, Discovery Channel
The Elephant Princess
Elephant Tales, 2006
Elephant Walk (Elizabeth Taylor), 1960
Ernest Goes to Africa
George of the Jungle
Hatari
Horton Hears a Who
The Impossible Elephant
National Geographic
One Lucky Elephant
The Prince and Me: The Elephant Adventure
Reflections on Elephants, National Geographic, 2010
Tarzan of the Apes
3D Safari Africa
The Vanishing Elephant (Houdini)
Whispers: An Elephant's Tale, Disney, 2000

24. F—Fawn

Fawn Activities

Songs to Sing and Play

Home on the Range

Cowboy Songs and Other Frontier Ballads, *sheet music, 1916.*

Oh, give me a home,
Where the buffalo roam,
Where the deer and the antelope play.
Where seldom is heard, a discouraging word,
And the skies are not cloudy all day.
Home, home on the range.
Where the deer and the antelope play.
Where seldom is heard, a discouraging word,
And the skies are not cloudy all day.

Tune: If You're Happy and You Know It

Words by Eunice Wright

If you know a fawn named Bambi, clap your hands. (clap, clap)
If you know a fawn named Bambi, clap your hands. (clap, clap)
If you know a fawn named Bambi,
Then you know that he's a dandy,
If you know a fawn named Bambi, clap your hands. (clap, clap)

If you know a skunk named Flower, hold your nose. (sniff, sniff)
If you know a skunk named Flower, hold your nose. (sniff, sniff)
If you know a skunk named Flower,
Hold your nose for an hour,
If you know a skunk named Flower, hold your nose. (sniff, sniff)

If you know a rabbit named Thumper, stomp your feet. (stomp, stomp)
If you know a rabbit named Thumper, stomp your feet. (stomp, stomp)
If you know a rabbit named Thumper,
With a powder puff on his bumper,
If you know a rabbit named Thumper, stomp your feet. (stomp, stomp)

Tune: Five Little Ducks

Traditional tune; words by Juli Wright. (Listen to Raffi sing this song. See Duck puppet for more verses.)

Five little fawns went out one day
Over the hills and far away,
Mommy (daddy) deer called, "Here, here, here,"
But only 4 little fawns came leaping near.

Poems and Nursery Rhymes

Five Frolicking Fawns (Count Down)

By Eunice Wright

Five frolicking fawns, went on a tour.
One found a friendly rabbit, then there were four.
Four frolicking fawns, playing by the tree.
One found a girl friend, then there were three.
Three frolicking fawns, wondering what to do.
One found a little skunk, then there were two.
Two frolicking fawns, having so much fun.
One went to hunt for food, then there was one.
One frolicking fawn, alone in the sun.
He decided to take a nap, then there were none.

The Cutest Baby Fawn

By Juli Wright

The cutest baby you'll ever see,
Has two big ears and soft eyes to see;
A little tail that flips and flops,
And boundless energy that never stops.

What's that I see out on the lawn?
It's a cute little baby fawn.
He wears a spotted coat all day,
And jumps and prances in his play.

The Doe. The Dodo.

Animal Analogues, by Robert Williams Wood, 1908.

The doe and her peculiar double
No longer are a source of trouble,

Because the dodo, it appears,
Has been extinct for many years.
She was too proud to disembark
With total strangers in Noah's Ark,
And we rejoice because her pride
Our Nature book has simplified.

Books

Anansi and the Moss-Covered Rock, by Eric A. Kimmel. *The spider uses a strange moss-covered rock in the forest to trick all the other animals, until Little Deer decides Spider needs to learn a lesson.*

Animal Neighbors: DEER, by Michael Leach (Power Kids Press, 2009). *Good information, nice photos.*

Animals-animals: DEER, by Wil Mara (Marshall Cavendish, 2009). *Nice photos, lots of text information.*

Bambi Count to Five, Walt Disney Golden Books, by Diane Muldrow. *A very cute simple-text board book for toddlers.*

Bambi Grows Up, Walt Disney Productions (Random House, 1979). *A lovely picture book about the movie of Bambi growing up.*

Bambi, Walt Disney (Twin Books, 1989). *A beautiful large picture book about the movie Bambi.*

Bambi's Children: The Story of a Forest Family, by Felix Salten.

Bambi's First Day, by Felix Salten (Sleeping Bear Press).

Deer at the Brook, by Jim Arnosky.

Goodnight Thumper, by Kitty Richards.

The Noble Stag, by Tales of Time, a Jataka Tale.

Shadow, the Deer, by Theresa Radcliffe.

WhiteTail Deer, Our Wild World series (NorthWord Press).

White-Tailed Deer, by Dorothy H. Patent (Lerner Pub., 2005). *Small book, photos and text OK.*

Wildlife of North America: The White Tailed Deer, by Michael Zwaschka (Capstone Press, 1997). *Nice photos, lots of text, good information.*

Movies and Television

Bambi, 1942, Walt Disney (sequel: *Bambi 2*)

Lost in the Woods, 2006, 30 min., a short family film. Shirley, an old box turtle, meets a lost raccoon and helps him. Together they learn about a newborn fawn who sleeps alone in the woods.

The Yearling, 1946. Family film drama made by MGM tells the story of a boy who adopts a fawn as a pet.

25. G—Giraffe

Giraffe Activities

Songs to Sing and Play

Tune: Mary Wore a Red Dress

Words by Eunice Wright

The giraffe has a long neck, long neck, long neck.
The giraffe has a long neck and eats tree leaves.

Substitute other animals and their characteristics.

Tune: Mary Had a Little Lamb

Words by Eunice Wright

Giraffe, you have the longest neck,
Longest neck, longest neck.
Giraffe, you have the longest neck,
You're sure to reach the trees.

Everywhere the giraffe went,
Giraffe went, giraffe went.
Everywhere the giraffe went,
The trees were sure to be.

He follows the path of leafy trees,
Leafy trees, leafy trees.
He follows the path of leafy trees,
And eats the highest tree top.

Tune: A Hunting We Will Go

Traditional

A hunting we will go, a hunting we will go,
Heigh ho, the dairy-o, a hunting we will go!
A hunting we will go, a hunting we will go,
We'll catch a giraffe and make him laugh,
And then we'll let him go!

Make up more rhyming verses.

Tune: Three Blind Mice

Words by Eunice Wright

Three tall giraffes
Three tall giraffes
See how they run,
See how they run,
They all run with their longs legs straight,
They gallop along at a steady gait,
Did you ever see a giraffe that was late?
Oh, three tall giraffes.

Poems and Nursery Rhymes

A Giraffe's Neck

By Eunice Wright

A giraffe's long neck allows him to see
Way up high, right over a tree.
He has long legs, and knobby knees.
He eats leaves up in the trees.
He's covered in spots from head to toe,
And has a hard time bending down low.

Five Giraffes (Count Down)

By Eunice Wright

Five giraffes went on a walking tour,
One found a watering hole, then there were four.
Four giraffes, eating from a tree,
One found a girl friend, then there were three.
Three giraffes, wondering what to do,
One found a little rhino, then there were two.
Two giraffes, having so much fun.
One went to find a hippo, then there was one.
One tired giraffe, alone in the sun,
Decided to take a nap, then there was one.

Books

Baby Giraffe, by San Diego Zoo Animal Library. *Cute photos of the baby giraffe.*
Big Max and the Mystery of the Missing Giraffe (I Can Read Book 2), by Kin Platt.
A Giraffe and a Half, by Shel Silverstein (HarperCollins). *Pencil drawings, story with repeating lines—for older children; not a colorful picture book.*

A Giraffe Goes to Paris, by Mary T. Holmes and John Harris (Marshall Cavendish, 2010).

Giraffe Graphs, by Melissa Stewart (Children's Press, 2006).

A Giraffe Grows Up, by Amanda D. Tourville (Picture Window Books, 2007).

Giraffe Sounds? by Debbie Buttar. *Good illustrations, cute board book.*

Giraffe: The World's Tallest Mammal, by Meish Goldish (Bearport Publishing, 2007).

Giraffes, Animals-animals, by Judith Jango-Cohen (Benchmark Books, 2002). *Beautiful photos, good text.*

Giraffes Can't Dance, by Giles Andreae. *Humorous story.*

The Lonely Giraffe, by Peter Blight (Bloomsbury, 2004). *Beautiful illustrations; good for young children. Giraffe helps save the animals.*

Meet the Giraffe, by Susanna Keller (PowerKids Press, 2010). Series: At the Zoo.

The Story of Giraffe, by Guido Pigui (Front Street, 2007).

Watching Giraffes in Africa, by Deborah Underwood (Heinemann, 2006). Series: Wild World.

The White Giraffe, by Lauren St. John (Dial, 1966).

Zarafa: The Giraffe Who Walked to the King, by Judith St. George (Philomel Books, 2009).

26. H—Hippopotamus

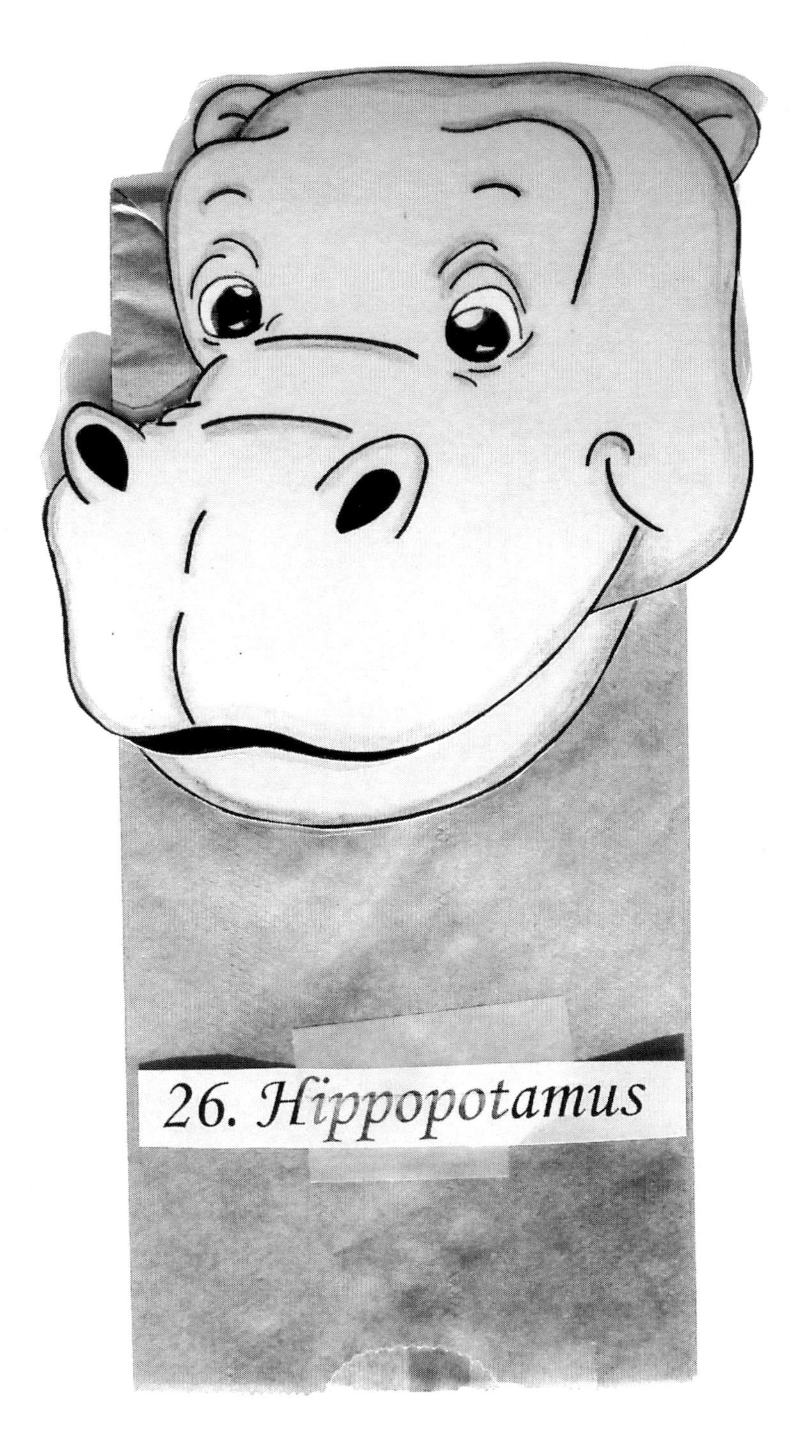

COPY THIS ENTIRE PATTERN AT 111%

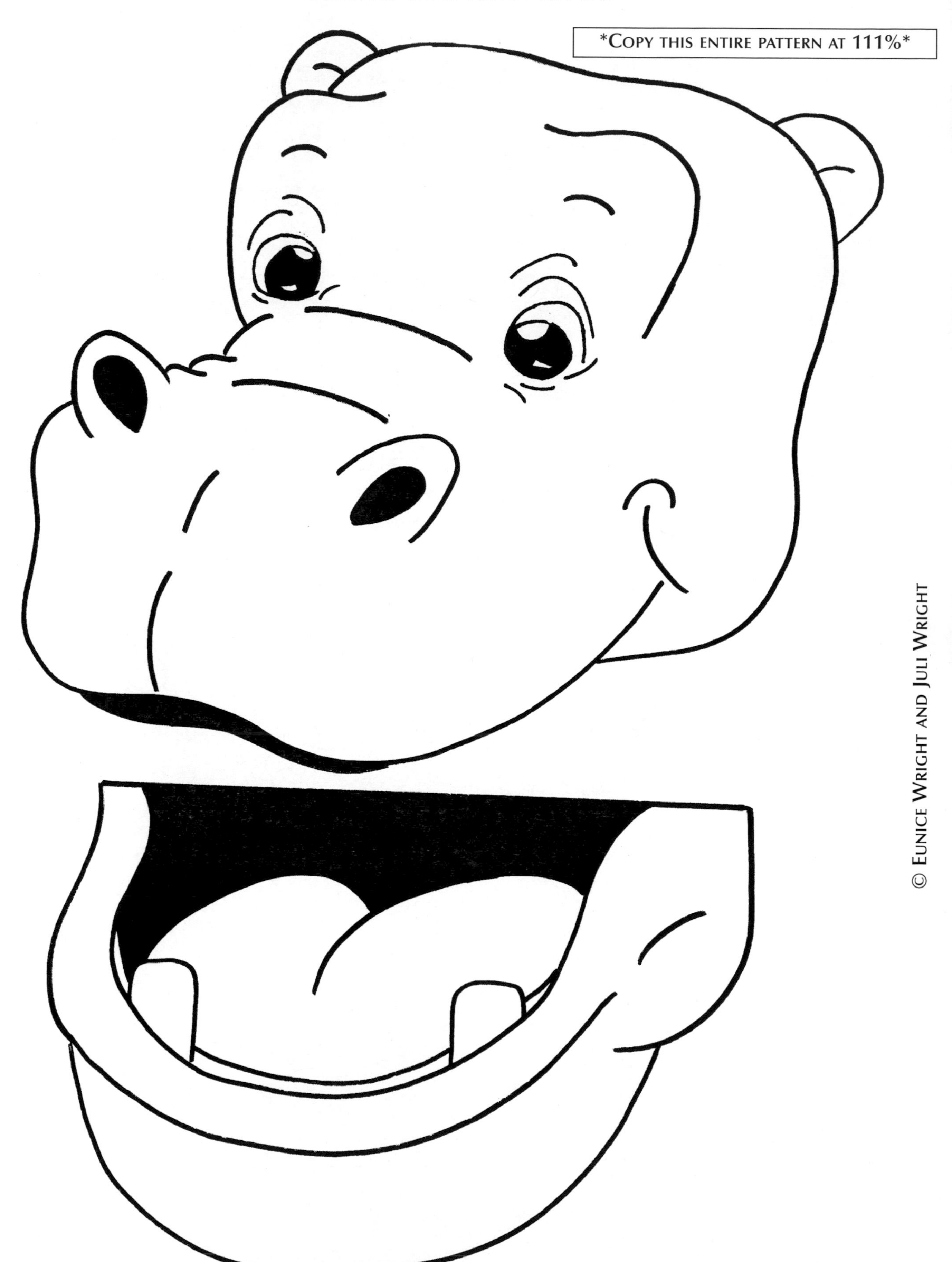

Hippopotamus Activities

Songs to Sing and Play

Tune: Yankee Doodle

Words by Eunice Wright

The hippo loves to float around,
He really loves the water.
With his body underneath,
Then he won't feel hotter.

Tune: Skip to My Lou

Words by Eunice Wright

Hip-po-pot-o-mus, we love you.
Hip-po-pot-o-mus, at the zoo.
Hip-po-pot-o-mus, swim and float.
Through the water, like a boat.

Tune: Where, Oh Where Has My Little Dog Gone?

Words by Eunice and Juli Wright

Where, oh where has my pink hippo gone?
Oh where, oh where can he be?
With his ears cut short and his tail cut long,
Oh where, oh where can he be?

I think he went down to the swimming pool.
To go for a little dip.
The water was nice and very cool,
But now he can't seem to be found.

I see him now playing peek-a-boo,
He likes to stay underneath.
He finds water plants on which to chew,
But can run really fast on land.

Tune: Brown Bear, Brown Bear (Hippo, Hippo) What Do You See?

Book by Bill Martin, Jr., Holt, 1983

Hippo, hippo, what do you see?
I see water all around me.

Tune: 10 Little Indians

Words by Eunice Wright

One little, two little, three little hippos,
Four little, five little, six little hippos,
Seven little, eight little, nine little hippos,
Ten little baby hippos.

Tune: Bingo

Words by Eunice Wright; traditional tune

There was a zoo, had an animal,
And Hippo was his name-o.
H-I-P-P-O!
H-I-P-P-O!
H-I-P-P-O!
And Hippo was his name-o!

Other Songs

"The Hippopotamus Song," by Michael Flanders and Donald Swann, 1999.
"Hooray for the Hippo," *I Have A Song for You*, Vol. 3, by Janeen Brady, p. 40.
"I Want a Hippopotamus for Christmas," 1953. A 10-year-old girl actually *did* receive a hippo for the holidays, which lived for 50 years. Funny-Christmas.com.
"There's a Hippo in My Tub," by Anne Murray.

Poems and Nursery Rhymes

Ten BIG Hippos

By Eunice Wright

Ten big hippos went for a swim,
Five of "her" and five of "him."
The hippos raced from shore to shore,
It wasn't enough—they wanted more!
All day long they stayed and played,
They splashed and danced and ate and sprayed.
When night came, the sleepy heads
Said, "Goodnight," from their water-beds.

Five Gray Hippos (Count Down)

By Eunice Wright

(This poem could be performed with five hippo puppets standing in a line. As each hippo leaves, a recording of a loud splash could be played.)

Five gray hippos, standing on the shore,
One ran to the river, (splash!) then there were four.
Four gray hippos, under a shady tree,
One ran to the river, then there were three.
Three gray hippos, under the sky so blue,
One ran to the river, then there were two.
Two gray hippos, sitting in the sun.
One ran to the river, then there was one.
One gray hippo, having lots of fun,
Splashing in the water, till the day was done.

The Hippopotamus

Bad Child's Book of Beasts, *by Hilaire Belloc, 1896.*

I shoot the Hippopotamus with bullets made of platinum,
Because if I use leaden ones his hide is sure to flatten 'em.

The Hippopotamus

I Am a Stranger Here Myself, *by Ogden Nash, 1938.*

"Behold the hippopotamus! We laugh at how he looks to us..."

Books

George and Martha, by James Marshall.

George and Martha One Fine Day, by James Marshall.

The Hiccupotamus, by Aaron Zenz.

Hippo Jogs for Health (Sweet Pickles Series), by Richard Hefter.

The Hippo-NOT-amus, by Tony and Jan Payne (Scholastic, 2003). *The little hippo wants to be anything but himself. Good preschool and up book; illustrations okay. Good introduction to other animals.*

Hippos (All About Wild Animals). A small book, photos okay, short text and information.

Hippos, by Sally M. Walker (A Carolrhoda Nature Watch Book, 1998). *Nice photos and text.*

Hippos Go Berserk, by Sandra Boynton.

I Want a Hippopotamus for Christmas, by John Rox.

Little Hippopotamuses, Born to Be Wild, by Colette Barbe-Julien (GarethStevens Pub., 2006). *Nice photos and information.*

Sergeant Hippo's Busy Week, by Wong H. Yee. *A very busy policeman.*

Ten Little Hippos, by Bobette McCarthy. *Ten talented hippos take to the stage, but silly mishaps cause the count to go down from 10 to 1.*

27. I—Ice Cream

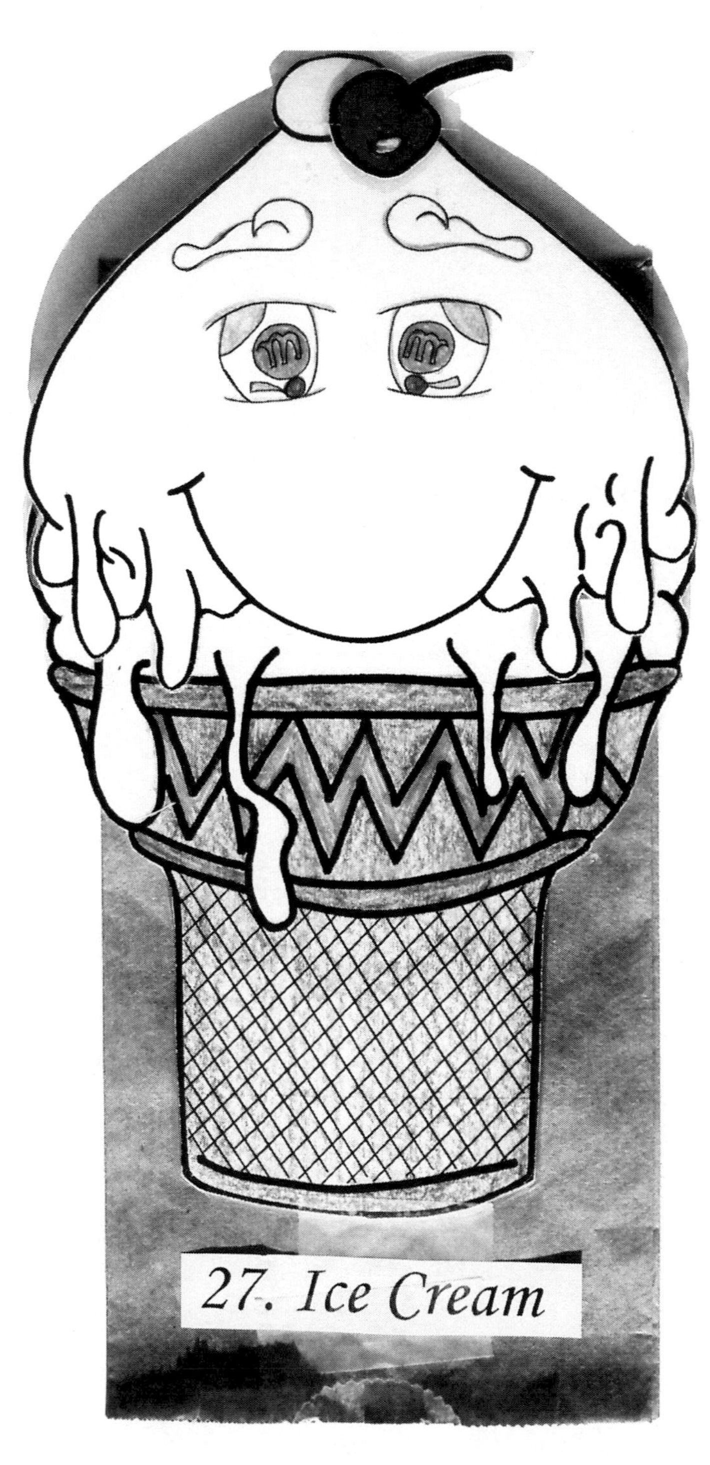

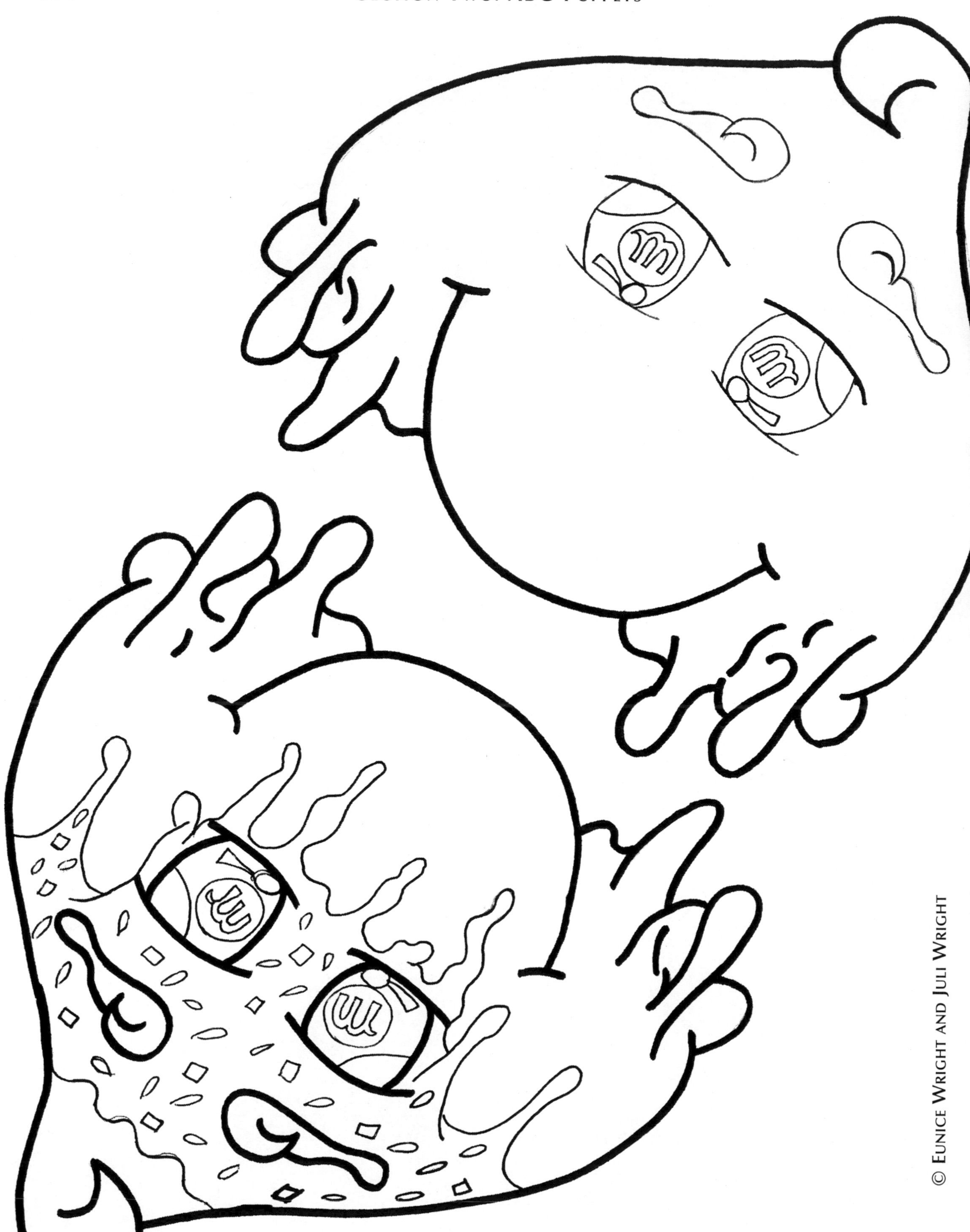

Ice Cream Activities

Songs to Sing and Play

Tune: On Top of Old Smokey

Words by Eunice and Juli Wright; traditional folk song and ballad

On top of my ice cream,
All ready to eat,
I lost my poor cherry,
When I turned up the heat.

It rolled off the table,
And onto the floor.
Then my poor cherry
Rolled out the front door.

It rolled in the garden,
And under a bush,
And then my poor cherry,
Was nothing but mush.

The mush was as tasty
As tasty could be.
And then the next summer,
It grew into a tree.

The tree was all covered,
All covered with moss.
And on it grew cherries
And choc-o-late sauce.

So if you like ice cream
All ready to eat,
Hold onto your cherry,
And DON'T turn up the heat!

Tune: Oh, Do You Know the Muffin Man?

Words by Eunice Wright

Oh, do you know the ice cream man,
The ice cream man, the ice cream man?
Oh, do you know the ice cream man,
Who drives an ice cream truck?
It plays a song that's very loud, very loud,
very loud.
It plays a song that's very loud,
All through the neighborhood.

He has so many ice cream flavors...
You can't choose just one flavor.

Tune: Mary Had a Little Lamb

Words by Eunice Wright

Mary had an ice cream cone,
Ice cream cone, ice cream cone.
Mary had an ice cream cone,
With a cherry on the top.

Everywhere that Mary went,
Mary went, Mary went,
Everywhere that Mary went,
The cone was sure to go.

She bought it at the store one day,
Store one day, store one day.
She bought it at the store one day,
And took it home to eat.

It followed her as it melted away,
Melted away, melted away.
It followed her as it melted away,
Dripping on the ground.

And so the ice cream melted away,
Melted away, melted away.
And so the ice cream melted away,
Even when it was licked.

Why does Mary love the ice cream so,
The Ice Cream so, The Ice cream so.
Why does Mary love the ice cream so,
It's because it tastes so good!

And so she bought some more ice cream,
More ice cream, more ice cream.
And so she bought some more ice cream,
The very next day!

Tune: Mary Had a Little Lamb

Words by Eunice Wright

I want an ice cream cone,
Ice cream cone, ice cream cone.
I want an ice cream cone,
With a cherry up on top.

(Name of child) wants (an ice cream cone banana split, sundae, milk shake, ice cream bar).

With a _____ _____ up on top (child's
favorite toppings)

Tune: Take Me Out to the Ballgame

By Jack Norworth and Albert Von Tilzer, 1908; words by Eunice Wright

Take me out for some ice cream,
Take me out to the store.
Buy me a cone, give me a great big scoop.
I'll be back when I want some more.
So it's scoop, scoop, scoop up the ice cream.
Give me a taste of each kind.
For it's one, two, three scoops I'll try
Give me more, I won't mind.

Tune: Swing Low, Sweet Chariot

By Wallace Willis, 1873, in the book The Jubilee Singers; *words by Eunice Wright*

I want a banana split,
Covered with chocolate ice cream.
With sprinkles and sauce and some whip
cream,
A cherry and some nuts!

I want a vanilla cone,
Dipped in chocolate sauce.
All covered with nuts in a waffle cone,
Served in the hot summer time.

I want a _____ shake,
With a _____ and a _____ and a _____.
I love ice cream, anyway you make it,
It's my favorite desert!

Tune: Mary Had a Little Lamb

Words by Eunice Wright

Once there was an ice cream cone,
Ice cream cone, ice cream cone.
Once there was an ice cream cone,
It's ice cream white as snow.

In the sun it melted, melted, melted.
In the sun it melted,
As fast as you can lick.

Tune: Twinkle, Twinkle Little Star

Words by Eunice Wright

Ice cream sundae, or a shake.
I like anything you make.
Banana split or in a cone,
I don't usually eat alone.
Any way it's fixed, I know,
I'll eat ice cream, fast or slow!

Tune: Twinkle, Twinkle Little Star

Words by Eunice Wright

On the top of my ice cream,
I like cherries and whip cream.
Sometimes chocolate sauce and crunch,
How I love to munch and munch.
Sprinkles on the top I see,
They are yummy, try and see.

Making Butter (Ice Cream) Tune: 99 Bottles of Pop

By Emilie Poulsson; adapted by Juli Wright

Scoop, scoop, scoop,
Every color so bright;
Add one scoop of rocky road,
And vanilla so white.

Higher, higher, higher
New flavors I want to try;
Till the ice cream is a tower
Strawberry, bubblegum, pumpkin pie.

Caramel, chocolate, cherry too;
All the flavors I will add.
If there's one I haven't tried,
It will make me really mad.

Taste! Oh, yummy taste,
Each flavor is so nice.
Eat it fast or it will melt—
Too late! It's melted ice.

Poems and Nursery Rhymes

Teddy Bear, Teddy Bear, Turn Around (Chant)

By Eunice Wright

I love ice cream, really, I do!
One scoop is not enough—
Please make it two.

Two scoops are nice, but I want more—
Three scoops is plenty,
Now run out the door!

I Love Ice Cream

By Eunice Wright

I love ice cream, really I do!
Just one scoop? No, make it two.
Yummmy! Now, two scoops for me.
I want more—let's make it three.
Three scoops, no, I want more.
Now I have 1, 2, 3, 4!

I Like Ice Cream

By Juli Wright

I like ice cream, yes I do!
I like ice cream, how about you?
I like ice cream, any where.
I like ice cream—I will share.

Books

Babe Ruth and the Ice Cream Mess, by Dan Gutman. A level 2 book. *Remember when ice cream sold for five cents and boys played stick ball in the streets?*

Curious George Goes to an Ice Cream Shop, by Margret and H.A. Rey.

Dora and the Stuck Truck, by Phoebe Bernstein. *Five different work trucks help to get the ice cream truck out of the mud.*

Fancy Nancy, by Jane O'Connor. *The story and illustrations are very cute. Definitely worth reading.*

Ice Cream, by Elisha Cooper. *Starting with a cow, this book describes the process of how ice cream is made—from milking the cow to the ice cream in the stores. The glossary at the end of the book contains complex and advanced vocabulary.*

Ice Cream Dreams (Sweet Pickles), by Jacquelyn Reinach.

Ice Cream, the Full Scoop, by Gail Gibbons. *The history and making of ice cream. Complicated illustrations, long text but good information.*

Isaac the Ice-Cream Truck, by Scott Santoro.

The Land Where the Ice Cream Grows, by Anthony Burgess.

Max Drives Away, by Rosemary Wells. *In this cute board book, Max wants ice cream for breakfast. (Most of us can relate to this.) But his sister says no.*

Milk to Ice Cream, by Julie Murray. *This book teaches young scientific minds about how cows are milked and how to make ice cream. It includes some ice cream facts and six vocabulary words that are highlighted on the pages. Older grades.*

Pearl and Wagner: Three Secrets, by Kate McMullan. *An easy-to-read book, three chapters; two friends love ice cream, but not necessarily secrets.*

Spike and Cubby's Ice cream Island Adventure, by Heather Sellers. *Two dogs that write and illustrate books together get distracted by the thought of a special treat on Ice Cream Island.*

The SpongeBob Squarepants Movie: Ice Cream Dreams, Nancy Krulik. *SpongeBob tries to cheer himself up by eating way too many ice cream sundaes.*

Wemberly's Ice-Cream Star, by Kevin Henkes. *Board book.*

Movies and Television

Ice Cream Man. Clint Howard. Movies and TV. Will the children be able to convince everyone the ice cream man is a little crazy?

The Shaggy D.A. (44 flavors—Tim Conway drives an ice cream truck), 1976.

Strawberry Shortcake—Adventures on Ice Cream Island. Strawberry Shortcake movies are one of the best selections you can get for your kids.

28. J—Jellyfish

COPY THE JELLYFISH HEAD PATTERN AT 143% AND COPY THE JELLYFISH BODY AT 167%

Jellyfish Activities

Songs to Sing and Play

Tune: You Are My Sunshine

Words by Eunice and Steven Wright

You beautiful Jellyfish, you lovely Jellyfish,
You make me smile when I see you.
You'll always be a fascinating show
Of lights, colors, shapes and sizes too.

Don't get too close, or you'll be sorry!
The jellyfish has stingers there.
Just one little touch, could be disaster—
It's beauty and deadliness to share.

Tune: Lollipop, Lollipop

By Julius Dixon, 1958; words by Eunice Wright

Chorus:

Jellyfish, jellyfish,
Better watch what you do!
Beware of the jellyfish,
That might sting you!

Verses:

Cute little jellyfish,
You have so many "arms."
You drift along,
With all your charms.

You glide and slide,
Through the sea so blue.
You float suspended,
It's just what you do.

Your lovely colors,
In a transparent cloud.
May be the attraction,
That shines so loud.

Tune: Mary Had A Little Lamb

Words by Eunice Wright

Once there was a jellyfish, jellyfish, jellyfish
Once there was a jellyfish, colorful, cloudy, and strong.
In the sea he floated, floated, floated.
In the sea he floated, all day long.

Tune: The Lion Sleeps Tonight

Words by Eunice Wright

In the ocean, the deep blue ocean, the jellyfish floats along.
In the ocean, the deep blue ocean, the jellyfish floats along.

By the island, the peaceful island, the jellyfish plays all day.
By the island, the peaceful island, the jellyfish plays all day.

Do not fe-ar, they are not ne-ar, The jellyfish sleep below.
Repeat—

Tune: Mary Had A Little Lamb

Words by Eunice Wright

The ocean has so many jellyfish,
Many jellyfish, many jellyfish.
The ocean has so many jellyfish,
Their floating tentacles will sting!

Tune: There Were Three Jolly Fishermen

Words by Eunice Wright

There were three floating jellyfish,
There were three floating jellyfish,
Jelly, jelly, fish, fish, fish.
Jelly, jelly, fish, fish, fish.
There were three floating jellyfish.

They all went deep into the sea,
They all went deep into the sea,
The, the, sea, sea, sea.
The, the, sea, sea, sea.
They all went deep into the sea.

Poems and Nursery Rhymes

Ten Little Fishes

By Eunice, Juli and Steven Wright

Ten little fishes were swimming by the shore,

1. This one said, "Let's swim where we can see more."
2. This one said, "Let's swim in the bay."
3. This one said, "I could swim there all day."
4. This one said, "Look what I see!"
5. This one said, "What could it be?"
6. This one said, "It floats and glows in the dark."
7. This one said, "I know it's not a shark!"
8. This one said, "It's soft and fluffy and pink."
9. This one said, "It's so beautiful! Don't you think?"
10. But the wise one said, "Let's be care-ful—and do not stay."

So they all left the jellyfish and swam away.

Merry Little Fishes

Finger Play Reader Part 2, *by John W. Davis, 1909; words adapted by Juli Wright*

Merry Little jellyfishes
In the ocean at play
Floating in the shallows,
Drifting far away.

Happy little jellyfishes ask,
"Come and play with me."
"NO, oh no!" I did say.
"That can never be."

Pretty bodies curving,
Bending like a bow,
Through the clear, bright water
See them swiftly go.

Happy little jellyfishes ask,
"Come and play with me."
"NO, oh no!" I did say.
"That would never do."

Jellyfish

By Juli Wright

Jellyfish swim high and low
Jellyfish go to and fro.
Jellyfish catch a fish
Jellyfish's favorite dish.
Jellyfish with long arms
Jellyfish that do no harm.

Jellyfish Floating

By Juli Wright

Floating, falling, like a leaf
The jellyfish swims among the reef
In the water, deep, blue, clear.
These jellyfish I don't fear—
Tranquil, as the Jellyfish swim
(They don't even use a fin!)
They like to eat little fish,
It is their favorite dish.

Games and Group Activities

Jellyfish Circle Game

Similar to Duck, Duck Goose, except: "I have a little jellyfish and he won't sting you, and he won't sting you, and he won't sting you, but he WILL sting you!!" Jellyfish chases fish.

Parachute Game

Pretend the parachute is a huge jellyfish. Children run into and out of the "floating" parachute, trying not to get stung (caught). Add water music and colored lights for effect.

Books

Australian Spotted Jellyfish (Animal Invaders), by Susan Heinrichs Gray.
Box Jellyfish: Killer Tentacles (Afraid of the Water), by Natalie Lunis.
Corals, Jellyfish, Sponges and Other Simple Animals (Grzimek's Student Animal Life Resource), by Catherine Judge Allen (2005).
Down in the Sea: The Jellyfish (Down in the Sea), by L. Patricia Kite (1993).
Floating Jellyfish (Pull Ahead Books), by Kathleen Martin-James.
Gooey Jellyfish (No Backbone! the World of Invertebrates), by Natalie Lunis.

Have You Ever Seen a Smack of Jellyfish? An Alphabet Book, by Sarah Asper-Smith.

Jellies, by Twig C. George (2001).

Jellyfish (Blastoff! Readers: Oceans Alive), by Ann Herriges (2006).

Jellyfish, by Bellwether Media, 2007. (Oceans Alive). *Beautiful photos, short text.*

Jellyfish (Early Bird Nature Books), by Elaine Landau (1999).

Jellyfish (Early Bird Nature Books), by Leighton R. Taylor and Norbert Wu (1998).

Jellyfish (Heinemann Read and Learn: A Day in the Life: Sea Animals), by Louise Spilsbury.

Jellyfish (True Books: Animals), by Lloyd G. Douglas (2005).

The Jellyfish (Weird Sea Creatures), by Miriam J. Gross (2006).

Jellyfish (Welcome Books), by Lloyd G. Douglas.

Jellyfish Can't Swim and Other Secrets from the Animal World, by Marjorie H. Parker and Tim Davis (1991).

Jellyfish (First Reports), by Mary K. Dornhoffer.

Jellyfish Inside Out, by Michelle McKenzie (2003).

Jellyfish (Marine Life), by Lynn M. Stone (2006).

Jellyfish (Ocean Life), by Martha E. H. Rustad (2006).

Jellyfish (Ooey-Gooey Animals), by Lola M. Schaefer (2002).

Jellyfish (Poison!), by Shane McFee (2007).

Jellyfish (Scary Creatures), by Gerard Cheshire.

Jellyfish (Under the Sea), by Carol K. Lindeen (2004).

Jellyfish (Underwater World), by Deborah Coldiron (2007).

Jellyfish (Wow World of Wonder), by Judy Wearing (2009).

Jellyfish: Animals with a Deadly Touch (Secrets of the Animal World), by Eulalia Garcia (1997).

A Jellyfish Is Not a Fish (Let's-Read-and-Find... Science Book), by John Frederick Waters.

Jellyfish: Sea Life (Naturebooks), by Sharon Sharth (2001).

The Jellyfish Season (Avon Camelot Books), by Mary Downing Hahn.

Jellyfish Shoes (Dingles Leveled Readers—Fiction Chapter Books and Classics), by Susan Gates (2008).

Jellyfish to Insects: Projects with Biology (Hands on Science), by William Hemsley (1991).

Jenny Jellyfish: A Tale of Wiggly Jellies, by Suzanne Tate (2001).

Jeremiah Jellyfish Flies High, by John Fardell, 2011. Hilarious; for older children.

Joy the Jellyfish, by Kristen Collier (Dragonflypubs.com, 2007). *Ages 3–5.*

Sea Jellies: From Corals to Jellyfish (Animals in Order), by Sharon Sharth.

Sponges, Jellyfish, and Other Simple Animals (Animal Kingdom Classification), by Steve Parker.

Wee on a Jellyfish Sting and Other Lies... (Bonkers Books), by Tracey TurnerClive Goddard.

Will Jellyfish Rule The World?: A Book About Climate Change, by Leo Hickman (2009).

Wonders of Jellyfish, by Morris K. Jacobson (1978).

Zeke, Ky and the Jellyfish, by Gwynneth Beasley (2010).

Movies and Television

Finding Nemo (Marlin & Dory in the field of jellyfish)

Mysteries of the Deep (Discovery Channel)

National Geographic, "Dance of the Jellyfish" Video

National Geographic, jellyfish facts and pictures for kids

National Geographic, monster jellyfish (plagues of giant jellyfish float toward Japan)

Nature's Perfect Predators—Box Jellyfish (recommended!)

Oceans in Glass: video by Nature

The SpongeBob Squarepants Movie

Super Animals—Super Jellyfish

Victims of Venom (venom from the sea)

29. K—Koala

COPY THE KOALA HEAD PATTERN AT 125%

Koala Activities

Songs to Sing and Play

Tune: Oh, Do You Know the Muffin Man?

Words by Eunice Wright

Oh, do you know the Koala bear?
The Koala bear?
The Koala bear?
Oh, do you know the Koala bear?
That lives in the tree tops?

Tune: Three Blind Mice

Words by Eunice Wright

Three Koala bears,
Three Koala bears.
See how they eat,
See how they eat,
Their paws have little black claws you can see,
A black nose and fluffy ears are as cute as can be,
Did you ever see such a sight in a tree?
As three Koala bears.

Tune: Bingo

Traditional. Words by Eunice Wright

There was a zoo had an animal,
And Koala was his name-o.
K-o-a-l-a!
K-o-a-l-a!
K-o-a-l-a!
And Koala was his name-o!

Tune: Did You Ever See a Lassie?

Words by Eunice Wright

Did you ever see a Koala,
A Koala, a Koala?
Did you ever see a Koala
With gray fluffy ears?

Tune: Jimmy Crack Corn

Words by Eunice Wright

The Koala's fur is fluffy and gray,
The Koala's fur is fluffy and gray,
The Koala's fur is fluffy and gray,
The Koala's in the zoo.

Tune: Row, Row Your Boat

Words by Eunice Wright

Koala, Koala, Koala Bear,
What do you eat?
"I eat eucalyptus leaves,
They are really neat."

Koala, Koala, Koala Bear,
Where can I see you?
"Australia is the place I'm from,
But look for me in the zoo."

Tune: 10 Little Indians

Words by Eunice Wright

One little, two little, three little Koala bears
... eating eucalyptus leaves.

Poems and Nursery Rhymes

Five Little Koala Bears

By Eunice Wright

Five little koala bears in a Eucalyptus tree.
The first one said, "Hey, look at me!"
The second one said, "I have pretty gray fur."
The third one said, "Yes, sir, that's for sure!"
The fourth one said, "Australia is my home."
The fifth one said, "Where is my comb?"
Five little koala bears in a eucalyptus tree,
Climbing and playing and eating leaves on the tree.

Koala Bear (Teddy Bear, Teddy Bear—Jump Rope Chant)

By Eunice Wright

Koala bear, koala bear, turn around,
Koala bear, koala bear, touch the ground.

Koala bear, koala bear, Dance on your toes,
Koala bear, koala bear, touch your nose.
Koala bear, koala bear, give a little clap,
Koala bear, koala bear, take a nap.
(or polar bear, brown bear, black bear, baby bear, Grizzly bear, Smokey Bear, etc.)

Little Koala

By Juli Wright

The little koala is cute; he wears a little gray suit.
He climbs the eucalyptus tree; he looks straight down at me.
He has leaves for lunch; he eats them by the bunch.
He has a little black nose; he's cute wherever he goes.

Books

Baby Koala (Nature Babies), by Aubrey Lang (2004).
Baby Koala and Mommy (Baby Animals), by Laura Gates (2007).
Can You Cuddle Like A Koala?, by John Butler (2003). Story Cove: A World of Stories.
I Am a Little Koala: Mini (Little Animals), by Francois Crozat (1995).
Koala (Natural World), by Michael Leach (2002).
Koala (Welcome Books), by Edana Eckart (2005).
Koala Bears (Real Readers), by Eliza Robbins (2002).
The Koala Book, by Ann Sharp (1995).
Koala Country: A Story of an Australian Eucalyptus Forest (Soundprints Wild Habitats), by Deborah Dennard (2001).
A Koala Is Not a Bear! by Hannelore Sotzek (Crabapples, 1997).
Koala, Koala, I'm Not a Bear, I'm a Koala, by David G. Earl (2009).
Koala Lou, by Mem Fox. *A young koala wants mother's loving attention.*
The Koala: The Bear That's Not a Bear (Bears of the World), by Dianastar Helmer (1998).
Koalas (Pebble Plus: Australian Animal), by Sara Louise Kras (2009).
Koalas and Other Australian Animals (Zoobook Series), by John Bonnett Wexo (1997).
Koalas and Other Marsupials (What Kind of Animal Is It?), by Bobbie Kalman (2005).
The Life Cycle of a Koala, by Bobbie Kalman (1997).
Princess Mia and the Magical Koala, by Vivian French (The Tiara Club), 2010.
Tales from the Outback (Koala Brothers), by Melissa Lagonegro (2004).
Why Koala Has a Stumpy Tail, by Martha Hamilton (2007).

Movies and Television

Animal Planet
Animal Rescue (baby Koala)
Noozles (the Koala Bear series). Linky, Pinky and Sandy, 1984–1993.
The Outback Koala Kid
Rescuers Down Under 2
Sam, the Koala
Sunny and Taemin (not in English)
Toby and the Koala Bear, 1981
The Wild, 2006 (many animals)

30. L—Lamb

Copy the lamb head pattern at 125%

Lamb Activities

Songs to Sing and Play

Baa Baa Black Sheep (tune: Twinkle, Twinkle Little Star)

The Baby's Opera, by Walter Crane, 1877 (sheet music)

Baa, baa, black sheep,
Have you any wool?
Yes sir, yes sir,
Three bags full.

One for my master,
One for my dame,
And one for the little boy
Who lives down the lane.

Baa, baa, black sheep,
Have you any wool?
Yes sir, yes sir,
Three bags full.

One to mend the jerseys
One to mend the socks
And one to mend the holes in
The little girls' frocks.

Baa, baa, black sheep,
Have you any wool?
Yes sir, yes sir,
Three bags full.

Throw It Out the Window (tune: Polly Wolly Doodle)

Nursery rhyme game. See Wee Sing Silly Songs for sheet music, or kididdles.com to listen to this song.

Mary had a little lamb,
Its fleece was white as snow,
And every where that Mary went—
She threw it out the window,
The window, the window, the second story window.
And everywhere that Mary went, she threw it out the window.

Little Bo Peep has lost her sheep,
And doesn't know where to find them,
Leave them alone and they'll come home,
And she'll throw them out the window,
The window, the window, the second story window.
And everywhere that Bo Peep went, she threw them out the window.

Baa, baa, black sheep, Have you any wool?
Yes, sir, yes, sir, 3 bags full.
One for my master, One for my dame, and One for the little boy
Who threw them out the window...

Repeat with other nursery rhymes: Old Mother Hubbard, Little Jack Horner, Old King Cole, Little Miss Muffet, Jack and Jill, Humpty Dumpty, etc.

Tune: Oh Where, Oh Where Has My Little Dog Gone?

Words by Eunice Wright

Oh where, oh where are the sheep today?
Oh where, oh where can they be?
Are they eating some grass, or growing some wool?
Oh where, oh where can they be?

Poems and Nursery Rhymes

Baa, Baa, Black Sheep

Kipling Stories and Poems Every Child Should Know

Baa, baa, black sheep, have you any wool?
Yes, sir; yes, sir; three bags full.
One for the master, one for the dame
None for the little boy that cries down the lane.

Little Bo-Peep

Harry's Ladder to Learning, with Two Hundred and Thirty Illustrations, by David Bogue and Joseph Cundall, 1850.

Little Bo-peep has lost her sheep,
And can't tell where to find them;
Leave them alone, and they'll come home,
And bring their tails behind them.

Little Bo-peep fell fast asleep,
And dreamed she heard them bleating;

But when she awoke, she found it a joke,
For they were still a-fleeting.

Then up she took her little crook,
Determined for to find them;
She found them indeed, but it made her
heart bleed,
For they'd left their tails behind them!

It happened one day, as Bo-peep did stray,
Unto a meadow hard by,
There she espied their tails side by side,
All hung on a tree to dry.

She heaved a sigh, and wiped her eye,
And over the hillocks she raced;
And tried what she could, as a shepherdess
should,
That each tail should be properly placed.

Little Bo Peep

The Home Book of Verse, *Vol. 1 (of 4). Author: Various; editor: Burton Egbert Stevenson, 1912.*

Little Bo-Peep has lost her sheep,
And can't tell (and doesn't know) where to
find them;
Leave them alone, and they'll come home,
And bring (bringing or wagging) their tails
behind them.
Little Bo-Peep fell fast asleep,
And dreamt she heard them bleating;
But when she awoke, she found it a joke,
For still they all were fleeting.
Then up she took her little crook,
Determined for to find them;
She, found them indeed, but it made her
heart bleed,
For they'd left all their tails behind them!
It happened one day, as Bo-peep did stray
Unto a meadow hard by.
There she espied their tails, side by side,
All hung on a tree to dry.
She heaved a sigh and wiped her eye,
And over the hillocks she raced;
And tried what she could, as a shepherdess
should,
That each tail should be properly placed.

Little Boy Blue

Harry's Ladder to Learning, with Two Hundred and Thirty Illustrations, *by David Bogue and Joseph Cundall, 1850.*

Little boy blue, come blow me your horn,
The sheep's in the meadow, the cow's in the
corn;
Where is the little boy tending the sheep?
Under the haycock fast asleep.

(Will you wake him? No, not I,
For if I do, He's sure to cry).

Mary Had a Little Lamb

The Home Book of Verse, *American and English, 1580–1918*

Mary had a little lamb.
Its fleece was white as snow;
And everywhere that Mary went,
The lamb was sure to go.

He followed her to school one day.
Which was against the rule;
It made the children laugh and play
To see a lamb at school.

And so the teacher turned him out,
But still he lingered near.
And waited patiently about
Till Mary did appear.

Then he ran to her, and laid
His head upon her arm.
As if he said, "I'm not afraid"
You'll keep me from all harm."

"What makes the lamb love Mary so? "
The eager children cried.
"Oh, Mary loves the lamb, you know,"
The teacher quick replied.

The Pet Lamb

Aunt Kitty's Stories, *1870, by various authors*

My own pet lamb, I long to be
From envy, pride, and malice free;
Patient, and mild, and meek like thee,
My own pet lamb.

I long to know my shepherd's voice,
To make his pleasant ways my choice
And in the fold like thee rejoice,
My own pet lamb.

The Lambs

Finger Plays for Nursery and Kindergarten, *by Emilie Poulsson, 1893. Sheet music and fingerplay actions.*

1. This is the meadow where all the long day
Ten little frolicsome lambs are at play.
These are the measures the good farmer brings
Salt in, or corn meal, and other good things.

2. This is the lambkins' own big water-trough;
Drink, little lambkins, and then scamper off!
This is the rack where in winter they feed;
Hay makes a very good dinner indeed.

3. These are the big shears to shear the old sheep;
Dear little lambkins their soft wool may keep.
Here, with its big double doors shut so tight,
This is the barn where they all sleep at night.

Eight White Sheep

Songs and Games for Little Ones, *by Harriet S. Jenks and Gertrude Walker, 1887. With sheet music.*

I've eight white sheep all fast asleep, and two old dogs close by;
All through the night their watch is bright, for fear a wolf come nigh.
A wild wolf comes, and then old thumbs (dogs), who like no better play, cry
"Bow, bow wow!" and "Bow, wow, wow!" and drive the wolf away!

Ha, ha, what fun! One sheep has run, and there goes number two!
Old thumbs now cry their "Bow, wow, wow!" and don't know what to do.
Now there goes three, and there goes four, all in a frightened pack,
And now old dogs cry, "Bow, wow, wow!" and try to drive them back!
Now there goes five, and there goes six, just see them jump the rails!
So now old dogs cry, "Bow, wow, wow!" and wag their bushy tails;
And there goes seven, and there goes eight, oh, look how fast they run!
And now old dogs cry, "Bow, wow, wow!" and think it is great fun.

The Lamb

Chinese Mother Goose Rhymes, *by Isaac Taylor, 1900.*

It jumped the chequered wall,
The bleating little lamb,
And snatched a bunch of grass
To feed its hungry dam.

Games and Group Activities

Pin the Tail on the Lamb

Make or find a poster of a tailless lamb to hang on the wall. Create separate tails for the lamb with cotton balls on paper. Each player is blindfolded and tries to attach the tail to the lamb in the correct spot. Whoever gets closest is the winner.

Books

Baa Baa Black Sheep, by Iza Trapani.
Baa-Choo! by Rosemary Wells. *A lamb that sneezes.*
"The Boy Who Cried Wolf." See #18.
Brave Charlotte and the Wolves, by Ann Stohner (Bloomsbury, 2009). *Beautiful large illustrations, but confusing story line for young children. Also see* Brave Charlotte.
Feeding the Sheep, by Leda Schubert (2010).
The Lamb and the Butterfly, by Arnold Sundgaard.
The Lamb Who Came for Dinner, by Steve Smallman, Tiger Tales. *A little lamb softens the heart of a mean old wolf. Excellent story for preschool children.*

The Little Lamb, Random House Picture-books.

Old MacDonald Had a Woodshop, by Lisa Shulman. *A sheep uses carpenter tools in his woodshop. Nice illustrations.*

Russell the Sheep, by Rob Scotton. *Russell can't get to sleep.*

Sheep in a Jeep, by Nancy Shaw (1986). *A rhyming tale of a group of sheep riding in a jeep.*

Sheep on the Farm, by Mari Schuh (2001). *Simple text and colorful photographs of sheep being raised on a farm. Nonfiction selection.*

Sneaky Sheep, by Chris Monroe.

Time for Bed, by Mem Fox (Houghton, 1997). Board book, ages 2–6. *Beautiful illustrations. Time for adult animals to put their babies to sleep. A book about getting ready for bed.*

Wee Little Lamb, by Lauren Thompson (2009). *Big illustrations of beautiful soft animals. A little lamb hides behind his mother until he finds a friend.*

When Sheep Sleep, by Laura Numeroff (Abrams Books, 2006). *Beautiful illustrations, short rhyming text.*

Where Is Green Sheep? by Mem Fox (2004). *Rhyming text about sheep; but where is green sheep? Fast asleep.*

"Wolf in Sheep's Clothing." See #18.

Movies and Television

Babe

Charlotte's Web

How to Train Your Dragon

Kung Foo Panda

The Muppets

Pixar Short Films (sheering sheep)

SERTA mattress commercials (the sheep are angry at the mattress company)

Sesame Street

Wallace and Grommet, in A Close Shave, 1995

31. M—Monkey

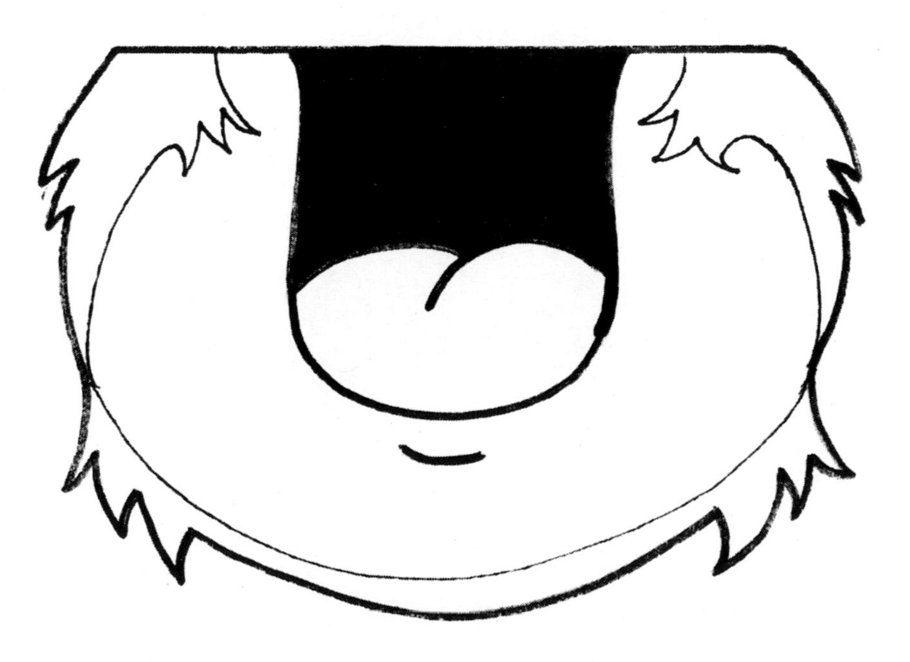

Monkey Activities

Songs to Sing and Play

Tune: The Bear Went Over the Mountain

Words by Eunice Wright

The monkey swung through the trees,
The monkey swung through the trees,
The monkey swung through the trees,
To see what he could see
To see what he could see,
To see what he could see

The other side of the jungle,
The other side of the jungle,
The other side of the jungle,
Was all that he could see

Was all that he could see,
Was all that he could see,
The other side of the jungle,
Was all that he could see!

Pop Goes the Weasel

Traditional

All around the Cobbler's bench
The monkey chased the weasel.
The monkey thought 'twas all in fun.
Pop! Goes the weasel.

Every night when I get home,
The monkey's on the table.
Take a stick and knock it off,
Pop! Goes the weasel.

Tune: The Itsy Bitsy Spider

Words by Eunice Wright

The itsy bitsy monkey climbed up the banana tree,
Yellow bananas were all that he could see.
He was so hungry, he gobbled two or three,
Then the itsy bitsy monkey climbed down the banana tree.

Tune: Sally, the Camel (Molly, the Monkey)

Camp song; adapt song, using other animals and traits. Alternate tune: "Dem Bones")

Sally the Camel has two humps (Molly, the monkey has one tail),
Sally the Camel has two humps,
Sally the Camel has two humps,
So ride Sally, ride! (So climb, Molly, climb!)
Boom, boom, boom.

Sally the Camel has one hump,
Sally the Camel has one hump,
Sally the Camel has one hump,
So ride Sally, ride!
Boom, boom, boom.

Sally the Camel has no humps,
Sally the Camel has no humps,
Sally the Camel has no humps,

Now Sally ... is a horse!! (Now Molly ... is a monkey!)

Alternate ending: (Because Sally is a horse ... of course!)

Try singing the song using other animals: Molly, the Monkey has one tail; Nellie, the Horse has four legs; Newton, the Newt has four legs; Tommy, the Turtle has one shell.

Tune: The Old Gray Mare

Oral traditional folk song, 1906. Collector E.C. Perrow

Here we sit like birds in the wilderness
Birds in the wilderness
Birds in the wilderness
Here we sit like birds in the wilderness
Waiting for our food.

Add things monkeys do, where they live, how they act, etc.

Here we sit like monkeys in the zoo...
Eating our bananas.
(or Swinging in the trees)

Other Songs

"Five Little Monkeys, Jumping on the Bed"
"Five Funky Little Monkeys," by Jack Hartmann.
"Monkey in the Treetop," *I Have a Song for You About Animals*, by Janeen Brady, p. 29.
"Monkey Motel," Scott Laningham. Presented as a Radio Aahs exclusive. 2:34.

Poems and Nursery Rhymes

The Monkeys and the Crocodile, or Teasing Mr. Alligator/Crocodile

Originated from: In My Nursery, A Book of Verse, *by Laura E. Richards, 1890.*

(See grandparents.com, and KingCountyLibrarySystem to watch this performed.)

Clap hands loudly on the word, "Snap!"

Three little monkeys
Swinging in a tree
Teasing Mister Alligator,
Can't catch me, can't catch me.

Along comes Mister Alligator,
Quiet as can be
And SNAPS that monkey
Right out of that tree!

Two little monkeys...

One little monkey
Swinging in a tree
Teasing Mister Alligator,
Can't catch me, can't catch me
Along comes Mister Alligator,
Quiet as can be
And SNAPS that monkey
Right out of that tree!

Alternate endings:

Quiet as can be... Snap! Missed me!
And SNAP! No more monkeys swinging in a tree!
But here's Mr. Alligator/Crocodile, full as can be!
Ha ha, missed me!

Five Dancing Monkeys (Count Up)

By Eunice Wright

One little monkey, dancing on his toes,
Up and down the music goes.
Two little monkeys, both politely bow,
Holding hands tightly, one yells, "OW!"
Three little monkeys, dancing the fox trot,
Three is a crowd, so I think not!
Four little monkeys, doing the limbo crawl,
One whacked his head & started to bawl.
Five little monkeys, having fun at last,
Dancing, singing, and twirling around fast.

Books

BIG Little Monkey, by Carole Schaefer (Candlewick Press, 2008). *A little monkey tries to grow up to be BIG. Simple illustrations.*
Caps for Sale, by Esphyr Slobodkina (Harper & Row, HarperCollins, 1947). *Monkeys take off with the cap peddler's goods while he takes a nap.*
Curious George, by H.A. Rey (Houghton Mifflin, 1973). *Curiosity seems to get George the monkey into lots of trouble—luckily the man in the yellow hat is always around to help him out.*
Curious George at the Parade, by Margret and H.A. Rey.
Eight Silly Monkeys Jumping on the Bed, by Steve Haskamp.
Five Little Monkeys Jumping on the Bed, by Eileen Christelow (Clarion). *Five monkeys would rather jump on the bed than sleep in it. A cute rhyming story for older children, humorous.*
Five Little Monkeys Sitting in a Tree, by Eileen Christelow (1993).
Monkey and Me, by Emily Gravett.
The Monkey and the Crocodile, by Paul Galdone (Houghton Mifflin, 1973).
Monkeys, by Patricia Whitehead (Troll, 1982).
So Say the Little Monkeys, by Nancy Van Laan (Simon & Schuster, 1998). *Very simple drawings, fair text.*

Spunky Monkeys on Parade, by Stuart J. Murphy. *Count the monkeys on parade. (Skip counting.)*
Summer of the Monkeys, by Wilson Rawls. *Older grades.*
There Was an Old Monkey Who Swallowed a Frog, by Jennifer Ward (2007). *In the jungle, this traditional tale with rhymes discusses the monkey's strange diet.*
Trouble Is His Name, by Elizabeth Montgomery (Garrard, 1976).

Movies and Television

Animals Are Beautiful People
Baby's Day Out (gorilla)
Born to Be Wild (gorilla)
Chimpanzee—Disney Nature Series, 2012
Chimpanzee Eden (Animal Planet)
Curious George
Dunston Checks In
George of the Jungle (gorilla)
Jumanji
Jungle Book
Little House on the Prairie (Edwards finds Clyde, the orangutan, to raise)
Mighty Joe Young (gorilla)
Monkeys Go Home
Monkey's Uncle (Merlin Jones), 1965
Orangutan Island
Robinson Crusoe
Rocket Man
Space Chimps, 2008 (Animation)
Tarzan

32. N—Newt

Copy this pattern at 111%

Newt Activities

Songs to Sing and Play

Newt of Earl (tune: Duke of Earl)

By Gene Chandler, penned by Bernice Williams, 1962; words adapted by Eunice Wright

Newt, newt, newt,
You're so cute, cute, cute!
You're so green, green, green,
With eyes that gleam, gleam, gleam!
Oh, newt! You are the only one...

Tune: Oh, the Noble Duke of York

Words by Eunice Wright

Oh, the newt I caught today,
Is slimy, slippery and green,
He walked right up the side of the wall,
And he walked back down again.

Oh, the newt upon the wall,
He has the cutest toes,
He climbs up the glass and back again,
And slides wherever he goes.

Tune: Did You Ever See a Lassie?

Words by Eunice Wright

Did you ever see a newt... with green slimy skin?

Tune: Itsy Bitsy Spider

Words by Eunice Wright

The itsy bitsy newt climbed up the slippery tree.
Down came a branch and hit him on the knee... Oww!
Out came a quail and bandaged up his knee... AND...
The itsy bitsy newt climbed up the other tree.

Tune: The Wheels on the Bus

Words by Eunice Wright

The newt crawls around the jungle all day ... he uses his suction toes.

Tune: Mary Had a Little Lamb

Words by Eunice Wright

_____ (name of child) had a little newt...
It's skin as _____ (color of puppet) as _____ (item).

Ex. Johnny had a little newt, little newt, little newt.
Johnny had a little newt, it's skin as green as grass.

Tune: I'm Bringing Home a Baby Bumble Bee

Chorus originated from the Arkansas Traveler, 1806; words by Eunice Wright

I'm bringing home a little baby newt,
Won't my mommy dry clean her new suit,
'Cause I'm bringing home a little baby newt...
Oh, it's all wet!

I'm hugging my little baby newt,
Won't my sister holler and hoot,
'Cause I'm hugging my little baby newt...
Oh, it's in her hair!

I'm chasing my little baby newt,
Won't my daddy think he's awful cute,
'Cause I'm chasing my little baby newt...
Oh, it's in the bowl of soup!

I'm singing to my little baby newt,
Won't my grandma pass out a new flute,
'Cause I'm singing to my little baby newt...
Oh, it's crawling on her glasses!

Add other actions that rhyme.

Tune: Sally, the Camel

Sing the song using other animals: Molly, the monkey has one tail; Nellie, the horse has four legs; Newton, the newt has four legs; Tommy, the Turtle has one shell.

Poems and Nursery Rhymes

Handsome Newt

By Eunice Wright

Long and slender, slimy too.
He likes the water, not the zoo.
His great big eyes and suction toes
Make him handsome wherever he goes.

A Salamander

Original author unknown; adapted by Eunice Wright

I saw a little creature that was slimy, smooth, and wet.
I thought it was the oddest thing that I had ever met.
It was something like a lizard, but it had no scales at all.
It was something like a frog, but it didn't hop—it crawled.
So I took it to my teacher and she told me right away,
"I see you brought a salamander (newt) into class today."

Little Newt

By Eunice and Juli Wright

Once there was a little newt
Who climbed a little tree.
He had his fingers spread out,
As wide as wide could be.

Do you know he climbs
With suckers on his toes?
They keep him from falling
Wherever he goes.

His colors can be so bright,
Of yellow, green and blue.
And polka dots so colorful
You wouldn't think it true!

Beware the brightest colors
The newt may care to wear;
It can be a warning
There may be poison there!

If the newt, by accident,
Should lose a toe or two,
He just grows another one,
Just as good as new!

The Gnu. The Newt

Animal Analogues, by Robert Williams Wood, 1887

The Gnu conspicuously wears
His coat of gnumerous bristling hairs,
While, as we see, the modest newt
Of such a coat is destitute.

(I'm only telling this to you,
And it is strictly "entre gnu.")

In point of fact the newt is nude,
And therefore he doest not obtrude,

But hides in some secluded gnook,
Beneath the surface of the brook:
It's almost more than he can bear,
To slyly take his breath of air,

His need of which is absolute,
Because, you see, his is a Pneu-t.

Our Tree-Toad

Child Songs of Cheer, *by Evaleen Stein, 1918; adapted by Juli and Eunice Wright*

Grandfather says the newt
That to our yard has come,
Is just a little wee newt
No bigger than his thumb!

And that his coat's so queer it
Can turn from green to blue!
Whatever color's near it,
Why, that's its color, too!

And then Grandfather snickers
And says, "Would you suppose
He climbs with little stickers
On all his little toes?

"And don't you wish your toes now
Were fixed like his? For, see,
Right up the elm he goes now
And sticks tight to the tree!"

Games and Group Activities

Have You Ever Seen a Newt?

By Eunice Wright

Color the NEWT puppets different colors for this activity. Make other puppets of different colors and repeat the activity. To the tune of "Have You Ever Seen a Lassie?"

Have you ever seen a newt, a newt, a newt?
(insert animal)
Have you ever seen a newt all dressed up
(or colored) in pink? (insert color)
With pink eyes, and pink nose,
And pink legs and pink toes.
Have you ever seen a newt all dressed up in
pink?

Have you ever seen a newt, a newt, a newt?
Have you ever seen a newt all dressed up in
white?
With white eyes, and white nose,
And white legs and white toes.
Have you ever seen a newt all dressed up in
white?

Have you ever seen a newt, a newt, a newt?
Have you ever seen a newt all dressed up in
purple?
With purple eyes, and purple nose,
And purple legs and purple toes.
Have you ever seen a newt all dressed up in
purple?

Have you ever seen a newt, a newt, a newt?
Have you ever seen a newt all dressed up in
blue?
With blue eyes, and blue nose,
And blue legs and blue toes.
Have you ever seen a newt all dressed up in
blue?

Bugs and Newt

Use five "bugs" such as small colored paper plates, poker chips, fig NEWTons, or plastic insects and one newt puppet which "eats" the insects as each verse subtracts a bug.

Five little bugs, flying through the door,
Along came a newt (slurp!), then there were
four.

Four little bugs, on a flowering tree.
Along came a newt (slurp!), then there were
three.

Three little bugs, flying around a old shoe,
Along came a newt (slurp!), then there were two.

Two little bugs, buzzing in the sun,
Along came a newt (slurp!), then there was one.

One little bug, on a honey bun,
Along came a newt (slurp!), then there were none (yum, yum!).

Books

Art and Max, by David Weisner. *Lizards who paint?*
I Wanna Iguana, by Karen Kaufman Orloff.
The Iguana Brothers, by Tony Johnston.
Little Newts, by Meish Goldish (Bearport Pub., 2010). *Great photos and good information. Recommended.*
Lizard's Song, by George Shannon (Greenwillow, 1981).
Manana, Iguana, by Ann Paul. *A twist on the Little Red Hen story.*
Me Too Iguana, Sweet Pickle Series (Holt).
The Mixed-Up Chameleon, by Eric Carle.
Newt, by Matt Novak (HarperCollins, 1997). An I Can Read Book.
One Newt in a Suit, by Andrew Weale.
Red-Spotted Newt, by Doris Gove.
The Salamander Room, by Anne Mazer and illustrated by Steve Johnson and Lou Fancher.
What Newt Could Do for Turtle, by Johnathan London.
Where's My Tail? by Susan Schafer (Marshall Cavendish, 2005). *Little lizard loses his tail and asks forest animals for help. Good illustrations, moderate text. Okay for early childhood.*

Movies and Television

Matilda
National Geographic: Fire Salamander and Alpine Newt, Amphibians
National Geographic: World's Weirdest—Swallowed Newt Escapes Death
Rio (lizard)

33. O—Owl

Copy this pattern at 105%

Owl Activities

Songs to Sing and Play

Barn Owl (tune: I'm a Little Teapot)

Words by Eunice Wright

I'm a little barn owl, gray and white.
I like hunting mice at night.
When I spread my wings, I'm quite a sight.
I like to sleep when it gets light.

Snowy Owl (tune: I'm a Little Teapot)

Words by Glen Wright

I'm a little owl, pure and white.
See my wings, I'm a beautiful sight.
When I see a mouse, in the moonlight,
Down I swoop, so quiet in the night.

Tune: Did You Ever See a Lassie?

Words by Eunice Wright

Did you ever see an owl, an owl, an owl?
Did you ever see a owl,
Fly this way and that?

Fly this way, and that way,
And this way, and that?
Did you ever see an owl,
Fly this way and that?

The Great Horned Owl (tune: She'll Be Coming Round the Mountain)

Words by Eunice Wright

The great horned owl has feathers on his head, "Who, who?"
The great horned owl has feathers on his head, "Who, who?"
The great horned owl has feathers,
The great horned owl has feathers,
The great horned owl has feathers on his head, "Who, who?"

Other verses:
The snowy owl has a white face and large wings, "Who, who?"
The Barn Owl is so beautiful and white, "Who, who?"

Tune: 10 Little Indians

Words by Eunice Wright

Replace the word "little" with another adjective: big, old, wise, sleepy, hungry, etc.
Sleeping all day long.

Poems and Nursery Rhymes

5 Little Owls (Count Down)

By Eunice Wright

5 little owls, by the barn door, 1 flew away, then there were four.
4 little owls, sitting in a tree, 1 flew away, then there were three.
3 little owls, calling, "Who, who?" 1 flew away, then there were two.
2 little owls, sleeping in the sun, 1 flew away, then there was one.
1 little owl, his work all done, flew home to mother,
Then there were none.

A Little Boy

Aunt Kitty's Stories, *Various Authors, 1870*

A little boy went into a barn,
And lay down on some hay;
An owl came out and flew about,
And the little boy ran away.

A Wise Old Owl

Punch, or the London Charivari, *April 10, 1875*

There once was an owl who sat in an oak,
The more he heard, the less he spoke.
The less he spoke, the more he heard.
Why can't we be like that wise old bird?

Nursery Rhyme

The Little Mother Goose, *by Jesse Wilcox Smith, 1918*

There was an owl lived in an oak.
Whiskey, whaskey, weedle!
And all the words he ever spoke,
Were fiddle, faddle, feedle!

A gunner chanced to come that road,
Whiskey, whaskey, weedle!
Says he, "I'll shoot you, silly bird!
So fiddle, faddle, feedle!"

The Owl and the Pussycat

Nonsense Songs, Stories, Botany, and Alphabets, *by Edward Lear, 1894; song composer: Elton Hayes.*

The owl and the pussycat went to sea in a beautiful pea-green boat
They took some honey and plenty of money wrapped up in a five-pound note.

The owl looked up to the stars above and sang to a small guitar,
"O, lovely pussy, o pussy my love, what a beautiful pussy you are, you are
What a beautiful pussy you are!"

Pussy said to the owl, "You elegant fowl, how charmingly sweet you sing.
O, let us be married, too long we have tarried, but what shall we do for a ring?"

They sailed away for a year and a day to the land where the bong-tree grows.
And there in a wood a piggy wig stood with a ring at the end of his nose,
His nose, his nose, with a ring at the end of his nose.

"Dear pig, are you willing to sell for one shilling your ring?" Said the piggy, "I will."
So they took it away and were married next day by the turkey who lives on the hill.

They dined on mince and slices of quince which they ate with a runcible spoon;
And hand in hand on the edge of the sand they danced by the light of the moon,
The moon, the moon, they danced by the light of the moon.

Awful Harbingers

Folk Rhymes Wise and Otherwise, *by Thomas W. Talley, 1922; adapted by Juli Wright*

When the big owl swoops
And the screech owl screeches,
And the wind makes a howling sound;
All the little children had better cover up,
The ghosts are coming around.

The Great Owl's Song

Folk Rhymes Wise and Otherwise, *by Thomas W. Talley, 1922; adapted by Juli Wright*

Who-woo-oo? Who-woo-oo? Who-woo-oo?
And who'll sing for brother and who'll sing for you?
I will sing to myself, but I won't sing for you.
Who-woo-oo! Who-woo-oo! Who-woo-oo!

Nonsense Books

Edward Lear, 1894

There was an old man with an owl,
Who continued to hoot and howl;
They sat on spade, and drank lemonade,
Which refreshed that old man and his owl.

A Howl About an Owl

In My Nursery: A Book of Verse, *by Laura E. Richards, 1890*

It was an owl lived in an oak,
Sing heigh ho! the prowly owl!
He often smiled, but he seldom spoke,
And he wore a wig and a camlet cloak.
Sing heigh ho! the howly fowl!
Tu-whit! tu-whit! Tu-whoo!

He fell in love with the chickadee,
Sing heigh ho! the prowly owl!
He asked her, would she marry he,
And they'd go and live in Crim Tartaree.
Sing heigh ho! the howly fowl!
Tu-whit! tu-whit! Tu-whoo!

"'Tis true," says he, "you are far from big."
Sing heigh ho! the prowly owl!
"But you'll look twice as well when I've bought you a wig,
And I'll teach you the Lancers and the Chorus Jig."
Sing heigh ho! the howly fowl!
Tu-whit! tu-whit! Tu-whoo!

"I'll feed you with honey when the moon grows pale."
Sing heigh ho! the prowly owl!
"I'll hum you a hymn, and I'll sing you a scale,
Till you quiver with delight to the tip of your tail!"
Sing heigh ho! the howly fowl!
Tu-whit! tu-whit! Tu-whoo!

So he went for to marry of the chickadee,
Sing heigh ho! the prowly owl!
But the sun was so bright that he could not see,
So he married the hoppergrass instead of she.
And wasn't that a sad disappointment for he!
Sing heigh ho! the howly fowl!
Tu-whit! tu-whit! Tu-whoo!

Games and Group Activities

Little Owl's Adventure

A puppet play by Richard Eaves. Mighty Books.com, Free-Text-To-Read. Make a mother owl and a baby owl puppet for this cute rhyming play.

Give a Hoot, Don't Pollute!

Use this U.S. Forest Service catchphrase to teach about littering. Make a puppet owl to pick up "litter" around the play area.

Books

Adopted by an Owl (The True Story of Jackson the Owl), by Robyn Smith van Frankenhuyzen. *A great horned owl is raised from an owlet.*

The Barn Owl (Animal Lives), by Sally Tagholm.

The Barn Owls, by Tony Johnston (Charlesbridge, 2000). *Good illustrations, short text.*

Bear's New Friend, by Karma Wilson. *Bear and friends play with a bashful owl.*

The Book of North American Owls, by Helen R. Sattler. *Beautiful illustrations.*

Good-Night, Owl! by Pat Hutchins (Macmillan, 1972).

The Happy Owls, by Celestino Piatti.

Hardy Boys 41: The Clue of the Screeching Owl, by Franklin Dixon (1962). *Older grades.*

The Littlest Owl, by Caroline Pitcher.

Look Whooo's Counting, Suse MacDonald.

The Owl and the Pussycat, by Edward Lear, illustrated by Jan Brett (Putnam, 1991). *Lear's poem about an owl in love with a cat first printed in 1870, and has since evolved into a dozen formats, including a board book.*

Owl and the Woodpecker, by Brian Wildsmith.

Owl Babies, by Martin Waddell (Candlewick Storybook Animations, 2010).

Owl Moon, by Jane Yolen (1987).

Owl (See How They Grow), by DK Publishing.

The Owl Who Hated the Dark, by Earle Goodenow.

The Owl Who Was Afraid of the Dark, by Jill Tomlinson.

Owls, by Gail Gibbons.

Owls (Animal Predators), by Sandra Markle.

Owls (Kids Can Press, Wildlife Owls), by Adrienne Mason.

Owls of the United States and Canada: A Complete Guide to Their Biology and Behavior, by Wayne Lynch. Beautiful illustrations.

Owls: The Silent Hunters (Animals in Order), by Sara Swan Miller.

Owly: The Way Home and the Bittersweet Summer, by Andy Runton. *Owly searches for new friends and adventures.*

Tell Me, Mr. Owl, by Doris Foster.
Those Outrageous Owls (Those Amazing Animals), by Laura Wyatt.
Welcome to the World of Owls (Welcome to the World Series).
White Owl, Barn Owl, by Nicola Davies (Candlewick Press, 2007). *Very nice illustrations, good story.*
The Wide-Awake Owl, by Louis Slobodkin.
Wow! Said the Owl, by Tim Hopgood.

Movies and Television

Harry Potter series (Hedwig)
Hoot, Disney movie. Several youth fight to protect endangered owls in Florida.
Legend of the Guardians: The Owls of Ga'hoole (Animated)
Magic of the Snowy Owl, 2012. Owls on the north slope of Alaska struggle to survive.
Owl Moon and Other Stories (1992)
The Sword in the Stone, Walt Disney, animated

34. P—Polar Bear

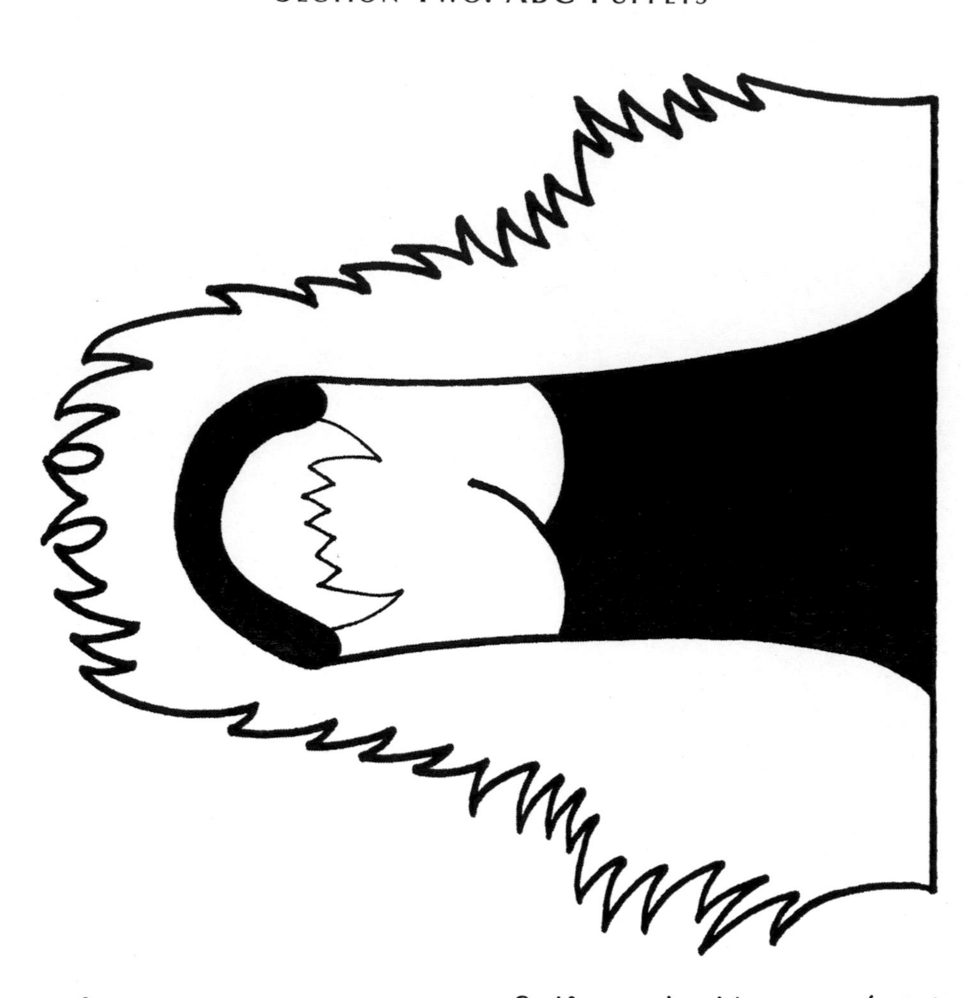

Polar Bear Activities

Songs to Sing and Play

If You Should Meet an Elephant (Polar Bear)

See DLTK Internet site for sheet music and tune.

1. If you should meet a (crocodile) on a spring-time day.
What would you do? What would you say?
I'd say, "Good morning (crocodile), how do you do?
I'm glad to meet you (crocodile), I'd like to dance with you."

2. If you should meet an (elephant) on a summer's day.
What would you do? What would you say?
I'd say, "Good morning (elephant), how do you do?
I'm glad to meet you (elephant), I'd like to dance with you."

3. If you should meet a (stinky skunk) on an autumn day.
What would you do? What would you say?
I'd say, "Good morning (stinky skunk), how do you do?
I'm glad to meet you (stinky skunk), I'd like to dance with you."

4. If you should meet a polar bear on a winter day.
What would you do? What would you say?
I'd say, "Good morning polar bear, how do you do?
I'm glad to meet you polar bear, I'd like to dance with you."

The Polar Bear Went Over the Ice Flow (tune: For He's a Jolly Good Fellow or The Bear Went Over the Mountain)

Words by Eunice Wright

The polar bear went over the ice flow,
The polar bear went over the ice flow,

The polar bear went over the ice flow,
To see what he could see.

To see (hear) what he could see (hear),
To see what he could see,
And all that he could see [hear] was—
The other side of the ice flow,
The other side of the ice flow,
The other side of the ice flow,
Was all that he could see.

Was all that he could see,
Was all that he could see,
The other side of the ice flow,
Was all that he could see!

(See: "Polar Bear, Polar Bear, What Do You Hear?" by Bill Martin, Jr.)

Tune: Mary Had a Little Lamb

Words by Eunice Wright

Substitute children's names and animals.

(Tommy) saw a polar bear, polar bear, polar bear,
(Tommy) saw a polar bear,
Its fur was white as snow.

Tune: 10 Little Indians

Words by Eunice Wright

1 little, 2 little, 3 little polar bears... (Black bears, bear cubs, brown bears, etc.)
All wearing white today. (All playing on the ice.)

Tune: Pop Goes the Weasel

Words by Eunice Wright

All around the ice flow,
The polar bear chased the _____ (walrus)
The polar bear thought 'twas all in fun.
"Help!" cried the ______ (walrus).

Tune: Teddy Bear, Teddy Bear (chant)

By Eunice Wright

Polar bear, polar bear, slide on the ice,
Polar bear, polar bear, that's real nice.
Polar bear, polar bear, snow is on your toes,
Polar bear, polar bear, some is on your nose.
Polar bear, polar bear, go find a cave,
Polar bear, polar bear, give us a wave. (Goodbye!)

Poems and Nursery Rhymes

Five Little Polar Bears (Count Down)

By Eunice Wright

Adapt animals as needed.

Five little polar bears, playing on the floor,
One found a friendly dog, then there were four.
Four little polar bears, running 'round the tree,
One found a friendly pig, then there were three.
Three little polar bears, chewing on a shoe,
One found a friendly cat, then there were two.
Two little polar bears, playing in the sun,
One found a friendly duck, then there was one.
One little polar bear, he just loved to run,
He found a friendly horse, then there were none.

This Little Pig (Polar Bear) Went to Market (Fishing)

By Eunice Wright

This little polar bear went fishing,
This little polar bear stayed home.
This little polar bear had fresh fish,
This little polar bear had none.
This little polar bear said, "Growl, growl, growl,"
All the way home. (or "I can't find my way home.")

The Polar Bear

Bad Child's Book of Beasts, *by Hilaire Belloc, 1896*

The polar bear is unaware
Of cold that cuts me through:
For why? He has a coat of hair.
I with I had one too!

The Two (Polar) Bears

The Jingle Book, *by Carolyn Wells, 1901*

Prince Curlilocks remarked one day
To Princess Dimplecheek,
"I haven't had a real good play
For more than 'most a week."

Said Princess Dimplecheek, "My dear,
Your majesty forgets—
This morning we played grenadier
With grandpa's epaulets.

"And yesterday we sailed to Spain—
We both were pirates bold,
And braved the wild and raging main
To seek for hidden gold."

"True," said the prince; "I mind me well—
Right hardily we fought,
And stormed a massive citadel
To gain the prize we sought.

"But if your ladyship agrees,
Methinks we'll go upstairs
And build a waste of arctic seas,
And we'll be polar bears."

"Yes, if you'll promise not to bite,"
Fair Dimplecheek replied,
Already half-way up the flight,
His highness by her side.

"Princess, on that far window-seat,
Go, sit thee down and wait,
While I ask nursie for a sheet,
Or maybe six or eight."

A pile of sheets his highness brought.
"Dear princess, pray take these;
Although our path with danger's fraught,
We'll reach the polar seas."

Two furry rugs his lordship bore,
Two pairs of mittens white;
He threw them on the nursery floor
And shouted with delight.

He spread those sheets—the funny boy—
O'er table, floor, and chair.
"Princess," said he, "don't you enjoy
This frosty, bracing air?

"These snowy sheets are fields of ice,
This is an iceberg grim."
"Yes, dear, I think it's very nice,"
She said, and smiled at him.

And then they donned the rugs of fur,
The mittens, too, they wore;
And Curlilocks remarked to her,
"Now you must roar and roar."

Dimplecheek looked out from the cowl
Formed by her furry rug.
"I'm 'fraid of bears that only growl—
I like the kind that hug."

Games and Group Activities

Tune: Boom, Boom, Ain't It Great to Be Crazy?

"Fill in the blanks" class activity.

Way up north where there's ice and snow,
There lived a polar bear and his name was Joe.
He got so tired of white, white, white,
That he wore _____ _____ (color, clothing) to the _____ (party, dance, school, meeting, convention) last night (yesterday, today, this morning).

Example below—use White Tiger puppet:

Way out east where there's sun and rain,
There lived a tiger and his name was Cain.
He got so tired of black and white,
That he wore purple pants to the party last night. (Chorus—Boom, Boom...)

See *Wee Sing Silly Songs*, p. 30, for penguin.

Walking Through the Arctic Snow

Modified by Eunice Wright

Classroom activity—adapt actions as needed; each line is an echo by children.

Walking through the arctic snow (echo)
And what do you think I saw? (echo)
A great big polar bear (or walrus, penguin, etc.)
He said Sta-and UP! (Everyone jump up)
(or He said Cra-wl!, Ru-un!, Sli-de!, Fre-eze!)
And shake, shake, this way (And boogey, woogey this way),
Shake, shake that way. (Everyone shake)
Shake, shake, this way,
And then sit down. (Sit down)

Books

Bears Out There, by Joanne Ryder.
The Little Polar Bear, by Hans De Beer.
Little Polar Bears (Born to Be Wild), by Gareth Stevens (2006). *Good information, nice photos.*
My Little Polar Bear, by Claudia Kueda (Scholastic Press, 2009). *Simple pictures, very short text.*
A Pair of Polar Bears, Twin Cubs Find a Home at the San Diego Zoo, by Joanne Ryder (Simon & Schuster for Young Readers, 2006). *Beautiful photos, simple easy text.*
Polar Bear (Natural World), by Penny Malcolm (Raintree, 2000). *Excellent photos; follows a polar bear cub in the Arctic Circle; shows habitats, life cycle, food chain, threats.*
Polar Bear Night, by Stephen Savage.
Polar Bear, Polar Bear What Do You Hear? by Bill Martin, Jr.
Polar Bears (Amazing Animals), by Christina Wilsdon (Gareth Stevens, 2009). *Beautiful photos, a great introduction to the polar bear.*
Polar Bears (Animal Predators), by Sandra Markle (Lerner Pub., 2004). *Very nice large photos.*
Polar Bears, by Gail Gibbons (Holiday House, 2001). *Drawings, good information.*
Polar Bears, by Lesley A. DuTemple. Early Bird Nature Books (Lerner Pub., 1997). *Beautiful photos, easy text, grades 1–3.*
Polar Bears on the Hudson Bay, by Dan Leathers (Mitchell Lane Pub., 2008). *Smaller photos, more information.*
Snow Bear's Christmas Countdown, by Theresa Smythe (Henry Holt, 2004). *Nice illustrations, short text, 25 days of Christmas.*
White Bear, Ice Bear, by Joanne Ryder.

Movies and Television

Balto
Crazy Polar Bear, Backkom, 2007, 1:33. RG Animation Studios.
The Cute Knut, YouTube, 2007, 7:43. The true story of the baby polar bear.
Mondays Suck, YouTube, 13 sec. short clip. Very cute!
National Geographic: Polar Bear Moms and Cubs.
Nature—Arctic Bears, PBS.
The Only Man in the World Who Can Swim with a Polar Bear, YouTube short clip, 2:16.
The Polar Bear King. A Northern Lights Production, 1991. A very cute movie young children might enjoy. A prince is turned into a polar bear. This movie shows (make-believe) village life in the snow.
Polar Bear: Spy on the Ice (PG)
Polar Bears and Dogs Playing, YouTube, 2007, 2:18.

35. Q—Quail

Quail Activities

Songs to Sing and Play

Tune: Did You Ever See a Lassie?

Words by Eunice Wright

Did you ever see a quail,
A quail, a quail,
Did you ever see a quail with feathers on her head?

Tune: 3 Blind Mice

Words by Eunice Wright

Mother quail,
Mother quail,
Leads her babies,
Leads her babies,
They follow her as she leads the way,
They never stop by the path to play,
Close to their mother they always stay,
Quail family,
Quail family.

Tune: I'm a Little Teapot

Words by Eunice Wright

I'm a mother quail with my chicks in a row,
Here are our head feathers, we love to show.
My chicks follow me, wherever I go,
All along the path, high or low.

Tune: How Much Is That Doggy in the Window

Words by Eunice Wright

How much is that quail in the bushes,
The one with the feather on top?
How much is that quail in the bushes?
I do think that quail's so cute.

Tune: Ten Little Indians

Words by Eunice Wright

1 little, 2 little, 3 little quails...
Following their mother.

Tune: Bingo

Words by Eunice Wright

There was a farmer had a bird,
And quail was her name-o.
Q-U-A-I-L!
Q-U-A-I-L!
Q-U-A-I-L!
And Quail was her name-o!

Poems and Nursery Rhymes

Five Little Mice and Five Little Quail

By Eunice Wright

Five little mice went out to play,
And met five quail that came their way.
The five little quail followed after their mother,
And the five little mice ran, chasing one another.

Five Little Quail

By Eunice Wright

Five little quails, running by the door,
One ran away, then there were four.
Four little quails, busy as a bee,
One ran away, then there were three.
Three little quails, playing "peek-a-boo,"
One ran away, then there were two.
Two little quails, playing in the sun.
One ran away, then there was one.
One little quail, having lots of fun,
He ran away, then there were none.
Five little quails, playing hide and seek,
All came running, when they heard mother shriek!

Quail

The Volta Review, *edited by Josephine B. Timberlake, 1921; adapted by Juli Wright*

Men are very fond of me.
You often hear them boast
Of my beauty and good taste,
I'm a quail that is better than most.

Books

Bobwhite Quail—From Egg to Chick to Egg, by Elizabeth and Charles Schwartz. *Nonfiction.*

Quail Can't Decide (Sweet Pickles Series), by Jacquelyn Reinach.

The Quail's Egg, by Joanna Troughton (Blackie Children's Books, 1988). *An additive tale, with each line repeated and another added; a good story to tell to small children, as they will enjoy saying, "NO," each time the quail asks for help. The mother quail tries to get her egg after it rolls into the crack of a rock.*

Quail's Song, by Valerie Scho Carey (Putnam Juvenile, 1990). *Ages 4–8. Large collage illustrations, quail versus coyote, a traditional Native American legend. Good for storytelling; a humorous story with added "sounds" for enrichment and entertainment. Fun for a children's puppet show.*

Movies and Television

Bambi

36. R—Rhinoceros

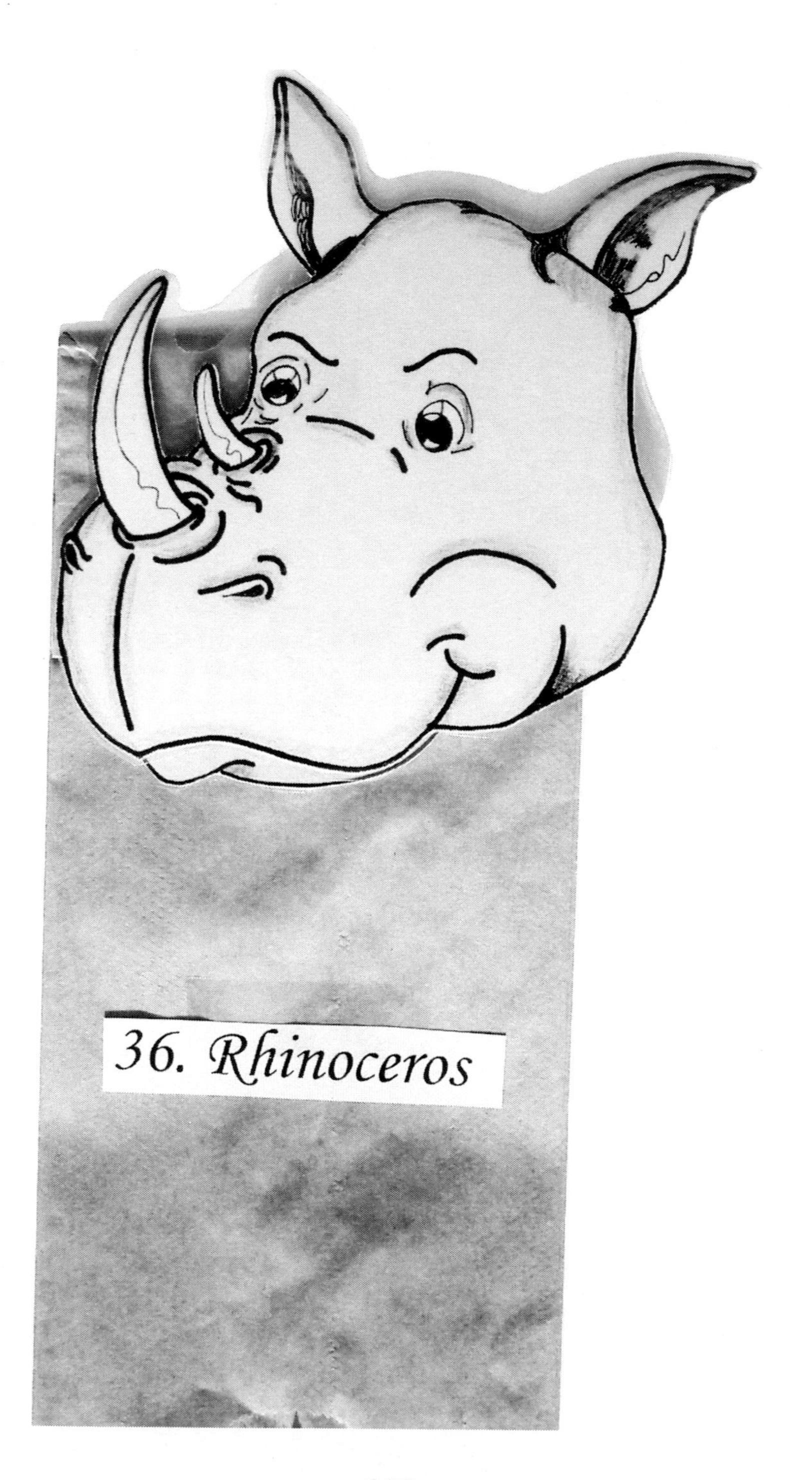

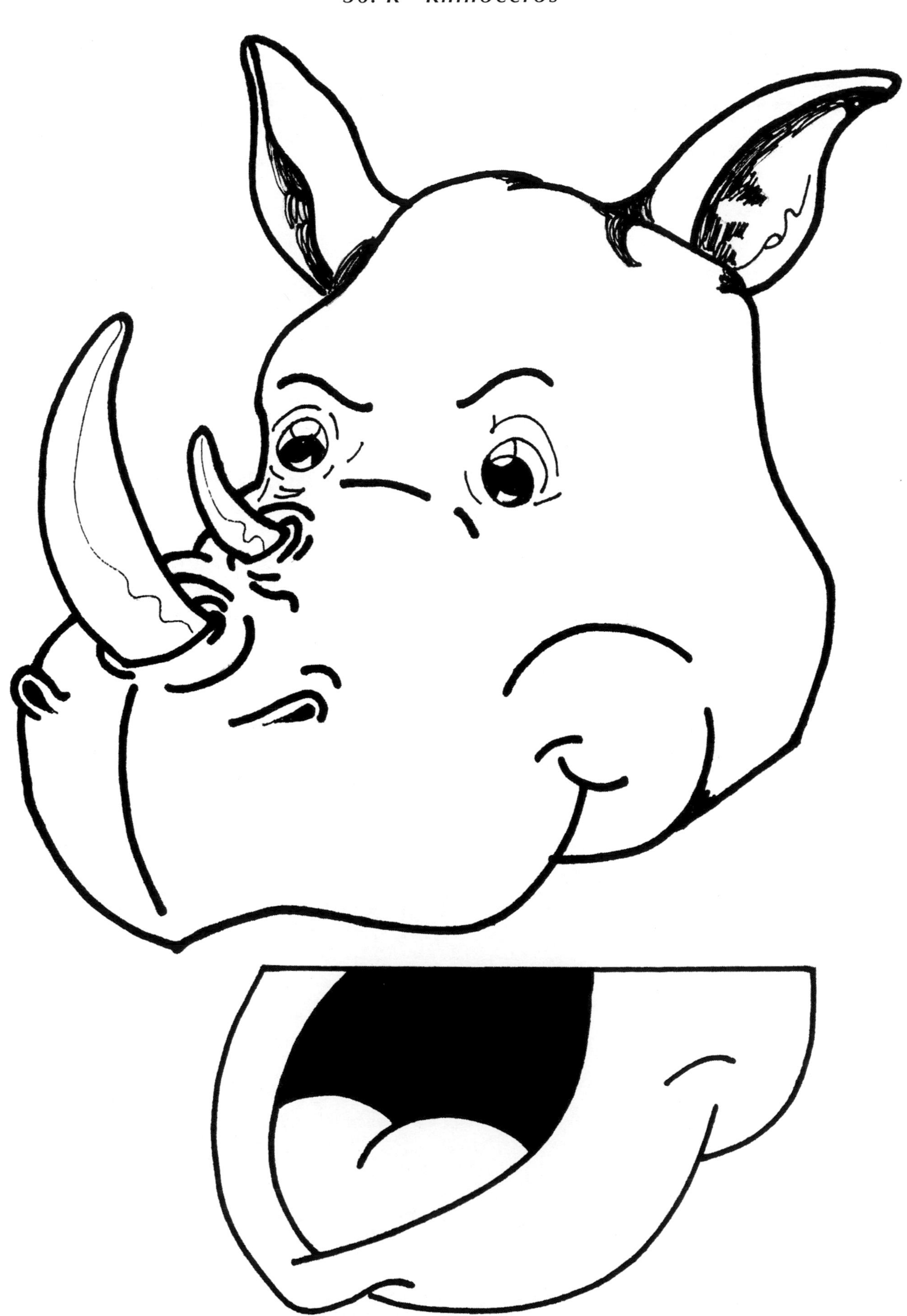

Rhinoceros Activities

Songs to Sing and Play

Tune: Oh Where, Oh Where Has My Little Dog Gone?

Words by Eunice Wright

Oh where, oh where are the rhinos today?
Oh where, oh where can they be?
Are they stomping out fires,
Or eating some grass?
Oh where, oh where can they be?

Tune: The Wheels on the Bus

Words by Eunice Wright

The rhinoceros at the zoo
Goes snort, snort, snort.
Snort, snort, snort.
Snort, snort, snort.
The rhinoceros at the zoo
Goes snort, snort, snort.
All around the zoo.

Tune: Three Blind Mice

Words by Eunice Wright

Three heavy rhinos,
Three heavy rhinos,
See how they run,
See how they run,
They blunder about with their heavy feet,
They charge at anything they happen to meet,
The pointy horns on their heads, don't greet.
Three heavy rhinos,
Three heavy rhinos.

Tune: 10 little Indians

Words by Eunice Wright

1 big, 2 big, 3 big rhinos, 4 big, 5 big, 6 big rhinos, 7 big, 8 big, 9 big rhinos,
10 big rhinoceroses.

Poems and Nursery Rhymes

The Rhino I Know

By Eunice Wright

The rhino I know,
Lives in the zoo.
There's a horn on his head,
Or maybe there's two.
He looks so scary,
He might chase you!
He's a great fire fighter—
(Well, they say it's true!)

Five Gray Rhinos

By Eunice Wright

Five gray rhinos, snorting past a boar.
One found a grassy hill, then there were four.
Four gray rhinos, playing under a tree.
One found a girl friend, then there were three.
Three gray rhinos, wondering what to do.
One found a bushy thicket, then there were two.
Two gray rhinos, having so much fun.
One went to hunt for food, then there was one.
One gray rhino, alone in the sun,
Decided to take a nap, then there were none.

The Rhinoceros

Bad Child's Book of Beasts, *by Hilaire Belloc, 1896*

Rhinoceros, your hide looks all undone,
You do not take my fancy in the least.
You have a horn where other brutes have none:
Rhinoceros, you are an ugly beast.

Books

Hippo! No, Rhino, by Jeff Newman (Little Brown, 2006). *An almost wordless small book; poor illustrations, story okay. The zookeeper gives the rhino the wrong label on his cage.*

I Know a Rhino, by Charles Fuge (Sterling Pub., 2002). *Good preschool book with a simple rhyming text. Beautiful animal illustrations.*

Who Wants a Cheap Rhinoceros? by Shel Silverstein. *Pencil drawings, simple text. No color; not for small children.*

Movies and Television

The Gods Must Be Crazy 2
Indiana Jones and the Last Crusade
Jumanji
Kung Fu Panda 1 and 2
The Lion King
Tarzan

37. S—Squirrel

Squirrel Activities

Songs to Sing and Play

Little Gray Squirrel (tune: Little Peter Rabbit Had a Fly Upon His Nose)

Words by Eunice Wright

Little gray squirrel had a flower in her hair,
Little gray squirrel had a flower in her hair,
Little gray squirrel had a flower in her hair,
And an acorn in her paws. *(or other item)*

Little gray squirrel had a nut in her mouth,
Little gray squirrel had a nut in her mouth,
Little gray squirrel had a nut in her mouth,
And a home full of acorns for the winter. *(or other items)*

Little gray squirrel had a hat upon her head,
Little gray squirrel had a hat upon her head,
Little gray squirrel had a hat upon her head,
And sunglasses on her nose. (or other item)

Substitute other animals and objects for other puppets.

Tune: Mary Had a Little Lamb

Words by Eunice Wright

Substitute child's name and animal.

(Susie) saw a gray squirrel, gray squirrel, gray squirrel,
(Susie) saw a gray squirrel,
Its tail was big and fluffy.

Acorn Camp Song

Traditional

I'm a little acorn round
Lying on the dusty ground
Everybody steps on me
That is why I'm cracked you see
I'm a nut (click) (click) (gently hit head on clicks)

I'm a nut (click) (click)
I'm a nut (click)
Nut (click)
Nut
Take myself to the movie grand
Just to hold my little hand
Wrap my arm around my waste
And when I squeeze I slap my own face!

I'm a nut (click) (click)
I'm a nut (click) (click)
I'm a nut (click)
Nut (click)
Nut

Alternate verse

I'm an acorn, small and round,
Lying on the cold, cold ground.
People pass and step on me (everyone walks all over me),
That's why I'm all cracked, you see (that is why I'm cracked, you see).

I'm a nut, (clap, clap)...

Poems and Nursery Rhymes

Little Nut Tree

Traditional

I had a little nut tree
And nothing would it bear
But a silver nutmeg, and a golden pear.
The queen of Spain's daughter
Came to visit me
And all because of my little nut tree.

Five Little Squirrels (Count Down)

By Eunice Wright

Five little squirrels, running on the floor,
One went up a tree, then there were four.
Four little squirrels, playing around the tree,
One went to find an acorn, then there were three.
Three little squirrels, had so much to do,
One went out on a limb, then there were two.
Two little squirrels, climbing in the sun,
One went to find a mate, then there was one,
One little squirrel, his work all done,

He had his store of acorns, then there was none.

4 Little Squirrels

By Eunice Wright

Four busy squirrels, high in a tree;
One dropped his acorn, then there were three.
Three gray squirrels, had so much to do;
One found a friend, then there were two.
Two scampering squirrels, their work never done;
One found another acorn, then there was one.
One tired squirrel, saw the setting sun;
Took a long nap, then there were none.

Squirrels

By Eunice Wright

Running, darting, he doesn't stop—
He climbs up to the tree top.
Scamper, twirling, chasing round.
Then he dashes down to the ground.

Whisky, Frisky

Traditional

Whisky, frisky, hippity hop.
Up he goes (climbs) to the treetop,
Whirly, twirly, round and round,
Down he scampers to the ground.
Furly, curly, what a tail,
Tall as a feather, broad as a sail.
Where's his supper? In the shell.
Snappy, cracky, out it fell.

The Squirrel

Aunt Kitty's Stories, *by various authors, 1870*

"The squirrel is happy, the squirrel is gay."
Little Mary once said to her brother.
"He has nothing to do, or think of but play,
And to jump from one bough to another."

The squirrel, dear Mary, is merry and wise,
For true wisdom and joy go together,
He lays up in summer his winter supplies,
And then he don't mind the cold weather.

Five Squirrels

The Volta Review, *edited by Josephine B. Timberlake, 1921*

Five little squirrels lived in a hollow tree.
The first little squirrel said, "What do I see?"
The next little squirrel said, "I smell a gun."
The third little squirrel said, "Come, let's run."
This little squirrel said, "Let's hide in the shade."
This little squirrel said, "I'm not afraid."
BANG! went the gun—
And away they all run.

The Squirrel

The Children's Book of Poetry, *illustrated by Henry T. Coates, 1879; written by Bernard Barton*

"The squirrel is happy, the squirrel is gay,"
Little Harry exclaimed to his brother;
"He has nothing to do or to think of but play,
And to jump from one bough to another."

But William was older and wiser, and knew
That all play and no work wouldn't answer,
So he asked what the squirrel in winter must do,
If he spent all the summer a dancer.

The squirrel, dear Harry, is merry and wise,
For true wisdom and mirth go together;
He lays up in summer his winter supplies,
And then he don't mind the cold weather."

The Squirrel

Finger Plays for Nursery and Kindergarten, *by Emilie Poulsson, 1893. Sheet music and fingerplay action.*

1. "Little Squirrel, living there
In the hollow tree,
I've a pretty cage for you;
Come and live with me!

You may turn the little wheel—
That will be great fun!
Slowly round, or very fast
If you faster run."

2. "Little Squirrel, I will bring
In my basket here
Every day a feast of nuts!
Come then, squirrel dear."
But the little squirrel said
From his hollow tree:
Oh! no, no! I'd rather far
Live here and be free."

3. So my cage is empty yet
And the wheel is still;
But my little basket here
Oft with nuts I fill.
If you like, I'll crack the nuts,
Some for you and me,
For the squirrel has enough
In his hollow tree.

The Robin and the Squirrel

The Peter Patter Book of Nursery Rhymes, *by Leroy F. Jackson 1918*

Said the robin to the squirrel,
"How d' you do?"
Said the squirrel to the robin,
"How are you?"
"Oh, I've got some cherry pies,
And a half a dozen flies,
And a kettle full of beetles on to stew."

Let Us Chase the Squirrel

Holiday Songs and Every Day Songs and Games, *by Emilie Poulsson, 1901*

With sheet music and some finger plays.

Let us chase the squirrel, up the hickory, down the hickory,
Let us chase the squirrel, up the hickory tree.

If you want to catch me, up the hickory, down the hickory,
If you want to catch me, learn to climb a tree.

Look, a Squirrel!

Folk Rhymes Wise and Otherwise, *by Thomas W. Talley, 1922; adapted by Juli Wright*

Look, a squirrel dressed in gray.
Look, the squirrel comes this way.
Look squirrel, it's almost day,
Look, the squirrel ran away.
I caught the squirrel! I caught the squirrel!
Now stay, I say. STAY!!!

Chasing the Squirrel

Songs and Games for Little Ones, *by Harriet S. Jenks and Gertrude Walker, 1887.*

With sheet music.

The squirrel loves a pleasant place,
To catch him you must run a race,
Hold out your hands, and you will see
Which of the two will quickest be
Now see our baby squirrels dear
We will not keep them prisoners here
We'll give them each, a nut to crack,
And then they'll gaily scamper back.

Games and Group Activities

Early Childhood Themes Through the Year, by Debbie Thompson and Darlene Hardwick; pp. 46–53 for fall and squirrel unit. Teacher Created Materials, 1993.
Yearful of Circle Times, by Liz and Dick Wilmes; pp. 20–23 for squirrel theme unit.

Books

Archie, the Acorn, by Tales of Time.
The Busy Little Squirrel, by Nancy Tafuri (Simon & Schuster, 2007). *Beautiful illustrations, short text, good introduction to animals. Recommended.*
Meanest Squirrel I Ever Met, by Gene Zion.
Scurry's Treasure, by Anne Carter.
Smarter Than Squirrels, by Lucy Nolan. *Two dogs keep the world safe.*
Squirrel Nutkin, by Beatrix Potter. *Excellent!*

Squirrels, by Brian Wildsmith (Franklin Watts, 1975).

Those Darn Squirrels! by Adam Rubin (Clarion Books). *The squirrels keep trying to reach the birdfeeders—as man and squirrel battle over feeders. Students may make squirrel feeders and tell of their own squirrel experiences after reading this book.*

What Will It Rain? by Jane Belk Moncure.

Movies and Television

Ice Age
Looney Tunes
Over the Hedge
The Sword in the Stone (Animated)

38. T—Tiger

Tiger Activities

Songs to Sing and Play

Tune: Three Blind Mice

Words by Eunice Wright

Tiger stripes,
Tiger stripes,
Black and orange *(black and white)*,
Black and orange,
He runs through the jungle or at the zoo,
He looks very scary to me and to you,
Did you ever see such a sight in your life,
As tiger stripes?

Tune: There Were Three Jolly Fishermen

Words by Eunice Wright

There were three jolly ti-gers,
There were three jolly ti-gers,
Ti, ti, gers, gers, gers.
Ti, ti, gers, gers, gers.
There were three jolly ti-gers.

They all went down the jungle trail,
They all went down the jungle trail.
Jungle, jungle, trail, trail, trail.
Jungle, jungle, trail, trail, trail.
They all went down the jungle trail.

Or

They all lived in the city zoo,...
City, city, zoo, zoo, zoo...

Tune: The Lion Sleeps Tonight

In the jungle, the scary jungle, the "tiger" roars all day...

Tune: Mary Had a Little Lamb

Words by Eunice Wright

Mary had a little tiger, little tiger, little tiger.
Mary had a little tiger
With black and orange stripes.

Everywhere that Mary went,...
The tiger was sure to go.

It followed her home late one night,...
Which surely would scare you!

And so her father put him out...
And told him to go home!

Tune: A Hunting We Will Go

Words by Eunice Wright

A hunting we will go, a hunting we will go,
We'll set a tiger trap and give him a little tap,
Then we'll scream and run away!

Found a Peanut

Traditional camp song

Found a (peanut) tiger
Found a tiger
Found a tiger just now
Just now I found a tiger
Found a tiger just now.

Ran away, ran away
Ran away just now.
Just now I ran away,
Ran away just now.

The tiger chased me,
The tiger chased me,
The tiger chased me just now.
Just now the tiger chased me,
The tiger chased me,
Just now.

Caught me anyway,
Caught me anyway,
Caught me anyway just now,
Just now, caught me anyway,
Caught me anyway,
Just now.

Ate me anyway
Ate me anyway
Ate me anyway just now
Just now he ate me anyway
Ate me anyway just now.

Got a tummy ache
Got a tummy ache
Got a tummy ache just now
Just now I got a tummy ache.
Got a tummy ache just now.

Went to the doctor
Went to the doctor
Went to the doctor just now
Just now I went to the doctor
Went to the doctor just now.

Had an operation
Had an operation
Had an operation just now
Just now I had an operation
Had an operation just now.

Died anyway
Died anyway
Died anyway just now
Just now I died anyway
Died anyway just now.

Got reincarnated
Got reincarnated
Got reincarnated just now
Just now I got reincarnated
Got reincarnated just now.

Found a tiger-man
Found a tiger-man
Found a tiger-man just now
Just now I found a tiger-man
Found a tiger-man just now.

Poems and Nursery Rhymes

Did You Ever Play Tag with a Tiger?

The Peter Patter Book of Nursery Rhymes, *by Leroy F. Jackson, 1918*

Did you ever play tag with a tiger,
Or ever play boo with a bear;
Did you ever put rats in the rain-barrel
To give poor old Granny a scare?

It's fun to play tag with a tiger,
It's fun for the bear to say "boo,"
But if rats are found in the rain-barrel
Old Granny will put you in too.

Eeny, Meeny, Miny, Mo.

Traditional

Eeny, meeny, miny, mo,
Catch a tiger by the toe.
If he hollers, make him pay
Fifty dollars every day.
My mother told me to
Choose the very best one.

Tiger

By Juli Wright and Glen Wright

Tiger creeping through the night.
Tiger's eyes are very bright.
Tiger creeping very slow.
When he sees you, he says, "Go!"

The Tiger's Tail

By Juli and Eunice Wright

Have you ever grabbed a tiger by the tail,
As he ran down the jungle trail?

Faster and faster he will run,
And you won't think it's very fun!

Dashing and smashing and bouncing about,
You'll have some bruises without a doubt.

But—why should the tiger run today,
When a tasty meal is just seconds away?

As he turns 'round to take a big bite,
You will have an awful fright!

Nose to nose, you will see him grin,
With his big teeth next to your chin.

The tiger has visions of steak so rare,
You on his plate will give you a scare!

Then he'll take one big lick of your dirty face,
And then—YUK! He'll be gone without a trace!

Scary Tiger

By Juli Wright

There once was a tiger who lived in a zoo,
He had black stripes and played the kazoo.

He had so many talents, he didn't know what to do.
Just don't get too close, he might scare YOU!

The Tiger

By Hilaire Belloc, 1896

The tiger on the other hand,
Is kittenish and mild,
He makes a pretty playfellow for any little child;
And mothers of large families (who claim to common sense)
Will find a tiger well repay the trouble and expense.

Games and Group Activities

Tiger Tag

Play tag, where "it" is a tiger and the other players are other jungle animals.

Pin the Tail on the Tiger

Make or find a poster of a tailless tiger to hang on the wall. Create separate tails for the tiger. Each player is blindfolded and tries to attach the tail to the tiger in the correct spot. Whoever gets closest is the winner.

Books

Auntie Tiger, by Laurence Yep (Harper, 2009). *Colorful pictures, silly story. The tiger eats the little girl as in Little Red Riding Hood.*

How the Tiger Lost Its Stripes, by Cory J. Meacham (1997).

How Tiger Got His Stripes: A Folktale from Vietnam, by Rob Cleveland (2006).

Little Black Sambo, by Helen Bannerman (HarperCollins, 1923). *The tale of a little boy who lost his red coat, his blue trousers and his purple shoes but who was saved from the tigers to eat 169 tiger pancakes for his supper. First written in 1899.*

Maya, Tiger Cub, by Theresa Radcliffe.

Moon Tiger, by Phyllis Root.

Rabbit's Tail, a Story from Korea, by Suzanne C. Han (Henry Holt). *The Tiger is really the main character—a very cute and funny book; excellent illustrations. Use a dried persimmon as a visual aid.*

Tiger on a Tree, by Anushka Ravishankar. *ALA Notable Children's Books. Younger Readers (Awards).*

Tiger Tales, Level 3 reader. Dorling Kindersley.

Tigers (True Books), by Ann O. Squire. *Very nice photos.*

Movies and Television

Dr. Doolittle
Dumbo
The Greatest Show on Earth
The Jungle Book
Madagascar
The Prince and Me
Sinbad and the Eye of the Tiger
Swiss Family Robinson
Tony, the Tiger (commercial cereal tiger)
Winnie the Pooh (Tigger)

39. U—Unicorn

Use Horse (#10d) for basic pattern, then add horn.

COPY HORN PATTERN AT 200%

Unicorn Activities

Songs to Sing and Play

Tune: There Were Three Jolly Fishermen

Words by Eunice Wright

There was a jolly unicorn.
There was a jolly unicorn.
Uni, uni, corn-corn-corn.
Uni, uni, corn-corn-corn.
There was a jolly unicorn.

His best friend was the dragon.
His best friend was the dragon.
Dra, dra, gon-gon-gon.
Dra, dra, gon-gon-gon.
His best friend was the dragon.

They both went out to play one day.
They both went out to play one day.
One, one, day, day, day.
One, one, day, day, day.
They both went out to play one day.
They had so much fun, they stayed to this day...

Tune: The Wheels on the Bus

Words by Eunice Wright

The unicorn says, "Please be quiet, Please be quiet, Please be quiet."
The unicorn says, "Please be quiet," when he hears you coming.

The unicorn lives in the forest...
All through his life.

The unicorn is magical...
He might never die.

The horn on his head is beautiful...
Sparkling, shining magic dust.

Tune: I'm a Little Teapot

Words by Eunice Wright

I am a unicorn, beautiful and sleek.
Here is my horn that comes to a peak.
I'm quiet and magical and never speak.
I am famous, for I'm unique.

Tune: Three Blind Mice

Words by Eunice Wright

U-ni-corn,
U-ni-corn.
See how they run,
See how they run.
They have magical powers, or so they say,
They have a spiked horn you don't see everyday,
Did you ever see how the unicorns play?
Oh, u-ni-corn.

Tune: Mary Had a Little Lamb

Words by Eunice Wright

Once there was a unicorn,
Unicorn, unicorn.
Once there was a unicorn,
Its coat was white as snow.

And everywhere the unicorn went...
The magic was sure to go.

Tune: Mr. Ed

Words by Eunice Wright

A unicorn is a kind of a horse,
A beautiful magical wonderful horse.
The magical horn upon its head
Grants wishes and dreams, or so it's said.

Tune: Five Elephants Went Out to Play

Words by Eunice Wright

One unicorn went out to play, out by a dragon's lair one day.
He had such magical fun, that he called for another unicorn to come.

Two unicorns went out to play...

The Unicorn Song

By Shel Silverstein, 1962. Made popular by a Canadian Band, The Irish Rovers, 1968.

Poems and Nursery Rhymes

The Lion and the Unicorn

Songs from *Alice in Wonderland* and *Through the Looking-Glass, by Lewis Carroll, 1921*

The lion and the unicorn were fighting for the crown,
The lion beat the unicorn all around the town.
Some gave them white bread, and some gave them brown,
Some gave them plum-cake, and sent them out of town.

Five Magical Unicorns

By Eunice Wright

Five magical unicorns, playing by the shore,
One found a pretty seashell, then there were four.
Four magical unicorns, running around the tree,
One saw a pretty fairy, then there were three.
Three magical unicorns, see the magic they can do.
One found a little elf, then there were two.
Two magical unicorns, hiding from the sun,
One saw a troll nearby, then there was one.
One magical unicorn, playing with the dragon,
He saw a rainbow, now there are none.

Wishes

By Eunice Wright

Once there was a magic unicorn,
Who met a pretty maid, all forlorn.
He said to her, if you make a wish,
I'll grant you one inside a fish.

As soon she was able, up she got
And ran to the favorite fishing spot.
With the first fish caught, she wished away,
But only one wish per person, the fish did say.

The pretty maid, all forlorn,
Went back to see the unicorn.
Too many wishes was the reason,
No wishes were granted to you this season.

Books

Claire and the Unicorn (Happy Ever After), by B.G. Hennessy (Simon & Schuster). *Good illustrations; the story is a little long for preschool children. Claire and her stuffed unicorn have a nice dream together.*

Dora and the Unicorn King.

The Dragon and the Unicorn, by Lynne Cherry.

The Eyes of the Unicorn, by Teresa Bateman.

Fairy Realm: The Unicorn, by Emily Rodda.

Happy Birthday Unicorn (Sweet Pickles Series), by Jacquelyn Reinach.

I Believe in Unicorns, by Michael Morpurgo.

If I Found a Wistful Unicorn, by Ann Ashford.

Into the Land of the Unicorns, by Bruce Coville.

The Magic Unicorn, by Alberto Melis.

Nobody Rides the Unicorn, by Adrian Mitchell.

The Princess and the Unicorn, by Carol Hughes.

The Unicorn Treasury, by Bruce Coville.

Unicorn Wings, by Mallory Loehr (Random House, 2006). *A unicorn can do magic, but wishes he had wings. Pretty illustrations, nice story.*

Unicorns and Other Magical Creatures, by John Hamilton.

Wish on a Unicorn, by Karen Hesse.

Movies and Television

Harry Potter

The Last Unicorn

The Little Unicorn

Nico, the Unicorn, 1998

Star Dust (PG-13)

40. V—Vulture

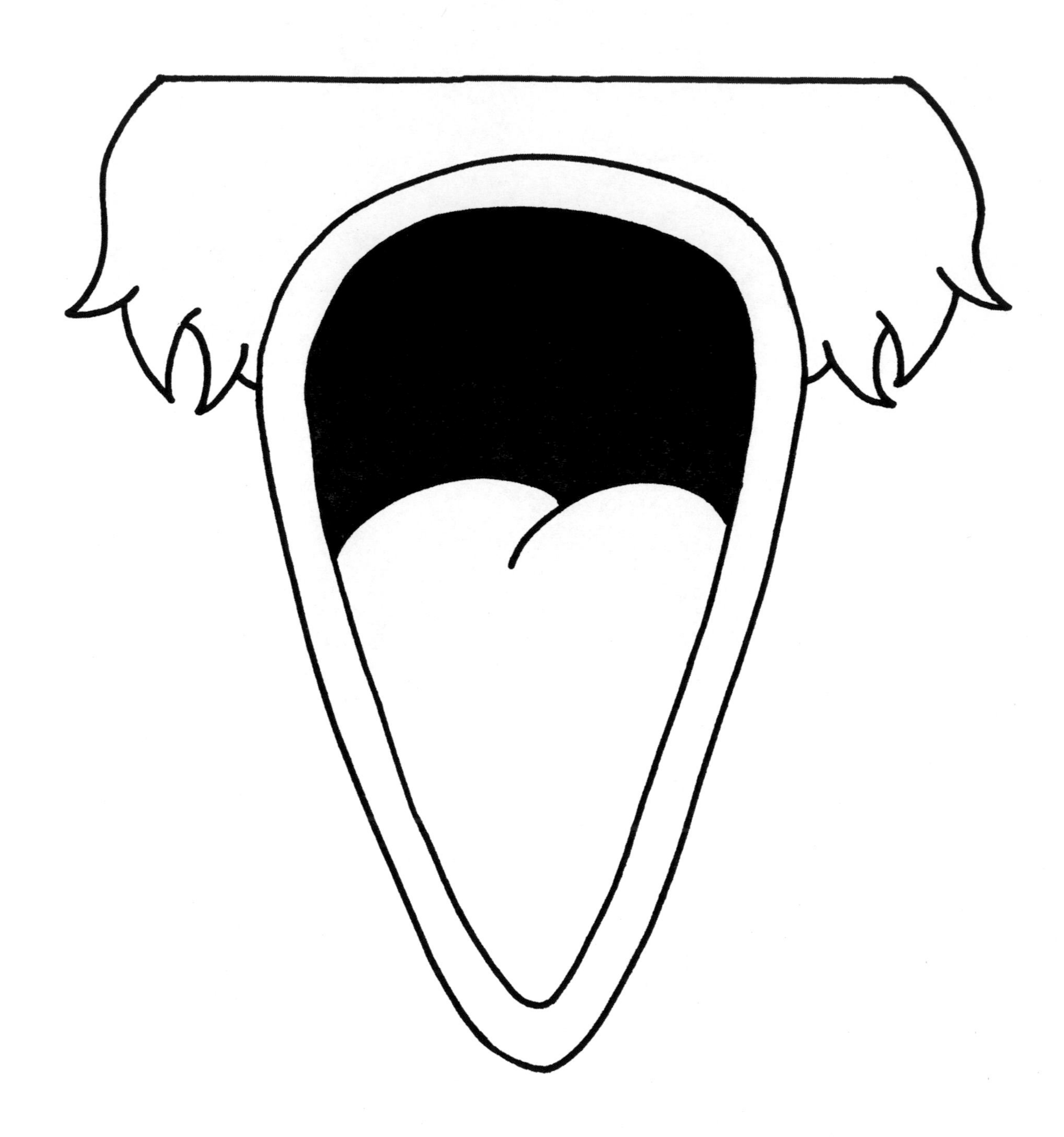

Vulture Activities

Songs to Sing and Play

Tune: The Wheels on The Bus

Words by Eunice Wright

The Vulture says, "It's time to eat, it's time to eat, it's time to eat."
The Vulture says, "It's time to eat," all day long.

The Vulture says, "I'll circle around..."

The Vulture says, "I'll wait my turn..."

Tune: Did You Ever See a Lassie?

Words by Eunice Wright

Did you ever see a vulture, a vulture, a vulture?
Did you ever see a vulture,
Fly this way and that?

Fly this way, and that way,
And this way, and that?
Did you ever see a vulture,
Fly this way and that?

Tune: Skip to My Lou

Words by Eunice Wright

Lost my dinner, what'll I do?...
Skip to my Lou, my darling.

I'll find another dinner, nicer too...
Skip to my Lou, my darling.

Flies on the carcass, shoo fly shoo...
Skip to my Lou, my darling.

Can't get a redbird, a vulture will do...
Skip to my Lou, my darling.

Vultures overhead, two by two...
Skip to my Lou, my darling.

Tune: Are You Sleeping?

Words by Eunice Wright

Creepy vulture,
Creepy vulture,
You have an evil eye.
You fly around and spy.
You wait for someone to die,
You're a rotten apple pie,
Creepy vulture,
Creepy vulture.

Sinister vulture!
Sinister vulture!
You circle 'round the weak,
A dead car-cass you seek.
You follow the meek,
To taste them in your beak.
Sinister vulture!
Sinister vulture!

Vile vulture!
Vile vulture!
The food that's on your list,
A dead menu you insist.
You're sure nothing's missed,
Your feathers are in a twist.
Vile vulture!
Vile vulture!

Poems and Nursery Rhymes

Five Hungry Vultures (Count Up)

By Eunice Wright

One hungry vulture, wondered what to do.
He waited and he waited, then there were two.
Two hungry vultures, sitting in a tree.
Along came another, then there were three.
Three hungry vultures, so sad and poor.
Along came another, then there were four.
Four hungry vultures, ready to dive.
As they swooped down, suddenly there were five.
Five hungry vultures, gobbled food fast.
Now the five vultures were full at last.

Five Hungry Vultures (Count Down)

by Eunice Wright

Five hungry vultures, staring at the floor,
One flew away, then there were four.

Four hungry vultures, up in a tree,
One flew away, then there were three.
Three hungry vultures, under the sky so blue,
One flew away, then there were two.
Two hungry vultures, sitting in the sun.
One flew away, then there was one.
One hungry vulture, his waiting now was done,
He flew away, then there were none.

The Vulture

By Hilaire Belloc, 1897

The vulture eats between his meals,
And that's the reason why
He very, very, rarely feels
As well as you and I.

His eye is dull, his head is bald,
His neck is growing thinner.
Oh! what a lesson for us all
To only eat at dinner!

The Vulture

By Juli Wright

The vulture sits in a slump,
He is a mean old grump.
He thinks himself real sly,
Waiting for his next meal to die.
For he wants to eat his lunch,
And on their bones he'll munch.

Books

Condors & Vultures, by David Houston (World Life Library). *Nice photos of some huge birds.*

Kiss Me, I'm Vulture (Sweet Pickles Series), by Richard Hefter.

Orlando, the Brave Vulture, by Tomi Ungerer.

Vulture: Nature's Ghastly Gourmet, by Wayne Grady. *Nice photos.*

Vulture View, by April P. Sayre.

Vultures, Animal Scavengers, by Sandra Markle (Lerner Pub., 2005). *Excellent photos and text. Great introduction to different kinds of vultures.*

Vultures (Early Bird Nature Books), by Roland Smith. *Very nice photographs of vultures.*

Vultures (First Books—Animals), by Mark J. Rauzon.

Movies and Television

I'll Be Home for Christmas, 1998. Short segment of vultures in the desert.

The Jungle Book (Disney Animation)

Snow White

41. W—Walrus

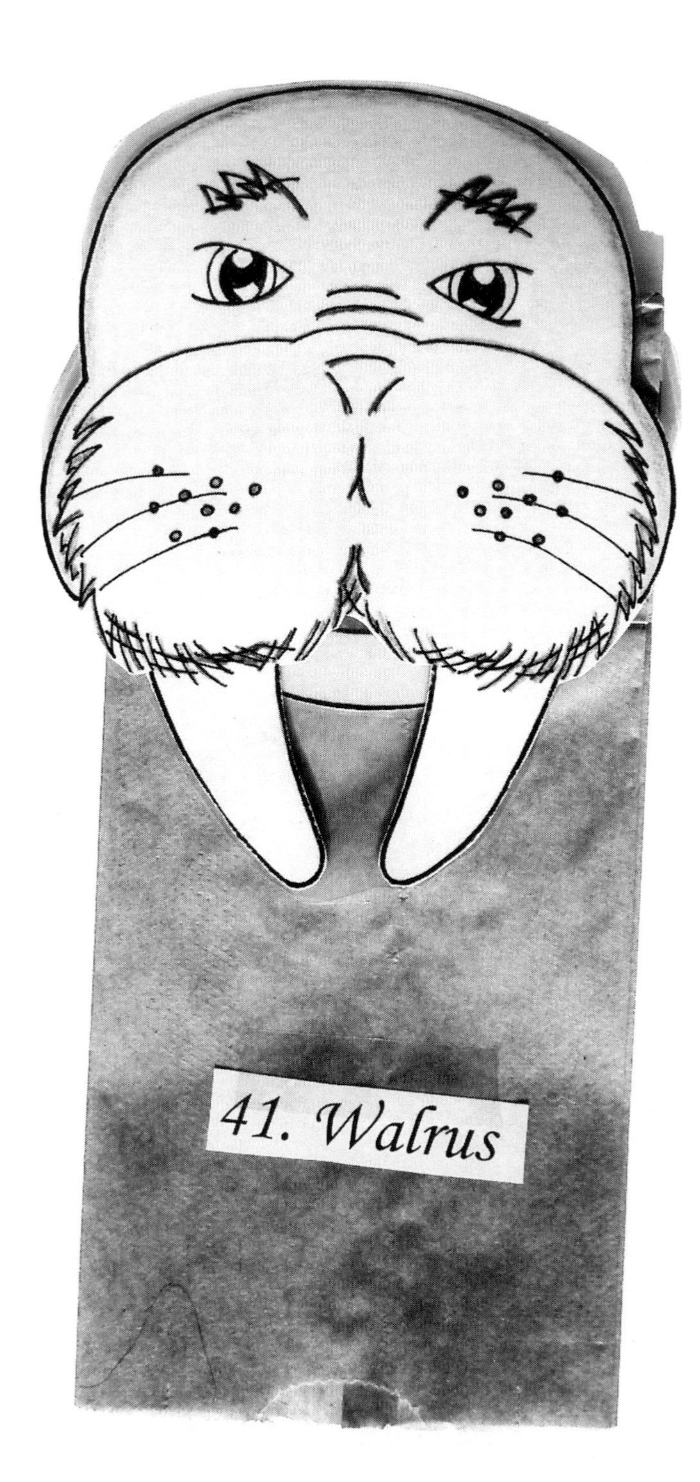

Walrus Activities

Songs to Sing and Play

Tune: There Were Three Jolly Fishermen

Words by Eunice Wright

There once was a wal-rus
There once was a wal-rus
Wal wal, rus, rus, rus,
Wal wal, rus, rus, rus,
There once was a wal-rus.

He sat on an iceberg all day
He sat on an iceberg all day
All, all, day, day, day.
All, all, day, day, day.
He sat on an iceberg all day.

His tusks were long and white
His tusks were long and white
And, and, white, white, white.
And, and, white, white, white.
His tusks were long and white.

Tune: Once There Was a Snowman

Words by Eunice Wright

Once there was a walrus, walrus, walrus.
Once there was a walrus, big, big, big.
On the ice he waited, waited, waited,
On the ice he waited, all day long.

Tune: Oh, Have You Seen the Muffin Man?

Words by Eunice Wright

Oh, have you seen the walrus yet?
The walrus yet, the walrus yet?
Oh, have you seen the walrus yet?
He's not here at the zoo.

He's in the ice house fast asleep...
And won't wake up 'til noon.

Tune: Ten Little Indians

Words by Eunice Wright

One big, two big, three big walruses...
All sliding on the ice.

Tune: The Wheels on the Bus

Words by Eunice Wright

The walrus says, "I'm the biggest...
On the ice today.

Tune: Brown Bear, Brown Bear, What Do You See?

Words by Eunice Wright

Walrus, walrus, what do you see?
I see a polar bear looking at me.

Song to Play

"A Seal and a Walrus," *I Have a Song for You*, Vol. 3, by Janeen Brady, p. 26.

Poems and Nursery Rhymes

Ice Party

By Eunice Wright

A walrus and a polar bear went out one day to play.
They built a snowman on the ice and told their friends to stay.

They had a party in the snow, and danced around all day.
For snacks they had some snowballs, in little bowls of clay.

When time to leave for home, their friends all waved goodbye.
"Let's play again another day, before the sun gets high."

The Walrus and the Carpenter

By Lewis Carroll (1832–1898); used in the movie Disney's Alice's Adventures in Wonderland.

Books

Little Walrus Saves the Day, by Carol Young.
Little Walrus Warning, by Carol Young and Walter Stuart.
Mr. Walrus and the Old School Bus

Very Worried Walrus, by Richard Hefter (Sweet Pickle Series, Holt).

Wally, the Lost Baby Walrus, by Chris Kiana and Minnie Kiana Morken.

The Walrus and the Carpenter, by Lewis Carroll.

Where's Walrus? by Stephen Savage (Scholastic Press, 2011). *A walrus escapes from the zoo...*

Movies and Television

Alice in Wonderland

Growing Up Walrus (baby walrus orphaned in Alaska)

Happy Feet 2

42. X—X-Ray

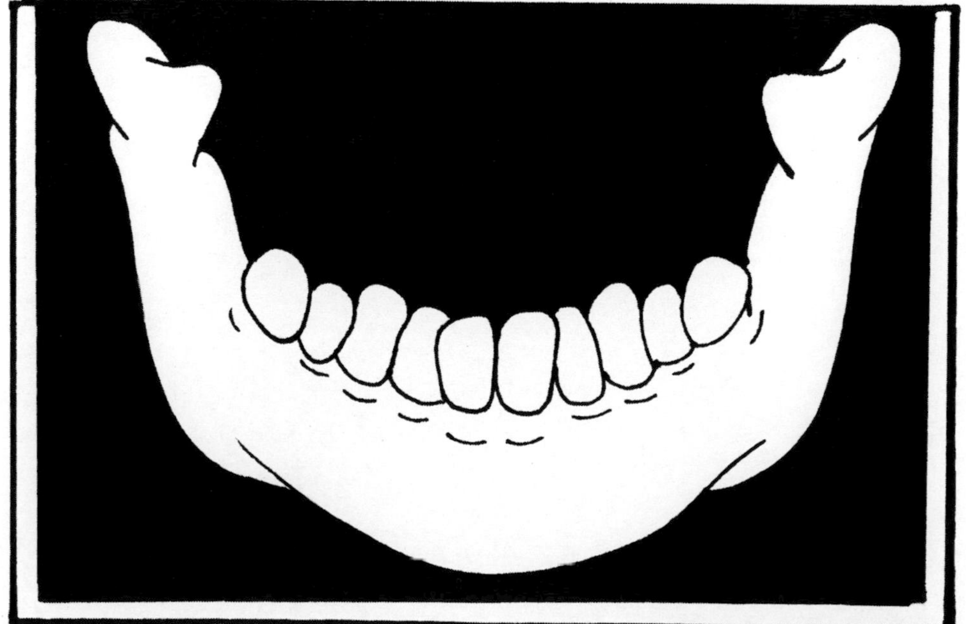

X-Ray Activities

Songs to Sing and Play

Dem Bones

Traditional by James Weldon Johnson, 1871–1933

(See Wee Sing Silly Songs *for words and music.)*

Ezekiel cried, "Dem dry bones!...

Skin and Bones

1813 version

There was an old woman, all skin and bone.
This old lady was very well known.
She lay in bed as I've heard say
For many years to fast and pray
When she has lain a twelvemonth space
The flesh was gone from her hands and face
When that another twelvemonth was gone
She was nothing at all but a skel-e-ton.

Skin and Bones Alternate

Traditional 1800 (see Raffi's version)

There was an old woman, all skin and bone (oooooo)
She lived down by the old graveyard (ooooooo)
One night she thought she'd take a walk (oooooooo)
She walked down by the old graveyard (ooooooo)
She saw the bones all layin' around (oooooooo)
She went to the closet to get a broom (oooooooo)
She opened the door and...
BOO!

Tune: Oh, Do You Know the Muffin Man?

Words by Eunice Wright

Oh, have you seen the X-ray tech,
The X-ray tech, the X-ray tech?
Oh, have you seen the X-ray tech,
Who works in the hospital?

Tune: If You're Happy and You Know It

Words by Eunice Wright

If you think you've broken a bone, get an X-ray!
If you think you've broken a bone, get an X-ray!
If you think you've broken a bone,
And it won't heal right on its own,
If you think you've broken a bone, get an X-ray!

Tune: Ten Little Indians

Words by Eunice Wright

One little, two little, three little X-rays...
All about our bones.

Tune: I'm a Little Teapot

Words by Eunice and Juli Wright

I'm a little X-ray, black and white,
To see me well, hold me up to the light.
I show your bones, oh what a sight!
I help the doctor to set your bones right.

Tune: Head, Shoulders, Knees and Toes

Words by Eunice and Juli Wright

Head, shoulders, knees and toes
Knees and toes, knees and toes.
Head, shoulders, knees and toes
That is what the X-Ray shows.

Song to Play

"A Skeleton Inside of You," by Joan Lisonbee Sowards. (Joansowards.com)

Poems and Nursery Rhymes

Five Little X-rays (Count Up)

By Eunice Wright

One little X-ray, see what I can do—
I show broken bones, maybe even two.
Two little X-rays, help the doctor see—
Under the skin; we may want three.

Three little X-rays, hanging above the floor—
That's not enough, we need four.
Four little X-rays, may help you survive—
Helping the doctor, he now has five.

Books

Bones, by Steve Jenkins. *Skeletons and how they work.*
A Book about Your Skeleton, by Ruth B. Gross.
The Dancing Skeleton, by Cynthia Defelice.
Dem Bones, by Bob Barner.
Head, Shoulders, Knees and Toes, by Annie Kubler. *A board book.*
Skeleton Hiccups, by Margery Cuyler (Simon & Schuster, 2002). *Cute story, short, easy; great illustrations; good for preschool children.*
The Skeleton in the Closet, by Alice Schertle (HarperCollins, 2003). *A cute rhyming text, good illustrations. A scary story.*
Skeleton Meets the Mummy, by Steve Metzger (Scholastic).
Skeleton Shake, illustrated by Lisa Conrad.
Skelly, the Skeleton Girl, by Jimmy Pickering (2007). *A little girl finds a bone one day...*
X Ray Picture Book of Dinosaurs and Other Prehistoric Creatures, by Kathryn Senior.
X Ray Picture Book of Everyday Things, by Peter Turvey.
The X-Ray Picture Book of Incredible Creatures, by Gerald Legg.
X-Treme X-Ray: See the World Inside Out! Photos by Nick Veasey (Scholastic, 2010).
Your Body: X Ray Picture Book, by Kathryn Senior.

Movies and Television

Classic *Sesame Street* animation (X for X-ray)
Classic *Sesame Street*—Kermit's X-Ray machine with Hairy Monster
Sesame Street—"The Letter X Song," by Cookie Monster
Sesame Street—"X" salute song

43. Y—Yak

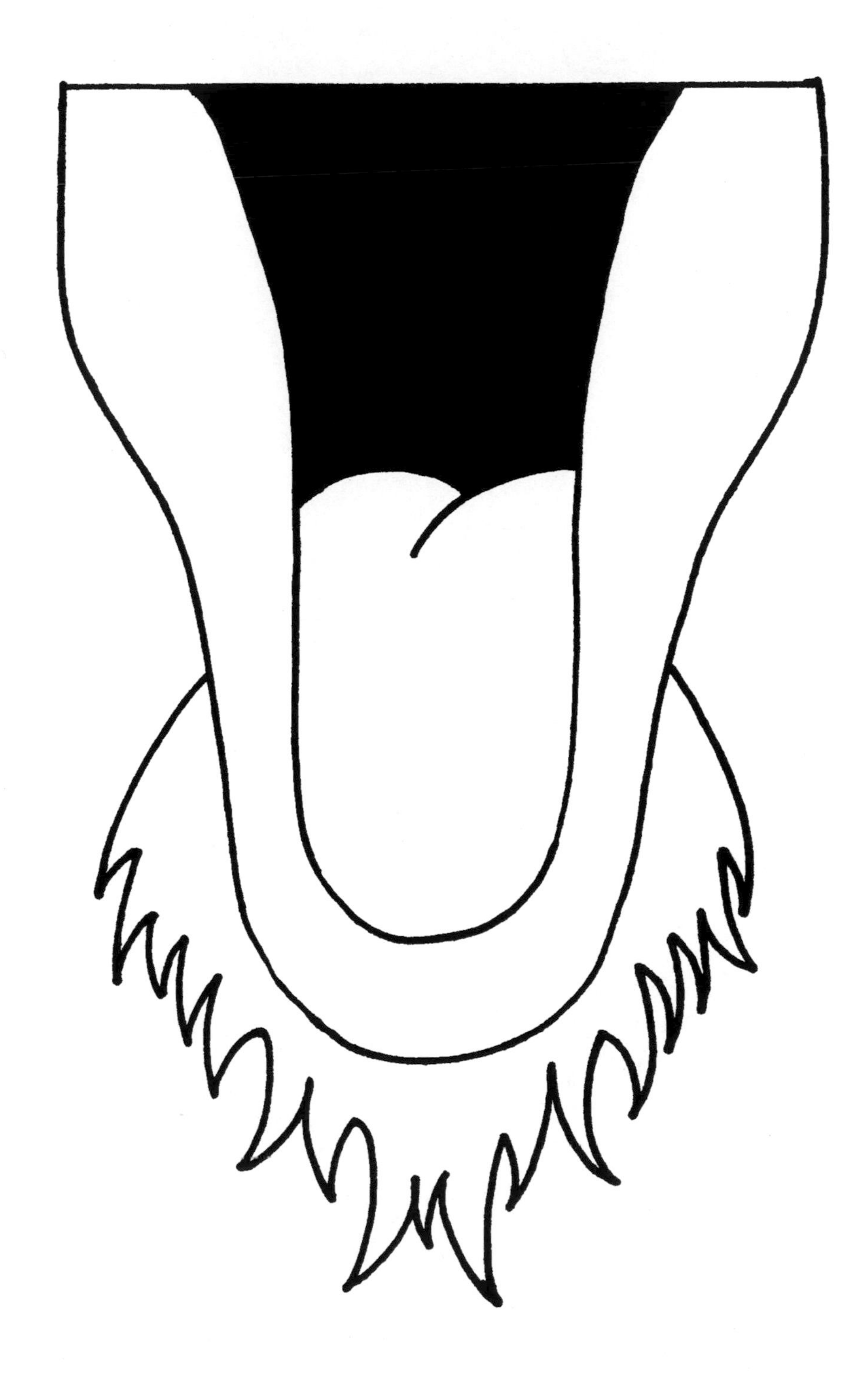

Yak Activities

Songs to Sing and Play

Tune: Mary Wore Her Red Dress

Words by Eunice Wright

Substitute any animal and its characteristics.

Mr. Yak has long hair, long hair, long hair.
Mr. Yak has long hair, and eats all day.

Tune: Did You Ever See a Lassie?

Words by Eunice Wright

Did you ever see a yak,
A yak, a yak,
Did you ever see a yak
With long shaggy hair?

Tune: A Hunting We Will Go

Words by Eunice Wright

A hunting we will go, a hunting we will go,
We'll catch a little yak,
And put him in a sack,
Then we'll take him to the show!

Tune: Ten Little Indians

Words by Eunice Wright

One brown, two brown, three brown yaks...
All in shaggy coats.

Tune: Are You Sleeping?

Words by Eunice Wright

Where is Mr. Yak?
Where is Mr. Yak?
Here I am.
Here I am.
How are you today, sir?
Very well, I thank you.
Graze away. Graze away.

Poems and Nursery Rhymes

Yawning Yaks

By Eunice Wright

Five yaks yawn a lot.
They work hard, believe it or not.
They yawn and yawn, yes they do.
Working hard is what they do.
Yesterday has come and gone,
And yaks can yawn and mow the lawn.
While all the day, hard work is done,
They'll go to sleep, one by one.

The Yak

By Eunice Wright

Yackity-yak, yackity-yak.
The yak likes to yack and yack and yack.
He has a brown coat and a nose that is black.
And lots of scruffily hair on his back.

The Yak

Bad Child's Book of Beasts, *by Hilaire Belloc, 1896*

As a friend to the children commend me the yak.
You will find it exactly the thing:
It will carry and fetch, you can ride on its back,
Or lead it about with a string.
The Tartar who dwells on the plains of Tibet
(A desolate region of snow)
Has for centuries made it a nursery pet,
And surely the Tartar should know!
Then tell your papa where the yak can be got,
And if he is awfully rich
He will buy you the creature—
or else he will not.
(I cannot be positive which.)

Five Brown Yaks

By Eunice Wright

Five brown yaks, grazing by the moor,
One drank from a stream, then there were four.

Four brown yaks, resting under a tree,
One found a girl friend, then there were three.
Three brown yaks, wondering what to do,
One found a lot of grass, then there were two.
Two brown yaks, having so much fun,
One went to hunt for food, then there was one.
One brown yak, alone in the sun.
Decided to take a nap, then there were none.

Books

All the Way to Lhasa: A Tale from Tibet, by Barbara Berger. *Beautiful illustrations, short text, about a trek to the Holy City. (Not too much written about a yak.)*

Does a Yak Get a Haircut? by Fred Ehrlich, M.D. (Blue Apple Books, 2003).

Go Track a Yak! by Tony Johnston (Simon & Schuster, 2003). *A humorous rhyming story with good illustrations, short text, repeating lines.*

Here Be Yaks: Travels in Far West Tibet, by Manosi Lahiri.

Kami and the Yaks, by Andrea Stenn Stryer.

See the Yak Yak, by Charles Ghingna.

The Yak Who Yelled Yuck, by Carol Pugliano-Martin.

Yakety Yak Yak Yak (Sweet Pickles Series), by Richard Hefter.

Zak, the Yak, Room to Read, by John Wood.

Movies and Television

Kung Fu Panda

The Mummy: Tomb of the Dragon Emperor (2008) PG-13. Small segment of a yak in the plane.

National Geographic

Our New Baby Yak! The Alaska Zoo footage of mom and baby Yak with music (2009)

Yaks Near Everest Base Camp. Everest Education Expedition, 2012. National Geographic.

44. Z—Zebra

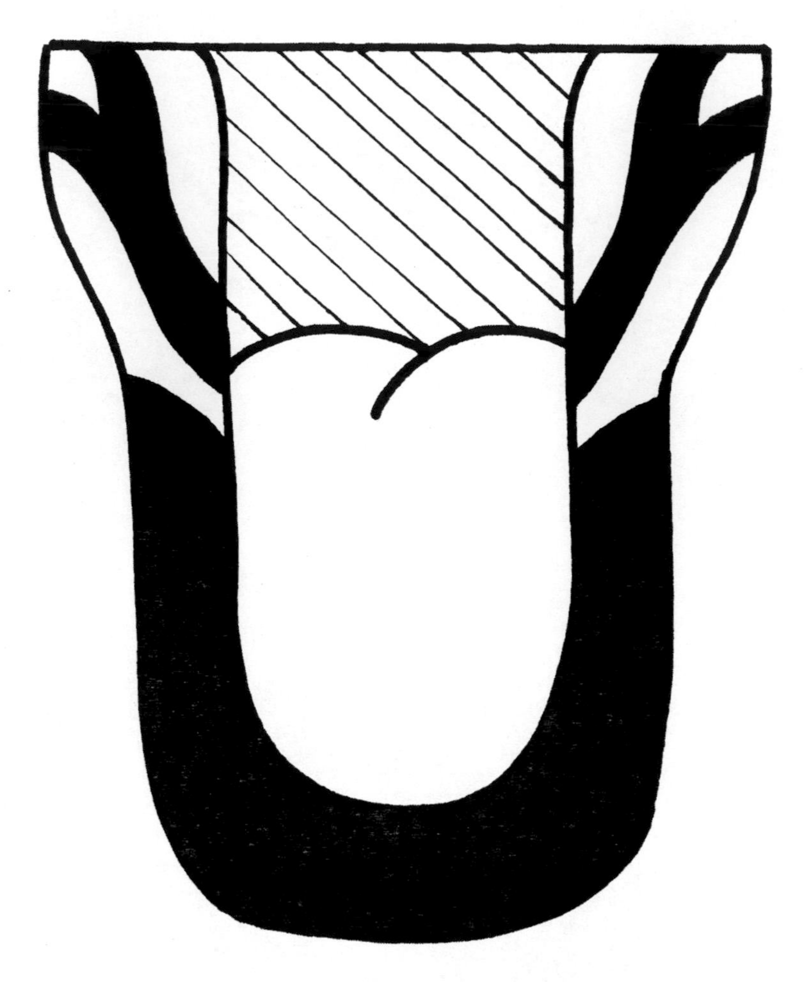

Zebra Activities

Songs to Sing and Play

Tune: The Farmer in the Dell

Words by Eunice Wright

The zebra in the zoo,
The zebra in the zoo,
Heigh ho, the zoo—oh,
The zebra in the zoo.

Tune: Bingo

Words by Eunice Wright

There was a zoo had an animal,
And Zebra was his name-o.
Z-E-B-R-A!
Z-E-B-R-A!
Z-E-B-R-A!
And Zebra was his name-o!

Tune: Did You Ever See a Lassie?

By Eunice Wright

Did you ever see a zebra
A zebra, a zebra,
Did you ever see a zebra
With black and white stripes?

Tune: Jimmy Crack Corn

Words by Eunice Wright

The zebra's stripes are black and white,
The zebra's stripes are black and white,
The zebra's stripes are black and white,
The zebra's in the zoo.

Tune: I'm a Little Teapot

Words by Eunice Wright

I'm a little zebra, with stripes of black and white,
See my cute face, I'm quite a sight!

When I get excited, I run with all my might.
Call me "Stripes," I'm as fast as light.

Tune: Ten Little Indians

Words by Eunice Wright

One little, two little, three little zebras...
All in black and white (*or all in racing stripes*)

Poems and Nursery Rhymes

Zippy Zany Zebras in a Zoo

By Eunice and Juli Wright

Five zippy zebras lived in a zoo.
The first one said, "I'm a zippy zebra, it's true."
The second one said, "Yes, I'm glad you're not blue!"
The third one said, "Yes, me too."
The fourth one said, "How do you do?"
The fifth one said, "It's nice to meet you!"
The five zippy zebras are all friends in the zoo.

Five Mice (Six Striped Zebras)

By Emilie Poulsson; adapted to zebras by Juli Wright

Six striped zebras running along the shore,
Looking for some grass or maybe something more;
Six striped zebras are thirsty and they know,
To the water's edge, they must surely go—
But the big round eyes of the alligator see
The six striped zebras hiding by the tree.
Quickly he snaps! but the zebras run away,
And hide in the fields, and that's where they stay.

Books

Baby Zebra, by Patricia A. Pingry (Ideals, 2004).
How the Zebra Got Its Stripes (Little Golden Book), by Ron Fontes.
It's a Baby Zebra, by Kelly Doudna (Abdo, 2008).
Lots and Lots of Zebra Stripes, by Stephen R. Swinburne (Boyds Mills Press, 2002).
On Beyond Zebra! (Classic Seuss), by Dr. Seuss and Theodor Seuss Geisel.
What If the Zebras Lost Their Stripes, by John Reitano.
Zebra Zips By, Sweet Pickle Series (Holt 1977).
Zebras, by Jill Anderson (Wild Ones, North-Word, 2005). *A cute preschool/early childhood picture book with photos of zebras and easy-read text.*
A Zebra's World, Caroline Arnold's Animals (Picture Window Books, 2006). *Large book and illustrations, simple text.*

Movies and Television

Jack, the Jumping Zebra, YouTube, 2011. (2:27)
The Lion King
Madagascar 1, 2, 3
National Geographic: Most Wanted: Highway Zebra (2:16)
National Geographic: Moving in Masses
Nature: Zebras! Zebras! Zebras!
Racing Stripes, Frankie Muniz, 2005.
Swiss Family Robinson, Disney, 1960. (Other animals: tiger, monkey, elephant, ostrich, dogs, pigs.) RKO, 1940, Edward Ludwig, based on novel.

Additional Activities

These activities can be used for Farm and Wild Animals, Zoo Animals and all kinds of other animals. Use them for inspiration of your own!

Songs to Sing and Play

Tune: The Wheels on the Bus

Words by Eunice Wright

Alligator/Crocodile (#19)
The alligator hisses, come on by, come on by, come on by.
The alligator hisses, come on by, I only want to visit.

The alligator (crocodile) has many sharp teeth, many sharp teeth, many sharp teeth.
The alligator has many sharp teeth, and hides beneath the water.

Bear (#2b)
The bear growls, where's my honey? Where's my honey? Where's my honey?
The bear growls, where's my honey? It's my favorite food.

A bear loves to hunt for honey ... it is his favorite food.

Beaver (#20)
The beaver says, move that log, move that log, move that log.
The beaver says, move that log, I'll make a house of wood.

A beaver chews on trees and sticks ... his home is made of wood.

Bird (#6d)
The birds sing, build a nest, build a nest, build a nest.
The birds sing, build a nest, let's have a family.

A bird can fly up in the sky ... his home is in a nest.

Cat (#6e)
The cat says, meow...
I want a mouse for lunch.

A cat hunts mice and drinks milk ... he is a nice pet.

Chick (#1a)
The chicks in the barnyard scratch, scratch, scratch...
For juicy little worms.

A chick is a baby chicken ... he lives on the farm.

Cow (#21)
The cow says, I make milk, I make milk, I make milk...
For you to drink at lunch.

The cow gives us milk to drink ... he lives on a farm.

Dog (#10f)
The dog barks, move on back...
All night long.

A dog can bark and chase a cat ... and cows and sheep and things like that.

Dolphin (#22)
The dolphin swims and jumps so high...
In the ocean blue.

Dolphins swim and jump up high ... they are fun to watch.

Duck (#1c)
The ducks in the pond dive and swim, dive and swim, dive and swim...
Looking for their food.

A duck swims in the water ... his home is on the farm.

Elephant (#23)
The elephant is so big and strong,...
He walks very slow.

An elephant has a long nose ... he sprays water with it.

Fawn (#24)
My name is Bambi,...
I have many forest friends.

A fawn is a baby deer ... I know one named "Bambi."

Fox (#1g)
The fox is smart usually...
He eats the gingerbread man.

A fox is smart and likes to hide ... he has a bushy tail.

Frog (#9a)
The frogs in the swamp croak all night long...
They love to make a noise.

A frog can hop and jump far ... he likes to eat bugs.

Giraffe (#25)
The giraffe has a long neck, long neck, long neck...
And loves to eat tree leaves.

A giraffe has a very long neck ... he eats the leaves of trees.

Goat (#14a)
A goat will eat anything...
He loves the greenest grass.

A goat may eat anything ... she can give us milk.

Goose (#1b)
Don't be a silly goose...
You may lay a golden egg.

The goose that laid the golden egg ... was stolen from the giant.

Hen (#1d)
The little red hen said, I'll do it myself...
And then she ate her bread.

The Little Red Hen and Henny Penny ... were both lady chickens.

Hippo (#26)
The hippopotamus likes the water...
He'll stay there all day long.

A hippopotamus loves the water ... he hides there when it's hot.

Horse (#10d)
The horse can gallop around the farm...
And gives rides on his back.

A horse is very fun to ride ... he can pull a cart.

Ice Cream (#27)
Ice cream is good to eat...
I want a triple scoop.

An ice cream cone is de-lic-ious! ... I want some more, please!

Jellyfish (#28)
The jellyfish is beautiful...
But you mustn't touch.

The jellyfish has stinging tentacles ... stay away from him!

Koala (#29)
The koala bear lives in the trees...
And eats delicious leaves.

The Koala bear eats eucalyptus leaves ... his home is Aus-tra-lia.

Lamb (#30)
Mary had a little lamb...
Its fleece was white as snow.

The lamb is a baby sheep ... his coat is made of wool.

Lion (#11a)
The lion roars so very loud...
He is the king of beasts.

The lion roars very loud ... he has very sharp teeth.

Monkey (#31)
Monkeys swing from tree to tree...
And love to eat bananas.

Monkeys climb and eat bananas ... I see them in the zoo.

Mouse (#8a)
A mouse loves to eat cheese...
And scurries all about.

The country mouse wanted to move ... and so did the town mouse.

Newt (#32)
A newt loves to swim in water...
And climb upon a rock.

A newt can climb on slippery rocks ... he really loves the water.

Owl (#33)
The owl is wise and gives a hoot...
He always gives advice.

An owl is a night bird ... with beautiful great big wings.

Polar Bear (#34)
The polar bear lives in the snow...
And swims in water, too.

A polar bear is big and white ... he lives in cold and snow.

Quail (#35)
A quail is a kind of bird...
She leads her babies safely.

The mother quail has baby chicks ... they follow her everywhere.

Rabbit (#7)
A rabbit can run and hop...
He loves to eat carrots.

Rabbits love to run and hop ... they eat leaves and carrots.

Rhinoceros (#36)
A rhino has a pointy horn...
And loves to stomp out fires.

The rhinoceros has pointed horns ... and loves to stomp out fires.

Rooster (#1f)
The rooster crows early in the morning...
And tries to wake us up.

The rooster crows so early every day ... he tries to wake us up.

Squirrel (#37)
Squirrels love to eat acorns...
They hide them in a tree.

Squirrels love to eat acorns ... they hide them in a tree.

Tiger (#38)
Tigers growl and prowl about...
With their stripes and very long tail.

The tiger has very sharp teeth ... and black and orange stripes.

Turkey (#1e)
The big fat turkey goes gobble, gobble, gobble...
Don't eat me Thanksgiving Day!

A great big turkey says, "gobble, gobble, gobble ... don't eat me on Thanksgiving Day!"

Turtle (#16a)
The turtle crawls so very slow...
But always wins the race.

The turtle crawls so very slow ... but always wins the race.

Unicorn (#39)
The unicorn is a magical horse...
And beautiful to behold.

A unicorn is magical ... his horn is beautiful.

Vulture (#40)
Vultures circle around overhead...
Waiting for something dead.

The vulture likes his food dead ... he waits and circles around.

Walrus (#41)
A walrus is a great big fellow...
He has two long white tusks.

The walrus has two long tusks ... he lives on cold, cold ice.

Wolf (#5c)
The wolf howls at the moon ... he has friends in a pack.

X-Ray (#42)
Getting an X-Ray doesn't hurt...
The picture shows your bones.

An X-ray helps to see your bones ... to see if they are broken.

Yak (#43)
The yak gives milk for newborn babies...
In a land far, far away.

The yak has shaggy long hair ... and gives milk like a cow.

Zebra (#44)
A zebra's stripes are black and white...
He is a funny fellow.

The zebra has black and white stripes ... all over his body.

Tune: Hush Little Baby, Don't Say a Word

Words by Eunice Wright

A is for alligator, ant and ape.
B is for bear and bird and beaver.
C is for cow and cat and chick...

Tune: Are You Sleeping?

Words by Eunice Wright

A-A Alligator, A-A Alligator,
Alligator begins with A.
Alligator begins with A.
A-A Alligator, A-A Alligator,
A-A-A, ... A-A-A.

Buh (sound of letter)-buh-bear,
[Repeat]
Bear starts with buh (sound of letter)
[Repeat]
Buh-buh-bear,
[Repeat]
Bear starts with buh
Bear starts with buh.

Alternate

X-X-X
X-X-fox (letter name or sound)
X-X-fox (letter name)
Fox ends with X
Fox ends with X
X-X-fox (letter name)
X-X-fox (letter name)
Fox ends with X (letter name)
Fox ends with X (letter name)

Tune: Mary Had a Little Lamb

Words by Eunice Wright

Bear starts with "buh, buh, buh" (letter sound)
"Buh, buh, buh," "buh, buh, buh"
Bear starts with "buh, buh, buh"
Bear starts with "buh."

Tune: Mary Had a Little Lamb

Words by Eunice Wright

Bear begins with B-B-B (letter name),
B-B-B, B-B-B.
Bear begins with B-B-B,
B-B-B-B-B.

Tune: The Wheels on the Bus

Words by Eunice Wright

The Dog begins with D, D, D,
D, D, D,— D, D, D.
The Dog begins with D, D, D,
D,— D,— D.

A Hunting We Will Go (Zoo)

Traditional. Adapted by Eunice Wright

Zoo Animals: fox, yak, bear, giraffe, rhino, elephant, lion, hippo, zebra, monkey, polar bear, walrus, tiger, koala

A hunting we will go, a hunting we will go,
Heigh ho, the dairy-o, a hunting we will go!
A hunting we will go, a hunting we will go,
We'll catch a fox and put him in a box,
And then we'll let him go!

We'll catch a yak and give him flack,
And then we'll let him go!

We'll catch a bear and cut his hair,
And then we'll let him go!

We'll catch a giraffe and make him laugh,
And then we'll let him go!

We'll catch a rhino and tell him all we know,
And then we'll let him go!

We'll catch an elephant and make him go on a hunt,
And then we'll let him go!

We'll catch a lion and make him cry on,
And then we'll let him go!

We'll catch a hippo and tell him zipp-o,
And then we'll let him go!

We'll catch a zebra and sell him to Lebra...

We'll catch a monkey and name him, "Spunky,..."

We'll catch a polar bear and blow some solar air...

We'll catch a walrus and let him call Mr. Russ...

We'll catch a tiger and make him say, "Grrr..."

We'll catch a koala and dress him like a doll-a...

A Hunting We Will Go (Farm)

Adapted by Eunice Wright

Farm Animals: cat, pig, dog, horse, chick, lamb, cow, duck, hen, turkey, goat, goose, mouse, rabbit, turtle

A hunting we will go, a hunting we will go,
Heigh ho, the dairy-o, a hunting we will go!
A hunting we will go, a hunting we will go,
We'll catch a cat and give him a hat,
And then we'll let him go!

We'll catch a pig and dance a little jig,
We'll catch a dog and give him a hog,
We'll catch a horse and cry, of course,
We'll catch a chick and give him a stick,
We'll catch a lamb and call him "Sam,"
We'll catch a cow and dance like WOW!
We'll catch a duck and his feathers pluck,
We'll catch a hen and put her in a pen,
We'll catch a turkey and name him "Perky,..."
We'll catch a goat and put on his coat...
We'll catch a goose and let him loose...
We'll catch a mouse and chase him out of the house..
We'll catch a rabbit and break his habit...
We'll catch a turtle and name her "Myrtle,..."

Ideas for Songs (zoo)

One elephant went out to play...
Five little monkeys, jumping on the bed
We're going to the zoo, to the zoo
The lady was inside, and the smile was on the crocodile
Five little monkeys, swinging in a tree, teasing Mr. Crocodile, "Can't catch me!"
I went to the animal fair
I'm being eaten by a boa constrictor
Tune: Oh do you know the muffin man (kangaroo) that lives in the zoo?
I want a hippopotamus for Christmas
The bear (lion, elephant, giraffe) went over the mountain
Brown bear, brown bear (hippo, hippo) what do you see?
Sally, the Camel Has One Hump (Molly, the monkey has one tail)

Tune: Battle Hymn of the Republic

Words by Eunice Wright

My eyes have seen the animals running 'round the zoo,

They have no cages, pens, or people to tell
them what to do.
They're free to roam about the grounds just
like me and you.
The animals are free at last!

Chorus:
Glory, glory, hallelujah!
Glory, glory, hallelujah!
Glory, glory, hallelujah!
The animals are free to go!

The cages were not locked last night when it
was time for bed,
So the animals went out exploring, by the
elephant they were led.
They liked the freedom that they found; the
lion roared and said,
"We're never coming back!" (Roar!!!)

Chorus:
Glory, glory, hallelujah!
Glory, glory, hallelujah!
Glory, glory, hallelujah!
It's fun to run around!

When it was time to eat their lunch, no food
could be found.
Their stomachs rumbled as loudly as a bay-
ing basset hound,
Where was the zookeeper with their lunch?
Not e-ven a sound.
We're as hungry as the bear!

Chorus:
Sorry, sorry that we left!
Sorry, sorry that we left!
Sorry, sorry that we left!
We're coming back for lunch!

As soon as the animals went back into their
pens,
They found their lunch was waiting there
right inside their dens.
Happily they ate their lunch, home to stay
like hens.
We're home to stay for good!

Chorus:
Glory, glory, hallelujah!
Glory, glory, hallelujah!
Glory, glory, hallelujah!
It's fun to run around...
(spoken) but it's nice to be home and eat!

Tune: I Went to the Animal Fair (zoo)

Adapted by Juli and Eunice Wright

I went to the city zoo,
And there was a kangaroo,
The big polar bear, sitting by his lair
Was fluffing his old gray hair.
The monkey was a "hunk,"
And sat on the elephant's trunk;
The elephant cried and called for a skunk,
And that was the end of the monk,
The monk, the monk, the monk,
The monk, the monk, the monk.
(Hold nose and say, "Peee—uuuuu!)

Tune: The Wheels on the Bus (zoo)

Words by Eunice Wright

The monkeys in the zoo say, "Eee, eee, eee..."
The tiger in the zoo says, "Growl, growl,
growl..."
The snake in the zoo says, "Hiss, hiss, hiss..."
The wolf in the zoo says, "Howl, howl..."

Tune: The Wheels on the Bus (farm)

Words by Eunice Wright

The chickens in the coop go cluck, cluck, cluck
Cluck, cluck, cluck—cluck, cluck, cluck.
The chickens in the coop go cluck, cluck,
cluck
Down on the farm.

The cows in the barn go moo, moo, moo...
The horses in the field go neigh, neigh, neigh...
The ducks in the pond go quack, quack,
quack...
The cats on the fence go meow, meow, meow
The dogs in the yard go arf, arf, arf...
The mice in the barn go squeak, squeak,
squeak...
The pigs in the pen go oink, oink, oink...
The hens in the coop go cluck, cluck, cluck...
The bunnies in the pen go hop, hop, hop...

The rooster on the fence goes cock-a-doodle-do;
The ducks on the pond go quack, quack, quack;
The lambs in the field go baa, baa, baa...

Tune: Are You Sleeping? (zoo)

Words by Eunice Wright.

(Optional: teacher sings first, children repeat it)

See the animals, see the animals,
In the zoo, in the zoo,
There are many kinds there,
There are many kinds there,
Which one are you? Which one are you?

Optional idea: A child has a puppet zoo animal which he names and describes or tells why he chose it.

Guess this animal, guess this animal,
See it move, hear its sound.
This animal lives in the (forest, zoo, farm, name of country, etc.)
This animal lives in the (forest, zoo, farm, name of country, etc.)
Guess this animal, guess this animal.

Optional ideas: children name the animal the teacher has picked, or children and teacher take turns acting like an animal and guessing which one it is, or a child has a paper sack puppet animal which he names and explains why he likes it.

Tune: The Farmer in the Dell (zoo)

Words by Eunice Wright

We're going to the zoo,
We're going to the zoo,
While we're there we'll see a bear,
We're going to the zoo.

We're going to the zoo,
We're going to the zoo,
Once inside we'll see the hide
Of the hippo and the seal.

We're going to the zoo,
We're going to the zoo,
On the way, the monkeys play,
While we're at the zoo.

We're going to the zoo,
We're going to the zoo,
The kangaroo who looks at you,
Will turn and hop away.

We're going to the zoo,
We're going to the zoo,
The lions roar along the shore
Of the lake with swans and geese.

We're going to the zoo,
We're going to the zoo,
Elephants spray and zebras play,
At the zoo all day.

We're going to the zoo,
We're going to the zoo,
Tigers growl and polar bears prowl,
The giraffe can see them all.

Tune: A Rig a Jig Jig (zoo)

Words by Eunice Wright

As I went walking down the street, down the street, down the street,
A _____ _____ _____ (big brown bear, snarling tiger, hungry polar bear) I happened to meet,
Hi ho, hi ho, hi ho...

Change actions to song while singing.

As I was *running* down the street,...
As I was *skipping*...
As I was *hopping*...
As I was *jumping*...
As I was *crawling*...

Tune: Mary Had a Little Lamb (farm)

Nursery rhyme adapted by Eunice Wright

Substitute child's name and animal—

Susie had a little mouse... (fluffy squirrel, prancing pony, etc.)

Tune: Mary Had a Little Lamb (zoo)

Words by Eunice Wright

Do you know where (the zebra) is?
The zebra is, the zebra is?
Do you know where the zebra is
With black and white stripes?

Tune: The Bear Went Over the Mountain (farm)

Words by Eunice Wright

The cow went into the barn,
The cow went into the barn,
The cow went into the barn,
To eat some oats and hay.

Tune: Did You Ever See a Lassie? (farm-zoo)

Words by Eunice Wright

Did you ever see a _____ (giraffe, cow), etc.
That lives in the zoo? (or jungle, farm, etc.)

Tune: London Bridge (farm)

Words by Eunice Wright

Now it's time to _____ _____ _____ (count the chicks, milk the cow, etc.)
My fair lady (There are six, I love milk, etc.)

Tune: She'll Be Coming 'Round the Mountain (careers)

Words by Eunice Wright

She'll (He'll) be driving ______ when she comes.

Use this verse for careers, people, and what they drive—old jalopy, a big red fire truck, a yellow school bus, a mail truck, rocket, old red tractor, airplane, etc.

She'll be wearing ______ when she comes.

Use this verse for what people wear—nurse's scrubs, space suit, sailor suit, lab coat, chef's coat, artist's apron, etc.

Tune: The Farmer in the Dell (farm-zoo)

Words by Eunice Wright

High ho, the dairy oh,
(a fly is on my nose, farm time is here, zoo trip is here, etc.
Animal time is here, oh, animal time is here,...)

Tune: Are You Sleeping? (farm)

Words by Eunice Wright

I hear dogs bark, bow-wow-wow... I hear birds sing, cats meow, cows moo, etc.

Tune: Camptown Races (farm-zoo)

Words by Eunice Wright

Today is _____ (theme) day all day long,
Doo dah, doo dah.
Today is _____ (theme) day all day long,
Oh, doo dah day.

Today is (farm, zoo) day all day long,
Doo dah, doo dah.
Today is farm day all day long,
Oh, doo dah day.

It is _____ day all day long,
Doo dah, doo dah.

Yesterday was _____ day all day long,
Tomorrow will be _____ day all day long,
Oh, doo dah day.

Today Is Monday (theme)

Words by Eunice Wright

Today is _____ (theme) day,
Today is _____ day,
Monday, farm day,
Tuesday, zoo day,
Wednesday, jungle day,
Thursday, nature day,
Friday, swamp day,
Come all you hungry animals,
Let's have a great big party!

Tune: The Wheels on the Bus (farm-zoo)

Words by Eunice Wright

The cows on the farm say, moo, moo, moo...
The farmer in the barn goes milk, milk, milk...
The tiger in the zoo goes roar, roar, roar...

Other Tunes to Use

Are You Sleeping?
Eensy Weensy Spider
For He's a Jolly Good Fellow
Found a Peanut
If You're Happy and You Know It (substitute if you're scared, sad, lonely, friendly)
I'm a Little Teapot
London Bridge
Mary Had a Little Lamb
The Mulberry Bush
The Paw Paw Patch
Pop Goes the Weasel
Row, Row, Row Your Boat
Skip to My Lou
Ten Little Indians
This Is the Way We Wash Our Clothes
Three Blind Mice
Three Jolly Fishermen
Twinkle, Twinkle, Little Star
The Wheels on the Bus
Yankee Doodle
You Are My Sunshine

See *Wee Sing Silly Songs* for more ideas.

Old MacDonald Had a Farm (farm)

Holiday Songs and Every Day Songs and Games, *by Emilie Poulsson, 1901. With sheet music and some finger plays.*

With a baa! baa! here, and a baa! baa! there,
Here a baa! there a baa! Here a baa! there a baa!
Hey, little lassie, will you come along with me,
And see the farmer's sheep?

With a moo! moo! here, etc.—cows.
With a grunt! grunt! here, etc.—pigs.
With a bow! wow! here, etc.—dogs.
With a cluck! cluck! here, etc.—hens.
With a peep! peep! here, etc.—chicks.
With a quack! quack! here, etc.—ducks.
With a meow! meow! here, etc.—cats.
Old MacDonald had a farm
E I E I O
And on that farm there were some ducks
E I E I O
With a quack-quack here
And a quack-quack there
Here a quack, there a quack
Everywhere a quack-quack
Old MacDonald had a farm
E I E I O

Repeat, substituting another animal for the duck, but repeat the last four lines, singing the duck sound before you start the song again.

Pig: oink-oink, chickens: peep-peep, dog: bow-wow, lambs: baa-baa, cow: moo-moo, horses: neigh-neigh, crows: caw-caw, cats: meow-meow, etc.

Tune: The Farmer in the Dell (farm)

Words by Eunice Wright

The farmer plants a garden...
The garden grows fast...
The farmer picks a squash...
The farmer feeds the chickens...
The farmer milks the cows...

Tune: The Wheels on the Bus (farm)

Words by Eunice Wright

The carrots in the garden
Grow underground, underground, underground.
The carrots in the garden
Grow under ground,
All summer long. (What else grows underground?)
The tomatoes in the garden grow above the ground...
All summer long. (What else grows above the ground?)
The watermelons (tomatoes, grapes, squash) in the garden grow on the vine...

The corn in the garden grows up straight and tall...
The peppers grow on a bush...

Tune: It's a Small World After All (garden)

Words by Eunice Wright

It's a vegetable garden after all...
It's a garden with squash and melons...
It's a garden with soil and seeds...

Template for Animal Song (Tune: The Old Gray Mare) (farm-zoo)

Words by Eunice Wright

Here we sit like birds in the wilderness
Birds in the wilderness
Birds in the wilderness
Here we sit like birds in the wilderness
Waiting for our food.

Here we sit like cows in a barn...
Waiting to be milked.

Here we sit like pigs in a pigpen...
Waiting to be slopped.

Here we sit like horses in a stall...
Waiting for our oats.

Here we sit like cats in a field of mice...
Waiting for our dinner.

Here we sit like chickens in a chicken coop...
Sitting on our nests.

Here we sit like brown monkeys in the zoo...
Eating our bananas.
(*or* swinging in the trees)

Baa Baa Black Sheep (tune: Twinkle, Twinkle Little Star) (farm)

Nursery rhyme; words by Eunice Wright

Baa, baa white sheep, have you any wool?
Cluck, cluck red hen, have you any eggs?
Bark bark, brown dog, have you chased anything today?
Moo, moo brown cow, have you been milked today?

Little Puppy (tune: Twinkle, Twinkle Little Star)

Words by Eunice Wright

Little puppy, you're so fun.
Soft brown fur; you like the sun.
You run and fetch and roll and play,
And sometimes come here when I say.
Little puppy, you're the one
I like to play with, while I run.

Hickety, Pickety, My Black Hen (nursery rhyme)

Hickety, Pickety, my black hen.
She lays eggs for gentlemen.
Gentlemen come every day
To see what my black hen doth lay.
Sometimes nine, and sometimes ten,
Hickety, Pickety, my black hen.

Baa Baa Black Sheep (tune: Twinkle Twinkle Little Star) (nursery rhyme)

Repeat "for the little girl who lives down the lane."

Baa, baa, black sheep,
Have you any wool?
Yes, sir, yes, sir,
Three bags full.
One for my master,
One for my dame,
And one for the little boy
Who lives down the lane.
Baa, baa, black sheep,
Have you any wool?
Yes, sir, yes, sir,
Three bags full.

Over in the Barnyard (tune: Down by the Station) (farm)

By Lee Ricks, 1948. Words by Eunice Wright

Over in the barnyard
Down by the haystack,
See all the cows (*name of an animal*)
Standing in a row.

Over in the barnyard
Down by the pigpen,

See all the pigs (*name of an animal*)
Eating in a row.

Over in the barnyard
Up in the barn loft,
See all the owls (*the name of an animal*)
Sleeping in a row.

Over in the barnyard
Down by the barn door,
See all the cats (*the name of an animal*)
Meowing in a row.

Over in the barnyard
Down by the farmhouse,
See all the dogs (*the name of an animal*)
Barking in a row.

Over in the barnyard
Down by the meadow,
See all the horses (*the name of an animal*)
Galloping in a row.

Ten Little Chickens (or other animals) (tune: Ten Little Indians) (farm)

Words by Eunice Wright

One little, two little, three little chickens...
Ran into the coop.

One little, two little, three little horses...
Galloped around the field.

One little, two little, three little ducklings...
Dove into the pond.

Tune: Little Boy Blue (nursery rhyme fun)

Words by Eunice Wright

Little girl pink, come play your flute;
The turkeys are gobbling, the owls give a hoot.
Where is the little girl who plays on her flute?
Under the shade tree, giving a toot.

Little boy/girl _____ (name)
Come _____ your _____ (verb, noun)
The _____'s in the _____, (animal, place)
The _____'s in the _____. (animal, place)

Where is the little _____ (name)
Who looked after the _____ (animal)
Under (Preposition: over, behind, between, inside, on top of, etc.) the _____ (noun)
Fast _____ (verb: asleep, wide awake, reading, singing, playing, laughing, etc.)

Farm Animals (Tune: Mary Wore Her Red Dress)

Words by Eunice Wright

Kitty drank her milk, milk, milk.
Kitty drank her milk, and now it's all gone.

Cows give their milk, milk, milk.
Cows give their milk, for us to drink.

Piggy wallows in mud, mud, mud.
Piggy wallows in mud, from his head to his toes.

Cows eat green grass, green grass, green grass.
Cows eat green grass, all day long.

Horses run around, around, around.
Horses run around, until the end of day.

Chickens lay eggs, egg, eggs.
Chickens lay eggs, in a nest.

Sheep grow wool, wool, wool.
Sheep grow wool, all winter long.

Goats eat everything, everything, everything.
Goats eat everything, all day long.

Tune: The Bear (or Other Animal) Went Over the Mountain

Words by Eunice Wright

(or swam across the river, ran through the jungle, jumped over the fence, lived in the zoo, etc.)

The mouse ran around the room ... to see what he could eat.

The cow ate all the grass ... until there was nothing left.

The horse jumped over the fence ... to see what he could eat.

The turtle swam across the river ... to race to the other side.

The tiger ran through the jungle ... to see what he could eat.

Tune: I'm a Little Teapot

Words by Eunice Wright

I'm a little kitty,
I like to drink milk.
Here is my nose, as soft as silk.
When you call, "Here, Kitty," I will come.
I'll jump in your lap and hum, hum, hum.

Tune: Pop! Goes the Weasel (farm)

Words by Eunice Wright

All around the barnyard,
The horse chased the cow.
The cow ran fast and jumped the fence..
Neigh! went the horse. (*or* Moo went the cow)

All around the barnyard,
The cat chased the mouse.
The mouse ran up the clock.
Bong! went the clock. (*or* squeak went the mouse)

Tune: Brown Bear, Brown Bear, What Do You See?

By Bill Martin, Jr. (He also wrote: Polar Bear, Baby Bear, Panda Bear, Chicka Chicka Boom, Boom.)

"Brown _____, brown _____, What do you see?..."
I see a _____ _____ looking at me.

(Repeat verses, using other animals)

Tune: This Is the Way We Wash Our Clothes *(Farm Activities)*

Words by Eunice Wright

This is the way we herd the sheep,
Herd the sheep, herd the sheep.
This is the way we herd the sheep, so early in the morning.

This is the way we gather the eggs,
Gather the eggs, gather the eggs.
This is the way we gather the eggs, so early in the morning.

This is the way we milk the cows,
Milk the cows, milk the cows.
This is the way we milk the cows, so early in the morning.

This is the way we ride the horse,
Ride the horse, ride the horse.
This is the way we ride the horse, so early in the morning.

This is the way we plant the seeds,
Plant the seeds, plant the seeds.
This is the way we plant the seeds, so early in the morning.

This is the way we feed the chickens,
Feed the chickens, feed the chickens.
This is the way we feed the chickens, so early in the morning.
(This is the way we plant the seeds, feed the chickens, weed the garden, etc.)

Tune: Did You Ever See a Lassie? (Farm Animal Sounds)

Words by Eunice Wright

Did you ever see a farm,
A farm, a farm?
Did you ever see a farm,
And all the animals there?

A pig who says oink, oink, oink.
And a horse who says neigh!
Did you ever see a farm,
And all the animals there?

Add animals as desired.

A rooster who says cock-a-doodle doo...
A cow who says moo...
A duck who says quack, quack, quack.. .

Did you ever see a farm,
And all the animals there?

Tune: Take Me Out to the Ballgame (farm)

Words by Eunice Wright

Take me out to the farm, dad.
Please take me there, right now.

Show me some horses and chickens, too.
I can't wait to see cows that moo.
For there are dogs, dogs, dogs in the barnyard,
If they don't bark its a shame.
For, its one, two, three animals and more,
At the old barnyard.

Animals on the Farm (tune: The Wheels on the Bus)

Words by Eunice Wright

The pigs on the farm go oink, oink, oink,
Oink, oink, oink, oink, oink, oink,
The pigs on the farm go oink, oink, oink,
All night long.

The sheep on the farm go bah, bah, bah,
Bah, bah, bah, bah, bah, bah,
The sheep on the farm go bah, bah, bah,
All night long.

The cows on the farm go moo, moo, moo,
Moo, moo, moo, moo, moo, moo,
The cows on the farm go moo, moo, moo,
All night long.

The ducks on the farm go quack, quack, quack,
Quack, quack, quack, quack, quack, quack,
The ducks on the farm go quack, quack, quack,
All night long.

Cluck, Cluck, Red Hen (tune: Twinkle, Twinkle Little Star)

For entire song, see: Adapted lyrics by Jacquelyn Reinach. Childways Music, 1970 (ASCAP) (traditional music)

1. Baa, baa black sheep, Have you any wool?..,
2. Cluck, cluck, red hen, Have you any eggs?...
3. Moo, moo, brown cow, Have you milk for me?...

Add verses with animals and products, rhyming the ending words.

Tune: Five Fat Turkeys Are We

Words by Eunice Wright

Hard-working farmers are we;
We get up each morning at three.
We milk every cow
And feed every sow
Until all our chores are done!

Tune: The Farmer in the Dell

Words by Eunice Wright

(Make up your own verses).

The animals on the farm, the animals on the farm
High-ho the dairy-oh, the animals on the farm.

The tractor plows the fields, the tractor plows the fields
High-ho the dairy-oh, the tractor plows the fields.

The barn is for the animals, the barn is for the animals
High-ho the dairy-oh, the barn is for the animals.

The pig rolls in the mud, the pig rolls in the mud
High-ho the dairy-oh, the pig rolls in the mud.

The horses like to run, the horses like to run
High-ho the dairy-oh, the horses like to run.

The chickens lay their eggs, the chickens lay their eggs
High-ho the dairy-oh, the chickens lay their eggs.

The ducks swim in the lake, the ducks swim in the lake
High-ho the dairy-oh, the ducks swim in the lake.

The farmer plants a garden, the farmer plants a garden
High-ho the dairy-oh, the farmer plants a garden.

Tune: Sally the Camel

Words by Eunice Wright

Bessie the cow has two horns, Bessie the cow has two horns,
Bessie the cow has two horns, moo, Bessie, moo—Boom, boom, boom—

Billy the goat has two horns—Billy the goat has two horns,
Billy the goat has two horns—charge Billy charge—Boom, boom, boom—

Sassy the cat has no horns—Sassy the cat has no horns...

(Spoken) Silly Sassy! you're just a cat—
(Sung very slowly) So meow, Sassy—Meow.

Tune: Are You Sleeping?

Words by Eunice Wright

Add other animals and sounds they make.

Are you talking, are you talking,
Little pig, little pig?
Hear the pig saying, Hear the pig saying,
"Oink, oink, oink, oink, oink, oink."

Tune: The Wheels on the Bus

Words by Eunice Wright

Add other animals and sounds they make.

The cows on the farm go _____ _____ _____ (children fill in blanks with correct sound),
The pigs on the farm go _____ _____ _____ All day long.

Mary Had a Little Lamb (nursery rhyme activity)

Words by Eunice Wright

Mary had a little lamb, little lamb, little lamb.
Mary had a little lamb, whose fleece was white as snow.

Add other animals and sounds they make.

Mary had a little _____, little _____, little _____,
Mary had a little _____, whose _____ was _____ as _____.

Tune: Paw Paw Patch (farm)

Words by Eunice Wright

Add other animals.

Bouncing up and down on my little brown pony,
Bouncing up and down on my little brown pony,
Bouncing up and down on my little brown pony,
All around the farm.

Feeding all the chickens and all the pigs,
Feeding all the chickens and all the pigs,
Feeding all the chickens and all the pigs,
All around the farm.

Riding the horse and chasing the cows,
Riding the horse and chasing the cows,
Riding the horse and chasing the cows,
All around the farm.

Other Songs

"Alphabet Animals at the Zoo," by John Kinderman Taylor.
"Babies (Animal Babies)," *I Have a Song for You About Seasons and Holidays*, by Janeen Brady, p. 28.
Children's Songs, Vol. V, Animals. Ages 4–10 (Music Made Easy), by A.W. Mickey Hart, Discovery Through Music, Inc. (Giraffe, Bear, Frog, Alligator, Beaver, Kangaroo, Hippopotamus, Cheetah, Panda, Wolf, Hyena.) Other volumes available are: Vol. 1 (moon, sun, rain, etc.), Vol. III (I'm Your Stomach, etc.), Vol. IV (Insects/Birds), Vol. VI (If I Were a Princess, etc.), Vol. VII (famous people, falcon, elephant, deer, cow, dinosaur, etc.)
"Down in the Jungle," by Jack Hartmann.
"Farm Songs," by Jack Hartmann (Hop 2 it Music).
"Fun at the Zoo," children's song, lyrics and

sound clip by Stephanie Burton. (Tune: "Let's do the Twist" or "Dance the Twist.") There are verses for many animals ... a very cute song!

"Going to the Zoo" by Tom Paxton. Verse 2—monkeys; verse 3—crocodiles.

"Hooray for the Hippo," *I Have a Song for You About Animals*, by Janeen Brady, p. 40.

Jack Hartmann's Animal Songs: "Rocco, the Rhyming Rhino," "The Animal Hokey Pokey," "Who Is at the Zoo?" "The Animal Alphabet Cheer."

"Old MacDonald," The Mother Goose Jazz Band, Josh Greenberg, 1994. Music, By Gosh! (ASCAP); from the music, By Gosh! Album *Go with the Flow*. 2:35. Also watch the Sesame Street Muppets sing this song.

"A Riddle" (An Elephant), *I Have a Song for You About Animals*, by Janeen Brady, p. 42.

Sing-Along Tunes for Tots, 1971, by Louise Stephens Baughman and Phyllis Juhlin Park. Contents: worms, pony, elephant, baby, birds, kitty, poor babes in the woods, clouds, pigs, mother, daddies, Halloween, etc.

"The Truth About Lions," *I Have a Song for You About Animals*, by Janeen Brady, p. 30.

"Who Built the Ark? (Noah built the ark)." Traditional.

"Your Neck's So Long," *I Have a Song for You About Animals*, by Janeen Brady, p. 37.

"The Zebra," *I Have a Song for You About Animals*, by Janeen Brady, p. 33.

Other recommended artists: Ron Brown, Phil Rosenthal, John Kinderman Taylor, Phil Rosenthal, Gary Rosen, Dennis Westphall.

Poems and Nursery Rhymes

An Alphabet Zoo

The Jingle Book, *by Carolyn Wells, 1901; words adapted for alphabet puppets by Eunice Wright*

A was an apt alligator,
Who wanted to be a head-waiter;
He said, "I opine
In that field I could shine,
Because I am such a good skater."

B was a beggarly bear,
Who carefully curled his front hair;
He said, "I would buy
A red-spotted tie,—
But I haven't a penny to spare."

C was a cool chicken,
Who went to an afternoon tea.
When they said, "Will you take
A caraway cake?"
She greedily took twenty-three!

D was a diligent duck,
In summer she shoveled the snow;
In the spring and the fall
She did nothing at all,
And in winter the grass she would mow.

E was an earnest elephant,
Who tried very hard to determine
If he should earn a cent,
How it ought to be spent,
And decided to purchase a sermon.

F was a fussy fawn,
Who remarked to his family, "By jingo!
I think I would go
To that animal show,
But they all talk such barbarous lingo."

G was a giddy giraffe,
Who never could learn how to spell;
But she managed to pass
To the head of her class,
Because she did fractions so well.

H was a haughty young hippo,
Who affected society talk;
But when introduced
At a large chicken roost
He excitedly screamed out, "Oh, Lawk!"

I was an icy ice cream,
Who carried a split banana;
With tears he'd protest

That he never could rest
Till he was topped with cherry-banana.

J was a jiggery jellyfish,
Who purchased a Spanish guitar;
He played popular airs
At fêtes and at fairs,
And down at the fancy bazaar.

K was a skittish koala,
Whose bonnet was always askew;
So they asked her to wait
While they put it on straight
And fastened it firmly with glue.

L was a leaping lion,
Who ate up twelve sheep and a shepherd,
But the real reason why
He continued to cry
Was his food was so lavishly peppered.

M was a mischievous monkey,
Who went to the free kindergarten;
When they asked him to plat
A gay-colored mat,
He tackled the job like a Spartan.

N was a naughty Newt,
Who wandered too near a buzz saw.
It cut off his toes,
And the shrieks that arose
Filled all of the neighbors with awe.

O was a stuffy old owl,
Who decided to enter the barn.
He could not return,
So continued to yearn
For his home in the tree-oh, darn!

P was a cold polar bear
Who had nothing to eat but a carrot,
And nothing to wear
But a wig of red hair,
And nowhere to live but a garret.

Q was a querulous quail,
Who at every trifle would sob;
He said, "I detest
To wear a plaid vest,
And I hate to eat corn from the cob!"

R was a rollicking rhino,
Attired in an old pillow sham.
When asked if he'd call
At the masquerade ball,
He said, "I'll go just as I am."

S was a shy busy squirrel,
Who slept on a sunny veranda.
She calmly reposed,
But, alas! while she dozed
They caught her and caged her and fed her.

T was a tidy young tiger,
Who went out to bring in the paper;
And when he came back
He made no muddy track,
For he wiped his feet clean on the scraper.

U was a young unicorn,
The bravest that ever was born.
They bought him a boat
And they set him afloat,
And straightway he sailed for Cape Horn.

V was a vigorous vulture,
Who taught animals physical culture;
When a pupil dropped dead,
The kind teacher said,
"You needn't consider sepulture."

W was a wild walrus,
All day he did nothing but squirm.
They sent him to school,
But he broke every rule,
And left at the end of the term.

X was a X-Ray brave,
Who took pictures for a living to save.
To each one he would say,
"Good day, sir, good day!"
And to each, a polite bill he gave.

Y was a youthful yak,
Who raised a ridiculous clamor;
And he chattered until
An owl said, "Keep still!
I'm trying to study my grammar."

Z was a zealous zebra,
A race he tried to provide.
If any one tried

To take a sly ride,
He refused and took them aside.

The Animals at the Zoo

Modified by Eunice Wright

At the zoo we saw a bear,
He had long, brown furry hair.

The lion growled and ran around,
He made a loud roaring sound.

The giraffe's neck is very long
You'll never hear him sing a song.

The elephant is so big and strong,
He could lift heavy logs all day long.

The monkeys climb up and down the tree,
And sometimes imitate you and me.

The tiger is so scary and big,
He wouldn't be if he wore a wig.

The zebra has stripes of black and white,
His beautiful coat is quite a sight.

But my favorite animal at the zoo
Is the _____, how about you?

Children can name their favorite animal—then make that puppet.

The Elephant's Trunk

By Eunice Wright

The elephant has a long trunk for a nose,
After a peanut it always goes.
He gets some water up inside,
And sprays it up all over his hide.

Over in the Meadow

Kit, Fan, Tot and the Rest of Them, *by Olive A. Wadsworth, 1870*

Traditional English Nursery Song—verses can be adapted for counting from 1 to 10 using the same puppet, using different kinds of puppets for each additional verse, or using a mother and baby puppets—reduce the puppet size for the baby.

Over in the meadow in the sand in the sun
Lived an old mother turtle and her little turtle(s) one (two, three, ...)
"Dig," said the mother. "I (we) dig," said the one (two, three, ...)
So they dug all day in the sand in the sun.

Over in the meadow in the sand in the sun
Lived an old mother frog and her little frog(s) one (two, three, ...).
"Hop," said the mother. "I (we) hop," said the one (two, three, ...).
So they hopped and were glad in the sand in the sun.

Ideas for additional verses:
Fish—where the stream runs blue (lived an old mother fish and her little fishes two).
Bird—in a nest in a tree (lived an old mother bird and her little birds three).
Rat—by an old barn door (lived an old mother rat and her little rats four).
Bee—in a snug beehive (lived an old mother bee and her little bees five).
Crow—in a nest built of sticks (lived an old mother crow and her little crows six).
Mouse—where the grass is heaven
Lizard—on a log by the gate
Duck—by a pond by the pine
Rabbit—in a big old den
(Others: **owl**, **beaver**, **chicken**, **turkey**, **pony**, **cow**, **cat**, **pig**, **goose**, etc.)

Or

Over in the zoo in the sand in the sun (in a cage in the zoo),
Lived a big old (tiger, lion, polar bear, elephant, rhino, hippo, zebra, giraffe, etc.).

To Market, to Market (nursery rhyme)

Clap your hands in rhythm

To market, to market, to buy a fat pig.
Home again, home again, jiggity jig.
To market, to market, to buy a fat hog.
Home again, home again, jiggity jog.
To market, to market to buy a plum bun,
Home again, home again, market is done.

Little Boy Blue (nursery rhyme)

Little Boy Blue
Come blow your horn!
The sheep's in the meadow,
The cow's in the corn.
Where is the boy
Who looks after the sheep?
He's under the haystack,
Fast asleep.
Will you wake him?
No, not I
For if I do,
He's sure to cry.

Two Mother Pigs

Original author unknown

Two mother pigs lived in a pen,
Each had four babies and that made ten.
These four babies were black and white.
These four babies were black as night.
All eight babies loved to play.
And they rolled and they rolled in the mud all day.
At night, with their mother,
They curled up in a heap,
And squealed and squealed
'Til they went to sleep.

Five Little Chicks

Original author unknown

Said the first little chick with a queer little squirm,
"I wish I could find a fat little worm."
Said the next little chick with an odd little shrug,
"I wish I could find a fat little slug."
Said the third little chick with a sharp little squeal,
"I wish I could find some nice yellow meal."
Said the fourth little chick with a sigh of grief,
"I wish I could find a little green leaf."
Said the fifth little chick with a faint little moan,
"I wish I could find a wee gravel stone."
"Now, see here," said the mother from the green garden patch,
"If you want any breakfast, just come here and scratch!"

This Little Cow

By Eunice Wright

This little cow went to the fields to graze,
This little cow stayed in the barn.
This little cow ate oats and hay,
This little cow had none.
And this little said, "Moo, moo, moo,
All the way home.

Five Little Ducks

Traditional. Words by Eunice Wright
(Change animals, voices, and numbers)

Five little _____ went out one day,
Over the hills, and far away.
Mommy (daddy) _____ called _____, _____, _____.
And four little _____ came _____ back.

Four little dogs went out one day,
Over the hills, and far away.
Mommy (daddy) dog called bow, wow, wow.
And three little dogs came running back.

Three little chickens went out one day,
Over the hills and far away.
Mommy (daddy) chicken called cluck, cluck, cluck,
And two little chickens came running back.

Two little horses went out one day,
Over the hills and far away.
Mommy (daddy) horse called neigh, neigh, neigh.
And one little horse came galloping back.

One little cow went out one day,
Over the hills and far away.
Mommy (daddy) cow called moo, moo, moo.
And no little cow came running back.

No little _____ went out one day,
Over the hills and far away.

Mommy (daddy) _____ called _____, _____, _____!
And five little _____ came _____ back (and very quickly, too!)

Oats, Peas, Beans, and Barley Grow

Traditional

Oats, peas, beans, and barley grow,
Oats, peas, beans, and barley grow,
Can you or I or anyone know
How oats, peas, beans, and barley grow?

Verse 1:
First the farmer sows his seed,
Stands erect and takes his ease,
He stamps his foot and claps his hands,
And turns around to view his lands.

Chorus:
Oats, peas, beans, and barley grow,
Oats, peas, beans, and barley grow,
Can you or I or anyone know
How oats, peas, beans, and barley grow?

Verse 2:
Next the farmer waters the seed,
Stands erect and takes his ease,
He stamps his foot and claps his hands,
And turns around to view his lands.

Chorus:
Oats, peas, beans, and barley grow,
Oats, peas, beans, and barley grow,
Can you or I or anyone know
How oats, peas, beans, and barley grow?

Verse 3:
Next the farmer hoes the weeds,
Stands erect and takes his ease,
He stamps his foot and claps his hands,
And turns around to view his lands.

Chorus:
Oats, peas, beans, and barley grow,
Oats, peas, beans, and barley grow,
Can you or I or anyone know
How oats, peas, beans, and barley grow?

Verse 4:
Last the farmer harvests his seed,
Stands erect and takes his ease,
He stamps his foot and claps his hands,
And turns around to view his lands.

Chorus:
Oats, peas, beans, and barley grow,
Oats, peas, beans, and barley grow,
Can you or I or anyone know
How oats, peas, beans, and barley grow?

Five Little Pigs

Original author unknown

Five little pigs went out to play.
The first little pig said,
"Let's go to the woods today."
The second little pig said,
"What will we do there?"
The third little pig said,
"We'll look for our mother."
The fourth little pig said,
"What will we do when we find her?"
"We'll hug her and kiss her and kiss her!"
Said the fifth little pig.

Farm Scarecrow (jumprope chant)

By Eunice Wright

Scarecrow, scarecrow, scare the crows.
Wave your arms and curl your toes.
Scarecrow, scarecrow, every day,
Scare the big black crows away!

Games and Group Activities

Tune: 99 Bottles of Pop (also see Nursery Rhyme Activities)

Chorus: Sing the alphabet to the tune of 99 Bottles of Pop.
Verses: Sing a nursery rhyme to the same tune.

Example: Group game, all sit in a circle. All sing the alphabet. First person sings a nursery rhyme. Repeat. Continue around the circle. A person is "out" if he can't think of a nursery rhyme.

All sing: ABCDEFGHIJKLMNOPQRSTUVWXYZ.
First person: Oh, Mary had a little lamb, its fleece was white as snow, and everywhere that Mary went, the lamb was sure to go.
All sing: ABC...
Second person: Jack and Jill went up the hill...
All sing: ABC...

Other Adaptable Games

By Eunice Wright

Animal sorting or matching game. Use colors, sizes, foods, habitats, sounds, etc.
Duck, duck, goose circle game, changing the animal names.
Guess the animal: Leader gives clues for the players to guess the animal (color, sound they make, size, etc.).
Instead of Mother May I, play Zoo Keeper May I.
Simon Says: During game play, Simon can say, "Walk like an elephant"; "Sound like a monkey"; "Waddle like a duck"; "Roar like a lion"; etc.
"We're going on a lion (bear, tiger, elephant) hunt..."
See bear activities for more suggestions.

Snack Suggestions

Make Zoo Stew, Elephant Surprise, Brown Bear Porridge, Zebra Zingers, Crocodile Tears, Penguin Punch, Koala Leaves, Lion Lunch, Tiger Butter, Hippo Lettuce, Rhino Radish, Polar Bear Fish Sticks, etc.

Internet Resources

Heidi Songs

www.heidisongs.com. Concepts covered are: Alphabet Action, The A Song, The B Song, The C Song, The D Song, The E Song, The F Song, The G Song, The H Song, The I Song, The J Song, The K Song, The L Song, The M Song, The N Song, The O Song, The P Song, The Q Song, The R Song, The S Song, The T Song, The U Song, The V Song, The W Song, The X Song, The Y Song, The Z Song, Sounds to Letters.

Singable Songs for Letters & Words has a song for every letter of the alphabet. Each song includes the sound of the letter, and a reference to what the letter looks like or how it is formed. There are also two other songs that practice all of the letters and their sounds from A to Z.

ABC Letter of the Week Book List

letteroftheweek.com. Preschool Age 3+, compiled by Katrina Lybbert. She suggests you choose one book to read for the whole week, or a different book for each day. See her list online: Copyright © 2000–2005 by Katrina Lybbert. All rights reserved.

Other Sites

"Alphabet Animals at the Zoo" (Children's Song Lyrics and Sound Clip, John "Kinderman" Taylor).
"The Animal Dance," "The Bird Song," by Phil Rosenthal
Barnyard Talkin', Song for Teaching Sounds of Farm Animals to Young Children, Dennis Westphall.
"The Chickens in the Coop," Children's song lyrics and sound clip
Child's Play Family Daycare has a unit full of ideas and activities for zoo animals.
Educational Children's Music from SongsforTeaching.com (recommended!)
Everything Preschool, Songs for Teaching.com
Farmer Game: KIDiddles.com (song with actions)
"Fun at the Zoo," Children's Song Lyrics and Sound Clip, by Stephanie Burton. (Tune: "Let's Do the Twist" or "Dance the Twist") A verse for each animal ... a very cute song!

Gary Rosen's Pet Sounds (Tiny Toes Music)
Jack Hartmann
Songsforteaching.com
Tickle Tune Typhoon

Books

Aesop's Fables, selected and illustrated by Michael Hague. *Simple stories, beautiful illustrations.*

The Alphabet Book, Random House Picture-backs.

AlphaOops! The Day Z Went First, by Alethea Kontis (Candlewick, 2006).

Amazing Beguiling Curious, 26 Fascinating Creatures, by Anne E.G. Nydam.

Animal Alphabet, Little Golden Book, by Barbara Shook Hazen (1973).

Animal Babies, Random House Picture-backs.

Animal Babies Around the House and Animal Babies in Towns and Cities, by Kingfisher Publications.

Animal Hospital, by Judith Walker-Hodge (Dorling Kindersley). Level 1 reader.

Animalia Midi, by Graeme Base.

Animals Are Sleeping, by Suzanne Slade (Sylvan Dell, 2008). *The rhymes give information on animals, where they live and sleep. Beautiful illustrations, very simple story line. The names of the animals are listed in the front of the book, not in the story with the animal picture.*

Animals in Winter (Let's Read About), by Henrietta Bancroft.

Animals Should Definitely NOT Wear Clothing, by Judi Barrett (Scholastic, 1970). *A cute book; the animals are nicely drawn and very comical. Easy reading.*

Baby Animals of the Grasslands, by Carmen Bredeson (Enslow, 2009).

Baby Farm Animals, by Garth Williams.

Baby Pets, illustrated by Robin James (Price/Stern/Sloan, 1983). *A beautifully illustrated board book. 8 pages.*

Barn, by Debby Atwell.

Barnyard Dance, by Sandra Boynton.

Barnyard Lullaby, by Frank Asch.

Barnyard Prayers, by Laura Godwin and illustrated by Brian Selznick.

Beautiful Moments in the Wild: Animals and Their Colors, by Stephanie Maze.

Big Red Barn, by Margaret Wise Brown.

The Big Storm, a Very Soggy Counting Book, by Nancy Tafuri, a Caldecott Honor Artist (Simon & Schuster, 2009). *For young readers and preschool children; beautiful illustrations of animals. This cute story will lead to discussion of different animals and storms.*

The Bird Alphabet Book, by Jerry Pallotta.

Brian Wildsmith's Amazing Animal Alphabet, by Brian Wildsmith.

Bubble Gum, Bubble Gum, by Lisa Wheeler. *Animals stuck in gum have trouble.*

Bunny Reads Back: Old MacDonald, by Rosemary Wells.

The Butterfly Alphabet Book, by Brian Cassie and Jerry Pallotta.

The Cat on the Mat Is Flat, by Andy Griffiths. *A collection of nine humorous stories in rhyme.*

Chicka Chicka Boom Boom, by Bill Martin, Jr. *The alphabet letters try to climb a coconut tree.*

Chickens Aren't the Only Ones, by Ruth Heller.

Click, Clack, Quackity Quack: An Alphabet Letter Book, by Doreen Cronin and Betsy Lewin.

Clickety Clack, by Rob and Amy Spence.

Cock-a-Doodle-Moo, by Bernard Most.

Color Farm, by Lois Ehlert. *Various cut paper shapes combine to create magnificent, colorful farm animals.*

Color Zoo, by Lois Ehlert. *Various cut paper shapes combine to create magnificent, colorful zoo animals.*

Come to the Meadow, by Anna Grossnickle Hines.

Count the Farm Animals 1—2—3, by Rosalinda Kightley.

Counting on the Woods, by George Ella Lyon.

Beautiful color photos with rhymes that describe animals and objects seen and counted on a nature walk. Read before a nature walk or field trip. Make animal puppets afterwards.

A Day at Greenhill Farm, by Sue Nicholson (Dorling Kindersley). Level 1 reader.

The Day Jimmy's Boa Ate the Wash, by Tinka Hakes Noble; illustrated by Steven Kellogg (Dial, 1980; Puffin Paperback, 1992). *When Jimmy's class visits the farm, he brings his pet boa constrictor. After a mix-up, Jimmy comes home with a pig, and the farmer and wife find a new pet.*

The Day the Sheep Showed Up, by David M. McPhail.

Dear Zoo: A Lift-the-Flap Book (board book), by Rod Campbell.

Dear Zoo: A Pop-up Book, by Rod Campbell.

Doing the Animal Bop, by Jan Ormerod.

Dooby Dooby Moo, by Doreen Cronin. *Grades K—3. Duck, cows, sheep, pigs and Farmer Brown are a wild combination as they all compete in the talent show.*

Dora's Eggs, by Julie Sykes and pictures by Jane Chapman.

Down on the Funny Farm, by P.E. King.

Eating the Alphabet: Fruits and Vegetables from A to Z, by Lois Ehlert.

Egg Poems, by John Foster.

Farm Alphabet Book, by Jane Miller.

Farm Animals, Random House Picturebooks.

Farm Counting Book, by Jane Miller.

Farm Life, by Elizabeth Spurr. *Farmer Dan and children count things on the farm.*

The Farmer in the Dell (Traditional Songs), by Ann Owen.

Farmer Mack Measures His Pig, by Tony Johnston.

Farmyard Animals, by Staff, Sterling Publishing Company.

The Fresh Water Alphabet Book, by Jerry Pallotta.

The Frog Alphabet Book, by Jerry Pallotta.

The Furry Animal Alphabet Book, by Jerry Pallotta.

The Gardener, by Sarah Stewart.

Going to the Zoo, by Tom Paxton.

Here Come Poppy and Max, by Lindsey Gardiner. *Poppy and her dog: The two imitate animals. A great book to supplement a zoo theme.*

I Love Animals, by Flora McDonnell (Candlewick Press, 2001). *Preschool age, farm animals.*

The Icky Bug Alphabet Board Book, by Jerry Pallotta.

If Anything Ever Goes Wrong at the Zoo, by Mary Jean Hendrick.

If I Ran the Zoo, by Dr. Seuss.

Inside a Barn in the Country, by Alyssa Satin Capucilli.

The Lion Storyteller Book of Animal Tales, by Bob Hartman (Lion Children's Books, 2002). *A collection of animal tales from around the world; includes Aesop's fables, and others. Simple illustrations and stories.*

Little Zeng's ABC's, by Chris Acemandese Hall.

Missing Mittens, by Stuart J. Murphy. *Farmer and animals are missing mittens. Who took them?*

The Mitten, by Jan Brett (Putnam, 1990). *Nicely illustrated forest animals find and use a child's lost mitten. In the sequel, The Hat, a hedgehog wears a woolen stocking as a new hat. A Ukrainian folktale.*

The Mitten, retold by Jim Aylesworth (Scholastic Press, 2009). *A lost mitten becomes a home for too many animals. Cute illustrations and rhyming story line. Great dramatizations, puppet show story and picture discussions.*

Moo Baa La La La! by Sandra Boynton. *A board book.*

Mrs. Wishy-Washy's Farm, by Joy Cowley.

My Big Animal Book, by Roger Priddy.

My School's a Zoo! by Stu Smith (HarperCollins, 2004). *Imagination runs wild with animals you've never ever seen before! A cute rhyming story. Good story for first day of school.*

Night in the Country, by Cynthia Rylant and illustrated by Mary Szilagi.

Noah's Ark, Random House Picturebacks.

The Ocean Alphabet Board Book, by Jerry Pallotta.

Old MacDonald, by Amy Schwartz.

Old Macdonald Had a Farm, by Tiger Tales and Hannah Wood (2012).

Once in the Country: Poems of a Farm, by Tony Johnston.

One Two Three: An Animal Counting Book, by Marc Brown.

1, 2, 3 to the Zoo, by Eric Carle. *Come take a ride on a zoo train and have some math fun by counting all the animals you see.*

Over in the Meadow, by Ezra Jack Keats. *This traditional counting rhyme focuses on animals and their babies in their natural habitats.*

Over in the Meadow, by Olive A. Wadsworth and illustrated by Mary Maki Rae.

Over in the Meadow at the Big Ballet, by Lisa Shulman (Putnam's Sons, 2007). *A good story for girls aspiring to be ballet dancers. A twist to the old familiar song. Very busy illustrations; not for young children.*

Over on the Farm: A Counting Picture Book Rhyme, by Christopher Gunson.

A Pet for Me: Poems, by Lee B. Hopkins. *A collection of poems about friendship between children and their pets.*

Pet Show, by Ezra Jack Keats (Macmillan, 1972).

Put Me in the Zoo, by Robert Lopshire. *A strange large spotted animal discovers he really belongs in a circus, not the zoo.*

Richard Scarry's Find Your ABC'S, Random House Picturebacks.

Roar! A Noisey Counting Book, by Pamela D. Edwards.

Rock-a-Bye Farm, by Diane Johnston Hamm.

Sesame Street Animal Alphabet, from A to Z, Random House.

The Sesame Street Pet Show, by Emily Perl Kingsley (Western, 1980).

Silly Tilly, by Eileen Spinelli. *The barnyard animals go crazy.*

Tales from Aesop, Random House Picturebacks.

Ten Friends, by Bruce Goldstone. *If you could invite 10 friends to tea, who would they be? Counting fun as different animal combinations add up.*

That's Good! No, That's Bad!, by Margery Cuyler (Henry Holt). *A very cute story with great illustrations. Great for a jungle unit for young children. Recommended. Teachers, please read with good dramatization!*

The 3D Animal Alphabet Book, by Donald Ebert and Barbara Schwartz.

The Tiny, Tiny Boy and the Big, Big Cow, by Nancy VanLaan.

Today I Will Fly! by Mo Willems. *While Piggie is determined to fly, Elephant is skeptical. He needs some help from his friends.*

Turtle and Snake Go Camping, by Kate Spohn. *Turtle and Snake go camping, but are scared by a strange sound in the dark.*

'Twas the Day Before Zoo Day, by Catherine Ipcizade (Sylvan Dell Publishing). *In this clever adaptation of 'Twas the Night Before Christmas, all the animals are preparing for Zoo Day—they burp, they spit, and they act like animals. What will Zoo Day bring?*

Unwitting Wisdom, and Anthology of Aesop's Fables (Chronicle Books, 2004). *A collection of Aesop's fables, beautiful illustrations, very long and complicated text.*

Wake Up, Sun! by David L. Harrison (Random House, 1986). *The farm animals can't get the sun to wake up! But someone special can. Nice illustrations and cute, short story.*

What Do You Do with a Tail Like This? by Steve Jenkins. *Great information about the amazing eyes, ears, noses, and tails of our animal friends. Second grade level.*

What's New at the Zoo? An Animal Adding Adventure, by Suzanne Slade (Sylvan Dell,

2009). *A cute rhyming zoo animal addition book for young children; math learning activities at the back of the book.*

When Animals Are Babies, by Elizabeth and Charles Schwartz (Holiday House, 1964). *Beautifully drawn illustrations with easy-to-read text. A nice, simple explanation of baby animals and their lives. Names of baby animals are included at the end of the book.*

When Lulu Went to the Zoo, by Andy Ellis (Andersen Press, 2008). *Cartoon-style artwork, rhyming text, cute story. Lulu brings home some zoo animals.*

Who Took the Farmer's Hat? by Joan Nodset.

"Whooo's There?" by Mary Serfozo (Random House, 2007). *A cute rhyming story of forest creatures at night. Nice illustrations.*

Who's Been Here? A Tale in Tracks, by Fran Hodgkins. Follow the paws.

Wild Animals, World Book, 2008.

Wild Animals from Alligator to Zebra, Random House Picturebooks.

Wild Baby Animals, by Karen Wallace (Dorling Kindersley). Level 1 reader.

The Year at Maple Hill Farm, by Alice Provensen.

Movies and Television

Abbott and Costello (season 1, episode 26: Safari, 26 min.)

Animals Are Beautiful People

Babe

Back at the Barnyard

Barnyard

Cats and Dogs 1 and 2

Charlotte's Web

Garfield and Friends

Home on the Range

Homeward Bound 2

Lady and the Tramp

Madagascar

Tarzan

The Wild

• Section Three. Family Members •

45. FATHER/MAN

Father Activities

Songs to Sing and Play

Tune: Mary Had a Little Lamb

Words by Eunice Wright

Daddy loves me very much, very much, very much,
Daddy loves me very much, he hugs and kisses me.

I followed him to work one day, work one day, work one day,
I followed him to work one day, but then he sent me back.

Daddy told me to be good, to be good, to be good,
Daddy told me to be good, and stay home with mommy.

Why does my daddy love me so, love me so, love me so?
Why does my daddy love me so, he says I'm special!

Tune: Are You Sleeping?

Words by Eunice Wright

Dad-dy loves me,
Dad-dy loves me,
I love him,
I love him,
Every day he hugs me tight,
Then I know everything's all right,
I love him!
I love him!

Tune: Pop Goes the Weasel

Words by Eunice Wright

Every day when daddy comes home,
He stops and says hello.
He bends down low and gives me a kiss,
"Smooch," goes the kiss. (blow a kiss)

Tune: BINGO

Words by Eunice Wright

I know someone who loves me lots,
And this is what his name is:
D-A-D-D-Y, D-A-D-D-Y, D-A-D-D-Y,
And this is what his name is.

Father's Whiskers
(tune: 99 Bottles of Pop)

Original song: "Who Threw Mush in Grandpa's Whiskers?" Traditional obscure origins.

I have a dear old daddy,
For whom I nightly pray,
He has a set of whiskers
That are always in the way.

Chorus:
Oh, they're always in the way,
The cows eat them for hay,
They hide the dirt on Daddy's shirt,
They're always in the way.
Father had a strong back,
Now it's all caved in,
He stepped upon his whiskers
And walked up to his chin.

Chorus

Father has a daughter,
Her name is Ella Mae,
She climbs up father's whiskers
And braids them all the way.

Chorus

I have a dear old mother,
She likes the whiskers, too,
She uses them for dusting
And cleaning out the flue.

Chorus

Alternative:
We have a dear old father,
For whom we dearly pray,
He has a set of whiskers,
They're always in the way.

Chorus

Oh, they're always in the way
The cows eat them for hay,
They hide the dirt on Father's shirt,
They're always in the way.
We have a dear old mother,
With him at night she sleeps,

She wakes up in the morning,
Eating shredded wheat.

Chorus

We have a dear old brother,
He has a Ford machine,
He uses Father's whiskers
To strain the gasoline.

Chorus

We have a dear old sister,
It really is a laugh,
She sprinkles Father's whiskers,
As bath salt in her bath.

Chorus

Father has a son,
His name is Sonny Jim,
He wants to grow some whiskers,
But Father won't let him.

Chorus

Father has a daughter,
Her name is Ella Mae,
She climbs up Father's whiskers,
And braids them all the way.

Chorus

Around the supper table,
We make a merry group,
Until dear Father's whiskers
Get tangled in the soup.

Chorus

Father fought in Flanders,
He wasn't killed, you see;
His whiskers looked like bushes,
And fooled the enemy.

Chorus

When Father goes in swimming,
No bathing suit for him,
He ties his whiskers 'round his waist,
And gaily plunges in.

Chorus

Father went out sailing,
The wind blew down the mast;
He hoisted up his whiskers,
And never went so fast.

Chorus

When father goes a-fishing
No fishing line needs he
He throws his whiskers in the lake
And pulls out two or three.

Chorus

Tune: Twinkle, Twinkle Little Star

Words by Eunice Wright

Every day you hug me tight,
Then a kiss on my cheek light.
Daddy, daddy, I love you!
You're the best dad, it is true.

Lloyd George Knew My Father (tune: Onward Christian Soldiers)

For earlier versions of this song, see: Songs of the Ridings, *by F. W. Moorman, ed. Of Yorkshire Dialect Poems, 1918.*

Lloyd George knew my father, father knew Lloyd George, ... (repeat 6 times)

Other Songs

"Daddy," sung by Anne Murray.
"Fathers Are Forever," I Have a Song for You About Seasons and Holidays, by Janeen Brady, p. 35.
"I Walk and Talk with Father," by Gladys Pitcher, C.C. Birchard & Co.
"I'm So Glad When Daddy Comes Home," Words anon., Music: Frances K. Taylor, Arr. Copyright 1989.
"My Dad," by Janeen Jacobs Brady. National Music Publishers, 1975.
"My Dad," words and music by Carol Graff Gunn. Copyright 1957.

Poems and Nursery Rhymes

Father at Play

The Children's Book of Poetry, *illustrated by Henry T. Coates, 1879. By Hannah More Johnson.*

Such fun as we had one rainy day,
When father was home and helped us play,
And made a ship and hoisted sail,
And crossed the sea in a fearful gale!

But we hadn't sail'd into London town.
When captain, and crew, and vessel went down—
Down, down in a jolly wreck,
With the captain rolling under the deck.

But he broke out again with a lion's roar,
And we on two legs, he on four,
We ran out of the parlor, and up the stair,
And frightened mamma and the baby there.
So mamma said she would be p'liceman now,
And tried to 'rest us. She didn't know how!
Then the lion laughed, and forgot to roar,
Till we chased him out of the nursery door;

And then he turned to a pony gay,
And carried us all on his back away.
Whippity, lickity, kickity, ho!
If we hadn't fun, then I don't know!
Till we tumbled off, and he cantered on,
Never stopping to see if his load was gone.
And I couldn't tell any more than he
Which was Charlie and which was me,

Or which was Towser, for, all in a mix,
You'd think three people had turn'd to six,
Till Towser's tail had caught in a door;
And mamma came out the rumpus to quiet,
And told us a story to break up the riot.

Bandy Legs

The Real Mother Goose, *by Blanche Fisher Wright, 1916.*

As I was going to sell my eggs
I met a man with bandy legs,
Bandy legs and crooked toes;
I tripped up his heels, and he fell on his nose.

When I Was a Bachelor

The Real Mother Goose, *by Blanche Fisher Wright, 1916.*

When I was a bachelor I lived by myself,
And all the meat I got I put upon a shelf;
The rats and mice did lead me such a life
That I went to London to get myself a wife.

The streets were so broad and the lanes were so narrow,
I could not get my wife home without a wheel-barrow;
The wheel-barrow broke, my wife got a fall,
Down tumbled wheel-barrow, little wife, and all.

Books

Because Your Daddy Loves You, by Andrew Clements, 2009.
Daddies Give You Horsie Rides, by Abby Levine.
Daddy and Me, by Karen Katz.
The Daddy Book, by Todd Parr.
Daddy Goes to Work, by Jabari Asim.
Daddy Hugs, by Karen Katz, 2007.
Daddy Hugs 1 2 3, by Karen Katz.
The Father Who Had 10 Children, by Bénédicte Guettier.
Guess How Much I Love You, by Sam Mcbratney.
I Love My Daddy Because..., by Laurel Porter-Gaylord, 2004.
I Love You, Daddy, by Jillian Harker (Parragon, 2011).
Just Me and My Dad, by Mercer Mayer.
Mister Seahorse, by Eric Carle.
My Dad, by Anthony Browne.
My Daddy Is a Giant, by Carl Norac.
Papa Please Get the Moon for Me, by Eric Carle.
Pete's a Pizza, by William Steig.
Ten, Nine, Eight, by Molly Bang.
We're Going on a Bear Hunt, by Michael Rosen.

Movies and Television

Andy Griffith Show (TV series)
Are We Done Yet?
Are We There Yet?
The Brady Bunch
Father Knows Best (TV series)
Father of the Bride
It's a Wonderful Life
Jingle All the Way
Little House on the Prairie
Mary Poppins
Mr. Incredible
My Three Sons (TV series)
Nanny McPhee
Pursuit of Happyness
The Rifleman (TV series)
The Sound of Music
Superman
To Kill a Mockingbird
Touched by an Angel

46. MOTHER/WOMAN

Mother Activities

Songs to Sing and Play

Tune: Yankee Doodle

Words by Eunice Wright

When I grow up I want to be
A mother, it's true—
She works so very hard all day,
But that is nothing new.

A mother, I want to be one,
Mother, my dear.
Mother, I love you so!
Let's all help her right here.

Tune: London Bridge

Words by Eunice Wright

Mothers work very hard, very hard, very hard,
Mothers work very hard, all day long.

Other Songs

"Copying Mother," by Floy A. Rossman, C.C. Birchard & Co.
"Dearest Mother, I Love You," by Emily Yates.
"The First Bouquet," by Eleanor Smith, Milton-Bradley Co.
"I Help Mother with the Dishes," by Faith Chambers Wilson, Silver Burdett Co.
"I Want to Be a Mother," by Janeen Jacobs Brady, 1975. National Music Publishers.
"Mother and Father," by Mabel E. Bray, Silver Burdett Co.
"Mother Dear," by Mildred Tanner Pettit, Silver Burdett Co.
"Mother Needs Me," *I Have a Song for You About Seasons and Holidays*, by Janeen Brady, page 36.
"Mother's Day," by Von Flotow, C.C. Birchard & Co.
"When Mother Sews," by Gladys Pitcher, C.C. Birchard & Co.

Poems and Nursery Rhymes

There Was an Old Woman Who Lived in a Shoe (nursery rhyme)

There was an old woman who lived in a shoe,
She had so many children, she didn't know what to do.
She gave them some broth without any bread,
Then whipped them all soundly and sent them to bed.

Mother Dear, Where Are You Going?

Traditional. Can be read in two parts, with one person being "Mother" and the other being the child.

Mother dear, where are you going?
Tra la la, tra la la
Mother dear, where are you going?
Tra la la la la!

I am going to my garden
Tra la la, tra la la
I am going to my garden
Tra la la la la!

What shall you do in your garden?
Tra la la, tra la la
What shall you do in your garden?
Tra la la la la!

I shall pick a bunch of flowers.
Tra la la, tra la la
I shall pick a bunch of flowers.
Tra la la la la!

To whom will you give your flowers?
Tra la la, tra la la
To whom will you give your flowers?
Tra la la la la!

They are for my very best friend.
Tra la la, tra la la
They are for my very best friend.
Tra la la la la!

And who is your very best friend?
Tra la la, tra la la
And who is your very best friend?
Tra la la la la!

This is my very best friend.
Tra la la, tra la la
This is my very best friend.
Tra la la la la!

Old Mother Hubbard

See Dog (#10f) for entire poem.

Mother, May I Go Out to Swim?

Traditional

"Mother, may I go out to swim?
Out to swim, out to swim?
Mother, may I go out to swim?"
"Yes, my darling daughter.

Fold your clothes up neat and trim,
Neat and trim, neat and trim,
Fold your clothes up neat and trim,
But don't go near the water."

Games and Group Activities

Mother, May I?

One child is picked as the "Mother," who stands on one end of a room with her back turned to the other children. Across the room, the other children, in turn, ask Mother's permission to move forward. (Ex. "Mother, may I take five steps forward?") The Mother either gives permission ("Yes, you may [do the movement]") or answers in the negative ("No, you may not do that, but you may [insert another instruction]"). Possible movements include giant steps, baby steps, backward steps, hopping steps, twirling steps, crab steps, etc. The goal is to be the first to reach Mother and take her place.

Books

Anne of Green Gables, by L.M. Montgomery. *There are several books in this series.*
Are You My Mother? by P. D. Eastman.
The Cat in the Hat, by Dr. Seuss, 1957.
Clifford's Happy Mother's Day, by Norman Bridwell.
Hanging Out with Mom, by Sonia W. Black.
Jonathan and His Mommy, by Smalls.
Just Me and My Mom, by Mercer Mayer.
Mama, Do You Love Me? by Barbara M. Joosse.
Mommy Doesn't Know My Name, by Suzanne Williams.
The Night Before Mother's Day, by Natasha Wing.
On Mother's Lap, by Ann Herbert Scott (Board Book).
T. Rex and the Mother's Day Hug, by Lois G. Grambling.
We're Making Breakfast for Mother, by Shirley Neitzel.
What Mommies Do Best, by Laura Numeroff.

Movies and Television

Anne of Green Gables
The Brady Bunch
The Christmas Box, 1995
Dr. Quinn, Medicine Woman
Freaky Friday
The Incredibles
Little House on the Prairie
A Mom for Christmas, Disney, 1990
Mrs. Miniver (World War II)
The Parent Trap
Please Don't Eat the Daisies
The Sound of Music

47. Brother/Boy

48. SISTER/GIRL

Brother and Sister/Boy and Girl Activities

Songs to Sing and Play

"A Happy Family," by Moiselle Remstrom. Pioneer Music Press, Inc. (Jackman Music Corporation). ("I love sister, she loves me")

"How Many People Do You Love," by Janeen Brady, *I Have a Song for You About People and Nature*, 1979, Vol. 1, p. 13.

"I'm a V.I.P.," by Janeen Brady, *I Have a Song for You About People and Nature*, 1979, Vol. 1, p. 7.

"My Brother and I," by Janeen Brady, *I Have a Song for You About People and Nature*, 1979, Vol. 1, p. 16.

"No One Else Can Smile My Smile," by Janeen Brady, *I Have a Song for You About People and Nature*, 1979, Vol. 1, p. 9.

"One Little Girl," by Janeen Brady, *I Have a Song for You About People and Nature*, 1979, Vol. 1, p. 10.

"She's My Sister," by Janeen Brady, *I Have a Song for You About People and Nature*, 1979, Vol. 1, p. 18.

"Somebody Loves," by Janeen Brady, *I Have a Song for You About People and Nature*, 1979, Vol. 1, p. 16.

Poems and Nursery Rhymes

Jack Be Nimble

The Real Mother Goose, *by Blanche Fisher Wright, 1916.*

Jack be nimble, Jack be quick,
Jack jump over the candlestick.

Jack jumped high, Jack jumped low,
Jack jumped over and burned his toe.

Bobby Shaftoe

The Real Mother Goose, by Blanche Fisher Wright, 1916.

Bobby Shaftoe's gone to sea,
With silver buckles on his knee:
He'll come back and marry me,
Pretty Bobby Shaftoe!

Bobby Shaftoe's fat and fair,
Combing down his yellow hair;
He's my love for evermore,
Pretty Bobby Shaftoe.

The Bunch of Blue Ribbons

The Real Mother Goose, *by Blanche Fisher Wright, 1916.*

Oh, dear, what can the matter be?
Oh, dear, what can the matter be?
Oh, dear, what can the matter be?
Johnny's so long at the fair.

He promised he'd buy me a bunch of blue ribbons,
He promised he'd buy me a bunch of blue ribbons,
He promised he'd buy me a bunch of blue ribbons,
To tie up my bonny brown hair.

Bobby Snooks

The Real Mother Goose, *by Blanche Fisher Wright, 1916.*

Little Bobby Snooks was fond of his books,
And loved by his usher and master;
But naughty Jack Spry, he got a black eye,
And carries his nose in a plaster.

Blue Bell Boy

The Real Mother Goose, *by Blanche Fisher Wright, 1916.*

I had a little boy,
And called him Blue Bell;
Gave him a little work,
He did it very well.

I bade him go upstairs
To bring me a gold pin;
In coal scuttle fell he,
Up to his little chin.

He went to the garden
To pick a little sage;
He tumbled on his nose,
And fell into a rage.

He went to the cellar
To draw a little beer;
And quickly did return
To say there was none there.

Boy and Girl

The Real Mother Goose, *by Blanche Fisher Wright, 1916.*

There was a little boy and a little girl
Lived in an alley;
Says the little boy to the little girl,
"Shall I, oh, shall I?"
Says the little girl to the little boy,
"What shall we do?"
Says the little boy to the little girl,
"I will kiss you."

Girls and Boys

The Baby's Opera, *by Walter Crane, 1877.*

Girls and boys come out to play,
The moon doth shine as bright as day;
Leave your supper, and leave your sleep;
Come to your playfellows in the street;
Come with a whoop, and come with a call.
Come with a good will or not at all.
Up the ladder and down the wall,
A penny loaf will serve you all.

Boy and the Sparrow

The Real Mother Goose, *by Blanche Fisher Wright, 1916.*

A little cock-sparrow sat on a green tree,
And he chirruped, he chirruped, so merry was he;
A naughty boy came with his wee bow and arrow,
Determined to shoot this little cock-sparrow.
"This little cock-sparrow shall make me a stew,
And his giblets shall make me a little pie, too."
"Oh, no," says the sparrow "I won't make a stew."
So he flapped his wings and away he flew.

The Boy in the Barn

The Real Mother Goose, *by Blanche Fisher Wright, 1916. This poem can also be used for the Owl puppet.*

A little boy went, into a barn,
And lay down on some hay.
An owl came out, and flew about,
And the little boy ran away.

Little Fred

The Home Book of Verse, *by Burton Stevenson, 1872.*

When little Fred was called to bed,
He always acted right;
He kissed Mamma, and then Papa,
And wished them all good night.
He made no noise, like naughty boys,
But gently upstairs
Directly went, when he was sent,
And always said his prayer.

Bessy Bell and Mary Gray

The Real Mother Goose, *by Blanche Fisher Wright, 1916.*

Bessy Bell and Mary Gray,
They were two bonny lasses;
They built their house upon the lea,
And covered it with rushes.
Bessy kept the garden gate,
And Mary kept the pantry;
Bessy always had to wait,
While Mary lived in plenty.

Betty Blue

The Real Mother Goose, *by Blanche Fisher Wright, 1916.*

Little Betty Blue
Lost her holiday shoe;
What shall little Betty do?
Give her another
To match the other
And then she'll walk upon two.

Billy, Billy

The Real Mother Goose, *by Blanche Fisher Wright, 1916.*

"Billy, Billy, come and play,
While the sun shines bright as day."
"Yes, my Polly, so I will,
For I love to please you still."
"Billy, Billy, have you seen
Sam and Betsy on the green?"
"Yes, my Poll, I saw them pass,
Skipping o'er the new-mown grass."
"Billy, Billy, come along,
And I will sing a pretty song."

Diddle Diddle Dumpling

The Real Mother Goose, *by Blanche Fisher Wright, 1916.*

Diddle diddle dumpling, my son John
Went to bed with his breeches on,
One stocking off, and one stocking on;
Diddle diddle dumpling, my son John.

Dance to Your Daddie

The Real Mother Goose, *by Blanche Fisher Wright, 1916.*

Dance to your daddie,
My bonnie laddie;
Dance to your daddie, my bonnie lamb;
You shall get a fishy,
On a little dishy;
You shall get a fishy, when the boat comes
home.

Elizabeth

The Little Mother Goose, *by Jesse Wilcox Smith, 1918.*

Elizabeth, Elspeth, Betsy, and Bess,
They all went together to seek a bird's nest;
They found a bird's nest with five eggs in,
They all took one, and left four in.

Elsie Marley

The Little Mother Goose, *by Jesse Wilcox Smith, 1918.*

Elsie Marley's grown so fine,
She won't get up to feed the swine,
But lies in bed 'til eight or nine!
Lazy Elsie Marley.

Little Jack Horner

The Little Mother Goose, *by Jesse Wilcox Smith, 1918.*

Little Jack Horner
Sat in the corner,
Eating of Christmas pie:
He put in his thumb,
And pulled out a plum,
And said, "What a good boy am I!"

Little Polly Flinders

The Little Mother Goose, *by Jesse Wilcox Smith, 1918.*

Little Polly Flinders
Sat among the cinders
Warming her pretty little toes;
Her mother came and caught her,
Whipped her little daughter
For spoiling her nice new clothes.

Little Tom Tucker

The Little Mother Goose, *by Jesse Wilcox Smith, 1918.*

Little Tom Tucker
Sings for his supper.
What shall he eat?
White bread and butter.

How will he cut it
Without e'er a knife?
How will he be married
Without e'er a wife?

Pretty Little Dutch Girl

Oral Traditional Action Rhyme

I am a pretty little Dutch girl
As pretty as can be
And all the boys in the neighborhood
Are crazy over me. (Come chasing after me)

My boyfriend's name is Mello
He comes from the land of Jello.
With pickles for his toes and a cherry for his nose
And that's the way my story goes.

Alternate verses:
My boyfriend gave me peaches
My boyfriend gave me pears
My boyfriend gave me fifty cents
And kissed me on the stairs.

I gave him back his peaches
I gave him back his pears
I gave him back his fifty cents
And kicked him down the stairs!

Alternate verses:
I hate to do the dishes
I hate to do the chores
But I love to kiss my boyfriend
Behind the kitchen door.

One day while I was walking
I heard my boyfriend talking
To a pretty little girl
With a strawberry curl.

And this is what he said:
I L-O-V-E love you
All the T-I-M-E time.
And I will K-I-S-S kiss you
In the D-A-R-K dark.

Alternate verse:
...*And* I kicked him down the stairs.
With a pickle on his nose and three sore toes.
That's the way it goes.

Little Boy Blue

The Real Mother Goose, *by Blanche Fisher Wright, 1916. Use this poem also for the sheep or cow puppet.*

Little boy blue, come blow your horn,
The sheep's in the meadow,
The cow's in the corn.
Where is the little boy who looks after the sheep?
He's under the haystack, fast asleep.
Will you wake him? No, not I—
For if I do, he'll surely cry.

Natural History

The Baby's Opera, *by Walter Crane, 1877.*

What are little boys made of?
Frogs and snails and puppy-dog's tails,
And that's what little boys made of.

What are little girls made of?
Sugar and spice and all that's nice,
And that's what little girls made of.

What are young men made of?
Sighs and leers, and crocodile tears,
And that's what young men made of.

What are young women made of?
Ribbons and laces, and sweet pretty faces,
And that's what young women made of.

Georgie Porgie

The Real Mother Goose, *by Blanche Fisher Wright, 1916.*

Georgie Porgie, pudding and pie,
Kissed the girls and made them cry.
When the boys came out to play,
Georgie Porgie ran away.

Wee Willie Winkie

The Little Mother Goose, *by Jessie Willcox Smith, 1918.*

Wee Willie Winkie runs through the town,
Upstairs and downstairs in his nightgown.
Tapping at the window and crying through the lock,

Are all the children in their beds?
It's past 8 o'clock.

Monday's Child

The Real Mother Goose, *by Blanche Fisher Wright, 1916.*

Monday's child is fair of face,
Tuesday's child is full of grace.
Wednesday's child is full of woe,
Thursday's child has far to go.
Friday's child is loving and giving,
Saturday's child works hard for his living.
And the child that is born on the Sabbath
day
Is bonny and blithe, and good and gay.

Mary, Mary Quite Contrary

The Real Mother Goose, *by Blanche Fisher Wright, 1916.*

Mary, Mary, quite contrary,
How does your garden grow?
With silver bells and cockle shells,
And pretty maids all in a row.

Good Children

Struwwelpeter, Merry Stories and Funny Pictures, *by Heinrich Hoffman, 1848.*

When the children have been good,
That is, be it understood,
Good at meal-times, good at play,
Good all night and good all day—
They shall have the pretty things
Merry Christmas always brings.

One and One

The Home Book of Verse, *Vol. 1 (of 4) Author: Various. Editor: Burton Egbert Stevenson 1912, by John Hookham Frere [1769–1846]*

Two little girls are better than one,
Two little boys can double the fun,
Two little birds can build a fine nest,
Two little arms can love mother best.
Two little ponies must go to a span;
Two little pockets has my little man;
Two little eyes to open and close,
Two little ears and one little nose,
Two little elbows, dimpled and sweet,
Two little shoes on two little feet,
Two little lips and one little chin,
Two little cheeks with a rose shut in;
Two little shoulders, chubby and strong,
Two little legs running all day long.
Two little prayers does my darling say,
Twice does he kneel by my side each day,
Two little folded hands, soft and brown,
Two little eyelids cast meekly down,
And two little angels guard him in bed,
"One at the foot, and one at the head."

Shock-headed Peter

Struwwelpeter, Merry Stories and Funny Pictures, *by Heinrich Hoffman, 1848.*

Just look at him! there he stands,
With his nasty hair and hands.
See! his nails are never cut;
They are grimed as black as soot;
And the sloven, I declare,
Never once has combed his hair;
Anything to me is sweeter
Than to see Shock-headed Peter.

There Was a Young Lady

Nonsense Books, *by Edward Lear, 1894.*

There was a Young Lady of Hull,
Who was chased by a virulent Bull;
But she seized on a spade, and called out,
"Who's afraid?"
Which distracted that virulent Bull.

There was a Young Lady of Bute,
Who played on a silver-gilt flute;
She played several jigs to her Uncle's white
Pigs:
That amusing Young Lady of Bute.

Courting

The Volta Review, *edited by Josephine B. Timberlake, 1921.*

"The time I've lost in wooing,
In watching and pursuing

The light that lies
In women's eyes,
Has been my heart's undoing."

There Was a Little Girl

The Home Book of Verse, *Vol. 1 (of 4). Authors: Various. Editor: Burton Egbert Stevenson 1912, by Henry Wadsworth Longfellow [1807–1882]*

There was a little girl, who had a little curl
Right in the middle of her forehead,
And when she was good she was very, very good,
But when she was bad she was horrid.

She stood on her head, on her little trundle-bed,
With nobody by for to hinder;
She screamed and she squalled, she yelled and she bawled,
And drummed her little heels against the winder.

Her mother heard the noise, and thought it was the boys
Playing in the empty attic,
She rushed upstairs, and caught her unawares,
And spanked her, most emphatic.

Books

ABC I Like Me! by Nancy Carlson.
All Kinds of Children, by Norma Simon.
Children Make Terrible Pets, by Peter Brown. 2010. Series, Primary Grades.
The Chronicles of Narnia, by C.S. Lewis.
Did I Ever Tell You How Lucky You Are? by Dr. Seuss.
Girl of Mine, by Jabari Asim.
The Going to Bed Book, by Sandra Boynton, 1982.
The Horse and His Boy, by C.S. Lewis.
I Am Big Brother/I Am Big Sister, by Joanna Cole.
I Am Not Going to Get Up Today! by Dr. Seuss.
I Can, Can You? by Marjorie W. Pitzer.
I Like Me! by Nancy Carlson.
I Like Myself, by Karen Beaumont.
I'm a Big Brother, by Joanna Cole (HarperCollins).
I'm a Big Sister, by Joanna Cole (HarperCollins).
Marvelous Me: Inside and Out (All About Me), by Lisa Bullard.
My Book About Me, by Dr. Seuss.
My Friend Isabelle, by Eliza Woloson.
The Night Before Preschool, by Natasha Wing.
Papa, Please Get the Moon for Me, by Eric Carle.
A Rainbow of Friends, by P.K. Hallinan.
Susan Laughs, by Jeanne Willis.
Twenty and Ten, by Claire H. Bishop (Scholastic). *Twenty children hide 10 others from Nazis.*
What I Like About Me, by Allia Z. Nolan. Board Book.
Where the Wild Things Are, by Maurice Sendak, 1988.
Whoever You Are, by Mem Fox. Reading Rainbow.
Winnie the Pooh and Christopher Robin, by A.A. Milne, 1998.

Movies and Television

The Adventures of Shark Boy and Lava Girl (2005, Disney)
Agent Cody Banks
Alice in Wonderland
Annie
The Apple Dumpling Gang
The Brady Bunch
The Cat in the Hat
Dennis the Menace
Ernest Goes to Camp
The Ewok Adventures
Goonies
Heavyweights
Home Alone
Honey, We Shrunk the Kids
Hotel for Dogs
The Incredibles

Jupiter Jones
Lassie
Little House on the Prairie
Little Lies
The Little Rascals
Madeline, 1998
Mary Poppins
Matilda
Nancy Drew
Narnia movies
The Parent Trap
Peter Pan
Pollyanna
Race to Witch Mountain
Return to Witch Mountain
Rin Tin Tin
The Sandlot
The Secret Garden
Seven Alone
Shirley Temple films
The Sound of Music
The Spy Kids
The Sword in the Stone
The Three Investigators

49. BABY/YOUNG CHILD

Baby/Young Child Activities

Songs to Sing and Play

Miss Lucy Had a Baby (tune: Pretty Little Dutch Girl *or* Ninety Nine Bottles of Pop)

Traditional oral jump rope rhyme (derived from "Miss Polly Had a Dolly")

Miss Lucy had a baby,
She named it Tiny Tim,
She put him in the bathtub
To see if he could swim.

He drank up all the water,
He ate up all the soap,
He tried to eat the bathtub,
But it wouldn't go down his throat.

He floated up the river,
He floated down the lake.
And now Miss Lucy's baby
Has got a belly ache.

Miss Lucy called the Doctor,
Miss Lucy called the Nurse,
Miss Lucy called the lady
With the alligator purse.

"Measles," said the doctor,
"Mumps," said the nurse.
"A virus," said the lady with the alligator purse.

"Penicillin," said the doctor,
"Bed rest," said the nurse.
"Pizza," said the lady with the alligator purse.

"He'll live," said the doctor,
"He's all right," said the nurse.
"I'm leaving," said the lady with the alligator purse.

Miss Lucy slapped the doctor,
Miss Lucy smacked the nurse.
Miss Lucy thanked the lady with the alligator purse.

Hush-a-by baby

The Baby's Opera, *by Walter Crane, 1877. Has sheet music.*

Hush-a-by baby on the tree-top,
When the wind blows the cradle will rock;
When the bough breaks the cradle will fall—
Down comes baby, cradle and all!

Tune: There Were Ten in the Bed

American traditional. (See Wee Sing Silly Songs, *p. 35, for sheet music, and Supersimplelearning.com for animation and music.)*

There were 10 in the bed, (or—Five little babies in the bed)
And the little one said,
"Roll over, roll over."
So they all rolled over and one fell out.

There were 9 (four) in the bed,
And the little one said,
"Roll over, roll over."...

(Continue until there is one baby left.)

And the little one said, "Good Night!" *(spoken in a baby voice)* or "I'm Lonely!"

Tune: Happy Birthday to You

Traditional, obscure origins

Good morning to you, (or name)
Good morning to (you,)
Good morning dear (baby)
Good morning to (you.)

John Brown's Baby Had a Cold Upon His Chest (tune: Battle Hymn)

American Traditional, originated in 1800s. (See Wee Sing Silly Songs, *page 8 for the sheet music.)*

John Brown's baby had a cold upon his chest,
John Brown's baby had a cold upon his chest,
John Brown's baby had a cold upon his chest,
And they rubbed it with camphorated oil.

John Brown's _____ had a cold upon his chest,
John Brown's _____ had a cold upon his chest,
John Brown's _____ had a cold upon his chest,
And they rubbed it with camphorated oil.

John Brown's _____ had a _____ upon his chest,
John Brown's _____ had a _____ upon his chest,
John Brown's _____ had a _____ upon his chest,
And they rubbed it with camphorated oil.

John Brown's _____ had a _____ upon his _____,
John Brown's _____ had a _____ upon his _____,
John Brown's _____ had a _____ upon his _____,
And they rubbed it with camphorated oil.

John Brown's _____ had a _____ upon his _____,
John Brown's _____ had a _____ upon his _____,
John Brown's _____ had a _____ upon his _____,
And they _____ it with camphorated oil.

John Brown's _____ had a _____ upon his _____,
John Brown's _____ had a _____ upon his _____,
John Brown's _____ had a _____ upon his _____,
And they _____ it with _____ _____.

Motions: not done on verse 1 (do it when words are omitted, which are the hyphens).
ACTIONS:
Baby—rock baby in arms
Cold—sneeze
Chest—slap chest
Rubbed—rub chest
camphorated oil—hold nose and make a face

Poems and Nursery Rhymes

Hush Little Baby

The Real Mother Goose, *by Blanche Fisher Wright, 1916.*

Hush, little baby, don't say a word,
Mama's going to buy you a mockingbird.

If that mockingbird won't sing,
Mama's going to buy you a diamond ring.

If that diamond ring turns to brass,
Mama's going to buy you a looking glass.

If that looking glass gets broke,
Mama's going to buy you a billy goat.

If that billy goat won't pull,
Mama's going to buy you a cart and bull.

If that cart and bull turn over,
Mama's going to buy you a dog named Rover.

If that dog named Rover won't bark,
Mama's going to buy you a horse and cart.

If that horse and cart fall down,
You'll still be the sweetest little baby in town.

So hush little baby, don't you cry,
Daddy loves you and so do I.

Come to the Window

The Little Mother Goose, *by Jesse Wilcox Smith, 1918.*

Come to the window,
My baby, with me,
And look at the stars
That shine on the sea!
There are two little stars
That play bo-peep
With two little fish
Far down in the deep;
And two little frogs
Cry "Neap, neap, neap";
I see a dear baby
That should be asleep.

Cry Baby

The Real Mother Goose, *by Blanche Fisher Wright, 1916.*

Cry, baby, cry,
Put your finger in your eye,
And tell your mother it wasn't I.

Baby Dear, Goodnight

Little Max, *by Rudolf Geissler, 1869, p. 58.*

Baby dear, good night, good night,
Doggie lies in slumbers deep;
Hush-a-bye, my treasure bright,
Pussy, too, is fast asleep.
Don't you wake them! If you do,
Pups will bark, and Puss will mew.
Go to sleep, and never fear,
Mother will call when morning's near.

The Girl and the Birds

The Real Mother Goose, *by Blanche Fisher Wright, 1916.*

When I was a little girl, about seven years old,
I hadn't got a petticoat, to cover me from the cold.
So I went into Darlington, that pretty little town,
And there I bought a petticoat, a cloak, and a gown.
I went into the woods and built me a kirk,
And all the birds of the air, they helped me to work.
The hawk with his long claws pulled down the stone,
The dove with her rough bill brought me them home.
The parrot was the clergyman, the peacock was the clerk,
The bullfinch played the organ,—we made merry work.

For Baby

The Real Mother Goose, *by Blanche Fisher Wright, 1916.*

You shall have an apple,
You shall have a plum,
You shall have a rattle,
When papa comes home.

Bye Baby Bunting

The Real Mother Goose, *by Blanche Fisher Wright, 1916.*

Bye, baby bunting,
Father's gone a-hunting,
Mother's gone a-milking,
Sister's gone a-silking,
And brother's gone to buy a skin
To wrap the baby bunting in.

Baby Dolly

The Real Mother Goose, *by Blanche Fisher Wright, 1916.*

Hush, baby, my dolly, I pray you don't cry,
And I'll give you some bread, and some milk by-and-by;
Or perhaps you like custard, or, maybe, a tart,
Then to either you're welcome, with all my heart.

Dance, Little Baby

The Real Mother Goose, *by Blanche Fisher Wright, 1916.*

Dance, little Baby, dance up high!
Never mind, Baby, Mother is by.

Dance, little Baby, dance up high!
Never mind, Baby, Mother is by.

Crow and caper, caper and crow,
There, little Baby, there you go!

Up to the ceiling, down to the ground,
Backwards and forwards, round and round;

Dance, little Baby and Mother will sing,
With the merry coral, ding, ding, ding

Hush-A-Bye

The Real Mother Goose, by Blanche Fisher Wright, 1916.

Hush-a-bye, baby, lie still with thy daddy,
Thy mammy has gone to the mill,
To get some meal to bake a cake,
So pray, my dear baby, lie still.

Hush-A-Bye

The Real Mother Goose, by Blanche Fisher Wright, 1916.

Hush-a-bye, baby,
Daddy is near;
Mamma is a lady,
And that's very clear.

Five Little Fingers

Obscure origin

5 little fingers on this hand *(hold up 5 fingers)*
5 little fingers on that *(hold up 5 fingers on the other hand)*
A dear little nose *(point to nose)*
A mouth like a rose *(point to mouth)*
Two little cheeks so tiny and fat *(point to cheeks)*
Two eyes and two ears *(point to eyes and then ears)*
And ten little toes *(point to toes)*
That is the way the baby grows.

Baby's Fingers

Obscure origin

These are Baby's fingers
These are baby's toes,
This is baby's belly button,
Round and round it goes.

My Treasure

By Juli Wright

My baby, don't you cry,
I will give you wings to fly.
My baby, you are a pleasure,
My sacred little treasure.

Adorable from your little nose,
Straight down to your little toes.
Your gentle, tiny smile,
Makes everything worthwhile.

Now I hold your tiny hand,
As you try to walk and stand.
Sweet little dream with lovely curls,
You fill my life with everyday pearls.

Dance to Your Daddy

The Little Mother Goose, by Jesse Wilcox Smith, 1918.

Dance to your daddy,
My little babby;
Dance to your daddy, my little lamb.

You shall have a fishy,
In a little dishy;
You shall have a fishy
When the boat comes in.

Rock-A-Bye, Baby

Harry's Ladder to Learning, with Two Hundred and Thirty Illustrations. London: David Bogue and Joseph Cundall, 1850. Printed by G. Barclay.

Rock-a-bye, baby, thy cradle is green;
Father's a nobleman, mother's a queen;
And Betty's a lady, and wears a gold ring;
And Harry's a drummer, and drums for the king.

Hush-a-bye, baby, on the tree-top!
When the wind blows, the cradle will rock;
When the bough breaks, the cradle will fall,
Down will come baby, cradle, and all.

Bye, oh, my baby!
When I was a lady,
Oh then my poor babe didn't cry!
But my baby is weeping
For want of good keeping.
Oh, I fear my poor baby will die.

Hush-a-bye, babby, lie still with thy daddy;
Thy mammy is gone to the mill
To get some wheat, to make some meat,
So pray, my dear babby, lie still.

How many days has my baby to play?
Saturday, Sunday, Monday,
Tuesday, Wednesday, Thursday, Friday.
Saturday, Sunday, Monday.

Hush-a-bye, baby,
Daddy is near,
Mammy's a lady,
And that's very clear.

Dance to your daddy
My bonny laddy,
Dance to your ninny,
My sweet lamb;
You shall have a fishy
In a little dishy,
And a whirligiggy,
And some nice jam.

Dance, little baby, dance up high,
Never mind, baby, mother is nigh;
Crow and caper, caper and crow;
There, little baby, there you go,
Up to the ceiling, down to the ground,
Backwards and forwards, round and round;
Dance, little baby, and mother will sing,
With the merry coral, ding, ding, ding!

Here we go up, up, up,
And here we go down, down, downy,
And here we go backwards and forwards,
And here we go round, round, roundy.

All for Baby

Finger Plays for Nursery and Kindergarten, *by Emilie Poulsson, 1893. Sheet music and fingerplay actions.*

Here's a ball for Baby,
Big and soft and round!
Here is Baby's hammer—
O, how he can pound!

Here is Baby's music—
Clapping, clapping so!
Here are Baby's soldiers,
Standing in a row!

Here's the Baby's trumpet,
Toot-too-toot! too-too!
Here's the way that Baby
Plays at "Peep-a-boo!"

Here's a big umbrella—
Keeps the Baby dry!
Here's the Baby's cradle—
Rock-a-baby-by!

Baby-Land

The Home Book of Verse, *Vol. 1 (of 4). Author: Various. Editor: Burton Egbert Stevenson 1912, by George Cooper (1840–1927)*

"Which is the way to Baby-land?"
"Any one can tell;
Up one flight,
To your right;
Please to ring the bell."

"What can you see in Baby-land?"
"Little folks in white—
Downy heads,
Cradle-beds,
Faces pure and bright!"

"What do they do in Baby-land?"
"Dream and wake and play,
Laugh and crow,
Shout and grow;
Jolly times have they!"

"What do they say in Baby-land?"
"Why, the oddest things;
Might as well
Try to tell
What a birdie sings!"

"Who is the Queen of Baby-land?"
"Mother, kind and sweet;
And her love,
Born above,
Guides the little feet."

Baby's Breakfast

The Home Book of Verse, *Vol. 1 (of 4). Author: Various. Editor: Burton Egbert Stevenson 1912, by Emilie Poulsson*

Baby wants his breakfast,
Oh! what shall I do?
Said the cow, "I'll give him
Nice fresh milk—moo-oo!"

Said the hen, "Cut-dah cut!
I have laid an egg
For the Baby's breakfast—
Take it now, I beg!"

And the buzzing bee said,
"Here is honey sweet.
Don't you think the Baby
Would like that to eat?"

Then the baker kindly
Brought the Baby's bread.
"Breakfast is all ready,"
Baby's mother said;

"But before the Baby
Eats his dainty food,
Will he not say 'Thank you!'
To his friends so good?"

Then the bonny Baby
Laughed and laughed away.
That was all the "Thank you"
He knew how to say.

Babies

The Peter Patter Book of Nursery Rhymes, *by Leroy F. Jackson, 1918.*

Come to the land where the babies grow,
Like flowers in the green, green grass.
Tiny babes that swing and crow
Whenever the warm winds pass,
And laugh at their own bright eyes aglow
In a fairy looking-glass.

Come to the sea where the babies sail
In ships of shining pearl,
Borne to the west by a golden gale
Of sun-beams all awhirl;
And perhaps a baby brother will sail
To you, my little girl.

Knock at the Door

Love and Law in Child Training—A Book for Mothers, *by Emilie Poulsson, 1899. (Many more in this book: cute fingerplays to do with a baby).*

Knock at the door.
Peep in!
Lift up the latch,
And walk in!
Take a seat right down there!"

Kicking Song

Love and Law in Child Training—A Book for Mothers, *by Emilie Poulsson, 1899.*

Kick, little Baby,
Kick and grow strong
Press against Mother,
List to her song.
Such a strong baby
How his legs go!
That's the way, Baby,
Stronger to grow.
Kicking and tossing
Up and then down,
Soon shall my baby
Trot through the town.
ALL GONE!
All gone! All gone!
Where did the good supper go?

All gone! All gone!
Gone to help Babykin grow.

Here in his face all so rosy and sweet,
Here in his arms and his hands and his feet
Here from the top of his head to his toes,
This is where Babykin's good supper goes.

All gone! All gone!
Where did the good supper go?

Baby Mine

Marigold Garden, *by Kate Greenaway, 1885.*

Baby mine, over the trees;
Baby mine, over the flowers;
Baby mine, over the sunshine;
Baby mine, over the showers.

Baby mine, over the land;
Baby mine, over the water.
Oh, when had a mother before
Such a sweet—such a sweet, little daughter!

Baby

The Home Book of Verse, *Vol. 1 (of 4). Editor: Burton Egbert Stevenson, 1912, by George Macdonald. From "At the Back of the North Wind"*

Where did you come from, baby dear?
Out of the everywhere into the here.

Where did you get those eyes so blue?
Out of the sky as I came through.

What makes the light in them sparkle and spin?
Some of the starry spikes left in.

Where did you get that little tear?
I found it waiting when I got here.

What makes your forehead so smooth and high?
A soft hand stroked it as I went by.

What makes your cheek like a warm white rose?
I saw something better than any one knows.

Whence that three-cornered smile of bliss?
Three angels gave me at once a kiss.

Where did you get this pearly ear?
God spoke, and it came out to hear.

Where did you get those arms and hands?
Love made itself into bonds and bands.

Feet, where did you come, you darling things?
From the same box as the cherubs' wings.

How did they all just come to be you?
God thought about me, and so I grew.

But how did you come to us, you dear?
God thought about you, and so I am here.

Rock-a-bye, Baby

The Home Book of Verse, *Vol. 1 (of 4). Author: Various. Editor: Burton Egbert Stevenson, 1912.*

Rock-a-bye, baby, thy cradle is green;
Father's a nobleman, mother's a queen;
And Betty's a lady, and wears a gold ring;
And Johnny's a drummer, and drums for the King.
Hush-a-bye, baby, on the tree-top,
When the wind blows the cradle will rock;
When the bough breaks, the cradle will fall,
Down will come baby, bough, cradle, and all.

Baby at Play

The Home Book of Verse, *Vol. 1 (of 4). Author: Various. Editor: Burton Egbert Stevenson, 1912.*

Brow bender, Eye peeper,
Nose smeller, Mouth eater,
Chin chopper,
Knock at the door—peep in,
Lift up the latch—walk in.

Here sits the Lord Mayor, here sit his two men,
Here sits the cock, and here sits the hen;
Here sit the chickens, and here they go in,
Chippety, chippety, chippety, chin.

The Difference

The Home Book of Verse, *Vol. 1 (of 4). Author: Various. Editor: Burton Egbert Stevenson, 1912, by Laura E. Richards [1850–1943]*

Eight fingers,
Ten toes,
Two eyes,
And one nose.
Baby said
When she smelt the rose,
"Oh! what a pity
I've only one nose!"

Ten teeth
In even rows,
Three dimples,
And one nose.
Baby said
When she smelt the stuff,
"Deary me!
One nose is enough."

Foot Soldiers

The Home Book of Verse, *Vol. 1 (of 4). Author: Various. Editor: Burton Egbert Stevenson 1912, by John Banister Tabb (1845–1909)*

'Tis all the way to Toe-town,
Beyond the Knee-high hill,
That Baby has to travel down
To see the soldiers drill.

One, two, three, four, five, a-row—
A captain and his men—
And on the other side, you know,
Are six, seven, eight, nine, ten.

Trot, Trot!

The Home Book of Verse, *Vol. 1 (of 4). Author: Various. Editor: Burton Egbert Stevenson, 1912, by Mary F. Butts (1836–1902)*

Every evening Baby goes
Trot, trot, to town,
Across the river, through the fields,
Up hill and down.

Trot, trot, the Baby goes,
Up hill and down,
To buy a feather for her hat,
To buy a woolen gown.

Trot, trot, the Baby goes;
The birds fly down, alack!
"You cannot have our feathers, dear,"
They say, "so please trot back."

Trot, trot, the Baby goes;
The lambs come bleating near.
"You cannot have our wool," they say,
"But we are sorry, dear."

Trot, trot, the Baby goes,
Trot, trot, to town;
She buys a red rose for her hat,
She buys a cotton gown.

Only a Baby Small

The Home Book of Verse, *Vol. 1 (of 4). Author: Various. Editor: Burton Egbert Stevenson 1912, by Matthias Barr*

Only a baby small,
Dropped from the skies,
Only a laughing face,
Two sunny eyes;
Only two cherry lips,
One chubby nose;
Only two little hands,
Ten little toes.

Only a golden head,
Curly and soft;
Only a tongue that wags
Loudly and oft;
Only a little brain,
Empty of thought;
Only a little heart,
Troubled with naught.

Only a tender flower
Sent us to rear;
Only a life to love
While we are here;
Only a baby small,
Never at rest;
Small, but how dear to us,
God knoweth best.

Counting Baby's Toes

The Children's Book of Poetry, by Henry T. Coates, 1879.

Dear little bare feet,
Dimpled and white,
In your long night-gown
Wrapped for the night,
Come, let me count all
Your queer little toes,
Pink as the heart
Of a shell or a rose.

One is a lady
That sits in the sun;
Two is a baby,
And three is a nun;
Four is a lily
With innocent breast;
And five is a birdie
Asleep on her nest.

My Little Sister

The Children's Book of Poetry, by Henry T. Coates, 1879. (This is an excerpt. See book for rest of poem, p. 37.)

I have a little sister,
She's only two years old
But she's a little darling,
And worth her weight in gold.

She often runs to kiss me
When I'm at work or play,
Twining her arms about me
In such a pretty way;

And then she'll say so sweetly,
In innocence and joy,
"Tell me a story, sister dear,
About the little boy."

Poems by Evaleen Stein

"Sleepy Time"
"Baby's Baking"

Books

A You're Adorable, by Buddy Kaye (Candlewick Press, 1996).
Are You My Mother?, by P.D. Eastman (Random House, 1986).
Babies, by Rachel Isadora.
Baby Baby Blah Blah Blah!, by Jonathan Shipton (Holiday House, 2009). *Very basic large child-like illustrations. An only child learns there will be a new baby in the family.*
Baby Born, by Anastasia Suen (Lee & Low, 1999).
Baby Dance, by Ann Taylor.
Baby High, Baby Low, by Stella Blackstone. *Groups of loving parents and their babies demonstrate opposites. Teaches patterns, sequences.*
Baby Says, by John Steptoe.
A Baby Sister for Frances, by Russell Hoban and illustrated by Lillian Hoban.
Baby's Catalogue, by Janet and Allan Ahlberg.
The Baby's Lap Book, by Kay Chorao (Dutton, 1991).
The Bad Babies Counting Book, by Tony Bradman.
Big Boy, Little Boy, by Betty Jo Stanovich and illustrated by Virginia Wright-Frierson.
Big Sister Now, by Annette Sheldon (Magination Press, 2006). *Cute short story, good preschool book. "New baby" notes to parents.*
Daddy's Lullaby, by Tony Bradman (McElderry, 2002).
Everywhere Babies, by Susan Meyers (HMH, 2004). *Rhyming preschool book, cute illustrations and text.*
Global Babies, by The Global Fund for Children.
Good Babies: A Tale of Trolls, Humans, a Witch, and a Switch, by Tim Meyers (Candlewick Press, 2005). *A troll baby living with humans and a human baby living with trolls have been switched by a witch. Good illustrations, long text.*
Goodnight, Moon, by Margaret Wise Brown (Harper, 1947).
Hello, Baby, by Lizzy Rockwell (Dragonfly, 2000).
Here Come the Babies, by Catherine and Laurence Anholt.
How Do You Make a Baby Smile? by Philemon Sturges (Harper Collins, 2007). *A very basic text, for very young children. Short lines, cute story involving animals and their young. Big sisters make baby smile. Nice large illustrations.*
Hush Little Baby, by Sylvia Long.
Hush, Little Baby: A Folk Song with Pictures, by Marla Frazee.
I Kissed the Baby! by Mary Murphy (Candlewick Press, 2003).
Love Song for a Baby, by Marion Dane Bauer (Simon & Schuster, 2002).
More, More, More, Said the Baby, by Vera B. Williams (Greenwillow, 1990).
The New Baby, by Mercer Mayer (Grossman).
Oh My Baby, Little One, by Kathi Appelt.

Peek-A-Boo, by Roberta G. Intrater (Cartwheel Books, 1997).
Please, Baby, Please, by Spike Lee.
She Come Bringing Me That Little Baby Girl, by Eloise Greenfield and illustrated by John Steptoe.
10 in the Bed, by Penny Dale.
We Have a Baby, by Cathryn Falwell.
When You Were a Baby, by Ann Jonas.
Where Is Baby's Belly Button? by Karen Katz (Little Simon, 2000).
Whose Baby? by Masayuki Yabuuchi.

Movies and Television

Babies eating lemons for the first time (YouTube)
Baby Einstein videos
Baby Geniuses
Baby's Day Out
Bath time fun (YouTube)
Bewitched
Bugs Bunny and the disguised robber baby (Looney Tunes)
The Good Witch's Charm
The Labyrinth
Sky High
Tom and Jerry (save the baby, and babysit)
Top Ten funny baby videos—YouTube
Willow

50. Grandmother/Old Woman

Copy this pattern at 111%

51. GRANDFATHER/OLD MAN

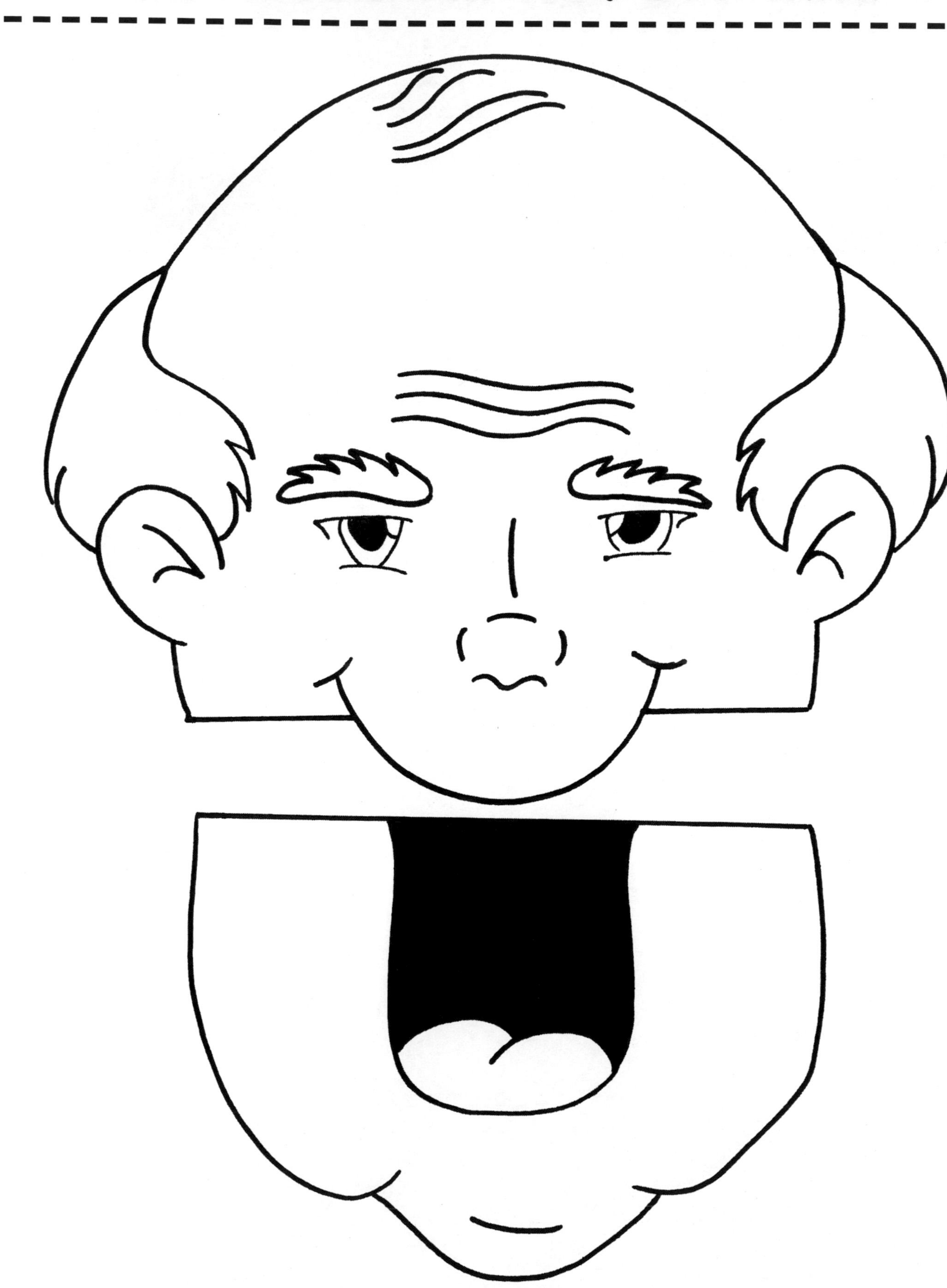

Grandmother and Grandfather Activities

Songs to Sing and Play

I Know an Old Lady Who Swallowed a Fly

Traditional folk song lyrics; adapted by Jack Hartmann. This song is available on Jack Hartmann's Rhymin' to the Beat, Volume 2.

I know an old lady who swallowed a fly
I don't know why she swallowed a fly
Oh, my, my!!

I know an old lady who swallowed a spider
That giggled and tickled inside her
She swallowed a spider to catch a fly
But I don't know why she swallowed the fly
Oh my, my!!

I know an old woman who swallowed a cat
Now fancy that, to swallow a cat!
She swallowed the cat to catch the bird
She swallowed the bird to catch the spider
She swallowed the spider to catch the fly
But I don't know why she swallowed the fly
Oh my, my!

I know an old lady who swallowed a dog...

I know an old lady who swallowed a cow...

I know an old lady who swallowed a horse
And that's the last thing she swallowed, of course!

Tune: Take Me Out to the Ball Game

Words by Eunice Wright

Let's go see our grandpar-ents,
It's time for a visit with them.
We haven't been there in the longest time,
We miss them and I guess they miss us,
So, we want to thank our grandparents
For all the things that they do.
So it's time ... to ... say you're the best,
And that we ... love ... you!

My Grandfather's Clock

By Henry Clay Work, 1876

My grandfather's clock
Was too large for the shelf,
So it stood ninety years on the floor;
It was taller by half
Than the old man himself,
Though it weighed not a pennyweight more.
It was bought on the morn
Of the day that he was born,
It was always his treasure and pride;

Chorus:
But it stopped short
Never to go again,
When the old man died.
Ninety years without slumbering,
Tick, tock, tick, tock,
His life seconds numbering,
Tick, tock, tick, tock,
It stopped short
Never to go again,
When the old man died.

In watching its pendulum
Swing to and fro,
Many hours had he spent while a boy;
And in childhood and manhood
The clock seemed to know,
And share both his grief and his joy.
And it struck twenty-four
When he entered at the door,
With a blooming and beautiful bride.

Chorus

My grandfather said
That of those he could hire,
Not a servant so faithful he found;
For it wasted no time,
And had but one desire,
At the close of each week to be wound.
And it kept in its place,
Not a frown upon its face,
And its hand never hung by its side.

Chorus

It rang an alarm
In the dead of the night,
An alarm that for years had been dumb;
And we knew that his spirit
Was pluming his flight,
That his hour of departure had come.
Still the clock kept the time,
With a soft and muffled chime,
As we silently stood by his side.

Chorus

Other Songs

"Grandma Got Run Over by a Reindeer," by Randy Brooks, 1979.
"Grandma's Feather Bed" (by Jim Connor); sung by John Denver. (The Muppets and John Denver sing a great version of this song.)
"Grandma's Patchwork Quilt," by Phil Rosenthal. Songsforteaching.com
"Grandmother," by Nonie Nelson Sorenson, 1989.
"Grandmother's Old Fashioned Garden," by Mildred T. Pettit, p. 191. *The Children Sing*, Deseret Book Co., 1951.
"I Know an Old Lady Who Swallowed a Pie," by Allison Jackson.
"I Love My Grandpa," *I Have a Song for You About People and Nature*, by Janeen Brady, p. 20.
"Oh, Grandpa," words and music by Pat Kelsey Graham, 1980.
"Old Folks at Home," by Stephen Foster, 1851.
"Old MacDonald Had a Farm." Traditional folk song.
"Over the River and Through the Woods," by Lydia Maria Child, 1844.
"Thank Goodness for Grandmas," by Janeen Jacobs Brady, 1978.
"This Old Man, he played one..." (see dog puppet activities for song).
"We Are Going to Grandma's House," *I Have a Song for You About People and Nature*, Vol. 1, by Janeen Brady, p. 19.
"When Grandpa (Grandma) Comes," by Marian Major, 1959.

Poems and Nursery Rhymes

Grandpa Dropped His Glasses

By Leroy F. Jackson, 1918

Make purple glasses by gluing purple cellophane in the lenses or coloring the lenses purple.

Grandpa dropped his glasses once
In a pot of dye,
And when he put them on again
He saw a purple sky.
Purple fires were rising up
From a purple hill,
Men were grinding purple cider
At a purple mill.
Purple Adeline was playing
With a purple doll;
Little purple dragon flies
Were crawling up the wall.
And at the supper-table
He got crazy as a loon
From eating purple apple dumplings
With a purple spoon.

Grandpapa's Spectacles

The Children's Book of Poetry, *illustrated by Henry T. Coates, 1879; by Elizabeth Sill.*

Grandpapa's spectacles cannot be found;
He has searched all the rooms, high and low, round and round;
Now he calls to the young ones, and what does he say?
"Ten cents for the child who will find them to-day."

Then Henry and Nelly and Edward all ran,
And a most thorough hunt for the glasses began,
And dear little Nell, in her generous way,
Said, "I'll look for them, grandpa, without any pay."

All through the big book she searches with care.

That lies on the table by grandpapa's chair;
They feel in his pockets, they peep in his hat,
They pull out the sofa, they shake out the mat.

Then down on all-fours, like two good natured bears,
Go Harry and Ned under tables and chairs,
Till, quite out of breath, Ned is heard to declare
He believes that those glasses are not any-where.

But Nelly, who, leaning on grandpapa's knee,
Was thinking most earnestly where they could be,
Looked suddenly up in the kind, faded eyes,
And her own shining brown ones grew big with surprise.

She clapped both her hands—all her dimples came out,—
She turned to the boys with a bright, rogu-ish shout:
"You may leave off your looking, both Harry and Ned,
For there are the glasses on grandpapa's head!"

Grandmother's Glasses

Obscure origins, finger-play

Use glasses, hats, and moving puppet arms for the grandmother. Adjust puppet pattern as necessary. Recite this first verse of the chant in a high-pitched voice:

These are Grandma's glasses. *(Put "glasses" over eyes or point to glasses.)*
This is Grandma's hat. *(Point to or place hat on head.)*
And this is the way she folds her hands.
And lays them in her lap.

Recite this second verse in a deep, low voice:

These are Grandpa's glasses. *(Put "glasses" over eyes.)*
This is Grandpa's hat. *(Place hat on head.)*
And this is the way he folds his arms.
And takes a little nap.

Grandmother Grundy

The Peter Patter Book of Nursery Rhymes, *by Leroy F. Jackson, 1918.*

O Grandmother Grundy,
Now what would you say
If the katydids carried
Your glasses away—

Carried them off
To the top of the sky
And used them to watch
The eclipses go by?

The Old Woman Who Lived in a Shoe

The Real Mother Goose, *by Blanche Fisher Wright, 1916.*

There was an old woman who lived in a shoe
She had so many children she didn't know what to do.
She gave them some broth and a big slice of bread
Kissed them all soundly and tucked them in bed.

The Old Woman Tossed Up in a Basket

The Real Mother Goose, *by Blanche Fisher Wright, 1916.*

There was an old woman
Tossed up in a basket
Seventeen times as high as the moon.
Where she was going
I just had to ask it,
For in her hand she carried a broom.

"Old woman, old woman,
Old woman," said I,
"Please tell me, please tell me,
Why you're up so high?"
"I'm sweeping the cobwebs
Down from the sky,
And I'll be with you
By and by."

Alternate:
Harry's Ladder to Learning, with Two Hundred and Thirty Illustrations, by David Bogue and Joseph Cundall, 1850.

There was an old woman went up in a basket,
Seventy times as high as the moon;
What she did there I could not but ask it,
For in her hand she carried a broom.
Old woman, old woman, old woman," said I,
Whither, oh whither, oh whither, so high?"
To sweep the cobwebs from the sky,
And I shall be back again by and by."

The Old Woman's Pie

Chinese Mother Goose Rhymes, *by Isaac Taylor, 1900.*

There was an old woman,
As I have heard tell
She went to sell pie,
But her pie would not sell.

She hurried back home,
But her doorstep was high,
She stumbled and fell,
And a dog ate her pie.

The Crooked Sixpence

The Real Mother Goose, *by Blanche Fisher Wright, 1916.*

There was a crooked man, and he went a crooked mile,
He found a crooked sixpence beside a crooked stile;
He bought a crooked cat, which caught a crooked mouse,
And they all lived together in a little crooked house.

Old Woman

The Real Mother Goose, *by Blanche Fisher Wright, 1916.*

"Old Woman, old woman, shall we go a-shearing?"
"Speak a little louder, sir, I am very thick o' hearing."
"Old woman, old woman, shall I kiss you dearly?"
"Thank you, kind sir, I hear you very clearly."

The Old Man in Leather

The Baby's Opera, *by Walter Crane, 1877. Has Sheet music.*

One misty, moisty morning, when cloudy was the weather,
There I met an old man clothed all in leather, clothed all in leather,
With cap under his chin,
How do you do, how do you do, how do you do, again, again.

Grandpa Feeds Baby

Chinese Mother Goose Rhymes, *by Isaac Taylor, 1900.*

Grandpa holds the baby,
He's sitting on his knee
Eating mutton dumplings
With vinegar and tea.
Then grandpa says to baby,
"When you have had enough,
You'll be a saucy baby
And treat your grandpa rough."

There Was an Old Man with a Beard

Nonsense Books, *by Edward Lear, 1894.*

There was an old man with a beard,
Who said, "It is just as I feared!
Two owls and a hen, four larks and a wren,
Have all built their nests in my beard!"

There was an old man who said, "Hush!
I perceive a young bird in this bush!"
When they said, "Is it small?" he replied, "not at all;
It is four times as big as the bush!"

There was an old man with a beard,
Who sat on a horse when he reared;
But they said, "Never mind! You will fall off behind,
You propitious old man with a beard!"

There was an old man who said, "How
Shall I flee from this horrible cow?
I will sit on this stile, and continue to
smile,
Which may soften the heart of that cow."

There was an old person whose habits
Induced him to feed upon rabbits;
When he'd eaten eighteen, he turned perfectly green,
Upon which he relinquished those habits.

There was an old man of Whitehaven,
Who danced a quadrille with a raven;
But they said, "It's absurd to encourage
this bird!"
So they lashed that old man of Whitehaven.

There was an old man of Peru.
Who never knew what he should do;
So he tore off his hair, and behaved like a
bear,
That intrinsic old man of Peru.

Going to See Grandmamma

Marigold Garden, *by Kate Greenaway (1846–1901)*

Little Molly and Damon
Are walking so far,
For they're going to see
Their kind Grandmamma.

And they very well know,
When they get there she'll take
From out of her cupboard
Some very nice cake.

And into her garden
They know they may run,
And pick some red currants,
And have lots of fun.

So Damon to doggie
Says, "How do you do?"
And asks his mamma
If he may not go too.

Games and Group Activities

My Grandfather's Clock

Use with "My Grandfather's Clock" song. Help children make clocks to tell the time. Show clocks with different times and different types of clocks. Let the children listen to a ticking clock and chimes.

To Grandma's House We Go!

A board game designed especially for grandparents to play with grandchildren to have fun, bond and enjoy being together. (Match shapes, recognize colors, refine social skills, think creatively.)

Books

All My Bad Habits I Learned from Grandpa, by Laurel Burnvoll, 2007.
All My Good Habits I Learned from Grandma, by Laurel Brunvoll, 2007.
Big Mama's, by Donald Crews. *Ages 3–6.*
Cherries and Lullabies, by Lynn Reiser. *Ages 3–6.*
Georgie Lee, by Sharon Denslow. *Ages 6–9.*
The Grandads' Book: For the Grandad Who's Best at Everything, by John Gribble.
The Grandma Book, by Todd Parr, 2006.
A Grandma Is a Gift from God, by Emilie Barnes, 2004.
Grandma's Smile, by Randy Siegel.
Grandma's Wedding Album, by Harriet Aiefert. *Ages 5–8.*
Grandpa and Bo, by Kevin Henkes, 1986.
Grandpa Green, by Lane Smith.
A Grandparents Book: Answers to a Grandchild's Questions, by Milton Kamen, 1995.
The Grannies' Book: For the Granny Who's Best at Everything, by Alison Maloney. *Good advice for new or old grandparents.*
Gus and Grandpa at Basketball, by Claudia Mills. *Ages 6–9.*
The Hello, Goodbye Window, by Norton Juster and Chris Raschka, 2005.

Henry and Mudge and the Great Grandpas, by Cynthia Rowland, 2006.
Here Comes Grandma, by Janet Lord, 2005.
I Love Saturdays y Domingos, by Alma Flor Ada. *Ages 3–6.*
I Unpacked My Grandmother's Trunk, by Susan Hoguet.
Lily's Garden, by Deborah Ray. *Ages 6–9.*
Little Critter: Grandma, Grandpa, and Me, by Mercer Mayer.
Lots of Grandparents, by Shelly Rotner. *Ages 3–6.*
Me with You, by Kristy Dempsey, 2009.
The Moon Ring, by Randy DuBurke. *Ages 6–9.*
More, More, More Said the Baby, by Vera Williams. *Ages 0–3.*
My Grandma and I, by P.K. Hallinan. A Board Book, 2002.
Off to School, Baby Duck!, by Amy Hest, 2007.
Old MacDonald, by Rosemary Wells.
Old MacDonald Had a Farm (Classic Books with Holes), by Pam Adams.
Over the River—A Turkey's Tale, by Derek Anderson, 2005.
Precautionary Tales for Grandparents, by James Muirden. *Belloc poetry.*
Show Some Respect, by Jan and Mike Berenstain. *Ages 4–7.*
Song and Dance Man, by Karen Ackerman, 1988. *Ages 3–6.*
There Was an Old Lady (Classic Books with Holes), by Pam Adams.
This Old Man (Classic Books with Holes), by Pam Adams.
Visiting Day, by Jacqueline Woodson. *Ages 6–9.*
What My Grandma Means to Say, by JC Sulzenko. *Grades 4–6. Addresses Alzheimer's.*
Where Is Coco Going? by Sloane Tanen, 2004.
Your Mommy Was Just Like You, by Kelly Bennett. *Ages 3–5.*
You're Going to Be a Grandma! by Deborah Zupancic. *A keepsake book.*

Movies and Television

The Addams Family
Ben 10 (animated series—Grandfather character)
Come Away Home
Dr. Quinn, Medicine Woman
Dolphin Tale (Grandfather)
Generation Gap (Grandfather)
Grandma Got Run Over by a Reindeer
A Grandpa for Christmas
Heidi (lives with grandfather)
Homecoming (grandmother)
Hoodwinked (Grandmother)
In Her Shoes (Grandmother)
Little House on the Prairie
Little Red Riding Hood (she takes grandmother a treat)
Looney Tunes (Tweety and Grandma)
Meet Me in St. Louis (Grandfather)
Meet My Mom (a soldier love story)
The Munsters
Pocahontas (Grandmother tree)
The Princess Bride (Grandfather)
The Princess Diaries (Grandmother)
Three Ninjas (Grandfather)
To Grandmother's House We Go, starring the Olsen twins.
Whale Rider (Grandfather)
Willy Wonka and the Chocolate Factory
Witches (boy lives with grandmother)

Additional Activities

Songs to Sing and Play

Tune: Oh, Do You Know the Muffin Man?

Words by Eunice Wright

Oh do you know the Muffin Man, (animal, person)
The Muffin Man, the Muffin Man,
Oh do you know the Muffin Man,
Who lives in Drury Lane? (the zoo, on the farm, works in the hospital)

Oh yes, I know the Muffin Man,
The Muffin Man, Muffin Man,
Oh do you know the Muffin Man,
Who lives in Drury Lane? *(Replace with appropriate word)*

Tune: Pop, Goes the Weasel (add animals)

Words by Eunice Wright

All around the barnyard,
The farmer chased the ______ (chicken).
The ______ (chicken) thought 'twas all in fun.
("Squawk,") goes the ______ (chicken).

Poems and Nursery Rhymes

Comical Folk

The Real Mother Goose, *by Blanche Fisher Wright, 1916.*

In a cottage in Fife
Lived a man and his wife
Who, believe me, were comical folk;
For, to people's surprise,
They both saw with their eyes,
And their tongues moved whenever they spoke!
When they were asleep,
I'm told, that to keep
Their eyes open they could not contrive;
They both walked on their feet,
And 'twas thought what they eat
Helped, with drinking, to keep, them alive!

The Dusty Miller

The Real Mother Goose, *by Blanche Fisher Wright, 1916.*

Margaret wrote a letter,
Sealed it with her finger,
Threw it in the dam
For the dusty miller.
Dusty was his coat,
Dusty was the siller,
Dusty was the kiss
I'd from the dusty miller.
If I had my pockets
Full of gold and silver,
I would give it all
To my dusty miller.

Fingers and Toes

The Real Mother Goose, *by Blanche Fisher Wright, 1916.*

Every lady in this land
Has twenty nails, upon each hand
Five, and twenty on hands and feet:
All this is true, without deceit.

The First of May

The Real Mother Goose, *by Blanche Fisher Wright, 1916.*

The fair maid who, the first of May,
Goes to the fields at break of day,
And washes in dew from the hawthorn-tree,
Will ever after handsome be.

The Greedy Man

The Little Mother Goose, *by Jesse Wilcox Smith, 1918.*

The greedy man is he who sits
And bites bits out of plates,
Or else takes up an almanac
And gobbles all the dates.

The Girl in the Lane

The Little Mother Goose, *by Jesse Wilcox Smith, 1918.*

The girl in the lane, that couldn't speak
plain,
Cried, "Gobble, gobble, gobble":
The man on the hill that couldn't stand still,
Went hobble hobble, hobble.

Jack Jingle

The Real Mother Goose, *by Blanche Fisher Wright, 1916.*

Little Jack Jingle,
He used to live single;
But when he got tired of this kind of life,
He left off being single and lived with his
wife.
Now what do you think of little Jack Jingle?
Before he was married he used to live
single.

Jack Sprat

The Little Mother Goose, *by Jesse Wilcox Smith, 1918.*

Jack Sprat
Could eat no fat,
His wife could eat no lean;
And so, betwixt them both,
They licked the platter clean.

A Man and a Maid

The Real Mother Goose, *by Blanche Fisher Wright, 1916.*

There was a little man,
Who wooed a little maid,
And he said, "Little maid, will you wed, wed,
wed?
I have little more to say,
So will you, yea or nay,
For least said is soonest mended-ded, ded,
ded."
The little maid replied,
"Should I be your little bride,
Pray what must we have for to eat, eat,
eat?
Will the flame that you're so rich in
Light a fire in the kitchen?
Or the little god of love turn the spit, spit,
spit?"

The Man in Our Town

The Real Mother Goose, *by Blanche Fisher Wright, 1916.*

There was a man in our town,
And he was wondrous wise,
He jumped into a bramble bush,
And scratched out both his eyes;
But when he saw his eyes were out,
With all his might and main,
He jumped into another bush,
And scratched 'em in again.

The Family

Songs and Games for Little Ones, *by Harriet S. Jenks and Gertrude Walker, 1887. (With sheet music)*

This is the grandma-ma,
This is the grandpa-pa,
This is the mother dear,
This is the father dear,
This is the little child,
See the whole family here!

The Family

Finger Play Reader Part 2, *by John W. Davis, 1909; words adapted by Juli Wright.*

This is the mother, good and dear;
This is the father, with hearty cheer;
This is the brother, stout and tall;
This is the sister, that plays with her doll;
This is the little one, pet of all;
Behold the good family great and small.

The Family

The Volta Review, *edited by Josephine B. Timberlake, 1921.*

This is the mother,
This is the father,
This is the brother tall.
This is the sister,
This is the baby.
Oh, how we love them all!

A Family Finger-play

A version of this poem can be found in The Volta Review, *edited by Josephine B. Timberlake, 1921.*

Adapt this finger play for the family and dog puppets.

This is a family
Let's count them and see,
How many there are,
And who they can be.
This is the mother
Who loves everyone.
And this is the father
Who is lots of fun.
This is my sister
She helps and she plays,
And this is the baby
He's growing each day.

But who is this one?
He's out there alone,
Why it's Jackie, the dog,
And he's chewing a bone.

The Old Man and His Wife

English Folk-Songs for Schools, *by S. Garing Gould, M.A., and Cecil J. Sharp, B.A., 1920.*

1. There was an old man in a wood,
As you shall plainly see, sir,
He said he'd harder work in a day
Than his wife could do in three, sir.

If that be so, the old wife said.
And this you will allow, sir,
Why, I'll go drive the plow to-day.
And you shall milk the cow, sir.

2. But you must watch the speckled hen
For fear she lay away, sir,
And you must watch the spool of yarn,
That I spun yesterday, sir.

The old wife took the stick in hand.
And went to drive the plow, sir,
The old man took the pail in hand,
And went to milk the cow, sir.

3. But Tiney winced and fussed about,
And Tiney cocked her nose, sir,
And Tiney gave the man a kick,
That blood ran from the blows, sir.

Tiney! pretty Tiney, dear,
My pretty cow, stand still, ah!
If you I milk another day-
it's sore against my will, ah!

4. He went to feed the little pigs
That were within the stye, sir,
But knocked his head against the door,
Which made the blood to fly, sir.

He went to watch the speckled hen
Lest she should lay away, sir,
But clean forgot the spool of yarn
His wife spun yesterday, sir.

5. He went within to fetch a stick
To give the pig his hire, sir,
But she ran in between his legs
And cast him in the mire, sir.

And as he looked at pig and cow
He said, I do agree, sir,
If my wife never works again
She'll not be blamed by me, sir.

Sweet Nightingale

English Folk-Songs for Schools, *by S. Garing Gould, M.A., and Cecil J. Sharp, B.A., 1920.*

1. My sweetheart, come along,
Don't you hear the sweet song,
The sweet notes of the nightingale flow?
Don't you hear the fond tale
Of the sweet nightingale,
As she sings in the valleys below?

2. Pretty Betty, don't fail,
For I'll carry your pail
Safe home to your cot as we go;
You shall hear the fond tale
Of the sweet nightingale,
As she sings in the valleys below.

3. Pray let me alone,
I have hands of my own,
Along with you, sir, I'll not go,
To hear the fond tale
Of the sweet nightingale,
As she sings in the valleys below.

4. Pray sit yourself down
With me on the ground,
On this bank where the primroses grow,
You shall hear the fond tale
Of the sweet nightingale,
As she sings in the valleys below.

5. The couple agreed,
And were married with speed,
And soon to the church they did go;
No more is she afraid
For to walk in the shade.
Nor to sit in those valleys below.

Books

Abby, by Jeannette Caines.
Abuela, by Arthur Dorros.
All Families Are Special, by Norma Simon.
All Kinds of Families, by Mary Ann Hoberman.
Are You My Mother? by P.D. Eastman.
Ask Mr. Bear, by Marjorie Flack (Macmillan, 1986).
Aunt Flossie's Hats, by James Ransome.
Baby Sister for Frances, by Russell Hoban.
Big Boy, Little Boy, by Betty Jo Stanovich.
Come to the Meadow, by Anna Grossnickle Hines.
Do Like Kyla, by Angela Johnson.
Don't Wake Up Mama! by Eileen Christelow.
Families, by Ann Morris.
Families (Babies Everywhere), by Rena D. Grossman, Star Bright Books. *Board book.*
The Family Book, by Todd Parr.
Five Minutes Peace, by Jill Murphy.
Grandfather Twilight, by Barbara Berger.
Grandma's Feather Bed, illustrated by Christopher Canyon (Dawn Publications, 2007.) *Includes John Denver CD.*
Grandpa and Bo, by Kevin Henkes (Greenwillow, 1986).
Happy Birthday, Sam, by Pat Hutchins.
Here Are My Hands, by Bill Martin, Jr., and John Archambault.
I Dance in My Red Pajamas, by Edith Thacher Hurd.
I Don't Want to Be Me, by Patricia Davis.
Make Way for Ducklings, by Robert McCloskey.
Mama, Daddy, Baby and Me, by Lisa Gewing (Spirit, 1989).
Mama, Do You Love Me? by Barbara M. Joose.
Me and My Family Tree, by Joan Sweeney.
Me Too! by Mercer Mayer.
Nobody Asked Me if I Wanted a Baby Sister, by Martha Alexander (Dial, 1971).
The Patchwork Quilt, by Valerie Flourney.
The Perfect Family, by Nancy Carlson (Carolrhoda Books, 1985).
She Come Bringing Me That Little Baby Girl, by Eloise Greenfield.
Stevie, by John Steptoe.
There Was an Old Lady Who Swallowed a Fly, by Simms Taback.
Titch, by Pat Hutchins.
Twin to Twin, by Margaret O'Hair.
What Mary Jo Shared, by Janice May Udry.
When I Go Visiting, by Anne and Harlow Rockwell.

Who's in a Family? by Robert Skutch.
Whose Mouse Are You? by Robert Kraus.

Movies and Television

The Addams Family
The Adventures of the Wilderness Family
Andy Griffith
Babe
Back at the Barnyard
Barnyard
The Brady Bunch
Cats and Dogs 1 and 2
Charlotte's Web
Dr. Quinn, Medicine Woman
The Flintstones
Garfield and Friends
Home on the Range
Homeward Bound 2
The Incredibles
The Jetsons
Leave It to Beaver
Little House on the Prairie
The Munsters
My Three Sons
Seventh Heaven
Swiss Family Robinson
The Waltons

Appendix A. Animal Puppets

All Animals

alligator (19)
bear (2b)
beaver (20)
bird (6d)
cat (6e)
chick (1a)
chicken (1a)
cow (21)
crocodile (19)
dog (10f)
dolphin (22)
duck (1c)
elephant (23)
fawn (24)
fox (1g)
frog (9a)
giraffe (25)
goat (14a)
goose (1b)
hen (1d)
hippopotamus (26)
horse (10d)
jellyfish (28)
koala (29)
lamb (30)
lion (11a)
monkey (31)
mouse (8a)
newt (32)
owl (33)
pig (15a)
polar bear (34)
quail (35)
rabbit (7a)
rhinoceros (36)
rooster (1f)
squirrel (37)
swan (13b)
tiger (38)
turkey (1e)
turtle (16a)
unicorn (39)
vulture (40)
walrus (41)
wolf (5c)
yak (43)
zebra (44)

Animal Groups and Themes

Aquatic

dolphin (22)
jellyfish (28)

Arctic Animals

Arctic fox (1g)
Arctic hare (7a)
Dall sheep (goat-like, with horns) (14c)
polar bear (34)
snowy owl (33)
walrus (41)
wolf (5c)

Circus Animals

bear (2b)
elephant (23)
giraffe (25)
horse (10d)
lion (11a)
monkey (31)
tiger (38)

Farm & Domestic Animals

cat (6e)
chick (1a)
cow (21)
dog (10f)
duck (1c)
goat (14a)
goose (1b)
hen (1d)
horse (10d)
lamb (30)
pig (15a)
rabbit (7a)
swan (13b)
turkey (1e)
turtle/tortoise (16a)

Jungle/Zoo Animals

alligator/crocodile (19)
bear (2b)
elephant (23)
frog (9a)
giraffe (25)
hippopotamus (26)
koala (29)
lion (11a)
monkey (31)
polar bear (34)
rhinoceros (36)
tiger (38)
turtle (16a)
vulture (40)
walrus (41)
wolf (5c)
yak (43)
zebra (44)

Wild Animals

alligator (19)
bear (2b)
beaver (20)
bird (6d)
crocodile (19)
fawn (24)
fox (1g)
frog (9a)
goat (14a)
mouse (8a)
newt (32)
owl (33)
quail (35)
rabbit (7a)
squirrel (37)
swan (13b)
turkey (1e)
turtle (16a)
vulture (40)
wolf (5c)

Appendix B. Resources

Websites

The following websites contain innumerable ideas for songs, stories, poems, etc., that you can use in crafting your story time or lesson.

Animals.NationalGeographic.com
AtoZkidsstuff.com
atozteacherstuff.com
brighthubeducation.com
BusSongs.com (nursery rhymes and children's songs)
Childcarelounge.com
DLTK-kids.com
enchantedlearning.com/categories/preschool.shtml (requires a membership, good information, ideas)
everythingpreschool.com (themes, zoo animals, etc.—lots of poems and finger plays submitted by teachers. Over 30,000 preschool education activities; 100 themes, 26 alphabet areas, and lesson plans)
first-school.ws/theme/alphabet.html (alphabet preschool activities and crafts)
fun.familyeducation.com
gregandsteve.com (a musical group)
Heidisongs.com
hummingbird.com
janbrett.com
KIDiddles.com
kidnkaboodle.net
kids.nationalgeographic.com
Kindercare.com
kinderkorner.com
kindermusick.com
kinderthemes.com
Koala-bears.org
learningplanet.com
makinglearningfun.com
Midgefrazel.net/gingerbread.html
MrsCowan.com/gingerbreadmanthemeunit.html.
nursery-rhymes-collection.com
parents.com/familyfun-magazine/
pbskids.org/zoom/activities/preschool/
Perpetualpreschool.com (ideas submitted by preschool teachers—lots of finger plays and activities. Over 12,000 free ideas for parents and educators of young children)
preschoolcorner.com
Preschooleducation.com
preschoolexpress.com by Jean Warren (excellent site. Preschool activities, games, ideas for teachers, parents, and grandparents-themes, booklists, lots of songs and fingerplays)
Preschoolrainbow.org (an excellent site for finding ideas. Has great books lists, activities, themes, music, units).
savethekoala.com
sharonmacdonald.com
shirleys-preschool-activities.com (good collection of activities, good for homeschooling, early childhood development)
Songs for Teaching, Using Music to Promote Learning (songsforteaching.com)
Step by Step Child Care (stepbystepcc.com)
storyplace.org/preschool (library stories and themes)
storytimesongs.com
theKoala.com
time4learning.com/preschool
todaysparent.com
treehousetv.com
Turtlepondpublications.com
2care2teach4kids.com

Music

Jack Hartmann (Hop to It Music): A Place on the Farm; Alphabet Zoo (appropriate for many puppets in Section Two); Counting Piggy Tails (#15).

Ron Brown (Intelli-Tunes): Fairy Tales (appropriate for many puppets in Section One); The Gingerbread Man (#10); The Three Billy Goats Gruff (#14); The Little Red Hen (#12); Little Henny Penny (#1); The Three Little Pigs (#15); Goldilocks and the Three Bears (#2).

Books

The following sources are in the public domain, making them free to use without any need for obtaining permission to use them in a public setting. Most, if not all, can be found online.

Altemus Wee Books for Wee Folks, 1917.

Aunt Fanny. *The Apple Dumpling and Other Stories for Young Boys and Girls*, 1852/1894.

Aunt Kitty's Stories, 1870.

Bancroft, Jessie H. *Games for the Playground, Home, School and Gymnasium*, 1922.

The Best College Songs for Union College, 1897.

Blake, William. *Songs of Innocence and Songs of Experience*, 1794.

Bogue, David, and Joseph Cundall. *Harry's Ladder to Learning, with Two Hundred and Thirty Illustrations*, 1850. Printed by G. Barclay, Castle St., Leicester Sq., London. (Note: No page numbers in the book or titles to separate nursery rhymes.)

Bonke, Willard. *Fun and Nonsense*, 1904.

Burchill, Georgine. *The Progressive Road to Reading*, 1913.

Burdick, Jennie Ellis, ed. *Childhood's Favorites and Fairy Stories the Young Folks Treasury*, Volume 1, 1919.

Carroll, Lewis. *Songs from Alice in Wonderland and Through the Looking-glass*, 1921.

Children's Corner, June 11, 1904.

Children's Folk Songs, Byron Arnold Collection, 1947.

Crane, Walter. *The Baby's Bouquet*, 1877.

Crane, Walter. *The Baby's Opera*, 1877. Includes sheet music.

Crane, Walter. *Mother Goose's Nursery Rhymes*, 1877.

Crane, Walter. *Mother Hubbard's Picture Book*, 1897. Contents: "Mother Hubbard," "The Three Bears," and "The Absurd A, B, C."

Davis, John W. *Finger Play Reader Part 2*, 1909. Sheet music.

Dennis, Clarence Michael James. *A Book for Kids*, 1921.

Denslow, W.W., adaptor and illustrator. *Denslow's Three Bears*, 1903.

Elliott, James William. *Nursery Rhymes and Nursery Songs*, 1870.

The European Magazine, April 1782.

Follen, Eliza Lee. "A Cat's Tale, with Additions," in *New Nursery Songs for All Good Children*, 1843.

Ford, Robert. *Children's Rhymes, Children's Games, Children's Songs, Children's Stories: A Book for Bairns and Big Folk*, 1904.

Greenway, Kate. *Mother Goose*, 1910.

Hoffman, Heinrich. *Struwwelpeter Merry Stories and Funny Pictures*, 1848.

Hofmann, May C. *Games for Everybody, Games for Children*, Dodge Publishing Co., 1905,

Jackson, Leroy F. *The Peter Patter Book of Nursery Rhymes*, 1918.

Jenks, Harriet S., and Gertrude Walker. *Songs and Games for Little Ones*, 1887, Includes sheet music.

Kipling Stories and Poems Every Child Should Know, 1909.

Lang, Edward. *The Nursery Rhyme Book*, 1897.

Lear, Edward. *Nonsense Books*, 1894.

Lomax, John A. *Cowboy Songs and Other Frontier Ballads*, Sturgis & Walton Company, 1910, 1916.

Mother Goose: The Complete Book of Nursery Rhymes, 1941. See donaldsauter.com.
The Only True Mother Goose Melodies, Munroe and Francis, 1833.
Poems by Alice and Phoebe Cary, Book 2, 1850.
Poems Teachers Ask For, Book 1, 1922.
Poulsson, Emilie. *Finger Plays for Nursery and Kindergarten*, 1893.
Poulsson, Emilie. *Holiday Songs and Every Day Songs and Games*, 1901. Has sheet music and some finger plays.
Poulsson, Emilie. *Love and Law in Child Training: A Book for Mothers*, 1899.
Riley, Alice C.D. *A Rat a Tat Tat*, Songs of the Child-World, 1897.
Runciman, Terry Richard. *The Shanty Book Sailor Shanties*, 1921.
School Committee of the City of Boston, 1921.
Smith, Jessie Willcox. *The Little Mother Goose*, Dodd, Mead: 1918.
Stevenson, Burton Egbert, ed. *The Home Book of Verse, Vol. 1 (of 4)*, 1912.
Talley, Thomas W. *Negro Folk Rhymes Wise and Otherwise*, 1922.
Taylor, Isaac. *Chinese Mother Goose Rhymes*, 1900.
Taylor, Jane, and Ann Taylor. *Little Ann and Other Poems*, 1883.
Thompson, Peter G. *Little Curly-Locks* (series), 1885.
Wadsworth, Olive A. *Over in the Meadow: Kit, Fan, Tot and the Rest of Them*, 1870.
Wright, Blanche Fisher. *The Real Mother Goose*, 1916.

Tunes and Songs

The following tunes and songs were referenced in this book. This listing can help you find them.

"A Hunting We Will Go," by Thomas Arne, 1777.
"All the Pretty Little Horses." Traditional American folk song (first printed in *On the Trail of Negro Folk Songs*, by Dorothy Scarborough, 1925). Believed to pre-date first printing.
"Are You Sleeping?" *The Home Book of Verse*, Vol. 1 (of 4). Author: Various. Editor: Burton Egbert Stevenson, 1912.
"Ballad of Jed Clampett," by Paul Henning, 1962.
"The Bear Went Over the Mountain," The American Folk Lore Society, 1920. *The Journal of American Folk Lore*, Vol. 55, Boston: Houghton, p. 91.
"Bill Grogan's Goat," oral traditional campfire echo song. Earliest printed version, 1904 (*The Tale of a Shirt*). Also, Will Hayes' song, "O Grady's Goat," published 1890, in *Shoemaker's Best Selections*, by Silas Nef. *Frank C. Brown Collection of North Carolina Folklore*, Vol. 3, 1913, "The Billy Goat."
"Bingo." *A Book of Nursery Rhymes and Songs*, by Sabine Baring, 1895, "Little Bingo."
The Book of Knowledge, Vol. 7, 1910 (some verses missing).
"Boom, Boom, Ain't It Great to Be Crazy," thought to be oral traditional camp song.
Bought Me a Cat Folk Rhymes, by Thomas W. Talley, 1922. (Song: "Bought Me a Wife.")
"Brown Bear, Brown Bear, What Do You See?" by Bill Martin, 1967. Also: "Polar Bear, Polar Bear, What Do You Hear?" 1991, and "Panda Bear, Panda Bear, What Do You See?" 2003, "Baby Bear, Baby Bear, What Do You See?" 2007. These are not songs per se, but can be easily adapted for singing.
"Dem Bones." Traditional spiritual song, by James Weldon Johnson (1871–1938).
"Did You Ever See a Lassie?" *Games for the Playground, Home, School and Gymnasium*, by Jessie Hubbell Bancroft, 1909.
"Do Your Ears Hang Low?" Tune from "Turkey in the Straw." Origin obscure. Oldest published work, "Do Your Balls Hang Low?" 1956, but pre-dates to Civil War.
"Down by the Station," by Lee Ricks and Slim Gaillard, 1948.
"Down on Grandpa's Farm," written by Robert

D. Singleton/Traditional (*One Light, One Sun*, Raffi).

"The Farmer in the Dell." *Games and Songs of American Children*, by William Wells Newell, 1883.

"Found a Peanut" (tune: "Oh My Darling, Clementine"). Earliest reference: 1949 film, *A Letter to 3 Wives.*

"The Fox Went Out on a Chilly Night," *The Nursery Rhymes of England*, by Halliewell Phillipps, 1842. Also: *A Book of Nursery Songs and Rhymes*, by Sabine Baring, 1895.

"Go In and Out the Window," Melody 1762. Composed by Lew Pollack (1895–1946). Earliest date for U.S. version, 1911, English versions, 1898. (*Round and Round the Village.*)

"Grizzly Bear," song performed by Harry Belafonte, 1960. Second version by Jack Scott, 1962.

"Here We Sit Like Birds in the Wilderness" (camp song). Tune: "The Old Gray Mare," folk song, by Stephen Foster, around 1843.

"A Home on the Range," *Cowboy Songs and Other Frontier Ballads*, sheet music, 1916.

"Horsey, Horsey" (a round), by Paddy Roberts, 1938.

"I Had a Rooster," oral traditional, performed by Pete Seeger.

"I'm a Little Teapot," by George Harold Sanders and Clarence Z. Kelley, 1939.

"I'm Bringing Home a Baby Bumble Bee." Chorus originated from Arkansas Traveler, 1806.

"I'm Bringing Home a Baby Bumble Bee." Music composed in 19th century by Colonel Sanford C. "Sandy" Faulkner, 1806–1874.

"In My Nursery," *A Book of Verse*, by Laura E. Richards, 1890. (Contains an older version of this song.) (See grandparents.com, and KingCountyLibrarySystem to watch this performed.)

"Jimmy Crack Corn" ("Blue Tail Fly"), folk song, 1844.

"The Kingdom of the Birds," published in 1719–1720 in Thomas D'Urfey's *Wit and Mirth, or Pills to Purge Melancholy.*

"Kookaburra," by Marion Sinclair, 1932.

"The Lion Sleeps Tonight," by Solomon Linda, 1920. Copyright Abilene Music Publishers, Disney, 2006.

"Little Bunny Foo Foo" (tune of "Down by the Station"). *Peter, Mopsy, Flopsy, Foo Foo Rabbit*, by B. Potter, 1910.

"Lollipop, Lollipop," by Julius Dixon, 1958.

"London Bridge," *Tommy Thumb's Pretty Song Book*, by John Newberry, 1744.

"Mary Had a Little Lamb," by Sarah Josepha Hale, 1830.

"Mary Wore a Red Dress, or Mary Wore Her Red Dress," oral traditional ("Mary Was a Red Bird"). Sung by Raffi.

"Mrs. O'Leary's Cow," also called "Old Mother Leary" and "There'll Be a Hot Time in the Old Town Tonight." Music by Theodore August Metz, lyrics by Joe Hayden, 1896.

"My Grandfather's Clock," by Henry Clay Work, 1876.

"Newt of Earl," "Duke of Earl," by Gene Chandler, penned by Bernice Williams, 1962.

"Oh, Do You Know the Muffin Man?" *The Young Lady's Book*, by Miss Henry Mackarness, 1888. First recorded in a British manuscript in 1820.

"Oh My Darling, Clementine," by Percy Montrose, 1884.

"Oh Where, Oh Where Has My Little Dog Gone?" Original words by Septimus Winner (1864). Also wrote "10 Little Injuns," 1868.

"The Old Gray Mare" (oral traditional), *Roud Folk Song Index* 751, 1906, Collector E.C. Perrow.

"Old MacDonald Had a Farm," 1917, *Tommy's Tunes.*

"The Old Woman and Her Pig," *English Fairy Tales*, by Joseph Jacobs, 1890.

"The Other Day I Met a Bear," traditional American camp echo song.

"Over the River and Through the Woods," by Lydia Maria Child. In *Flowers for Children*, Vol. 2, 1844, original piece with 6 verses.
"Polly Wolly Doodle," Harvard student songbook of 1880.
"Pop Goes the Weasel," Boston, 1858. New York, 1901 and 1914. Originated in England.
"Rig a Jig Jig." *The Best College Songs for Union College*, 1897, p. 185.
"Row, Row, Row Your Boat," *The Franklin Square Song Collection*, 1881.
"She'll Be Coming Round the Mountain," *The American Song Bag*, written pre–1800.
"Sipping Cider Through a Straw." Traditional American camp echo song.
"Skip to My Lou" (Version 1), *Popular Folk Games*, 1907.
Stephen Foster (1826–1864) wrote over 200 songs, including "Oh Susanna," "Camptown Races," "Old Folks at Home," "Jeanie with the Light Brown Hair," "Beautiful Dreamer" and possibly "The Old Gray Mare."
"Swing Low, Sweet Chariot," by Wallace Willis, 1873, in the book: *The Jubilee Singers*.
"Take Me Out to the Ballgame," by Jack Norworth and Albert Von Tilzer, 1908.
"There Was an Old Lady Who Swallowed a Fly." Music by Alan Mills, lyrics by Rose Bonne, copyright 1952.
"There Were Three Jolly Fishermen," by Roy Palmer, 1986. Inspired from the song: "Caller Herring," by W. and T. Fordyce, 1840.
"This Is the Way We Wash Our Clothes" (same tune as, and originating from, "Here We Go Round the Mulberry Bush").
"This Old Man," *English Folk Songs for Schools*, by S.B. Gould and C.J. Sharp, 1906.
"Three Blind Mice" in *The Baby's Opera*, by Walter Crane, 1877. Has sheet music.
"Today Is Monday," *Everybody's Favorite Songs*, 1933.
"Turkey in the Straw." Earliest lyrics under the name "Zip Coon," by Dan Bryant, 1861.
"Twinkle Twinkle Little Star: The Star," by Jane Taylor (1783–1824) in *The Home Book of Verse*, Vol. 1 (of 4) Author: Various. Editor: Burton Egbert Stevenson, 1912.
"The Wheels on the Bus," American folk song, mid–20th century. Based on the traditional British song, "Here We Go Round the Mulberry Bush."
"Who Did Swallow Jonah?" by Barton, 1899, p. 40.
"The Yellow Rose of Texas," Firth, Pond and Company of New York, 1858, by J.K.
"You Are My Sunshine," lyrics by Jimmy Davis and Charles Mitchell, 1939.

INDEX

Numbers in bold italic refer to pages where puppet patterns appear.